WHICH? WAY TO
SAVE AND INVEST

Which?
BOOKS

KU-594-243

**Published by Consumers' Association
and Hodder & Stoughton**

Which? Books are commissioned and researched by
The Association for Consumer Research
and published by Consumers' Association,
2 Marylebone Road, London NW1 4DX
and Hodder & Stoughton, 47 Bedford Square,
London WC1B 3DP

First edition 1982
Second edition 1983
Copyright © 1988 Consumers' Association Ltd

British Library Cataloguing in Publication Data

Which? way to save and invest. —— 3rd ed.
   1. Great Britain. Investment
   I. Consumers' Association.
   II. The Which? book of saving and investing
   332.6'0941

ISBN 0 340 48934 0

Typographic design by Paul Saunders
Cover illustration by John Holder
Index compiled by Moira Greenhalgh

Typeset by Gee Graphics, Crayford, Kent
Printed and bound in Great Britain by Butler & Tanner Ltd,
Frome and London

Acknowledgements

Editor: Jane Vass

With thanks to the following for their contributions:
Kathryn Deane, Simon Hinde, Amanda Jarvis, Deborah
Lamb, Jonquil Lowe, Veronica McGrath, Simon
Richmond, Mark Shanahan, Sue Thomas, Sue Ward, Sara
Williams, John Willman

CONTENTS

Introduction   9

Section I: Choosing a home for your money

1   Investment strategy   13
2   Investment choices   29
3   Investing for retirement   43
4   Investing for children   55
5   Safety first   73
6   Getting advice   81
7   Tax   93
8   A bird's eye view   117

Section II: Where to put your money first

9   Your home   141
10   Building societies   151
11   Bank and finance company accounts   165
12   National Savings investments   171
13   Pensions from employers and the state   187
14   Personal pension plans   213

Section III: Other ways of investing

15	Shares	241
16	Unit trusts	267
17	British Government stocks	287
18	Local authority investments	303
19	Endowment policies	311
20	Unit-linked life insurance	327
21	Guaranteed income and growth bonds	351
22	Annuities	355
23	Commodities	367
24	Investing abroad	381
25	Alternative investments	403

Index	419

INTRODUCTION

A little cash to spare? A lump sum on retirement or redundancy? Or are you already a seasoned investor? Whatever your situation, you'll want to know how you can help your investments come up trumps – and how to avoid the joker in the pack. This book draws on *Which?* magazine's many years of experience in answering these questions, with help from experts and consultants in the field.

Since we first published the forerunner of this book – *The Which? Book of Saving and Investing* – in 1982, the financial picture has changed considerably. The rate of inflation has halved; the top rate of income tax has fallen from 60 to 40 per cent; and a new framework of investor protection has been established.

The cards in your investment pack have changed too. Some types of investment have disappeared, new ones have been devised, and others have grown in importance. Largely as a result of the Government's privatisation programme, the number of private shareholders has risen, so that around one in five of us now owns shares. Yet the October 1987 stock market crash reminded us that investing in shares can be a gamble. You may feel tempted to put your money in the building society instead. But even building societies have changed, as the huge range of accounts and interest rates on offer testifies.

All change?
Not entirely. The underlying principles of sensible investment have remained the same – and the first section of this book, *Choosing a home for your money*, explains how to work out an investment strategy, the investment choices open to you, how tax can affect those choices, and what protection you have if things go wrong.

9

First steps

The second section of the book, *Where to put your money first*, looks at some of the basic homes for your money. However much money you've got, you're almost certain to have some of it stashed away in one of these homes.

The first card in your hand is a low-risk savings scheme, such as a bank, building society or National Savings account. As well as providing a secure home for at least some of your money, these accounts can be a good place to keep an 'emergency fund' of easily accessible money in case of an unforeseen crisis.

But in this section you'll also find information about buying a home and a pension. This is where saving and investing overlap with financial planning generally. For example, if you own your own home, it may be your most valuable asset as well as somewhere to live; and as well as being a tax-efficient way and secure way of saving, a pension is a sensible way of making sure that you've something to live on in retirement.

More risk for more reward?

Once you've sorted out your own investment strategy, and looked at the basic types of investment, you may feel that you are prepared to accept a little more risk for the rest of your money, in return for the chance of a higher return. If so, the book's third section, *Other ways of investing*, looks at the other types of investment available. These range from shares, unit trusts, British Government stocks and commodities, to life insurance and annuities.

The section also looks at the pros and cons of other investments you might not have considered – investing abroad, or even linking your investment to a hobby through alternative investments such as stamps, diamonds and vintage wine.

Play your cards right

No one investment can be all things to all people. Although this book covers most of the types of saving and investment available, your final guide will be *your* needs. So, our overall aim is to guide you through the complexities of the money business to build up your own hand of savings and investments. We hope that it increases the odds in your favour.

SECTION I

Choosing a Home for Your Money

1

INVESTMENT STRATEGY

Whether you're a small-scale investor, or looking for a home for many thousands of £££, your problem will not be lack of choice. The difficulty arises in making sensible choices among all the investments available – and, in some cases, finding out all the details needed to come to these decisions. Your aim should be to end up with a number of different investments, covering your differing needs. So before getting down to the nitty gritty of the different investments, we've set out a plan for working out your overall investment strategy.

In the next chapter we give examples of different people putting their individual strategies into effect. The two chapters after that look in detail at the particular questions to be answered when investing for retirement and for children. We then look at where to go for advice and what to do if things go wrong. Chapter 7 explains how tax affects your investments. And in Chapter 8, we give a bird's eye view of the different investments open to you – you'll find more details on each in the rest of the book.

Of course, deciding now on a particular set of investments isn't the end of the story. It's important to keep a close eye on your investments and to review them periodically – see p25 for things to bear in mind.

Investment priorities checklist

Your personal circumstances are bound to affect your choice of investments. But no matter what your situation is, some things are worth considering *before* you start thinking about investments in detail.

Are your dependants protected?
What would happen if you died tomorrow? Would your mortgage be paid off? Would your wife have to go back to

work earlier than planned? Would your husband have a big enough income to pay someone to look after the children?

For most people, the solution to this protection problem is life insurance, not saving and investing. A cheap type of life insurance is *term insurance* – see p315.

Have you put some money aside for emergencies?

Could you cope with an unexpected disaster (major car repairs or damage to your home, say)? If not, concentrate on building up an emergency fund in some place where you'll be able to withdraw it at short notice (within a week, say). See p22, and Chapter 2 for investments to consider.

Are you buying your own home?

Buying a home has proved a good long-term investment in the past. Buying your home also has tax advantages – under current rules, you get tax relief on the interest you pay on a mortgage of up to £30,000, and there's normally no capital gains tax to pay on the increase in value of your home. If you aren't buying a home (and don't already own one), pause for thought – and read Chapter 9 – before you go for any other long-term investment.

Are you planning for your retirement?

Don't assume that the state pension on its own will safeguard your standard of living – especially with the changes introduced in 1988. In Chapter 13, we give details of pension schemes – both from the state and from employers. Try to work out how well off the state pension together with any employer's pension and income from your savings will leave you – see Chapter 3. If you're self-employed, or not in an employer's pension scheme, consider taking out a personal pension plan – see Chapter 14 for details.

Investment strategy checklist

Once you have covered the priorities set out above, your next step is to choose the investments which are best for you – taking your own personal circumstances and aims into account.

Some investments make sense only for people of a certain age (annuities for the over-70's, say); others (eg school fees policies) are obviously only suited to those with children to educate. These are extreme cases of the ways in which your personal circumstances can shape your investment strategy – but there may be less dramatic repercussions too. Most

people will be saving and investing for a number of purposes. Are you saving for something in particular – eg a trip
to the Bahamas? Or just to accumulate cash?

Different investments may be suitable for each purpose –
so most people ought to end up putting their money into a
variety of investments. It's worth thinking about the points
below, and reading the sections on keeping up with inflation
(see p16) and on risk (see p19), before you decide on a particular investment. And when comparing interest rates on
different investments, see p25.

Age

If you are 50, for example, you are more likely to be concerned with saving up for retirement and thinking about
how to invest any lump sum you get, than with building up
a deposit for your first home. Your children are likely to be
off your hands too, and you may have more spare cash to
save than you had in your thirties.

Health

If you have a weak heart, for example, you may find it
difficult (or expensive) to get the right kind or amount of life
insurance. You may want to supplement your life cover
with additional savings. Investing through a life insurance
policy is likely to be less worthwhile for you than for those
in good health.

Family

You may want to save up (or invest a lump sum) for your
children's education. And you need to think about how your
assets will be passed on when you die. You may want to
build up a capital sum for your heirs to inherit.

Expectations

If you expect your income to drop at some point (when you
start a family, perhaps, or when you retire), you may want
to build up savings to draw on when you're hard up. On the
other hand, if you expect a big rise in salary (when you get
an additional qualification, say, or finish training) you may
feel you can run down your savings a bit since you expect to
be better off later. Or you may be coming into a large
inheritance – and need to find a suitable home for it.

Tax

Some investments are particularly suitable for non-taxpayers, while others may be particularly good for higher rate

taxpayers. We cover tax in Chapter 7. Elderly people should look out for the effect of losing age allowance – see p40.

What you want from your investments
If you want to build up a fund for next year's holiday, you probably need to consider a different range of investments from someone saving up for retirement, or to pass on a capital sum to their heirs. Similarly, if you are looking for a fixed income from your investments, the investments you select will differ from those chosen by someone prepared to accept an income that varies with general interest rates. For more details, see p22.

How much you can invest
How much money can you afford to invest? Some invest-ments are open to you only if you have a sufficiently large lump sum. And other investments are open only to those who can save a regular sum each month. Still others are more flexible and can take your savings as and when they arise.

How long you can invest for
Think carefully before you commit yourself to saving a definite amount each month for a long time (25 years, say), or locking up a lump sum for a lengthy period. All sorts of changes could happen over the period of the investment that might make it hard to continue, and most long-term savings plans penalise you if you cash in early.

Keeping up with inflation

With some investments the value of the capital you invest stays the same – but, of course, this doesn't allow for the effects of inflation. If you invest £1,000 now, spend the income from the investment and get your £1,000 back in four years' time, it will be worth only £820 or so in terms of today's buying power if inflation averages 5 per cent a year. And (with the same rate of inflation) if you got your money back in 20 years' time, it would be worth only £380 in terms of today's buying power.

Looked at another way, an inflation rate of 5 per cent means that you have to see the value of your investments (after allowing for tax) rise by at least 5 per cent a year on average just for them to be worth the same to you in the future as they are now. That's before you draw an income from your investment.

The Diagram below shows the devastating effect of inflation – bear this in mind when considering how much your investments (or the income from them) will be worth in the future.

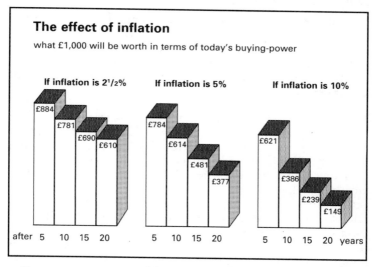

The effect of inflation

what £1,000 will be worth in terms of today's buying-power

If inflation is 2¹/₂%: £884, £781, £690, £610

If inflation is 5%: £784, £614, £481, £377

If inflation is 10%: £621, £386, £239, £149

after 5 10 15 20 years

One strategy you could consider for long-term investing is to go for index-linked investments which guarantee to keep pace with inflation (and perhaps give a little extra interest too). Alternatively, you could go for riskier investments like unit trusts, shares, property or alternative investments which might do a lot better than keep up with inflation (but could do a lot worse, or even end up worth less than at the start).

In the Diagram on pp20–21, we compare the rates of return you might have got over different periods of time for various lump sum investments. You can see that over the longer period some of the riskier investments such as shares and gold sovereigns have done a better job of keeping up with inflation than safer ones such as building societies. On the other hand, looking at the shorter period, you would have lost money invested in gold sovereigns over only five years, while money in the building society would have more than kept pace with inflation. (Note that over different periods the results could have been very different – so don't use this Diagram to draw conclusions about where to invest your money.)

Of course, you may be prepared to put up with a drop in purchasing power because, for example, you're looking for a particularly 'safe' investment, or you want to be able to withdraw your money at short notice (eg for your emergency fund).

Don't be taken in by ads

You may well come across advertisements similar to the one shown below.

The figures sound very attractive. The plan is worth £115,000 on retirement – providing you with a pension of £15,000 a year, or a lump sum of £35,000 plus a pension of £10,000 a year.

And the assumption about growth in your investment of 10 per cent a year may seem fairly reasonable.

But what will the money be worth when the plan ends in 20 years' time? Inflation could make mincemeat of the figures quoted in the advertisement. For example, if inflation averaged 5 per cent, the £15,000 a year pension will be worth only £5,653 in 20 years.

Of course, the buying-power of your contributions will fall over the years and you could mitigate the effect of inflation, to some extent, by raising your contributions from time to time in line with inflation. And the value of your investment may grow by more than 10 per cent a year (though it could also grow by less!).

But looking behind adverts like this (and ones that tell you how a lump sum investment will grow) does illustrate the dramatic effect of inflation – something to be aware of when you're planning for some time in the future.

onal Pension Plan.

all very well

:ompany employed?
al Pension

an its main
ns get full tax
ix-free.
ent funds for
Managed
ension Fund

: the
mate

ch as 17½%
increased by

What can you expect when you retire?
It depends entirely on the amount you pay and the investment performance, but as an example take a man aged 40 who plans to retire at 65.

He makes regular contributions of £1,200 each year and if he pays tax at the basic rate that's equivalent to £900.

Even assuming his investment grew by only 10% a year, his plan would be worth £115,000 on retirement.

That would provide him with a pension of £15,000 a year or a tax-free sum of £35,000 and a pension of £10,000 a year.

The Personal Pension Plan is a very flexible scheme and it can be tailor-made to suit your particular circumstances.

If you'd like more details post us the

Risk

One of the major risks you face is seeing the purchasing power of your investments drop over time as a result of inflation. This applies to practically any investment. But there are two additional risks you face:

■ **risk to capital** – the value of what you've invested in shares, unit trusts, property and so on is likely to fluctuate. You may find that when you need to cash in your investment the value of, say, your shares or unit trusts is particularly low. Alternative investments (eg antiques, jewellery, Persian carpets) are at risk in this way too – when you want to sell, you may not be able to find a buyer at a price which gives you a reasonable return. And a dealer's mark-up may be particularly high

■ **risk to income** – the size of the interest (or dividend) you get may vary considerably, depending on the performance of the company, fund, investment or whatever. In the worst case, you might get no income from the investments at all.

To minimise the impact of these risks on your investments, the golden rule is to spread your money around. Decide first what proportion of your capital (if any) you are prepared to put into risky investments, what proportion you want in safe ones. Accepting a degree of risk is, in the main, a price you may have to pay to stand at least some chance of increasing the buying-power of your investments.

Aim to spread your money among different types of investments – eg single-premium bonds, unit trusts, building societies. Particularly with riskier investments, try to put your money with a number of different companies issuing each type of investment. Also try to stagger investing over a long period (at least a year, preferably longer). By spreading your investments in these ways you'll reduce your risk of doing very badly. Bear in mind though that you'll also reduce your chances of doing extraordinarily well.

If you decide to go for a relatively high-risk investment (like shares or alternative investments), don't be tempted to withdraw your emergency fund from its safe home and invest it in the same way. This should cut down the risk of having to sell your investments (to pay for a new roof, say) when prices are low. And steer clear of direct investment in shares unless you've got a substantial amount to invest – see p246.

If you know you'll need your money on a particular future date, be prepared to cash in investments beforehand – a few

Investments compared: What you'd get back in first quarter of 1988 on £1,000 invested 5, 10, 15 and 20 years before in various investments

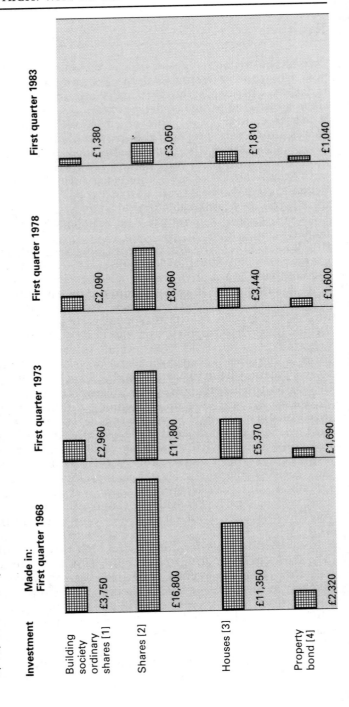

Investment	Made in: First quarter 1968	First quarter 1973	First quarter 1978	First quarter 1983
Building society ordinary shares [1]	£3,750	£2,960	£2,090	£1,380
Shares [2]	£16,800	£11,800	£8,060	£3,050
Houses [3]	£11,350	£5,370	£3,440	£1,810
Property bond [4]	£2,320	£1,690	£1,600	£1,040

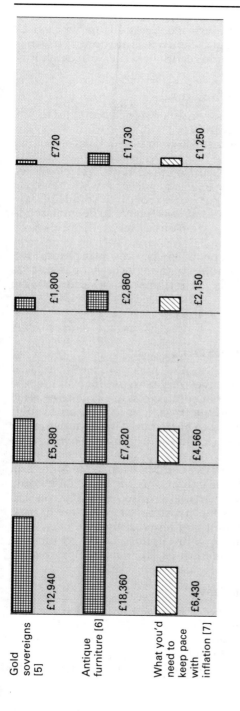

[1] Figures supplied by Nationwide Anglia Building Society. Assumes income reinvested
[2] Based on the FT Actuaries All-Share Index, assuming income reinvested and with allowances for buying and selling costs (but no allowance for capital gains tax)
[3] Based on Nationwide Anglia Index of Average House Prices, with allowances for buying and selling costs (but not capital gains tax)
[4] Based on longest running property bond introduced by Abbey Life Assurance in 1967, and with allowances for buying and selling costs. No tax would be payable on the proceeds unless an income had been withdrawn by cashing in part of the investment
[5] Source: Sharps Pixley Ltd, with allowances for VAT and differences between buying and selling price
[6] Based on Antique Collectors' Club Antique Furniture Price Index, with allowances for costs of buying and selling at auction
[7] Based on Retail Prices Index

years in advance, if need be – ideally at a time when their value is high. If you wait until you need the money, you may find you have to cash your investments when prices are low.

Investing your emergency fund

When deciding on a home for this part of your capital, you want to look for three things:

■ safety – no risk that when you cash in you'll get fewer £££ back than you put in

■ instant accessibility – you don't usually get even two weeks' notice of an emergency, so you want to be able to get the money back on the spot, or at most in a couple of days

■ highest possible return – but you'll have to be prepared to take less than you'd get for an investment that ties your money up for longer.

See the Route Maps on pp32–35 for some suggestions. Remember to update the amount of money you keep in reserve for emergencies regularly. Inflation will erode its buying power.

Your aims in investing

Many people want their investments to produce an income now. Others will invest for capital growth, either to provide an income later (on retirement, say), or to pass on to their heirs, or to build up a fund to buy something (a house or car for example). Below we outline some factors to consider in each of these cases.

You might in fact want a combination of income and growth – although to some extent, the line between income and capital growth is an artificial one. After all, you can always cash in some of your investments from time to time to give you income. And if you reinvest income from your investments the value of your capital should go up over time. There are tax considerations, though (see Box on p25).

Investing for income now

You need to consider how long you're likely to go on needing the income from your investments. If it's for more than a couple of years, you can't afford to ignore the effect of inflation on the purchasing power of any income your investments produce. You'll need a rising income. To achieve this, you are likely to have to put some of your capital at risk, or buy an index-linked investment. It may be sensible to invest some of your money for capital growth, with a view to cashing part of it in on a regular basis to provide income.

You have to make your own choice about how much of your capital to risk. Put the remainder in a place where the income from it will be safe – see the Route Maps on pp32–35 for suggestions.

If you don't anticipate having to rely on your extra investment income for longer than a year or two, you may well decide there is no point taking risks to get an income that will keep up with inflation.

If you don't pay tax, some investments may be particularly attractive if the interest is paid without deduction of tax. We have marked these investments (mainly National Savings schemes) with ● in the Route Maps on pp32–35 – but check that things have not changed since we went to press.

On the other hand some investments, where the return is tax-free, look more attractive the higher your rate of tax. These investments are marked with ★ in the Route Maps. Check in the Route Maps (and with current rates of return) that your investments are giving you as good a return as possible.

Investing to provide income later

If you're going to need your capital to give you an income later, you can't afford to risk all of it. But you do need to try to make up for the effects of inflation on its buying-power over the years between now and the time you plan to draw the income.

You could consider investing part of your money in Index-Linked National Savings Certificates. With this investment, the value of what you've invested is adjusted each month in line with inflation (provided you've held the certificate for at least a year). You can invest up to £5,000 (April 1988). A married couple can each invest up to the maximum – ie up to £10,000 in all. You could also consider index-linked British Government stocks – see Chapter 17.

If you have capital left over, it makes sense to put some of your money into investments which may give a return high enough to make up for inflation. To minimise the chances of all your risky investments doing a nose-dive at once, follow the advice on p19.

Investing to pass on more for your heirs

You may feel you can take risks with more of your capital for longer if your primary aim is to pass money on to your heirs.

What you need to be particularly aware of is the impact of inheritance tax on what your heirs will get when you die – though it won't strike unless what you leave (together with taxable gifts made in the seven years before your death) tops £110,000 (in the 1988–89 tax year). To minimise the effect of inheritance tax, consider:

■ giving away each year as much as is allowed without incurring any liability to inheritance tax
■ taking out life insurance with the proceeds going straight to your children
■ leaving your possessions directly to the youngest generation (your grandchildren rather than your children) if you want the possessions to go to them eventually.

For more details on inheritance tax, see p114.

Investing to build up a fund to buy something

If you are investing in order to buy something in the future, bear in mind that the value of some investments (eg shares, property, alternative investments) tends to fluctuate, so you may find that when you want to cash in your investments the return is not very good. It makes sense to steer clear of these investments if the time when you are going to want to use the money is very close at hand.

If, on the other hand, you'll need the money in, say, 10 years' time, you could still go for investments which fluctuate in value – but be prepared to cash the investments *before* you need the money (preferably when they're doing well). Don't be forced into cashing your investment when its value is depressed – eg by a slump in the share or property markets.

And before you decide to take extra risks with your capital in the hope of getting a greater gain, consider borrowing money to buy now rather than waiting until you have built up a larger fund.

Cashing in investments to give income

With certain lump sum investments (eg single-premium bonds), it's possible to cash in part of the investment each year to give yourself an income. But note that with, for example, single-premium bonds or unit trusts which run a withdrawal scheme, because the value of your investment fluctuates, you may have to cash in a higher proportion of your investment from time to time – or else face a drop in your income. And if you cash in more than the growth of your bond, you'll be eating into your capital.

With other investments (eg shares, alternative investments etc) there are no special schemes. And you may get a poor price at the time you want to cash part of the investment to provide income.

Building capital by reinvesting income

As the tax system stands at present, if you invest for income with a view to reinvesting it to build up capital, you may pay more tax than if you had got an equivalent rise in value through a straight capital gain. Investment income is taxed at either 25 per cent or 40 per cent for the 1988–89 tax year, the rate depending on your taxable income. Capital gains are taxed at the same rate, but the first £5,000 of capital gains you make by disposing of assets in the 1988–89 tax year is tax-free. If you haven't used up all of this tax-free allowance it may be sensible to invest for capital gains rather than income.

Review your investments regularly

You can't assume that the best investments for you today will still be the best in a few months' time. For example, the rates of return offered by different investments will change. New types of investment may come on the market. Tax laws may change too. Inflation will mean that your investments need topping up. And changes in your circumstances, not to mention the effect of external factors (like political pressures throughout the world), could make a nonsense of your original choice. So it's vital to keep an eye on what's happening and change your investments when necessary.

Keep an eye on interest rates

One difficulty in comparing the return you can get with different types of investment is that the rates of interest quoted with some investments aren't strictly comparable. This is because they don't make any allowance for how frequently interest is paid out. To make comparison easier, banks, building societies and finance companies now follow a Code of Practice which lays down rules about how rates of interest should be advertised. The only problem with this is that the Code allows them to quote *four* different rates in an advertisement – and sorting out which to use for comparison can be tricky. See Box on p28.

Interest rates aren't always what they seem

When interest is paid out to you, you can spend it or reinvest it: if you reinvest it, you earn interest on the interest. The more frequently interest is paid out to you, the sooner you can reinvest it and the higher will be the overall return.

Suppose, for example, that you invest £1,000 for a year at 8% a year. If the interest is paid out just once a year, £80 is all you can get. But if the interest is paid out at six-monthly intervals and you reinvest it, you will end up with more. This is because after six months, £40 (4% of £1,000) will be added to the £1,000 giving £1,040; in the second six months, another 4% interest will be earned on this £1,040 – ie £41.60. £40 plus £41.60 gives interest of £81.60 for the year – the same as you'd get if you put your money in an investment paying 8.16% just once a year.

If the interest is paid quarterly, the return is even higher at £1,082.40. Monthly interest would bring the return up to £1,083. And these differences would build up over the years – as Table 1 below shows. So the true rate of return depends not just on the amount of interest paid out, but also the frequency with which it is paid out.

Table 1: how £1,000 grows if interest at 8% is added

	yearly	half-yearly	quarterly	monthly
after 1 year	£1080	£1082	£1082	£1083
after 2 years	£1166	£1170	£1172	£1173
after 5 years	£1469	£1480	£1486	£1490
after 10 years	£2159	£2191	£2208	£2220
true return	8%	8.16%	8.24%	8.30%

Finding the true rate of return

The rates quoted on investments where interest is added once a year are true rates of return – this applies to National Savings Investment Account, for example. The returns quoted on National Savings Certificates and the redemption yields on British Government stocks are also true returns which can be directly compared one with another.

But many other investments add interest more often than once a year: with most building society accounts other than regular savings accounts, local authority loans, bank deposit and savings accounts and finance company deposits, interest is added twice a year (sometimes quarterly). National Savings Income Bonds pay out income monthly, and you can ask for monthly interest with some other savings accounts. In all these cases, you need to know the true rate of return to compare them with investments paying out interest less frequently.

Table 2, below, sets out the true rates of return for a variety of quoted rates, when the interest is paid out half-yearly, quarterly or monthly. Banks, building societies and finance companies now quote true rates in their advertising – they call them the 'compounded annual rates', or CAR.

Note that with National Savings Ordinary Account, interest is paid once a year but only for complete calendar months. So if you pay in or withdraw money during a month, the true return may be *lower* than the quoted rate.

Table 2: true rates of return

quoted rate	true rate if interest is paid out or added		
	half-yearly	quarterly	monthly
5%	5.06%	5.10%	5.12%
6%	6.09%	6.14%	6.17%
7%	7.12%	7.19%	7.23%
8%	8.16%	8.24%	8.30%
9%	9.20%	9.31%	9.38%
10%	10.25%	10.38%	10.47%
11%	11.30%	11.46%	11.57%
12%	12.36%	12.55%	12.68%

Gross rates of return

Interest on most types of savings account is now paid after deduction of tax at the composite rate (see p99). There is no more basic rate tax to be paid on the interest, and the rate is usually known as the net rate.

Advertisements for such investments often quote a 'gross equivalent' rate of return to compare with the return from investments which pay interest without deduction of tax (mainly National Savings schemes). The gross equivalent is the rate which a basic rate taxpayer would have to earn from an investment which pays interest before tax is deducted, to give the same after-tax return as from a bank or building society (for how to work out the gross equivalent, see p100).

Suppose, for example, that you get 6% net interest from a building society account. With a basic rate of tax of 25%, you'd have to earn a before-tax rate of interest of 8% to have 6% left after tax (8% less 25% of 8% = 8% less 2% = 6%). So the gross equivalent rate would be 8%.

Note that quoting a gross equivalent rate does not mean that you can actually get that rate if you don't pay tax. Even if you don't pay any tax at all, you can't claim back any composite rate tax that's been deducted. So non-taxpayers should ignore gross equivalent rates and concentrate on what you'd actually get.

The different rates – what they mean

Four different rates of return may be quoted in savings advertisements by banks, building societies and finance companies which follow the voluntary Code of Practice:

- **net** – if you draw out the income and don't reinvest it, the rate you'll get with no more basic rate tax to pay
- **gross equivalent** – the rate you'd have to get before deduction of tax to end up with the net rate after basic rate tax had been deducted
- **net compounded annual rate (CAR)** – if you reinvest the income, the rate you'll get with no more basic rate tax to pay
- **gross equivalent compounded rate** – the rate you'd have to get before deduction of tax to end up with the net compounded annual rate after tax had been deducted at the basic rate.

If you're choosing between different investments, some paying interest after deduction of tax and some before tax, make sure you compare like with like to see which gives the better return. Suppose, for example, you want to compare National Savings Investment Account (interest paid before tax) with a building society account (interest paid after tax). The National Savings Investment Account pays out interest once a year, so the quoted interest rate is the true rate of return. Compare this with the following rate for the building society account:

- if you pay tax, the gross equivalent compounded rate
- if you don't pay tax, the net compounded annual rate.

2

INVESTMENT CHOICES

Once you've worked out your investment strategy, you can start to think about the investments themselves. To help narrow down the choice of investments to those which would be most suitable for you, use the Route Maps on pp32–35. One is for lump sums, the other for savings (either on a regular basis or piecemeal).

Follow the Route Maps for each sum of money you want to invest – eg your emergency fund, money you're willing to see fluctuate in value, money you can invest for 10 years, and so on. You'll end up with a different shortlist for each sum.

For any investments which you think might suit you, read the relevant chapter in the book. Then find out what is happening to that investment at the moment. In each chapter, we tell you where to get more information. And check in the newspapers for the up-to-date rates of return being offered by the investments you have in mind. There's a bird's eye view of different types of investment in Chapter 8.

Armed with these facts, narrow down the investments on your shortlists to those which suit you best. Don't forget that work on your investments doesn't end there – you'll need to keep them under review to make sure that they continue to suit you.

To show you how this can be done, we look at the choices facing a number of investors. For example, Roger and Rose Steele want to find homes for both a lump sum and for their savings. Their strategy and decisions are followed through from start to finish. The remaining six examples look at only one of the problems each investor faces. Three investors have lump sums of varying sizes to invest; with the other three, it's savings of various amounts which are presenting difficulties.

Of course, your own final choice out of the shortlist each investor ends up with, might – because of your particular preferences – be different from that in our examples.

Planning your investments

Roger and Rose Steele have one child, Alex. Roger earns around £12,000 a year as a teacher. They want to save for quite a few things – a holiday next year, and then a car, new furniture and so on. They don't want to lock their money away for too long. They've already got some money saved up in a building society ordinary share account and wonder whether that's the best place for it.

How Roger and Rose decide what to do with their money

First, they look at the investment priorities checklist on p13.

Both Roger and Rose have life insurance cover. They have policies which will pay out lump sums and a regular income if either dies. At present they have £2,100 put aside in a building society ordinary share account. But they feel that £500 is as much as they need in an emergency fund.

Roger and Rose are buying their own home with a mortgage and don't intend to move in the next few years. Roger is in the teachers' pension scheme – which offers quite good benefits.

Roger and Rose would like to save something each month. So they've got to decide how to invest:
- their £500 emergency fund
- the additional £1,600 lump sum
- the money they manage to save in future.

They use the investment strategy checklist (see p14) to help sort out their investment plan:
- age – Roger is 34 and Rose 28. Rose is hoping to go back to work when Alex, their 3-year-old, goes to school – but they're not going to rely on this
- health – both are in good health
- family – apart from Alex, there are no immediate dependants. But they feel that if any of the parents were widowed or became ill, they'd like to help out. At the moment, this prospect seems unlikely, but it means they don't feel like committing themselves to very long-term savings – which they might not be able to keep up if they do have to help out. They don't intend giving Alex a private education. If they did, they would consider saving in a school-fees scheme
- expectations – if Rose can't go back to her old job, she would like to consider some sort of retraining. This might involve some expense – they don't really know. There are no

large inheritances coming their way – though eventually they will share in the proceeds from the sale of their parents' houses

■ tax – Roger is a basic rate taxpayer, and any investment income won't put him into a higher tax bracket

■ what they want from their investments – their main aims are: to pay for a holiday next year and later for a new car; to pay for any retraining that Rose may need in a couple of years or so; and to enable them to help out their parents should the need arise. They aren't looking for income from their investments

■ how much they can invest – apart from the £2,100 in the building society, they reckon they can save about £50 a month – but most of this is earmarked for their holiday next year

■ how long they can invest for – the Steeles have decided to keep £500 handy as an emergency fund. And they need £40 a month of their regular savings available for their planned holiday. The other lump sum of £1,600 and £10-a-month regular savings can be invested for somewhat longer. But long-term investment clearly doesn't suit their needs.

Once Roger and Rose have chosen their investments they'll keep an eye on what's happening and may move their money around from time to time. But first they follow the route map overleaf to see the choices open to them.

How Roger and Rose choose their investments

Lump sum

First of all they try to sort out what to do with the £2,100 they have. They intend keeping £500 of this as an emergency fund and following the Route Map find three types of investment where they can put this money and get it out at short notice – a bank or finance company deposit account, building society instant access accounts or National Savings Ordinary Account. They read about these and check on the rates of return currently offered by these alternatives. They choose a building society tiered interest account which pays a higher than normal rate of interest on £500 or more. (There's the added advantage of the society being open on Saturdays.) They'll keep a close watch on rates of return in the future in case other investments offer a better return.

Now they follow the Route Map again to see what they could do with the £1,600. They skip the next few steps – they're buying their own house, are in a pension scheme, not close to retirement and can leave their money invested for at least a year. At the next step they see they should

Route map for lump sums

Start here for each chunk
of your money

Looking for a home for
your emergency fund
(available at short notice)? **NO** →

YES ↓

Bank and finance
company deposit
accounts
Building society ordinary
share or instant access
accounts
National Savings
Ordinary Account ★

Are you buying your
own home? **NO** →

Consider buying a home
– see Chapter 9

YES ↓

Are you in a pension
scheme, or already
retired? **NO** →

Single-premium
personal pension
plan ★

YES ↓

Are you coming up to
retirement? **YES** →

Consider turning part
of your lump sum
into additional voluntary
contributions ★

NO ↓

Can you leave your
money invested for at
least a year? **NO** →

Bank deposit, term and
notice accounts
Building society ordinary
share and notice
accounts
Finance company term
and notice accounts
National Savings
Investment Account ●
National Savings
Ordinary Account ★

YES ↓

Do you want to protect
your money against
inflation with an index-
linked investment? **YES** →

Prepared to take a slight
risk to get a slightly
higher return - and
looking mainly for
capital gain rather than
income?

NO ↓

Looking for income now? **NO** →

YES ↓

Are you at least 65,
preferably older? **NO** →

Are you prepared
to see the value of
your investment go
down rather than
up in the hope that
you will get a
better return?

YES ↓

Consider a home income
scheme or an annuity

YES ↓

**For longer-term
investments (seven
years, say):**
Shares, unit trusts or
investment trusts
Personal Equity Plans
(PEPs)
Single-premium
investment bonds ★
Could also consider:
British Government
stocks (and there's no
risk if held to maturity)

● May be particularly
worth considering for non-
taxpayers
★ May be particularly
worth considering if
you pay tax at the
higher rate

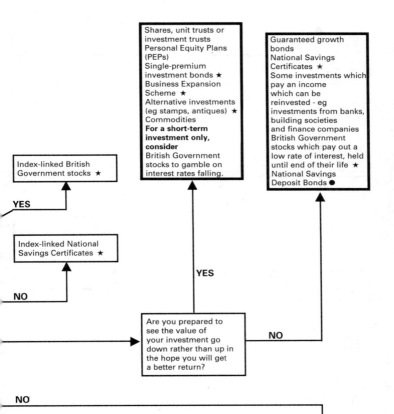

Shares, unit trusts or investment trusts
Personal Equity Plans (PEPs)
Single-premium investment bonds ★
Business Expansion Scheme ★
Alternative investments (eg stamps, antiques) ★
Commodities
For a short-term investment only, consider
British Government stocks to gamble on interest rates falling.

Guaranteed growth bonds
National Savings Certificates ★
Some investments which pay an income which can be reinvested - eg investments from banks, building societies and finance companies
British Government stocks which pay out a low rate of interest, held until end of their life ★
National Savings Deposit Bonds ●

Index-linked British Government stocks ★

YES

Index-linked National Savings Certificates ★

NO

YES

Are you prepared to see the value of your investment go down rather than up in the hope you will get a better return?

NO

NO

Notice and term accounts from banks, building societies and finance companies
Building society instant access and monthly income accounts
Guaranteed income bonds
Local authority loans
National Savings Income Bonds ●
National Savings Investment Account ●

Route map for savings

Start here for each chunk
of your money

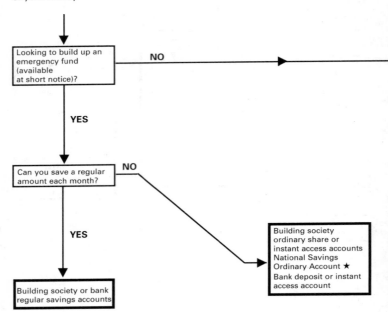

Looking to build up an
emergency fund
(available
at short notice)?

NO

YES

Can you save a regular
amount each month?

NO

YES

Building society or bank
regular savings accounts

Building society
ordinary share or
instant access accounts
National Savings
Ordinary Account ★
Bank deposit or instant
access account

● May be particularly
worth considering for
non-taxpayers

★ May be particularly
worth considering if
you pay tax at the
higher rate

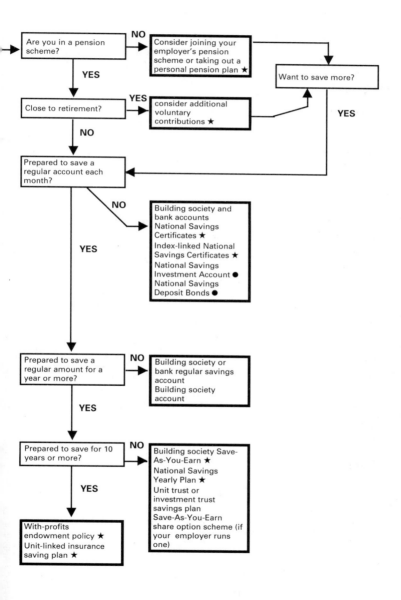

Are you in a pension scheme?

NO → Consider joining your employer's pension scheme or taking out a personal pension plan ★

YES ↓

Close to retirement?

YES → consider additional voluntary contributions ★

NO ↓

Want to save more? **YES**

Prepared to save a regular account each month?

NO → Building society and bank accounts
National Savings Certificates ★
Index-linked National Savings Certificates ★
National Savings Investment Account ●
National Savings Deposit Bonds ●

YES ↓

Prepared to save a regular amount for a year or more?

NO → Building society or bank regular savings account
Building society account

YES ↓

Prepared to save for 10 years or more?

NO → Building society Save-As-You-Earn ★
National Savings Yearly Plan ★
Unit trust or investment trust savings plan
Save-As-You-Earn share option scheme (if your employer runs one)

YES ↓

With-profits endowment policy ★
Unit-linked insurance saving plan ★

consider an index-linked investment. They'd like to put about half the money somewhere it won't lose its buying power so that it can pay for their new car. And, as they think that inflation might rise from its current low level, they decide to put it in Index-linked National Savings Certificates.

They go through the Route Map again for the last part of their lump sum which they are prepared to risk in the hope of a windfall. After answering *No* to the question *Looking for income now?* they come to investments they should consider if they're prepared to see the value of their investments go down rather than up in the hope of a better return. They see that these include shares, unit trusts, investment trusts and single premium investment bonds. Believing that the prospects for the stock market look good, they plump for a couple of unit trusts (they haven't enough money to make a sensible investment in shares).

Regular saving
They follow the Route Map on the previous pages to see what to do with the £50 they reckon they'll be able to save each month. They come to the question *Prepared to save a regular amount for a year or more?* for the £40 a month they're saving for their next year's holiday. As the answer is *No*, they have a choice of building society and bank savings schemes. After checking on current interest rates, they decide that a building society account with a high interest rate will offer them the best overall return and the opportunity to withdraw their money at short notice without losing out. For the remaining £10 a month, they are prepared to consider saving for more than a year, but not as long as 10 years. At £20 a month, the minimum monthly investment for National Savings Yearly Plan is too high. They plump for building society SAYE, a five-year investment which offers a fixed rate of return.

Summary
They're going to invest £500 in a building society account, £800 in Index-linked National Savings Certificates and £800 in unit trusts. They're going to save £40 a month in a building society high interest account and £10 a month in building society SAYE.

Saving for something special

Anne Stevens is a basic rate taxpayer. She wants to go to Australia to see her daughter and her grandchildren, but the cheapest return fare is over £1,000. She can afford to save around £25 a month – so will need an investment lasting four or five years to save up the fare (which is likely to rise further through inflation).

She follows the Route Map until she comes to the question: *Prepared to save a regular amount each month?* Answering *Yes*, she moves on to consider just how long she can commit herself – over one year but not as long as 10 years. That presents four options: share option schemes (not an option for Anne – her employer isn't offering one); unit trust or investment trust savings plans, which are a mite too risky for her liking; and building society SAYE and National Savings Yearly Plan. Both the latter offer a fixed return over five years, according to the Table on p120 onwards.

Yearly Plan doesn't quite fit her needs: each year's savings have to be left for a further four years to get the maximum rate of return – so her second year's savings wouldn't earn the full rate unless left until year six, the third year's till year seven and so on. She is likely to want all the money back at the end of five years and so would lose out on the full rate of return.

That leaves building society SAYE, which does pay the top rate of return on every £ paid in over five years (and a bonus if the money is left for another two years). Anne could get a slightly higher rate of interest in some types of building society account, but their interest rates can go down (or up) – so she decides to plump for the fixed rate of interest offered by SAYE. To help build up the sum she'll need for her trip Anne decides that whenever she has spare money she'll try to put it in another building society account – a suitable home for small, irregular sums of money. She also decides to approach her bank manager to see whether, once she's saved for some time, she could get a loan.

Investing with an eye on the taxman

Paul and Sheila Plantin, in their late-40s, find themselves with £25,000 to invest when Sheila's mother dies, leaving her a legacy. They live in their own home, have an adequate emergency fund and enough insurance for their needs. Paul belongs to an excellent company pension scheme (though won't quite qualify for a full pension when he reaches 65 – he only joined it in his thirties).

Despite Paul's high salary, private school fees make a big dent in their income, and will continue to do so for some time. So they'd like to invest £20,000 of the legacy to increase their income while these fees continue, but are worried about extra income tax they might have to pay (they pay tax at the higher rate of 40 per cent). They'll invest the remaining £5,000 with as little risk as possible (they're hoping to buy a boat in five years' time when the children are older).

First they follow the Route Map for the safe investment. They check investments with a ★ next to them carefully (these are particularly worth considering if you pay tax at the higher rate). They come early on to Index-linked National Savings Certificates which guarantee to maintain the buying power of their money. After a year, they can withdraw some money (tax-free) if they need it and still get index-linking. They see they should also consider index-linked British Government stocks if they're prepared to take a slight risk. They check on the current prices for the stocks, and find that, for their rate of tax, the return should just beat inflation. They decide to put £2,500 into each of these index-linked investments.

Next they follow the Route Map for their longer-term investment until they come to the question about whether they are looking for income now. Yes, they are. They pass over the next question about age and are then asked if they are prepared to see the value of their money go down rather than up in the hope of a better return. Once again the answer is *Yes*. They see they can choose between shares, unit trusts, investment trusts, Personal Equity Plans and single-premium investment bonds plus riskier investments still like antiques and commodities. Deciding to give the riskier options a miss they decide to invest £10,000 in single-premium bonds. They can withdraw up to 5% of their investment each year for 20 years without paying tax. In 20 years' time, they'll have retired and are unlikely to be paying higher rates of tax – so may avoid paying any extra tax on this investment. They decide to split the £10,000 equally between two managed bonds.

They then invest the maximum £3,000 in a Personal Equity Plan to get the tax advantages. The remaining £7,000 is invested in unit trusts – ones that aim for capital growth rather than income. They plan to cash in some of their units each year, but to make sure that they don't make net capital gains of more than the £5,000 limit free of capital gains tax. As they approach retirement and the school fees come to an end, they'll consider making additional voluntary contributions to Paul's pension scheme to make up for the missing years.

Saving for a rainy day

Mike and Sue English are in their late 20s, with one baby and another due soon. They pay no tax – and feel they've got little cash left over at the end of each month, what with food, rates, rent and so on. They are worried because they have no savings or life insurance.

For someone in their position with dependants, life insurance should come before any attempt to save money. If Mike died, Sue would have to rely on social security to make ends meet. And if Sue were to die, Mike would have a hard time looking after the baby and going to work. They realise that investment-type life insurance is not really for them. With this firmly sorted out in their minds, they decide to go to an insurance adviser to arrange protection-type life insurance, to cover them should one or other die.

Next they think about their emergency fund. They follow the Route Map on p32 and see that they are recommended to consider building society instant access accounts, a bank deposit account or National Savings Ordinary Account. None of these is marked as being especially suitable for non-taxpayers, so they check up on the rates of interest on offer. They go for a building society ordinary share account which seems to have the edge over the others. A bonus is that they'll get a cash card giving them access to their money round the clock from the machines outside hundreds of building society branches – useful in a real emergency.

Once they've built up a large enough emergency fund, they'll go through the Route Map again and look for a somewhat longer-term investment for their additional savings. One strong contender is likely to be National Savings Investment Account: this pays a particularly good rate of return to non-taxpayers, but needs a month's notice for withdrawals.

Investing a windfall

Marianne Fortune, 21, has just inherited £3,000 from her grandmother. She's single, lives with her parents and has a large enough emergency fund. She's a basic rate taxpayer. She reckons that some time in the future she'll want to buy a home, and decides to put £2,000 towards this. She decides to try to turn the remaining £1,000 into something bigger – she's prepared to take risks with it.

She follows the Route Map for lump sums, and sees that investing the £2,000 earmarked for a future home won't be easy: house prices have consistently risen faster than prices in general for many years, so Marianne needs an investment which offers the chance of outstripping inflation in the future. Index-linked investments do that – but only just, so she rules them out. Accepting that she is going to have to take some risk to keep up with house prices, Marianne plumps for a couple of unit trusts – both growth funds with any income reinvested.

She goes back to the Route Map, to see how she should invest the £1,000 she's going to gamble with. She looks up the shortlisted investments in the Table and in the Chapters later in the book. She toys with investing her money in shares but could really only afford to invest in one company – a very risky idea. She decides instead to put the £1,000 towards improving the 18th century glass collection she started a couple of years ago – even if the bottom drops out of antique glass, she'll get a bit of pleasure out of the collecting.

Investing for extra income

Miss Simmons is aged 80, and lives alone. She lives on her state pension and a small pension from her ex-employer and wonders what to do with the £5,000 she has to invest – which is at present in a bank deposit account. She's alarmed at the way inflation has made inroads into the buying-power of the interest she gets. She'd like to get a bit of extra income to allow herself a few more treats.

She realizes that she can leave some of her money in the bank deposit account to act as an emergency fund – but she reckons she won't need more than £300 for this. Thinking about it, though, she decides to leave twice this amount in her account – so that she can draw on it if she wants extra income.

Miss Simmons already owns her home, so doesn't need to worry about getting a mortgage. She hasn't got any Index-linked investments, and reckons that Index-linked National Savings Certificates will suit her very well. Although this investment does not pay out a regular income, she sees she could cash certificates to get an income. She realises that the value of what she invests will go up in line with the Retail Prices Index (though not if she cashes the certificates before a year is up). This index-linking seems a big plus to Miss Simmons. So she decides to put £2,000 into these and, after the first year, to cash bits of her investment if she feels particularly hard-pressed.

She decides not to put any money into index-linked British Government stocks – she wants to take no risks, and besides they don't pay a worthwhile income (nor can they be cashed cheaply in bits and pieces).

Since she's over 70, she could consider an annuity or cashing in on her home through a home income scheme. She's not really tempted by a home income scheme – she may want to move home later – so she decides to put the remaining £2,400 into an annuity. She realises that the income from this won't be protected against inflation. She decides to give more thought to moving to a smaller house, and investing any money from the sale to give her more income. She realises that there are heavy expenses involved in buying and selling property – and that she'll have to allow for these before going ahead.

Saving for retirement

Bob Mason, self-employed, earning around £10,000 a year, and his wife, Cathy, are in their mid-40s. Their three children have all left home and Cathy thinks it's time they started saving for Bob's retirement. They don't want to rely on their business for their retirement funds.

They already have an adequate emergency fund and are buying their home with a mortgage. They follow the Route Map for savings to the question: *Are you in a pension scheme?* Bob is self-employed, and already contributes £20 a month (£240 a year) towards a personal pension plan. He asks the insurance company which runs the pension plan what he might get in the way of a pension at 65 if he kept up this level of saving. They say about £300 a month, so Bob and Cathy decide to step up the amount they save.

Bob can get tax relief on up to $17^{1}/_{2}$% of his £10,000 a year – ie £1,750 a year or around £145 a month. The Masons reckon that they can afford another £30 a month without too much trouble, so take out a second personal pension plan for this amount (having plans with two companies means that they haven't got all their eggs in one company basket).

Like many self-employed people Bob's earnings fluctuate from month to month, and even with these higher pension contributions they would have something over to save in good months. So the Masons decide to add odd savings to their emergency fund in a building society ordinary share account. Their emergency fund is over £500, so they switch it to a tiered interest rate account where they get a higher than normal rate of interest. If the amount drops below £500, they won't lose out: the interest rate falls back to the basic ordinary share rate.

3

INVESTING FOR RETIREMENT

For many people, ensuring an adequate income in retirement is a major motive behind saving and investing. This chapter will help you formulate a strategy to achieve this, whether you're still working, close to retirement, or have already retired.

The first step in sorting out your retirement finances is to look at how your income measures up to your expenditure when you retire. Chapters 13 and 14 of this book look in detail at the various types of pension schemes – use these to work out how much you can expect from pensions. If the answer is not enough, then you will need to consider the options for boosting your income in retirement.

Of course, inflation makes budgeting for your retirement difficult if you're looking a good many years ahead. Currently, though, the state retirement pension is increased regularly in line with rising prices. And the amount you can expect from an employer's pension should go up too, at least in the period up to retirement. But the buying-power of the income you can expect from any savings could be drastically reduced by inflation. The best you can probably do is to work out what you'll get (and what you'll need) in terms of today's prices and pensions. Then make regular checks – once a year, say – that you aren't going too far off course.

What you'll get

Your chief sources of income are likely to be some or all of:
- your state retirement pension
- a pension from your job (and from any earlier jobs)
- pensions from personal pension plans
- income from working after retirement
- income from any savings.

How much state retirement pension you might expect [1]

tax year in which you'll retire	your earnings: typical yearly amount in today's money £	your yearly state pension: single person £	married couple £	married couple if each qualifies for own pension [2] £
1988–89	5,000	2,500	3,790	4,370
	7,500	2,810	4,100	4,680
(with 10 years'	10,000	3,120	4,410	5,000
additional	12,500	3,440	4,720	5,310
pension)	15,000	3,750	5,040	5,620
	20,000	3,860	5,140	6,250
	25,000	3,860	5,140	6,870
	30,000	3,860	5,140	7,500
1993–94	5,000	2,680	3,960	4,420
	7,500	3,150	4,430	4,890
(with 15 years'	10,000	3,620	4,900	5,360
additional	12,500	4,080	5,370	5,820
pension)	15,000	4,550	5,840	6,300
	20,000	4,710	6,000	7,230
	25,000	4,710	6,000	8,170
	30,000	4,710	6,000	9,110

1998–99

your earnings		(with 20 years' additional pension)	
5,000	2,860	4,140	4,460
7,500	3,480	4,770	5,090
10,000	4,110	5,390	5,710
12,500	4,730	6,020	6,340
15,000	5,360	6,640	6,960
20,000	5,570	6,860	8,210
25,000	5,570	6,860	9,460
30,000	5,570	6,860	10,710

2008–09

your earnings		(with 20 years' additional pension [3])	
5,000	2,710	4,000	4,430
7,500	3,210	4,500	4,600
10,000	3,710	5,000	5,430
12,500	4,210	5,500	5,930
15,000	4,710	6,000	6,430
20,000	4,890	6,170	7,430
25,000	4,890	6,170	8,430
30,000	4,890	6,170	9,430

[1] Assuming you retire at age 65 (men) or 60 (women) and that you are not contracted out of the state scheme. Includes the basic pension and additional pension, but not graduated pension. All the figures assume that you qualify for as much pension from the state as you possibly can, given your age and earnings. If you have gaps in your National Insurance contributions record, you may get a lower amount.

[2] Assuming husband and wife each earn half the amount shown in the *your earnings* column. If they don't, pension may be somewhat less – but never less than shown in the previous column.

[3] Amounts are lower than in 1998–99 because of changes to the additional pension (see p189).

Your state retirement pension

Everyone who has worked for long enough (and paid enough National Insurance contributions) is entitled to a *basic pension* – £41.15 a week for a single person, £65.90 for a married man, from 11 April 1988 onwards. Anyone who worked for an employer after April 1979 and who was not contracted-out of the state scheme will be entitled to an *additional pension* under the State Earnings Related Pension Scheme (SERPS) as well. People who were employed between April 1961 and April 1975 may also get a *graduated pension*. See Chapter 13.

The Table on pp44–45 shows, for different levels of income, what state retirement pension (basic plus additional) you could expect with different lengths of time to go to retirement. The pension we give is worked out at today's rates – but state pensions are currently increased each year broadly in line with prices in general.

A pension from your job

What you will get from an employer's pension scheme depends on how the scheme is set up. With *final pay schemes* you get a proportion (one-sixtieth, or one-eightieth, say) of your 'final pay' (as defined by your scheme) for each year you've been in the scheme. With *money purchase schemes*, your pension is the income that you and your employer's contributions can buy at the time you retire. See Chapter 13 for more details, and check with your employer how your scheme works, and approximately how much you could hope to get when you retire.

The problem with a pension from a job, is that though it may seem handsome when you first retire, it's likely to look less appealing after 10 years or so if it hasn't increased in line with inflation. The Table on p17 shows the effect of inflation on the buying-power of your money.

Many schemes have some pension increases built in. And some employers have, in the past, given special increases to help cope with inflation. But unless you belong to a scheme where the pension is index-linked (eg the Civil Service and other public sector schemes), you should allow for inflation in working out how well off you'll be after you retire.

If your scheme provides a lump sum in addition to your pension (or in place of part of your pension if you choose) deciding which to take isn't easy – see p202 for things to take into account.

It's unlikely that you'll stay in one job all your working

life – and unfortunately, changing jobs is likely to mean you end up with less pension than if you'd stayed with one employer.

You will have several options to consider:

■ a *deferred pension* from the job you leave (based on the number of years you were in the scheme)

■ a *transfer payment* from your old pension scheme into the new one you're joining, to increase the benefits you'll get from it

■ a *transfer payment* into a personal pension scheme (see below).

Any deferred pension from a final pay scheme for service since 1 January 1985 must be increased each year at least to match inflation (with a ceiling of 5 per cent, though many schemes in practice cover inflation in excess of 5 per cent a year). But if you've got a deferred pension from service before 1 January 1985, it is unlikely to be increased to keep pace with inflation since then (unless the scheme is in the public sector). So when taking deferred pensions for service before 1 January 1985 into account, be sure to allow for the erosion of its buying power through inflation (use the Table on p227).

With a transfer payment into another employer's pension scheme based on final pay, you may be credited with years of membership in the new scheme – this would ensure that your whole pension was linked to your final pay.

Personal pensions

If you're self-employed, or in a job but contracted out of the State Earnings Related Pension Scheme (SERPS), you may be contributing to personal pension plans (see Chapter 14). These are marketed by insurance companies, building societies, banks and other investment managers, and what you will get depends on the amount of contributions you have paid. Check up with the pension provider (if they haven't told you already) how much pension your payments have so far earned you, and how much you'll get if you keep paying a certain amount into a plan each year. You'll have to adjust the figure you're given to allow for inflation between now and retirement. To build up an adequate pension, you should aim to pay up to the maximum allowed for tax relief – see p236.

Working after retirement

Be wary of setting too much store by this. The economic situation may make jobs for people over retirement age hard to come by, your health may have deteriorated, or you may find yourself less and less inclined to go on working. So don't rely on this source of income to carry you through a major part of your retirement. And remember that the *earnings rule* means that what you earn could reduce your state pension – see p191. Note that if you do work after retirement age, you may be advised to put off drawing your state pension, and thereby build up more – see p190.

Income from savings

If you have money saved already, or plan to save in the future, you can add on to what you get in the way of pensions any income you'll get from investments. But bear in mind:

■ if you invest your money for maximum safety, its value (except with a few investments – see p51) may not keep pace with inflation – its buying-power, and that of the income you get from it, will fall over the years

■ if you've accepted some degree of risk in the attempt to safeguard the buying-power of your money, you stand the chance of losing at least some of it. So it's sensible to make a pessimistic estimate of the income your investments will provide in, say, 20 years' time.

Widows, widowers and other dependants

While planning your retirement finances, it's vital to check that your family wouldn't be left short should you die. Many employers' pension schemes provide a pension for widows (and some even for widowers), on the death of the employee – whether before or after retirement. If your family couldn't manage on this (together with any income from their job, your savings and state benefits) you need life insurance. This book doesn't cover this aspect of your family finances – for how to work out how much life insurance you need, see *Your money for your life, Which?*, September 1987 p430.

What you'll need

Around the time you retire, a shift in your spending pattern is very probable. You may be able to predict some of this change fairly easily, especially the part that relates to simply stopping work. You won't have to pay for fares to and from the office, for example, or for lunches at work. And you may also know that you'll spend more on particular hobbies – golf, gardening or painting, say – when you have the time to give to them. You may also know that some of your current financial commitments – the mortgage or school fees, for example – will have ended by the time you retire.

It's less easy to take into account the effects of simply growing older. As you get older, you may well want to spend more than you do now on, for example, staying warm, transport, labour-saving appliances, holidays (you may not want to rough it any more).

Giving realistic weight to this kind of age-related spending change is very hard – particularly if you're trying to look 20 or 30 years into the future. But it's still worth trying to allow for it when you work out your future spending needs: that way you stand a better chance of coming closer to the truth than you do if you assume you'll spend your money the same way in your retirement as in your thirties or forties.

Balancing your budget

If you are looking ahead some time to retirement, you need to be thinking of ways of protecting your long-term savings against inflation, until the time comes when you'll actually need them.

The first two chapters of this book will help you in making your choices. If you're not buying a home already, this may be one of the best forms of long-term investment you could make – see Chapter 9. If you're already buying a home, moving to a better, more expensive one might pay.

If you're employed and there's a pension scheme at work, this is likely to be a worthwhile way of saving – and you could consider making additional voluntary contributions (see p203), especially in the last few years before retirement. Both your own and your employer's pension contributions are normally free from income tax. And they go into a special fund which doesn't have to pay income tax or capital gains tax. In addition, a pension in a final pay scheme (the commonest type) is linked to your pay when you leave your job, so giving you some protection against inflation until you retire.

If you don't belong to an employer's pension scheme, or if you're self-employed, you should consider taking out a personal pension. This is, in effect, a pension scheme run by an investment manager (eg insurance company or unit trust manager) for individuals rather than for groups of employees. As with an employer's scheme, you get tax relief on your contributions, up to a certain limit. The fund your payments go into pays no income tax or capital gains tax. So you should get a good return on your money – but you won't be able to get it out before the age of 50 at the earliest.

If you've got the choice of an employer's scheme but feel its benefits are poor, check on whether you'd do better to go for a personal pension – though you're unlikely to get any help through employers' contributions.

Consider putting most of your other long-term savings into investments where your money at least stands a chance of maintaining its buying power. Index-linked National Savings Certificates guarantee inflation-proofing and a bit more. Index-linked British Government stocks can also protect savings against inflation, depending on when you buy and sell them. Investments in shares, property, commodities and alternative investments such as antique furniture or gold coins may keep pace with inflation over longer periods – but this will not be guaranteed. Be prepared to move your money around to take advantage of the investment opportunities of the day. Bear in mind the rate of tax you pay. Make sure your investments give you the best return – taking both income tax and capital gains tax into account (see p93).

Making ends meet in retirement

Your major sources of income in retirement are likely to be your pensions (from the state, and from any other schemes you were in) and the income from your savings. If you've already retired, there's likely to be little scope for building up extra savings to increase your income. And you may find that, because of inflation, an income which seemed adequate at the start of retirement, is looking on the low side now. The Table on p17 shows how inflation can whittle away your buying-power – bear this in mind when considering how much income you'll need over your retirement years.

Before checking on ways in which you could boost your income, consider ways of cutting your expenses. For example, check that you are claiming all the help that's available from social security (in the way of income support, and the like) or from your local authority (housing benefit, meals on wheels, home helps and the like). Check at your local social security office and Town Hall. Also make sure you're not paying more tax than you need – the current *Which? Tax-Saving Guide* should help. Look carefully at how you're spending your money *now* to see if there are any areas where you could cut back relatively painlessly.

You could also think about moving to a house which is cheaper to run – one with lower rates and fuel bills, or closer to shops, for example. But don't put off this decision for too long – it may be easier to make the move and establish new friends and social activities earlier in retirement.

If you've managed to cut down your expenses, you could either invest the money, or use some or all of it in ways which will cut costs later on – eg insulating your home, making repairs to your home. This sort of investment may not give you the best return on your money – but knowing that there'll be fewer large bills to meet later in retirement may be worth it in terms of peace of mind.

Boosting the income from your investments

Check that your investments are working as well for you as they can (taking into account the way you are taxed – see p52). You should be looking for investments that stand a chance of maintaining their buying-power – either through an increasing income as time passes, or through capital growth with the possibility of withdrawing regular amounts to use as income. No one investment can fully match these needs – so keep an eye on your investments overall to see how they're doing and likely to do. For general advice on planning your savings, see the first two chapters of this book.

Chapter 8 gives you a bird's eye view of a wide range of investments. But some investments are particularly worth considering in retirement. Index-linked National Savings Certificates, for example, can protect at least part of your capital against inflation. The limit on the amount you can invest is £5,000 (£10,000 for a married couple). See p176 for details. To protect more of your savings against inflation, consider Index-linked British Government stocks (see Chapter 17). Whether you get a return greater or less than inflation depends on the price you buy at, whether you can hang on until redemption, or if not, the price you sell at.

An annuity is an investment designed especially for the elderly. You hand over your capital to an insurance company in return for a guaranteed income for the rest of your life – see Chapter 22.

Getting an income from your home

You may be able to use your home to raise extra income in retirement. One way of doing this is to sell it and move to a cheaper one, chosen with an eye to lower running costs. This should leave you with a lump sum to invest.

If your home is of a convenient size and easy to run, you may feel there is no need for you to move. You could instead consider getting extra income through a home income scheme – which is specially designed for elderly people (the over-70s, say). See p363.

An alternative way to use your home to raise money – without moving out – is to let part of it, or to take in a lodger. Before you decide to try this however, get up-to-date information on your rights (and duties) as a landlord – in particular, what your rights are about getting your lodger or tenant out at some later date. The Department of the Environment publishes a series of leaflets which give the current rules – get them from your local Citizens' Advice Bureau. And remember that when you take a lodger or tenant you are going into business on a small scale: you should keep careful records of income and expenses, and keep an eye on changes in the law which may affect you. It would be prudent to get advice from a solicitor before becoming a landlord.

Tax after retirement

Like everybody else, the over-65s are liable for tax. But they can claim a higher personal allowance than younger people – so more of their income can be tax-free. The tax rules which currently apply to the over-65s are summarised below: there are changes in the pipeline for 1990 – see p54.

Age allowance

Anyone who reaches the age of 65 or over during the start of the tax year (or whose wife does) can claim age allowance – whether or not they have retired – instead of the ordinary single person's or married man's allowance. For the 1988–89 tax year the full age allowance is £3,180 for a single person, £5,035 for a married man. Those reaching 80 or over during the tax year can claim an even higher rate of age allowance: for the 1988–89 tax year, the 80-plus rate is £3,310 if single, £5,205 for a married man.

But age allowance is reduced by two-thirds of the amount

by which a person's 'total income' (see p95) exceeds a certain limit – £10,600 for the 1988–89 tax year. The allowance is never reduced below the level of the ordinary personal allowance, no matter how high 'total income' is. For the 1988–89 tax year, an elderly person with an income of not more than £11,463 if single, or £12,010 if married, could benefit from age allowance (those entitled to the 80-plus rate benefit up to £11,658 if single, £12,265 for a married man).

If your 'total income' is within the range where your age allowance is being reduced, bear in mind that each extra £ of taxable income you get will effectively be taxed at a fairly high rate – over 40 per cent in the 1988–89 tax year. This might make investments where the return is not taxable (eg National Savings Certificates) worth considering – look carefully at investments with a * next to them in the Route Maps on pp32–35.

See below for a complication which can arise if you cash in part of a life insurance policy.

Married women's pensions

If you're a married woman, a pension for which you qualify on your own contributions counts as your own earned income. This means that you can claim the wife's earned income allowance on it. For the 1988–89 tax year, up to £2,605 of your earnings (including any pension you earned in your own right) is tax-free.

If you get a pension based on your husband's contributions, it normally counts as your husband's income, and wife's earned income allowance cannot be set against it. If you're entitled to a pension of your own but choose to get a (higher) pension based on your husband's contributions, you can count as your earnings the amount of pension you were entitled to on your own contributions.

Gains on life insurance policies

If you've invested in a single-premium life insurance policy (see p332) and would like to cash part of it in, be careful. If you're getting age allowance there could be snags. Although any taxable gain you make when you cash in this type of life insurance policy is free of basic rate tax, it is counted as part of your investment income for the year. And increasing your income can mean you get less age allowance (see above) so pay more tax.

If you cash in part of a life insurance policy, for each year that you've held the policy, you're allowed to cash in 5 per cent of the premiums you've paid so far without it affecting your tax position at the time. If you cash in more than this, the excess is counted as a 'gain' in the year you make it, regardless of how much of it (if any) is in fact gain and how much is return of premiums. This would be added to your ·'total income' and could reduce your age allowance dramatically. So it's wise not to cash in more than the allowances you've built up – unless you cash in the whole of the policy (in which case only the actual gain is added to your income).

See p102 for more on the taxation of single-premium life insurance policies.

Tax for the over-65s from 1990

New tax rules are coming in from 6 April 1990 onwards, designed to give equal treatment to husband and wife.

Under the new system, everyone – married or single, man or woman – will be entitled to their own personal allowance. Anyone reaching 65 or over in a tax year will be entitled to a higher rate of personal allowance (just as the age allowance for over-65s is currently higher than the ordinary personal allowances). And there will continue to be an even higher rate for over-80s.

Married couples will be entitled to an extra **married couple's allowance** (the equivalent of the difference between the present single person's allowance and the married man's allowance). If either of a married couple is 65 or over during the tax year, the couple will be entitled to a higher rate of married couple's allowance (as at present the age allowance for married men is higher than the ordinary married man's allowance). The married couple's allowance will be set against the husband's income, but if his income is less than his tax allowances, the unused part of the married couple's allowance can be transferred to the wife.

As at present, the higher personal allowances for over-65s will be reduced if 'total income' exceeds a certain limit. But the allowance you are entitled to will depend on your own 'total income': if a wife's 'total income' does not exceed the limit, her over-65 personal allowance will not be reduced even if her husband has a huge 'total income'.

Finally, a wife will be able to set her personal allowance against any income she has, not just earnings as at present. And it can be set against any pension she gets, even if it is based on her husband's contributions.

There will be special rules to ensure that no-one is worse off under the new system (otherwise some married men under 65 with wives over 65 might lose out).

4

INVESTING FOR CHILDREN

Choosing an investment for a child under 18 involves much the same principles as for an adult: you have to take account of how much there is to invest, how long you want to invest it for, what rate of tax will be paid on the income and so on. But the range of investments to choose from is not quite the same as for adults:

■ there are age limits for some investments (7 or 16 are common ages), while some are not open at all to children under 18.

■ there are investments open only to children, usually offering perks and free gifts to win the custom of the next generation of money magnates. In general, these are variations on the standard accounts open to adults, but they may offer different rates of return to younger customers.

When investing for a child, follow the guidance in Chapters 1 and 2 on sorting out an investment strategy and finding a shortlist of likely investments. Then use the Table on pp56–57 to eliminate any investments which are barred to children or which require too high a minimum investment. You can find more details of particular investments in Chapters 9 to 25.

How tax affects your choices

Which alternative to choose will depend very much on the child's (or, in some cases, the parents') tax position.

The first point to note is that income of more than £5 a year which comes from investing money given by a child's parents is taxed as the parents' income. So passing on investments to your children won't save tax on the income from them – it will be taxed at your highest rate.

However, any other income the child gets is taxed as the child's – whether from investments handed on by doting grandparents, earnings from a paper round or appearance

Which investment suits your child

type of investment	age child can invest in own name [1]	minimum investment
Bank deposit accounts	from birth, but normally no withdrawals until 7	£1
British Government stocks bought through Post Office [2]	from birth, but not normally cashable until 7	none [3]
National Savings Certificates [2]	from birth, but not normally cashable until 7	£25
National Savings Ordinary Account [2]	from birth, but normally no withdrawals until 7	£1
National Savings Investment Account [2]	from birth, but normally no withdrawals until 7	£5
National Savings Income Bonds	from birth, but normally no withdrawals until 7	£2,000
National Savings Deposit Bonds	from birth, but normally no withdrawals until 7	£100
National Savings Yearly Plan	from birth, but normally no withdrawals until 7	£20 a month
Building society ordinary shares	varies – often 7	often £1
Building society regular savings accounts	varies – often 7	normally £1 a month

Building society notice or term shares	varies – often 7	£500 upwards
Premium Bonds [2]	from birth, but only in own name at 16	£10
Building society Save-As-You-Earn	16	£1 a month
Local authority loans	must be 18 when loan matures	often £250 to £500 – sometimes more
Finance company deposits	varies – often 18	often £100 to £1,000
Life insurance policies	varies widely – often 16 to 18, can be younger	often £5 to £10 a month; lump sum £250 to £1,000
Shares	18	none – but £1,200 a sensible minimum [3]
Unit trusts	varies – often 18	often £250 to £500
British Government stocks bought through stockbroker	18	none – but £1,000 a sensible minimum [3]

[1] See p59 for ways of investing on behalf of a child, if the child is too young to invest in his own name.

[2] National Savings gift tokens (value: £5, or in multiples of £5 up to £30) can be used. These tokens can't be exchanged for cash.

[3] You have to pay commission each time you buy or sell so investing or withdrawing small amounts may not be worthwhile.

fees from advertisements. And it won't be taxed at all unless it exceeds the single person's allowance (£2,605 for the 1988–89 tax year).

Most children are unlikely to have enough income to pay tax, and so should search out the investments described in the Route Maps in Chapter 2 as particularly worth considering for non-taxpayers. These are the investments which pay interest without deduction of composite rate tax (see p99): with investments where composite rate tax is deducted from the interest before it is paid out (eg building society and bank accounts), non-taxpayers cannot reclaim the tax.

For more details about children and tax, see p67. Note that a child under 18 ceases to be taxed as a child if married.

Special children's investments

Banks and building societies know that today's young savers are the next generation of investors – and aim to catch them young. Some offer higher rates of interest to young savers; others tempt the nation's youth with perks such as books, badges, magazines, school gear and the like. A few offer both, though not surprisingly, the higher the rate of interest, the fewer the goodies.

Some of the gifts are designed to help children learn about money and draw up budgets – you might find them worthwhile even if the rate of interest isn't top of the league. And if money boxes, torches, tee-shirts or real china piggy banks help children to learn thrift, you mightn't be too concerned at the loss of a £ or two in interest. If it's interest you want, check out National Savings Investment Account and your local building societies – and forget the goodies.

Example

Samantha (who is 16) is saving up for a portable stereo radio/cassette recorder costing £75. She has a £10 birthday present to start her off and reckons on saving £1 a week out of her pocket money. She earns the occasional few £££ from baby-sitting and any cash gifts at Christmas could also be added. She doesn't pay tax – and the interest from her savings isn't going to add up to more than £5 a year, so there's no need for her parents to worry about paying tax on her interest.

Using the Route Map on p34, she whittles her choice down to National Savings Investment Account or some sort of bank or building society account. But tax will be deducted from interest paid on bank or building society accounts, and she won't be able to claim it back. Only National Savings

Investment Account is particularly recommended for non-taxpayers, because it pays interest without deduction of tax.

After checking that she wouldn't get a higher return from local building societies even after deduction of tax, Samantha settles on National Savings Investment Account. Although she sees that she'll have to give a month's notice to withdraw money, she regards this as a good thing to stop her frittering it away.

Trusts

If you're planning on giving substantial amounts of money to a child, you may be worried that he or she might squander it. You could, of course, keep the money in your own name and hand it over when the child reaches 18, say. But doing this has disadvantages. For example, *you* may be tempted to squander the money, it might mean more inheritance to pay if you were to die within seven years of making the gift, and so on.

A way out of this problem is to set up a trust for the child. A trust is managed by *trustees* for the benefit of those for whom it was set up (the *beneficiaries* of the trust). The people setting up the trust – the parents, say – can act as trustees; or they can appoint friends or relatives; or a professional adviser (such as a solicitor or accountant) can be appointed as one of the trustees. Below we give brief details of how a trust is set up – and on p61 look at some short-cuts you can take.

A trust can have more than one beneficiary – so you can, for example, set up a trust for the benefit of all your 10 grandchildren (plus any more that come along). In this chapter we normally assume a trust has only one beneficiary – but what we say holds equally well for trusts with more than one.

When a trust is set up, the trustees may be given the power to invest in specified investments, or to invest *as they think fit*. If they aren't given these powers there are special rules about how they can invest the money.

Putting money into a trust could mean an inheritance tax bill, though – see p70.

Setting up a trust

The rules about trusts are extremely complicated so we recommend you ask a solicitor with experience of setting up trusts to draw up a **trust deed** for you. This will specify who the trustees are, who is entitled to benefits from the trust, when income and capital are to be paid out, ways in which the trustees can invest the money and so on.

Even a fairly straightforward trust might cost between £100 and £300 to set up – and there could be a charge each year from the trustees for running the trust (as much as £100 or more say). So it's probably not worth setting up a trust unless you plan to give a lot of money to your children (at least £5,000; possibly as much as £20,000, say) – and feel the cost of setting up and running the trust is worthwhile, or would be outweighed by tax savings.

There are two basic types of trust:

■ **fixed trusts** (often called *interest in possession* trusts) where a particular person (or people) has the right to the income from the trust (or the equivalent of income – eg the right to live in a rent-free home). The trustees have no choice but to hand over the income to the beneficiaries at the times stated in the trust

■ **discretionary trusts** where it is left to the discretion of the trustees which of the possible beneficiaries should be paid income. They may also be free to decide which should get capital. If the trustees have the power to accumulate income – ie not to pay it out at all (until the trust ends) – the trust is called an *accumulation trust*. An *accumulation and maintenance trust* is a type of accumulation trust from which income can be paid out only for the maintenance, education or benefit of the beneficiaries (until the beneficiaries get an interest in possession, that is).

The trust deed may say that beneficiaries shouldn't get any payments (or other benefits) from the trust unless some event happens – eg they get married, or reach the age of 25. This type of trust may be fixed or discretionary.

The distinction between fixed and discretionary trusts is important because there are special income tax and inheritance tax rules for the different types of trust – see p69.

Broadly, the current tax rules mean that:

■ setting up a fixed trust for your own child won't normally save you income tax – the income from the trust will be taxed as yours

■ *but* if you set up an accumulation trust, income which is accumulated will be taxed at 35 per cent (in the 1988–89 tax year) and there'll be no further income tax to pay so long as it isn't paid out until your child reaches 18. So this could be worthwhile if you pay tax at more than 35 per cent (ie 40 per cent)

WARNING: once you've set up a trust, you can't normally

change your mind and take the money back. And, while you can indicate your preferences to the trustees about how they should manage the trust's affairs, they do not have to follow them.

If you think you or your family could benefit from a trust, you should discuss it with a solicitor or other professional adviser.

Short-cut trusts

There are ways of making sure that money you invest for your children is held in trust for them without going to the expense of setting up a tailor-made trust.

Life insurance policies

You can take out a life insurance policy (on your, or your husband's or wife's life) with the proceeds made payable to your child. Perhaps the simplest way of doing this is to get a policy worded according to the *Married Woman's Property Act*. In this case, the policy (and any money it pays out) is held in trust for the child until he or she reaches an age you specify when taking out the policy.

The policy can be a single-premium one (eg a managed bond, property bond) or a regular-premium one (eg a unit-linked savings plan, an endowment policy).

The premiums you pay count as gifts for tax purposes (but will probably come into one of the tax-free categories – see p114). There's no inheritance tax to pay on money paid out by the policy. And if the policy is handed over to the child after the age of 18, any taxable gain on the policy is taxed as the child's, not the parents'. But if the policy ends before it is handed over, the gain is taxed as the parents' – though the trust pays the tax.

Unit trusts

A few unit trust management companies run schemes which set up accumulation and maintenance trusts if people want to invest for children.

The minimum investment ranges from £100 to £500, and there's sometimes a small fee for setting up the scheme. But before going ahead with one of these schemes, check whether the unit trusts available would be suitable for your child – see Chapter 16 for what to watch for.

Example

Leslie and Lucretia Lime pay tax on the top slice of their income at 40 per cent. They've got £5,000 from a with-profits endowment policy, and want to invest it for their 10-year old daughter, Sally. They don't want her to have the money until she's 18.

They consider whether to set up an *accumulation and maintenance* trust (which could save them income tax) – but they decide that the amount they're investing doesn't justify the expense of setting up a tailor-made trust. So they put £3,000 into a single-premium managed bond, taken out on Leslie's life, but with the proceeds payable to Sally and the policy being handed over to her when she is 18 – so that any gain on it will count as hers for tax purposes. They invest the remaining £2,000 in unit trusts on behalf of Sally – the income from this will count as the Limes' for tax purposes (though any gains will be taxed as Sally's).

The £5,000 will count as a gift for inheritance tax purposes. But Mr and Mrs Lime have not used their tax-free quota of £3,000 each for this year (ie they have £6,000 tax-free in hand). So they can invest the money for Sally without fear of inheritance tax. And there'll be no inheritance tax to pay when the investments are handed over to Sally.

Planning for school fees

If you've decided to send your child (or children) to a private school, you're going to be faced with substantial bills. School fees range from £1,250 a year for the cheapest day preparatory school to £7,500 for the most expensive senior boarding school.

You may well find paying fees out of your current income hard going. So if there's time in hand, it's worth looking into ways of saving now for school fees in the future. When working out how much you might need, don't forget that school fees – along with prices in general, and your earnings – are likely to rise over the years. In recent years school fee increases have outstripped the rise in the cost of living.

Various insurance companies and investment advisers specialise in arranging schemes to provide the money that's needed for fees at the time it's needed. In the main, these schemes are based on investment-type life insurance policies and annuities.

Below, we give details of the main types of school fees schemes. Broadly, they fall into two groups:

■ **capital** schemes where you invest a lump sum now to provide fees in the future

■ **income** schemes where you save on a regular basis to build up the money needed to pay school fees.

Depending on your circumstances a mixture of the different types may suit you best.

Note that these schemes do not *guarantee* to pay a child's school fees whatever they are – they simply pay out sums of money at various intervals (which may turn out to be less than, or more than, enough to pay the fees).

It's worth bearing in mind that there's nothing magical about school fees schemes. They are simply a way of investing money in order to make a set of payments some time in the future – and they use the sorts of investment which you might well choose to invest in yourself if you were arranging to save up for school fees independently. However, there has to be careful timing of the investments to make sure there's money around when the fees are due, and there are tax complications which have to be taken into account. So although you can go it alone, you may decide it's best to make your investments through a special school fees scheme.

Where to go for school fees schemes

Your bank or a reputable insurance broker should be able to help you – or put you in touch with an insurance company or broker specialising in school fees schemes. Or you could try the *Independent Schools Information Service* (ISIS) for help – write to 56 Buckingham Gate, London SW1E 6AG (Tel: 01-630 8793) for help. But get quotes from more than one source – different schemes suit different people, and you could save money by shopping around.

How capital schemes work

Educational trusts

You pay a lump sum to an educational trust either directly or via an insurance company or broker. Your lump sum is invested to provide guaranteed amounts each term for an agreed number of years – at a level decided by you at the outset. Your money can be used only for paying school fees – the trust will make out cheques for the fees only to the school – though you aren't tied to a particular school. If the fees have risen above the amounts guaranteed to be paid out, you'll have to meet the shortfall.

If, when the time comes, you don't need to pay school fees, you may be able to transfer the plan to a different child. Alternatively, you may be able to get back the amount of

Cutting the cost

Many schools offer scholarships to academically, musically or artistically gifted children, subject to entrance exam results. These can help pay part or all of the fees. A leaflet on grants and scholarships is available from the Independent Schools Information Service ISIS (for address, see p63). If you've already chosen a school ask the bursar.

If you have a joint gross income of less than £17,000 (1988–89 school year), the Government's Assisted Places Scheme can help with fees at selected senior schools for entry at 11, 13 or 16. For details, write to the Department of Education & Science, Room 3/65, Elizabeth House, York Road, London SE1 7PH (in Wales, the Welsh Office Education Department, Cathays Park, Cardiff CF1 3NQ; in Scotland, the Scottish Education Department, New St Andrews House, Edinburgh EH1 3SY).

Some employers may help with fees, especially for staff posted overseas (there are schemes, for example, for parents working for the Diplomatic Service or serving in the armed forces). Financial help from an employer can count as a taxable fringe benefit in some cases – check with the Inland Revenue.

your original investment (though it may then be worth much less because of inflation).

Investment bonds

If you don't want your lump sum to be tied to paying school fees, you can buy a single-premium investment bond from an insurance company (for more about these, see p332). The money buys units in a fund of investments (eg shares, British Government stocks). Your lump sum grows if the value of the units goes up, but falls if the value goes down. Fees are paid by cashing in your units – and there's a risk that their value may be low when you need to sell them to pay the fees.

How much do you need to invest?

With most schemes there's a minimum investment – usually £1,000. Beyond this, the amount you need to invest will depend on how long there is until the fees start and what the fees are expected to be. If you have a just-born child, you should think about investing a lump sum of at least £45,000 to pay for private boarding education (assuming fees went up from current levels by 10 per cent a year).

Tax

An educational trust has charitable status and doesn't have to pay tax on its investments, as long as the money is used for educational purposes. And you don't have to pay tax on the money which goes to pay fees. A future Government might choose to remove an educational trust's charitable status – you would then have to meet the shortfall in fees created by losing the tax benefits.

With investment bonds, there may be some income tax to pay on money drawn by cashing in the units – but normally only at the higher rate. No tax is due if the parents (or the child if the scheme was set up by anyone other than the parents) pay tax at the basic rate only. For more details about the taxation of income drawn from investment bonds, see p102.

How much inheritance tax has to be paid and when, depends on who gives the money:

■ **if the parents give the money** Payments made by the parents solely for the *maintenance, education or training* of their children are free of inheritance tax. So there's no inheritance tax to pay when the money is first invested, nor when the fees are paid. But if the money is not held in trust – or if it is held in trust and the parents keep the right to cash in the scheme – there may be inheritance tax to pay if the parent who gives the money dies. The cash-in value of the investment will form part of his or her estate, and will be taxed in the normal way. If the parent gives up the right to cash in a trust scheme, the money will remain in trust for the child and will be used for his or her maintenance, education or training – the money won't form part of the parent's estate

■ **if someone else (eg grandparents) gives the money** If the grandparents (or whoever) don't set up a trust scheme, the money they eventually pay over for school fees will count as gifts for inheritance tax.

If they do set up a trust scheme – and they give away the right to cash in the scheme – the money they invest in the first place counts as a gift for inheritance tax purposes. If they keep the right to cash in the scheme, what counts as a gift is the cash-in value of the scheme when fees start being paid (which will almost certainly be higher than the value of the original investment).

Note that even if there is a potential liability to inheritance tax, gifts of money can still be tax-free. For example, gifts made out of normal income are free of inheritance tax, as are gifts totalling up to £3,000 a year – for more details see p114.

Composition fees

You can, with many private schools, pay school fees in

advance by what's known as a **composition fee**. In this case, the school then invests the money, often in an annuity which starts paying out when the child goes to school. The amounts you have to invest will vary from school to school but are broadly similar to those involved in capital schemes.

How income schemes work

There are a number of different ways in which these schemes can be set up – but most involve saving regularly by taking out a series of investment-type life insurance policies, which mature year by year as the fees become due.

For example, suppose you plan to send your child to public school in 10 years' time for five years. You could take out five with-profits endowment policies which end after 10, 11, 12, 13 and 14 years respectively. For the first 10 years, you'd pay a flat amount (the premiums for all the policies). From the eleventh year onwards, the premiums would start to tail off, as each policy ended.

If you expect your income to go up over the years you might prefer to pay premiums which increase rather than decrease. In this case, it may be best to take out five 10-year policies in successive years. Your premiums will increase each year up to the fifth year, stay level for the next five years, then tail off as policies end.

Some companies use unit-linked policies (see Chapter 14) to provide part or all of the fees. With these, there's the risk that when you want to cash in a policy, the value of the units may be particularly low and you might get less than you'd hoped for.

If you change your mind about sending your child to private school, what happens depends on whether or not the policies are being held in trust for the child. If they are being held in trust (which gives a possible inheritance tax advantage – see opposite) the money from the policies must be used for the benefit of the child. If they are not being held in trust you can either cash in the policies, or keep them as a form of saving.

How much do you need to invest?

As with capital schemes, the amount you need to invest will depend on how long there is to go before your child is going to private school and what the fees are expected to be. If you were hoping to provide private boarding education for a child who's a baby now, (assuming fees went up from current levels at 10 per cent a year) you would have to think about investing around £6,000 a year.

Tax

There's normally no income tax to pay on the money paid out by these schemes (except, in certain circumstances, when a life insurance policy has to be cashed in early).

If it's the parents who pay for the scheme there's no inheritance tax to pay on the premiums or on the money paid out by the policies. If people other than the parents pay for the scheme, there's no inheritance tax to pay so long as the premiums are paid out of their normal income — or count as tax-free for some other reason (see p114). If the policies are being held in trust for the child, there's no inheritance tax to pay if the person who set up the scheme dies. But if the policies are not being held in trust, the proceeds on death count as part of the person's estate.

Failed to plan?

If you've left it too late – or the fees are more than you anticipated – you may be able to borrow the money for the fees. But first compare the monthly cost of any loan with the outlay if you pay as you go, to see whether you couldn't meet the cost out of your income. The occasional overdraft may be cheaper and you won't be committed to paying off loans for years to come.

Banks and insurance companies offer special loan packages for school fees, which usually involve a second mortgage on your home (and some sort of arrangement fee). The money is lent to you as the fees fall due, and you repay it after 25 years (or when you retire) with the proceeds of an investment-type insurance policy. The monthly cost – insurance premiums plus interest – rises as you draw more of the money to pay the fees.

If you can manage most of the cost out of day to day income but need to top it up with more than an overdraft, you could ask your bank manager for a straightforward bank loan. If you've got an investment-type life insurance policy, you may be able to borrow from the insurance company on the strength of it – see p319.

Children and tax

Tax-saving tips

We give details about tax as far as children are concerned on p55. And there's yet more on tax in Chapter 7. Here we point out the main things to bear in mind, and some ways you can take advantage of the income tax, inheritance tax and capital gains tax rules to keep tax bills when investing for children to a minimum.

■ **Giving money to your own children won't normally save you any income tax** Income of more than £5 a year which comes from gifts made to a child by his or her parents counts as the parents' income for tax purposes – and, if it's taxable, is taxed at their highest rate of tax.

■ **Giving money to your grandchildren (or any other children who aren't your own) could mean less tax to pay on the income it produces.** Income which comes from gifts made to a child by anyone other than his parents counts as the child's own income for tax purposes. A child can have income of at least as much as the single person's allowance (£2,605 a year in the 1988–89 tax year) before starting to pay tax.

■ **Giving money to your children during your lifetime could save inheritance tax** In general, you have to pay inheritance tax on anything over a set amount (£110,000 in the 1988–89 tax year) that you give away during the seven years before you die or on your death. But some types of gift are tax-free and don't count towards the £110,000 limit. It makes sense to take advantage of these tax-free ways of handing money to your children during your lifetime. For a list of the main tax-free gifts you can make, see p114.

And in general, gifts which are taxable are taxed at a lower rate if you make them at least three years before your death rather than leaving them in your will. If you live more than seven years after making a gift, there will be no inheritance tax to be paid on it at all.

Note that husband and wife are taxed separately for inheritance tax purposes – and can each make their quota of tax-free gifts.

■ **You can if you want invest money for your children without their being able to get their hands on it for the time being.** You can do this by taking out an insurance policy where the proceeds are made payable to your children – see *Short-cut trusts* on p61.

■ **Consider setting up an accumulation trust** if you pay income tax at 40 per cent, want to give your children large amounts of money and don't want to put the money into investment-type life insurance. Income which is accumulated is taxed at a flat rate – 35 per cent for the 1988–89 tax year.

Tax on income from fixed trusts

A *fixed* trust pays tax at the basic rate on its income. Any income paid out of the trust comes with a tax credit of the amount of tax deducted (25 per cent of the before-tax income for the 1988–89 tax year).

If the trust was set up by the parents, the income counts as theirs' (see opposite), and they get the 25 per cent tax credit. If the trust was set up by anyone other than the parents, the income counts as the child's and the child gets the tax credit.

If the parents (or child, as the case may be) don't pay tax, or pay less than the tax deducted, they can claim tax back. If the highest rate of tax the parents (or the child) pay is 25 per cent the tax liability on income from the trust is automatically met by the tax credit. If the parents (or child) pay tax at a rate of more than 25 per cent they will have to pay extra tax – calculated on the income paid out plus the tax credit.

Tax on income from discretionary trusts

These pay tax on their income at a special rate – 35 per cent for the 1988–89 tax year.

As with a fixed trust, any income paid out is taxed as either the parents' income (if the trust was set up by the parents) or the child's income (in any other case). But with a discretionary trust, the income comes with a tax credit of 35 per cent of the before-tax amount of income. Whether or not there's more tax to pay (or whether a rebate can be claimed) depends on whether the parents' (or child's) top rate of tax is more or less than 35 per cent. If the top rate is *less* than 35 per cent, it would be worth asking the trustees to pay as much income out as possible – as tax could then be claimed back from the taxman. With an accumulation trust, if the income is accumulated and not paid out until your children are 18 or over, there'll be no further income tax to pay – but neither you nor your children will be able to claim tax back.

Inheritance tax

For brief details of how inheritance tax works, see pp113–116 in Chapter 7.

If you make a gift to your child (or set up a trust under which he or she benefits) it normally counts as a gift for inheritance tax purposes. But some gifts you make are free of inheritance tax – we summarise the main ones to bear in mind on p114.

Below we tell you some of the special inheritance tax rules which apply to trusts. But the taxation of trust funds and settlements can be very complicated – one reason for getting professional advice if you're setting up a tailor-made trust.

Gifts to trusts

In general, the value of the money, property (or whatever) you put into the trust counts as a gift. With gifts to the following types of trust, there will be an inheritance tax bill if you die within seven years of making the gift (in the same way as for any other gift):
- an accumulation and maintenance trust
- a trust for disabled people
- a fixed trust – provided the gift was made on or after 17 March 1987.

With gifts to all other trusts, you may have to pay inheritance tax at the time you make the gift, even though you live for more than seven years after the gift. The gift is added to the value of other such gifts made within the previous seven years; if the total comes to more than £110,000, then inheritance tax is charged on the excess at 20 per cent (which is half the rate payable for gifts on death). If you survive for seven years after the gift, no further inheritance tax will be due on it, but if you die within seven years, then the gift is included in the reckoning for inheritance tax on your death (with credit for the tax already paid).

Note that gifts to trusts count as tax-free if they would be tax-free when made to an individual (for example, if made out of normal spending).

Inheritance tax on trusts

With a **fixed trust**, anyone with the right to income or the equivalent of income (eg the right to live in a rent-free home) from the trust is considered to own the trust's capital – or part of the trust's capital, if the rights to the benefits are shared among several people. When a person's right to the trust's benefit goes to someone else, this is considered to be making a gift. For example, your son may have the right to income from a trust once he reaches 18. If this right passes to his younger sister when he reaches 21, he is considered to make a gift at that time. The gift is valued as the share of the trust's capital which he is considered to own, at the time the right to the income is transferred. Inheritance tax will be due if the son dies within seven years of the gift – but this tax is paid by the trust.

When the trust finally comes to an end, and the capital is handed over to beneficiaries who until that time had the right to the income, there's no further inheritance tax to pay.

Discretionary trusts (other than accumulation and maintenance trusts – see below) may be charged inheritance tax even if payments aren't made out of the trust. Inheritance tax is automatically charged on everything in the trust every ten years – the *periodic charge*. The rules for calculating the periodic charge are complex, but the overall aim is to collect the same amount of tax as would be paid if the trust's property was owned by an individual and passed on at death every 33 years.

When payments are actually made from a discretionary trust's capital (or if fixed interests are created), the trust is also charged inheritance tax. The value of what's paid out (or turned into a fixed interest) is charged at the rate of tax which applied at the last periodic charge but this rate is scaled down in proportion to the time since the last 10-yearly charge – eg if it's one year since the 10-yearly charge the rate is one tenth of the rate at the last 10-yearly charge. If the payment from the trust is made within three months after a 10-yearly charge, there's no tax to be paid.

There are special rules for discretionary trusts set up before 27 March 1974.

Payments of capital from certain **accumulation and maintenance trusts** are free of inheritance tax. And these trusts are also free of the 10-yearly tax bills. To qualify, a trust must be for the benefit of one or more people under the age of 25, who must get the capital of the trust (or at least the right to the income, or use of the trust property) on or before their 25th birthday. If any income is paid out from the trust before this, it must be used only for the maintenance, education or training of the beneficiaries.

If the accumulation and maintenance trust was set up after 14 April 1976, it will be free of inheritance tax only if the children who benefit have a grandparent in common or the trust is less than 25 years old.

Capital gains tax

If you hand over assets (such as shares or your second home) to your children, or put them into a trust, you *dispose* of what you've given – and there may be some capital gains tax to pay (as well as inheritance tax) unless *hold-over relief* is claimed (see p111). The asset is valued at its market value at the time you make the gift. For the rules about capital gains tax, see p104 onwards in Chapter 7.

Bear in mind that the first £5,000 (for the 1988–89 tax year) of net capital gains you make from disposing of assets during a tax year is tax-free.

Once a gift has been made, how much capital gains tax has to be paid on any further gains depends on whether the child controls the investment, or whether it's in trust.

Gains made by a child

Capital gains made by a child are taxed as the child's own gains, not the parents'. The normal rules for working out capital gains tax apply – so, for example, the child can make £5,000 of gains in a tax year without paying tax.

Gains made by a trust

Trusts set up after 6 June 1978 pay capital gains tax at a flat rate of 25 per cent for a fixed trust, 35 per cent for a discretionary trust (including an accumulation and maintenance trust). But the first £2,500 (for the 1988–89 tax year) of net capital gains is free of capital gains tax. This lower tax-free limit for trusts means that trusts are often liable for more capital gains tax than an individual.

If a beneficiary becomes entitled to some or all of the assets of the trust – for example, when he reaches 18 – this counts as the trust disposing of the assets, and if there are gains, capital gains tax has to be paid by the trust (unless the trustees and beneficiary apply for *hold-over relief*).

5

SAFETY FIRST

Investment can be both profitable and interesting, but it's not without its risks – for example investing in shares that do badly. There's no law to protect you against such risks, but there are other risks you can guard against. The world of investment has its share of rogues who will not think twice before disappearing with your hard-earned cash. In this chapter we look at what legal protection there is to stop things going wrong, and to try and compensate you if they do. We also take a look at some things *you* can do to protect yourself from the rogues.

The past

Regulation of investment businesses used to consist of a piecemeal collection of acts of Parliament plus the self-regulation of such bodies as the Stock Exchange. For example, bank deposits were, and still are, protected by the Banking Act (which, among other things, guarantees 75 per cent of the first £20,000 of your deposit if the bank goes bust) and life insurance policyholders by the Policyholders Protection Act (which guarantees 90 per cent of your entitlement in a long-term policy).

But there were many loopholes and areas where there was no protection at all for the investor. For example, anybody could set themselves up as an 'investment consultant'. They might have belonged to a trade association or have professional indemnity insurance which might pay out if they lost your money through fraud or negligence. But if they didn't, you had no protection if you trusted your money to them and things went wrong.

The Financial Services Act

In 1986 Parliament passed the Financial Services Act (FSA) – a mammoth piece of legislation – designed both to fill the gaps in investor protection and to boost confidence in financial services. Below are the main points of the protection you get under the Act. Most of these came into operation in April and July 1988. The rest should be in effect by October 1988.

But however sensible the rules are, they won't work unless they're enforced – see 'How to complain' on p77 for what you can do if you suspect the FSA isn't being complied with. It's worth noting that the FSA does *not* apply to companies which provide general insurance (eg for your home or car) or which deal in *tangible* investments, such as gold coins or antiques, which you can inspect before buying. Existing criminal and civil laws dealing with fraud and breach of contract help protect you when buying tangible investments.

Under the FSA, statutory powers to authorise and regulate investment businesses have been delegated by the Department of Trade and Industry to the **Securities and Investments Board (SIB)**. SIB in turn recognises five **Self-Regulating Organisations (SROs)** and a number of **Recognised Professional Bodies (RPBs)** – see end of Chapter for a list of the SROs and RPBs. Between them, the SROs will cover investment business ranging from commodity and financial futures trading through to the selling of life insurance and unit trusts. RPBs will cover the investment activities of professionals such as solicitors and accountants.

Authorisation

All businesses dealing in or giving advice on investments, with certain very limited exceptions, must now be *authorised* to carry out their business. To become authorised, businesses have to show they are properly run, have sound financial backing and trained staff. Anyone who conducts an investment business without such authorisation will be committing a criminal offence, so any contracts you make with them will be void. Authorisation is given either by SIB or – more commonly – by an SRO or RPB. You can call SIB on 01-929 3652 to find out whether a firm is authorised or not, or consult the SIB Central Register on Prestel (available in some public libraries).

Until the system has run for some months, you may come

across a few firms with *interim authorisation*. This is a temporary arrangement to cover firms which are still in the process of having their applications for authorisation checked out. These businesses are subject to the same rules and regulations as fully authorised ones. But, until they're fully authorised, you can't tell whether they're 'fit and proper' persons to do business with. And they *won't* be covered by the compensation scheme — see p77.

'Fit and proper' businesses

Once authorised, investment firms which fail to abide by the rules of their regulating organisation can be disciplined or, at worst, have their authorisation removed and be banned from the industry. Each regulating organisation's rules must be at least as stringent as SIB's. The main points of these 'conduct of business' rules are:

■ investment businesses have to take into account *your* best interests when giving you advice

■ in most cases an adviser has to 'know their customer' – ie, be fully aware of your personal and financial situation

■ 'best advice' rules mean that independent advisers have to give you the best advice they can, taking into account the range of products on the market and your particular needs. Company representatives have to give you 'best advice' based on the range of products and services they provide and if nothing suits your needs they must tell you so

■ in most cases (but not when just buying life insurance or unit trusts), written 'customer agreements' are required, which give details of the services being provided and their cost, set out your investment objectives and the responsibilities of your adviser and warn of the risks of certain investments

■ 'best execution' rules apply for most transactions. This means that the firm must carry out the deal on the best terms available

■ you should get all the information you need about what you are buying and what you are being charged

■ a voluntary maximum commission scale has been set out. If a company pays a commission on its products above this scale an adviser selling that company's products must tell you how much the commission is. From January 1990, independent advisers will always have to tell you how much commission they receive on products they recommend

■ advertisements and illustrations of benefits have to comply with rules about comparisons, references to past performance and give risk warnings if necessary

■ proper arrangements must be made for keeping your money (eg money awaiting investment) separate from an adviser's. However, this rule won't come into effect until October 1988 for advisers dealing on the Stock Exchange. A really determined fraudster could still run off with your money, but at least the FSA should make it easier to get compensation – see opposite

■ some of this protection isn't available to you if you're classed as a professional or business investor, or if you're classed as an *experienced* investor in your customer agreement (ie one with plenty of recent experience in a particular field of investment). Watch out if this applies to you – read your customer agreement carefully and query it if you think your investor status should be different.

Independence

Advisers selling life insurance and unit trusts must either give completely independent advice on all the products of that type on the market, or act as representatives selling and advising on just one company's or group's products (unless you ask them to sell you another company's product). This has become known as 'polarisation' and has meant that banks and building societies, in particular, have had to change the way in which they operate.

In the past you could get general investment advice from your bank manager, say, yet he or she would also be able to sell you the bank's own products. Polarisation means that it now has to be made clear to you whether the company you're dealing with gives independent advice or advice on just one company's products. However, banks and building societies which have opted to be representatives can direct you to a subsidiary company for independent advice.

Cold-calling

Financial sales representatives are banned from cold-calling, ie visiting or telephoning you without your previous invitation – unless they're selling unit trusts, life insurance or pension plans.

If you buy life insurance, a pension or unit trusts as a result of a cold-call, you get a 'cooling-off' period – ie you can cancel within 14 days of getting a notice telling you of your rights (or before the first payment, if later). But this won't apply to unit trusts or single-premium life insurance bonds if you received no advice, or bought either through an ad or in line with your customer agreement.

Compensation

A compensation scheme is available if you lose money because your adviser goes bust or turns out to be a fraud. The scheme is financed by a levy on all investment businesses and run by SIB.

If you find yourself in the unfortunate position of having lost money in a bankrupt investment company you should write to SIB, with any proof you have of the amounts involved. The scheme can pay up to £48,000 – full protection for the first £30,000 invested, then protection for 90 per cent of the next £20,000. So, it's worth bearing in mind that, in most cases, you'll only be assured of getting all your money back if you've invested £30,000 or less. But some regulating organisations may pay more.

You also have the right to sue a company for damages if you believe that:

■ the company has broken the rules of its regulating organisation, and

■ as a result of this you have lost money.

This rule doesn't come into force until 3 October 1988, except for companies directly authorised by SIB.

How to complain

Under the FSA there are three stages which you can go through if you have a complaint about an authorised investment business. First, all authorised businesses must have a complaints procedure set up to deal with problems. You should approach the company in writing, providing evidence of your complaint.

Second, if your complaint isn't resolved satisfactorily, you can approach the appropriate regulating body – the stationery of all authorised businesses should tell you which this is. The regulating body involved will have a system set up to deal with investor complaints. If they think that the rules may have been broken, they will investigate. If the complaint is about some other aspect it may be passed on to another body – ie one of the Ombudsmen. Complaints procedures vary between SIB, the SROs and the RPBs, but all have a number of ways of dealing with a justified complaint, such as giving a private or public reprimand or withdrawing authorisation (so that the firm will have to stop business). Only SROs can order a company to repay you (including any costs you've incurred).

Finally, if you're unhappy about the way the SRO or RPB has handled your complaint, you can go to SIB. SIB's own complaints procedure will then come into operation.

The complaints procedure under the FSA applies only if you are dealing with an authorised firm – unauthorised firms are illegal anyway, and if you come across one you should get in touch with SIB.

As well as SIB, the SROs and the RPBs there are other organisations and associations that deal with complaints against investment businesses. If you have a complaint about an investment adviser, see Chapter 6 for further information; if your complaint is about a particular type of investment, see also the chapter dealing with that investment.

Self-protection

Even though the FSA gives you a safety net, it's still a good idea to take precautions before deciding where and with whom to put your money. You should weigh up both the potential risks and benefits of your planned investments. Chapter 6 outlines a number of points to consider when choosing someone to advise you on what to do with your money. Other things to watch out for are:

■ particularly good deals – don't allow greed to overcome your common sense. Investing money is a business like any other and a competitive one at that. If you come across an adviser who promises you returns way beyond the norm, the chances are that he or she's either not planning to return your money or there's a lot of risk involved – in which case you could also end up with nothing

■ 'guaranteed' returns – if the sales pitch refers to a 'guaranteed return', find out exactly who or what is giving this guarantee. Words alone are not enough (especially if the company is based abroad)

■ high pressure selling – one of the drawbacks of the FSA is that 'cold-calling' has been extended to the sale of unit trusts and personal pension plans (not previously allowed). Remember no deal is so urgent that you have to decide immediately whether to invest – it's your money, so don't allow yourself to be pushed into deciding what to do. Give yourself time to find out more

■ how much commission your adviser is getting. Commission rates do vary, making some investments more attractive for advisers to sell. Despite the 'best advice' rules of the

FSA, it's still a good idea to ask how much commission your adviser is getting on each proposed investment. If you don't get an answer you should consider finding another adviser who is prepared to tell you

■ never deal with anyone who doesn't have authorisation – report them to SIB (you can check with SIB as to who is authorised). And, if you find out that an authorised business is breaking the rules of their regulating body, report them too

■ being classed as an 'experienced investor' – if you are, some of the protection outlined earlier in this chapter will not apply, for example, the duty for an adviser to find out your needs before giving advice.

One final warning; remember that the FSA is there to protect you against rogues and the negligence of others, not the unavoidable perils of investment. Investment will never be totally risk-free.

Who are the regulators?

Securities and Investments Board (SIB)
3 Royal Exchange Buildings, London EC3V 3NL
Tel: 01-283 2474

Self-Regulating Organisations (SROs)

Association of Futures Brokers and Dealers (AFBD)
Made up of advisers, managers and dealers in futures and options.
B Section, 5th floor, Plantation House, 4–16 Mincing Lane, London EC3M 3DX
Tel: 01-626 9763

Financial Intermediaries, Managers and Brokers Regulatory Association (FIMBRA)
Made up of independent investment intermediaries who advise or manage portfolios for private individuals – for example life insurance and unit trust advisers.
Hertsmere House, Marsh Wall, London E14 9RW
Tel: 01-538 8860

Investment Management Regulatory Organisation (IMRO)
Made up of corporate investment managers and advisers – for example pension fund managers, unit trust managers, and some banks.
Centre Point, 103 New Oxford Street, London WC1A 1PT
Tel: 01-379 0601

Life Assurance and Unit Trust Regulatory Organisation (LAUTRO)
Made up of insurance companies, unit trusts and friendly societies, and mainly regulates the marketing of their investments.
Centre Point, 103 New Oxford Street, London WC1A 1QH
Tel: 01-379 0444

The Securities Association (TSA)
Made up of members of the Stock Exchange, plus dealers in international stocks and bonds and money market investments.
The Stock Exchange Tower, London EC2N 1HP
Tel: 01-256 9000

Recognised Professional Bodies (RPBs)

Chartered Association of Certified Accountants
29 Lincoln's Inn Fields, London WC2A 3EE
Tel: 01-242 6855

Institute of Actuaries
Staple Inn Hall, High Holborn, London WC1V 7QJ
Tel: 01-242 0106

Institute of Chartered Accountants in England and Wales
PO Box 433, Chartered Accountants' Hall, Moorgate Place, London EC2P 2BJ
Tel: 01-628 7060

Institute of Chartered Accountants in Ireland
Chartered Accountants House, 87–89 Pembroke Road, Dublin 4
Tel: 0001 680400

Institute of Chartered Accountants of Scotland
27 Queen Street, Edinburgh EH2 1LA
Tel: 031-255 5673

Insurance Brokers Registration Council (IBRC)
15 St Helen's Place, London EC3A 6DS
Tel: 01-588 4387

The Law Society
113 Chancery Lane, London WC2A 1PL
Tel: 01-242 1222

Law Society of Northern Ireland
Law Society House, 90–106 Victoria Street, Belfast BT1 3JZ
Tel: 0232 231614

Law Society of Scotland
Law Society Hall, 26 Drumsheugh Gardens, Edinburgh EH3 7YR
Tel: 031-266 7411

6

GETTING
ADVICE

Lots of people offer investment advice. But how good will
the advice be? In this chapter we look at the various sources
of professional advice, what they might offer, and what they
might cost.

Who's offering advice?

Various groups of people give investment advice of one sort
or another. For example:
- accountants
- banks
- building societies
- independent investment advisers
- independent insurance advisers and brokers
- insurance company representatives
- merchant banks
- solicitors
- stockbrokers.

In the past anyone could set themselves up as an investment adviser – there were some controls, but major loopholes existed through which the conmen could slip. As
outlined in Chapter 5, the Financial Services Act has reme-
died this. Advisers have to be 'authorised' and if they represent just one company, eg a particular insurance company,
they will have to make this clear. This doesn't mean that
their advice will always necessarily be good – you can only
be completely sure of that with the benefit of hindsight. But
you do have some comeback now if things go wrong.

What types of advice can you get?

Investment advice falls broadly into two categories:
- general advice – such as how your money should be split
between different types of investment

■ specialist advice – about, for example, which shares to invest in or which kind of investment-type life insurance to buy.

Ideally, someone who gives general advice should know a lot about all types of investment and about the tax rules affecting them. A specialist adviser should be an expert in one or two fields of investments – insurance or shares, for example. Both types of adviser now have a legal duty to be aware of your financial circumstances and of what you want from your investments – eg an income or capital growth. This rule doesn't apply when an adviser is acting for you on an 'execution-only' basis, for example buying or selling shares for you, under your instructions.

If your adviser manages all your investments for you (called portfolio management), you can often choose for the management to be *advisory*, where the adviser needs your prior approval to act, or *discretionary*, where he or she doesn't. Most advisers prefer discretionary management – so that they can act quickly when necessary. If you decide on discretionary management it's normal to agree broad limits to your adviser's discretion – for example not more than five per cent of your money to go into the shares of any one company.

Choosing an adviser

It's not hard to find an investment adviser – finding one that's right for you is the problem. Some general advisers – such as solicitors and accountants – normally give such advice as a sideline to their main business. Other advisers will not be interested in your business unless you've a lot of money to invest – £50,000 or even £100,000, say.

So it's best to do a bit of homework before you go out to look for an adviser. Opposite is a checklist of points which you should consider to help you decide what your investment needs and aims are. In going through this checklist you will have to put a bit of thought into exactly what you want from your investments – whether you are willing to risk losing money in hope of a capital gain, whether you want your money available at short notice and so on. See Chapters 1 and 2 for help in sorting out your priorities.

You should also expect to be asked about all these points by an adviser (unless your needs are very specific, for example you're just asking them to sell some shares). If an adviser doesn't ask about these points they won't be in a position to give you suitable advice and it's best to steer clear of them.

Checklist of points to consider

- your age
- your health
- whether you're married, single, separated or divorced
- number and ages of children and other dependants
- size and make-up of family income
- possible changes in your financial circumstances
- your regular financial commitments
- your tax position
- your investments
- your home and mortgage
- your pension
- existing insurance policies
- how long you want to invest for
- your reasons for investing, for example how important it is to you to get a high income, make a capital gain
- whether you want to be able to get your money back quickly
- what degree of risk you're prepared to take with your money.

Once you've decided on your investment aims, it should be a little easier to choose a suitable type of adviser – see our guide to the advisers for what each type offers. When you've found the adviser you want, check that they're authorised – you can do this either by contacting SIB or the appropriate regulating body (see pp79–80). Make sure you see more than one authorised adviser so that you can compare what they're offering.

It's not only the adviser who should ask questions – you should too. It's important that you are clear about exactly what kind of adviser you're dealing with. You should find out:

- whether they are independent or a company representative
- which SRO or RPB they're regulated by
- what compensation scheme they are covered by
- whether they have professional indemnity insurance which will pay out if they lose your money through fraud or negligence.

Another important question you should ask is how the adviser will be paid. Some advisers charge fees, usually a percentage of your investment. Others will get commission from the companies you invest money with. Of this latter group it's important to bear in mind that while the advice may seem free there *is* a cost involved. The commission will be deducted from the investors' funds. If you do pay a fee, the adviser may undertake to pass on to you any commission they receive. See next pages for how each type of adviser is paid.

Don't make your final decision until you're satisfied on all these points. Steer clear of advisers who make fantastic claims for what they can do for your money – investment that supposedly brings high returns may well be fraught with risk.

Once you've decided on your adviser, make sure you specify exactly what you want them to do and get it from them in writing. Under the Financial Services Act your adviser will, in most cases, have to draw up a customer agreement which sets out your investment objectives, the services to be provided, the responsibilities undertaken and the charges being made. Avoid making cheques out in your adviser's name if at all possible – make out your cheque to the company providing the investment. If a firm has *got* to handle your money, check that it's held in a separate client account. And, if an adviser is going to be looking after your money over a long period, make sure that they stick to your customer agreement. Ask how they'll keep in touch, who'll be dealing with you and how often. Expect a report on your investments at least once a year.

Guide to advisers

Accountants

Generally, these aren't investment specialists, but they may offer independent advice to customers, or refer you to a specialist.
■ **What they offer** – varies considerably, but includes general investment advice, tax planning, advice on wills and trusts, sometimes advisory or discretionary portfolio management, contact with specialist advisers, eg stockbrokers.
■ **What they charge** – their normal fees, which depend on the time spent (and can vary greatly, so shop around). They may get commission if you buy life insurance, unit trusts or shares through them. *Chartered* accountants are supposed to tell you in writing about any commission they expect to receive as a result of your investment. *Certified* accountants

are supposed to deduct any commission received from their fee and show this on the bill.

■ **What to watch out for** – some accountants may be well qualified to advise you about investments: others may not.

■ **Who to complain to** – the *recognised professional body* to which the accountant belongs – see p80. Check to see if your accountant has professional indemnity insurance – almost all should. If a large part of their business comes from advising on or managing investments, they may belong to **FIMBRA** as well – see p79.

Verdict
Worth trying if you want advice on an overall investment strategy and can afford the fees.

Banks

All the High-Street banks offer investment advice. Most advise about their own investment products only, but some advise about all products on the market – see p76. Banks that sell their own products at branch level generally also offer independent advice through a connected company, eg a trust company.

■ **What they offer** – varies from bank to bank and within banks themselves – but includes advice on the bank's own products (eg insurance and unit trusts), advice on buying and selling stocks and shares, advice on tax, advice on pensions, portfolio management.

■ **What they charge** – usually nothing if you buy life insurance or unit trusts, as the bank gets commission; normal stockbrokers' commission for buying and selling shares (maybe with an 'administration fee' on top); for managing a portfolio, either a flat fee or half to one per cent a year of the portfolio's value. There could be an extra fee for tax help.

■ **What to watch out for** – some banks operate wholly as independent advisers, but most banks' branches sell just their own products.

■ **Who to complain to** – if you can't get the head office of your bank to deal satisfactorily with your complaint, try the **Office of the Banking Ombudsman**, Citadel House, 5–11 Fetter Lane, London EC4A 1BR, Tel: 01-583 1395. Depending on the part of the bank you've dealt with and the type of investment you've purchased, you may also want to approach **FIMBRA, IMRO, LAUTRO** or the **TSA** – see pp79–80 for addresses.

Verdict

Useful if you want advice on or management of smaller sums of money – under £10,000, say. For management of larger amounts you may have to approach a bank's trust company. Or you could go to one of the 'private' banks, which offer a more personalised service and usually advise only customers with large sums of money.

Building societies

Since November 1987, building societies have been able to provide a wide range of financial services and products, eg share dealing services in conjunction with stockbrokers. In the future the range of services could be larger if societies decided to turn themselves into public limited companies.

■ **What they offer** – not all societies have taken or will take advantage of all their new powers but, as well as advice on their own products and services, you may be able to get the following: share-dealing or unit trust services (through links with other financial bodies), advice on Personal Equity Plans.

■ **What they charge** – normally nothing because the society gets commission from the company whose product you buy – though it's not unknown for societies to pass some of their commission on to you. If you are referred to another adviser, eg a stockbroker, you will pay that adviser's charges.

■ **What to watch out for** – most building societies offer independent advice, but some offer advice only on the products of one company – see Chapter 5, p76.

■ **Who to complain to** – if you can't get the society's head office to deal satisfactorily with your complaint, try the **Building Societies Ombudsman**, Grosvenor Gardens House, 35–37 Grosvenor Gardens, London SW1X 7AW, Tel: 01-931 0044. Under the Financial Services Act societies are generally authorised by **SIB** – see p79.

Verdict

An obvious (though not always independent) choice for advice on ways of investing to pay off a mortgage. And worth contacting if you want advice on their own products, for example instant access accounts, or if you want to find out about any of the new services or products they may offer.

Independent investment advisers

These may go under different titles, for example 'personal investment consultant', but, strictly speaking, they should all look at all types of investment when advising you.

■ **What they offer** – includes: general investment advice, advisory or discretionary portfolio management, advice on tax and pensions, advice on shares and unit trusts, advice on alternative types of investment.

■ **What they charge** – usually nothing if they're just selling a life insurance policy or unit trust, as they get commission. For managing a lump sum, charges can range from half to one per cent a year of the value of your portfolio. Charges may be less for very large amounts. Instead advisers may charge a flat fee, such as £100 a year or a slice of your profits – or even both. Services like tax help may cost extra.

■ **What to watch out for** – charges for advice can vary widely. If your adviser charges a fee, ask if it will be reduced if commission is paid on any of the investments purchased.

■ **Who to complain to** – if you have problems, get in touch with the appropriate regulating organisation, likely to be **FIMBRA, IMRO** or **TSA** – see pp79–80 for addresses. Some advisers have professional indemnity insurance which will pay out if you can prove your money was lost through their negligence or fraud.

Verdict

Worth trying if you want general advice or someone to manage a lump sum for you (say, £10,000 plus).

Independent insurance advisers and brokers

Anyone can call themselves an independent insurance *adviser* but to be a *broker* they must meet set conditions and register with the Insurance Brokers' Registration Council (IBRC). Under the Financial Services Act both advisers and brokers have to be authorised.

■ **What they offer** – advice on life insurance and pensions, plus sometimes: general insurance advice (for your home, car etc), tax advice, unit trust advice, portfolio management.

■ **What they charge** – usually nothing as they earn commission on what they sell. Charges for portfolio management are similar to those of general investment advisers.

■ **What to watch out for** – commission rates can vary from product to product and company to company. So ask your adviser what commission they will get on each investment they recommend. Research done for *Which?* in the past hasn't found registered brokers' advice to be any better than that of other independent insurance advisers.

■ **Who to complain to** – **FIMBRA** (see p79). For registered brokers you can also contact the **IBRC**, 15 St Helens Place,

London EC3A 6DS, Tel: 01-588 4387. This has a fund which may pay out if you lose money through a broker's negligence or fraud. Also, check that your adviser has professional indemnity insurance (brokers must have this).

Verdict
Worth trying, particularly if you've already decided on investment-type life insurance, pensions or unit trusts. Don't always expect general advice on all investments.

Insurance company representatives

Life insurance companies often employ representatives to deal with you in person. Some companies sell their products just through their representatives, press advertisements and direct mailing, others just through independent advisers, while some use both methods. Some companies have a policy of passing direct enquiries on to brokers.

■ **What they offer** – includes: advice on which of their products best suits your needs, advice on tax implications of their products, retirement planning advice, advice on their company's own unit trusts, general information on the financial markets (sometimes over the phone or through talks and seminars).

■ **What they charge** – nothing, since most representatives get commission from their company on the products that they sell.

■ **What to watch out for** – in the past, it was not unknown for company representatives to pass themselves off as independent – this is no longer allowed. Don't be pressurised into buying their products if you're not convinced they're right for you. Also, get quotations from more than one company. You may not save any money dealing directly with a company (rather than through an adviser) – commission costs are built into the price of an investment.

■ **Who to complain to** – **LAUTRO** covers insurance companies, unit trust management groups and friendly societies – see p80. If an insurance company head office won't deal satisfactorily with a complaint, see if the company belongs to the **Insurance Ombudsman Bureau**, 31 Southampton Row, London WC1B 5HJ, Tel: 01-242 8613 or **Personal Insurance Arbitration Service**, 75 Cannon Street, London, EC4N 5BH, Tel: 01-236 8761.

Verdict
Obviously, you will get advice on only one company's products. But if you know you want to invest with that

particular company, and you're sure you can't get a better deal elsewhere, worth trying.

Merchant banks

These generally deal with companies and institutions rather than individuals, offering services such as international banking, corporate finance and investment management. Few merchant banks (also called 'private' banks) will consider advising individuals unless you have a large sum of money to invest – over £100,000, say. Some will not take on individuals at all. Contact **The British Merchant Banking and Securities Houses Association**, 101 Cannon Street, London EC4N 5BA, Tel: 01-283 7332 for a list of members.

■ **What they offer** – services and products on offer will vary considerably, but include advisory and discretionary management of your investments (so long as you have a minimum amount to invest – commonly £100,000 but could be much more), advice on and purchase of stocks and shares, tax advice.

■ **What they charge** – usually a yearly fee, between half and one per cent of your investments, say. If selling their own investment products or those of other companies, they could earn commission – make sure you find out if this is the case.

■ **What to watch out for** – check whether the advice you're getting is independent or just about their own products. The bank has a duty to make this clear to you.

■ **Who to complain to** – the head office of the bank concerned, or the appropriate regulating body under the Financial Services Act.

Verdict
Only for the rich. Their main emphasis is on stocks and shares.

Solicitors

Solicitors aren't generally investment specialists, but nearly all will give existing clients advice; most will give it to anyone who comes to see them. All solicitors have to give independent advice.

■ **What they offer** – varies considerably, but includes general advice, contacts with specialist advisers (such as stockbrokers), sometimes advisory or discretionary portfolio management, tax planning, advice on wills and trusts.

■ **What they charge** – usually a fee based on the time spent (rates can vary so shop around). If commission is received it can only be kept with your permission. In practice fees are sometimes reduced by the amount of the commission.

■ **What to watch out for** – some may be well qualified to tell you where to put your money – others may not.

■ **Who to complain to** – their **recognised professional body** – for example the Law Society – see p80. They all have professional indemnity insurance. They may also belong to **FIMBRA** if a large part of their business comes from advising on or managing investments.

Verdict

Worth considering for general discussion of investments.

Stockbrokers

These specialise in shares and British Government stocks – but many have widened their services in recent years. Until 1987 you could also buy and sell shares through 'licensed dealers in securities' – financial organisations licensed by the Department of Trade and Industry (although there was little protection against rogues). Like stockbrokers, these share dealers must now be authorised and will be covered by the compensation fund set up under the Financial Services Act (unless only interim authorised – see p75).

■ **What they offer** – mainly advice on buying and selling shares and British Government stocks, usually unit trusts too; also advisory and discretionary portfolio management (for sums starting at £5,000, but usually much more), unit trust portfolio management, their own unit trusts and Personal Equity Plans, investment research, general investment advice (sometimes through a subsidiary company).

■ **What they charge** – commission for buying and selling shares on your behalf ranges from one to two per cent of the price of the shares, plus VAT. Most stockbrokers have minimum commissions of around £20 or £25. For portfolio management, there's an annual fee of, say, one per cent of the value of the portfolio.

■ **What to watch out for** – charges both for buying and selling shares and for general management of a portfolio vary a lot – so it's worth shopping around. *Buying, selling and owning shares: an Action Kit from Which?* includes a nationwide guide to stockbrokers who are prepared to deal with individuals, and their charges. But don't expect a stockbroker to be able to choose shares that consistently do better than average – investing in shares is a risky business (see Chapter 15). Not all stockbrokers are prepared to deal with individuals.

■ **Who to complain to** – the **TSA** (see p80). Some of the old dealers in securities may also belong to **FIMBRA** – see p79 for addresses.

Verdict

If you want advice on shares, British Government stock or unit trusts, a stockbroker may be your best bet. They are worth considering for management of a lump sum, say, £10,000 plus, though some stockbrokers manage only very large sums.

7

TAX

Why bother about tax? The short answer is that tax can affect the return on your investments. You can't know how good (or bad) an investment will be until you can gauge the effect of tax on it.

Let's take an extreme example. Dave Grabber has a very high income and pays income tax at the higher rate of 40 per cent. He has a choice between two investments:

■ investment A will pay him an income of 10 per cent a year

■ investment B won't pay any income, but will – he hopes – show a capital gain of 8 per cent a year.

Both these figures are before tax, and at first sight, Investment A looks more attractive. But let's assume that Investment A pays an income of £10,000. The effect of income tax at 40 per cent will be to reduce this to £6,000. Investment B on the other hand, producing a gain of £8,000, is liable for capital gains tax. This is also at 40 per cent, but the first slice of total yearly gains (£5,000 in the 1988–89 tax year) is tax-free. So Dave would pay tax at 40 per cent on only £3,000, ending up with an overall return of £6,800 – higher than that from Investment A.

This example shows how tax can affect the return on your investment. But tax can also affect the cost of an investment, particularly with pensions and mortgages. With both company and personal pension schemes, tax relief can save up to 40 per cent of the cost. And of course most people qualify for tax relief on the interest they pay on their mortgages, and so save tax at their highest rate.

What are the taxes?

The most common tax you'll have to pay on investment income is income tax. The other main tax to watch out for is capital gains tax. Inheritance tax, which replaced capital transfer tax in 1986, doesn't directly affect the return you get on your investments – but we give the basic rules at the end of this chapter.

Which tax will hurt you most depends very much on your investment choice. You have an annual slice of tax-free capital gains (see p93), and if your returns aren't likely to exceed this, you won't be hurt by tax at all if you go for investments which produce a capital gain rather than income. If, however, you've used all of your tax-free slice for capital gains tax, you'll have to pay tax at the same rate as your top rate of income tax. So you should look for investments offering the highest rate of return after tax – either as income or as capital gain.

Income tax

There are four ways in which investment income can be treated. It can be:
- tax-free
- taxable, but not taxed before you get it
- paid with basic rate tax deducted
- paid with composite rate tax deducted.

Tax-free investments are likely to appeal most to higher rate taxpayers, while non-taxpayers should be wary of investments with composite rate tax already deducted (as you can't claim back that tax). Instead, non-taxpayers should look at the types of investment which pay their income either before tax is deducted, or with basic rate tax deducted. If you are a non-taxpayer, you can claim back any basic rate tax that's been deducted, unless you get enough income to push you into the tax band.

Income tax is charged on your income for a tax year. Tax years run from 6 April in one year to 5 April the following year. So your tax bill for 1988–89, say, will normally be based on your income from 6 April 1988 to 5 April 1989. But in some cases it's difficult to know in which year your investment income will be taxed. Sometimes your bill is based on income you received in the tax year in question (current year basis), while sometimes it's based on the investment income you received in the previous year (preceding year basis). In this chapter, we tell you which basis applies to which types of income – and how you can sometimes juggle the figures to get a lower tax bill.

How much income tax?

All your income is added together, to arrive at your **gross income** .... say £12,000

From this you deduct your **outgoings** (certain payments you make, eg expenses paid in connection with your work) .... say £1,500

This leaves what the taxman calls your '**total income**' .... say £10,500

From this you deduct your **allowances** (eg single person's allowance, or married man's) .... say £4,095

This leaves your **taxable income** .... say £6,405

Tax is charged on your **taxable income**.

Rates of income tax for the 1988–89 tax year
The first £19,300 of your taxable income is taxed at the basic rate of 25 per cent. Anything more is taxed at the higher rate of 40 per cent.

Tax rates have fallen over the past few years, especially for higher rate taxpayers, and Parliament has also done away with the investment income surcharge. Until 1984, this surcharge meant that investors had to pay an extra 15 per cent tax on all investment income over a certain amount. The net result of these tax changes is that more of your investment income stays in your pocket.

Tax-free investment income

- proceeds from Save-As-You-Earn
- proceeds from National Savings Certificates (and, in most cases, Ulster Savings Certificates if you live in Northern Ireland)
- proceeds from a National Savings Yearly Plan
- proceeds from a qualifying life insurance policy (see p101 for details)
- premium bond prizes
- first £70 interest each year from a National Savings Ordinary Account
- interest received in connection with delayed settlement of damages for personal injury or death
- part of the income from many annuities
- income from a family income benefit life insurance policy

■ reinvested income from a qualifying Personal Equity Plan.

Investment income taxable but not taxed before you get it

Interest from the investments listed below comes into this category:
■ National Savings accounts and National Savings Income and Deposit Bonds
■ British Government stocks bought on the National Savings Stock Register – eg through a Post Office – and War Loan
■ interest on loans you make to private individuals
■ deposits at non-UK branches of UK or overseas banks
■ deposits made by people not ordinarily resident in the UK.

How it is taxed
The interest is paid gross, and you have to account to the taxman separately for any tax you owe.

If you've been getting interest from one of these sources for a few years, it will normally be taxed on a preceding year basis – ie your tax bill for the 1988–89 tax year will be based on the interest paid (or credited) to you in the 1987–88 tax year. This bill must normally be paid by 1 January 1989, or within 30 days of the date on the Notice of Assessment you'll get – whichever is later. But if your interest doesn't vary much from year to year, and you pay tax under PAYE, the tax on your interest will probably be collected along with tax on your earnings.

Special rules
Special rules apply to the first three and last two years in which you get interest of this type – see Table on p98 for details.

If you get interest of this type from more than one source, the taxman will normally apply his special rules to each source separately. But if there is a big change in the interest from a single source – eg if you greatly increase or decrease the size of your National Savings Investment Account – the taxman may treat such interest as coming from a new source, and apply his special rules.

You won't need to worry about these rules if your interest is much the same from year to year. But if it does vary, you may be able to reduce your tax bill.

If the amount of interest in year 3 is lower than in year 2, tell the taxman that you want your tax bill for year 3 to be based on the interest you actually got in year 3. (You can make this choice at any time within six years of the end of year 3).

If the amount of interest in years 2 and 3 is high compared with the interest in year 4, consider closing your account (eg a National Savings Investment Account) just before the end of year 4, and reopening it a week or so later (after the start of the next tax year). That way, your tax bill for year 4 will be based on the interest you actually got in that year, rather than on the higher amount of interest you got in year 3.

If you have more than one account, you may need to close them all.

Investment income paid with basic rate tax deducted

Examples of this type of income are:
- dividends from UK companies
- distributions from unit trusts
- interest on certain loans – eg loans to foreign governments
- interest on certain British Government stocks (normally all stocks bought through a stockbroker, except War Loan)
- interest on company fixed-income investments (loan stocks or debentures)
- part of the income from annuities
- income from certain income and growth bonds
- income from certain trusts and settlements
- income from a will, paid out to you during the administration period (ie while the details of who gets what under the will are being worked out).

How it is taxed

This type of income is taxed on a current year basis – ie your tax bill for the 1988–89 tax year is based on the income paid (or credited) to you in that tax year.

There's no basic rate tax for you to pay on this type of income – because the basic rate tax (or something equivalent to it) has been deducted before the income is handed over to you.

With dividends from UK companies and distributions from unit trusts, each dividend or distribution is accompanied by a tax credit. Your gross (before-tax) income is taken to be the dividend plus the tax credit. For the 1988-89 tax year, the tax credit is 25 per cent of the gross income. So if, say, the dividend is £75, the tax credit will be £25 and the gross income £100.

You get a tax voucher from the company (or unit trust)

Interest not taxed before you get it: what your tax bill is based on

	Tax is initially based on:	but for some years, there's a choice:
First year in which you get interest from this source (year 1)	interest you get in first tax year (current year basis)	no choice this year
Second tax year (year 2)	interest you get in second tax year (current year basis)	no choice this year, unless source of interest begins on 6 April in year 1. If it does, tax year 2 will normally be based on the interest you got in year 1 (*preceding year basis*) – and you can choose to have tax for year 2 based on interest in year 2 instead (*current year basis*). Consider doing this if interest in year 2 is lower than interest in year 1. Note, in this case, you have no further choice in year 3.
Third tax year (year 3)	interest you got in second tax year (preceding year basis)	**your choice:** you can choose to have tax based on interest you get in year 3 (current year basis). Do so if this is less than interest you got in year 2
Fourth and subsequent tax years. . . .	interest you got in preceding tax year (preceding year basis)	no choice for these years
Until the last-but-one tax year in which you get interest from this source	interest you got in preceding tax year (preceding year basis)	taxman's choice: when you tell him, at the end of the next tax year, that you've closed your account, the taxman can revise your tax bill. He will base it on the interest you actually got in the last-but-one tax year (current year basis) if this comes to more than your original bill
Last tax year in which you get interest from this source	interest you get in this tax year (current year basis)	no choice this year

showing the amount of the dividend (or distribution) and the amount of the tax credit.

With other types of income taxed before you get it, tax is deducted (usually at the 25 per cent basic rate) before the income is paid to you. Again, you normally get a tax voucher or a similar document from whoever pays you the money. This will tell you the gross (before-tax) amount of income, the tax deducted, and the actual sum you get. Keep any tax vouchers as proof that tax has been credited or deducted.

The outcome of all this is that:

■ if your income (including income of this type) is too low for you to pay tax, you can claim back all the tax that's been deducted or credited. And note that if your income is high enough for you to pay some tax, but not as much as has already been deducted, you can claim back the difference

■ if you are liable for basic rate tax (but no more) on the whole of your income of this type, your liability for tax on this income is automatically met by the tax deducted and credited

■ if you pay tax at the higher rate, you will have to pay extra tax – calculated on the gross (before-tax) income.

Any extra tax on income received between 6 April 1988 and 5 April 1989 has to be paid by 1 December 1989 – or within 30 days of the date on your Notice of Assessment, if later.

Investment income paid with composite rate tax deducted

Types of investment income taxed in this way include:
■ most building society interest
■ most bank interest
■ interest from other authorised institutions, eg finance companies
■ interest from foreign currency deposits made at UK banks
■ interest on most local authority loans issued after 18 November 1984.

How it is taxed

Banks, building societies and other institutions pay tax at a special composite rate (23.25 per cent in 1988–89) before paying out interest to you. Because of this, you don't have to pay basic rate tax on interest you get from them. But you can't claim back the tax that they have paid – even if your income is too low for you to pay tax. So non-taxpayers should look for better returns elsewhere.

If you have to pay tax at the higher rate, you will have to

pay extra tax on your interest. When working out your tax bill, the taxman includes the grossed-up amount of interest as part of your income. The grossed-up interest is the amount which, after deduction of tax at the basic rate, would leave the interest you actually got. To calculate the grossed-up interest for the 1988–89 tax year, take the net interest, and divide it by 0.75.

You are liable for tax on this grossed-up amount at the top rate of tax that you pay, in the year in which you receive the interest. But you are treated as already having paid basic rate tax on the interest – so you only have to hand over the difference.

Example

George Streatley got £450 in building society interest in the 1988–89 tax year. As he's a higher rate taxpayer, he will have to pay some extra tax on this interest. To work out how much, he divides £450 by 0.75 to find the grossed-up amount – £600. He's liable for tax at 40 per cent on £600 – ie £240. However, he's treated as having already paid tax on this interest at the 25 per cent basic rate (ie £150 in tax). So he has to hand over only an extra £240 – £150 = £90.

Points to watch

Annuities

If you've bought an annuity voluntarily with your own money (not, for example, as part of a personal pension plan), part of the income you get each year is treated as a return of capital, part as interest on the capital. Only the interest part is taxable – the insurance company will tell you how much this is.

Discretionary trusts

For the 1988–89 tax year, discretionary trusts pay tax at 35 per cent on most of their income. This applies whether the income is kept by the trust or paid out to you. If it is paid out to you, you get a credit of 35 per cent of the gross (before-tax) amount. If your income (including the income from the trust) is too low for you to pay tax, or you pay tax at a lower rate, you can claim back some (or all) of the tax deducted.

Income and growth bonds

There are several different types of bond, which work (and are taxed) in different ways. See Chapter 21.

Unit trusts

With the first distribution you get from a unit trust, you're likely to get an equalisation payment. This is a return of part of the money you first invested, so doesn't count as income and isn't taxable. But see p112 for how it affects any capital gains you make.

With an accumulation unit trust (where income is automatically reinvested for you) the amount reinvested – apart from any equalisation payment – counts as income and is taxable.

National Savings Investment and Ordinary Accounts

You and your spouse are each allowed £70 interest free of tax from an ordinary account with the National Savings Bank. But you are taxed on anything more.

Note that if you have, say, £100 interest and your spouse has £20, you will have to pay tax on £30 of your interest, even though the combined interest isn't more than 2 x £70 = £140. If you and your wife have a joint account, however, you can have £140 interest free of tax. Any one person is allowed only £70 free of tax – however many accounts he or she has.

All interest from National Savings Investment Accounts is taxable; how much tax (if any) you have to pay depends on the size of your income.

British Government (and some other) stocks

Since 28 February 1986, if you sell British Government stocks before a date when you're due to receive an interest payment (normally twice yearly), part of the price you get is deemed to be the interest you would otherwise have received. It is calculated on a daily basis and taxed as income. This is known as the 'accrued income scheme', and also applies to sales of local authority and company loan stocks. However it won't apply if the 'nominal' or face value of all the stocks covered by the scheme that you (or your spouse, up to 1990) hold does not exceed £5,000 at any time in the tax year. See p293 for how to work out your accrued income.

Income tax and life insurance

There are two main types of life insurance policy for tax purposes. These are:

■ **qualifying policies** – including most regular-premium policies, for example most endowment policies and low-cost endowment policies linked to mortgages

■ **non-qualifying policies** – eg single premium policies.

The insurance companies' investment funds are taxed, but you don't have to pay basic rate income tax on policy proceeds yourself (and as the proceeds always count as income, there's no capital gains tax to pay).

When you do have to pay tax

You have to pay tax only if you're a higher rate taxpayer (or would be once the gain from the policy is added to your income) and:

■ *either* the policy is a non-qualifying policy

■ *or* the policy is a qualifying policy but you cashed it in or made it paid up in its first 10 years (or the first three-quarters of its term, if less).

If this applies to you, you need to work out your **taxable gain**. This is the amount you get when a policy comes to an end (*plus* any amounts you've had from the policy in the past), *less* the total premiums paid (including any subsidy you got on the premiums).

If you cash in only part of a policy before it matures, you get an allowance for each 12-month period since you first took out the policy. If you've received more from the policy than the amount of your allowances, the excess counts as your gain. For the first 20 years of the policy, the allowance is five per cent of the total premiums paid so far. For each year after that, the allowance is five per cent of the total premiums paid in that year and in the previous 19 years.

This means that you can take a yearly income from non-qualifying policies up to the yearly allowance without paying any tax. Any income above the yearly allowance is free of basic rate tax, but if you are a higher rate taxpayer you will have to pay tax at the higher rate for the year in which you take the income. If you don't use the full five per cent allowed in any tax year, you can use it in future years.

Should a taxable gain arise because the person insured dies, you work out the gain by taking the cash-in value of the policy just before death, and deducting the total of premiums paid.

How the gain is taxed

Any gain is added to your income for the tax year in which the policy matures or is cashed in. There's no basic rate tax to pay on the gain – only any higher rate tax. For example, if you are liable to tax at the higher rate of 40 per cent, you'll pay tax at 40 – 25 = 15 per cent.

If adding the gain to your income means that part of your income is pushed from the basic to the higher tax bracket, you should claim **top-slicing relief**. This spreads the gain over the years that the policy has run. Your tax bill is based on the average gain for each complete year that the policy has run, multiplied by the number of years. If the average gain added to your other taxable income doesn't take you into the higher tax bracket, there's no further tax to pay.

Example: how top-slicing relief can save tax
Arnold Archer bought a £20,000 single premium bond in December 1983, and cashed it in for £30,000 in July 1988 – making a gain of £10,000. He already has taxable income for 1988–89 (after deducting his allowances and outgoings) of £15,000. His tax bill on the gain would normally be worked out by adding the gain to his investment income:

Without top-slicing relief

rate of tax %	income on which you pay this rate £	gain on bond £	amount of tax £
25	15,000		3,750
40	nil		
25		4,300	1,075
40		5,700	2,280
total gain		10,000	
basic and higher rate tax on gain			3,355
subtract tax at basic rate on gain (25% of £10,000)			2,500
total tax bill on gain			855

With top-slicing relief

rate of tax %	income on which you pay this rate £	gain on bond £	amount of tax £
25	15,000		3,750
40	nil		
25		2,500	625
40		nil	nil
average yearly gain		2,500	
tax on average yearly gain			625
subtract tax at basic rate on average yearly gain (25% of 2,500)			625
so tax bill on average yearly gain is			nil
total tax bill on gain (nil x 4)			nil

But Arnold realises he can claim top-slicing relief. With this, the average yearly gain of £2,500 (the £10,000 total gain divided by the four complete years the bond ran for) is added to his investment income for the year. His total tax bill on the gain is the tax on the average yearly gain multiplied by the number of complete years for which he held the bond. Top-slicing relief means that Arnold doesn't have to pay any tax on the gain and so saves £855 – see Table on p103.

Tax relief on your premiums

Premiums on qualifying policies taken out before 14 March 1984 get a subsidy from the taxman, irrespective of whether you pay tax or not. The subsidy is 15 per cent up to 6 April 1989, reducing to 12.5 per cent after that date.

You'll continue to get the subsidy *unless* you alter the policy in a way which increases the benefits payable. That could include taking up an option attached to the policy – for example, to increase your premiums and therefore your amount of cover, to extend the term, or to convert the policy into another kind of policy. You won't lose the subsidy if the increased benefits are due to an increase that's *built-in* – for example if premiums and cover automatically increase by a fixed percentage. But there's a limit on premiums of £1,500 or one sixth of your total income, whichever is greater, and if you pay premiums of more than this you won't get the subsidy on the excess.

Capital gains tax

You can make a capital gain (or loss) whenever you stop owning something – no matter how you came to own it. But you won't always be taxed on gains when you dispose of an asset.

Anything you own (whether in the UK or not) counts as an asset – for example houses, jewellery and shares.

You dispose of an asset not only if you sell it, but also if you give it away, exchange it, or lose it. You also dispose of an asset if it is destroyed or becomes worthless, if you sell rights to it (eg grant a lease), or if you get compensation for damage to it (eg insurance money) and don't spend it all on restoring the damage. But a transfer of an asset between a husband and wife who aren't separated doesn't count as a disposal, nor does the transfer of an asset you leave when you die. Some types of gain are tax-free altogether – see p106

– and the first slice of total chargeable gains made in the tax year is also tax-free. In the 1988–89 tax year, your tax-free slice was £5,000.

Working out the gain

To work out the gain you make when you dispose of an asset, you have to:
■ take the **final value** of the asset when you dispose of it –its sale price (or market value at the time, if you gave it away or sold it for less than its full worth)
■ deduct its **initial value** when you got it – the price paid (or the market value at the time if you were given or inherited it)
■ deduct any **allowable expenses** you incurred in acquiring, improving or disposing of the asset, such as the costs of advertising, commission, legal fees and stamp duty.

If the answer is a plus figure you have made a **gain**, and if the answer is a negative figure you've made a **loss**. You can subtract losses from gains to reduce the amount liable to capital gains tax.

An important allowance which can reduce or eliminate your taxable gain, or even turn it into a loss, is **indexation allowance**. This helps prevent you being taxed on gains caused purely by inflation. See p107 for how to calculate the allowance.

Gains after allowing for indexation are called **chargeable gains**, any losses after indexation are called **allowable losses**. You can deduct your losses from your gains, and any losses left over can be carried forward to future tax years, and used to reduce your chargeable gains to the level of the tax-free slice.

Your chargeable gains *less* your tax-free slice *less* any allowable losses leave your **net taxable gains**. In our **Route Map** on pp108–109 we take you through the sums involved, with an example of how the figures could work out.

Capital gains tax applies only to gains made after 31 March 1982. See p111 for how to work out your taxable gain for assets acquired before that date.

How much tax?

Capital gains tax is charged at the same rate you'd pay if your gain was your top slice of income. So if you pay only basic rate tax you'll pay capital gains tax at 25 per cent, and if you pay higher rate tax you'll pay tax at 40 per cent (1988–89 tax rates). If you don't pay tax at the higher rate, but your net taxable capital gains *plus* your taxable income (see p95) come to more than the amount of the basic rate tax band, you pay higher rate tax on the excess. Suppose you had net taxable gains of £10,000, and taxable income of £10,500, ie £20,500. You would pay higher rate tax on £20,500 minus the amount of the basic rate tax band (£19,300 in 1988–89), ie £1,200, and basic rate tax on the rest.

Any tax due has to be paid either on 1 December after the end of the tax year in which the gains were made, or 30 days after the date on your assessment, whichever is later. If you disagree with an assessment, take it up with your tax office in writing within 30 days.

Tax-free gains

The gains you make on some assets are tax-free, but any losses you make on them can't be used to offset chargeable gains. The main tax-free gains are those on:
■ your own home (see p148)
■ private cars
■ British money (including post-1837 gold sovereigns and Britannia gold coins)
■ foreign currency for personal and family expenditure (eg for a holiday abroad)
■ British Government stocks
■ National Savings Certificates, Save-As-You-Earn, National Savings Yearly Plan, Premium Bonds
■ personal belongings with a predictable life of less than 50 years when you got them (eg electronic equipment)
■ personal belongings expected to last more than 50 years (eg antiques, jewellery and other moveable items) provided their value when you dispose of them is £3,000, or less. If their value is higher, your gain is taken to be the lower of *either* the actual gain *or* the final value, minus £3,000 multiplied by 5/3. But if you dispose of something for less than £3,000 and make a loss, your loss is worked out as if you had actually got £3,000 for the item
■ gifts to charities
■ gifts to some 'national heritage bodies', eg some museums and the National Trust
■ proceeds from life insurance policies, unless you bought the policy from a previous holder
■ 'qualifying' corporate bonds – those quoted on the Stock Exchange or traded in the Unlisted Securities Market, and acquired after 13 March 1984
■ shares issued after 18 March 1986 under the Business Ex-

pansion Scheme (on their first disposals only)
■ disposals made after 1 July 1986 of futures and options in British Government stocks and qualifying corporate bonds. This doesn't apply to disposals of commodity futures, financial futures and traded options
■ shares and unit trusts held in a qualifying Personal Equity Plan
■ betting winnings.

Route Map: how much capital gains tax?

The Route Map overleaf takes you through the steps involved in working out your capital gains tax. It's illustrated with an example, showing how much tax Matthew Parsons had to pay when he sold his holiday cottage (Matthew's main home is exempt from capital gains tax, so there'll be no tax to pay when he sells that).

He bought his cottage in March 1982 for £20,000, and sold it at the end of April 1988 for £50,000. He had buying costs of £700, spent £2,000 installing central heating in June 1983, and had selling costs of £1,200 – £3,900 in all.

Matthew has made no other disposals for capital gains tax purposes, except for an unlucky share investment in 1983, when he made an allowable loss of £2,000. His taxable income is £20,000 so he is a higher rate taxpayer.

Indexation allowance

Indexation allowance allows for inflation by linking the values of your assets and expenses to changes in the Retail Prices Index (RPI). It is worked out from the date you acquired the asset or incurred the expense, or March 1982 if later (if you owned an asset on or before 31 March 1982, see p111 for how to work out the allowance). So if you incurred any expenses in a different month from acquiring the asset, you need to work out the indexation allowance for that expense separately. Costs of disposing of the asset cannot be index-linked.

To work out your indexation allowance you first need to find out the RPI for:
■ A – the month of disposal
■ B – the month in which the index-linking begins (the date you acquired the asset, or incurred the expense, or March 1982 if later).

The RPI is announced every month by the Department of Employment and published in the Department's *Employment Gazette* (try your local library). See Box on p110 for a list of RPI figures since March 1982.

Will you have to pay capital gains tax?

Have you made a gain?

Matthew's calculations

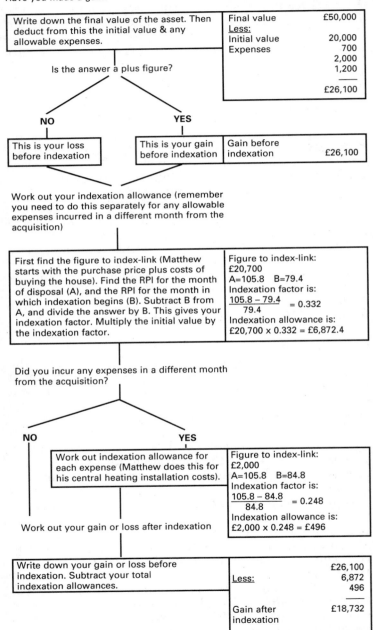

Write down the final value of the asset. Then deduct from this the initial value & any allowable expenses.	Final value	£50,000
	Less:	
	Initial value	20,000
	Expenses	700
		2,000
		1,200
Is the answer a plus figure?		———
		£26,100

NO → This is your loss before indexation

YES → This is your gain before indexation

Gain before indexation	£26,100

Work out your indexation allowance (remember you need to do this separately for any allowable expenses incurred in a different month from the acquisition)

First find the figure to index-link (Matthew starts with the purchase price plus costs of buying the house). Find the RPI for the month of disposal (A), and the RPI for the month in which indexation begins (B). Subtract B from A, and divide the answer by B. This gives your indexation factor. Multiply the initial value by the indexation factor.	Figure to index-link: £20,700 A=105.8 B=79.4 Indexation factor is: $\frac{105.8 - 79.4}{79.4} = 0.332$ Indexation allowance is: £20,700 x 0.332 = £6,872.4

Did you incur any expenses in a different month from the acquisition?

NO

YES → Work out indexation allowance for each expense (Matthew does this for his central heating installation costs).

	Figure to index-link: £2,000 A=105.8 B=84.8 Indexation factor is: $\frac{105.8 - 84.8}{84.8} = 0.248$ Indexation allowance is: £2,000 x 0.248 = £496

Work out your gain or loss after indexation

Write down your gain or loss before indexation. Subtract your total indexation allowances.		£26,100
	Less:	6,872
		496
		———
	Gain after indexation	£18,732

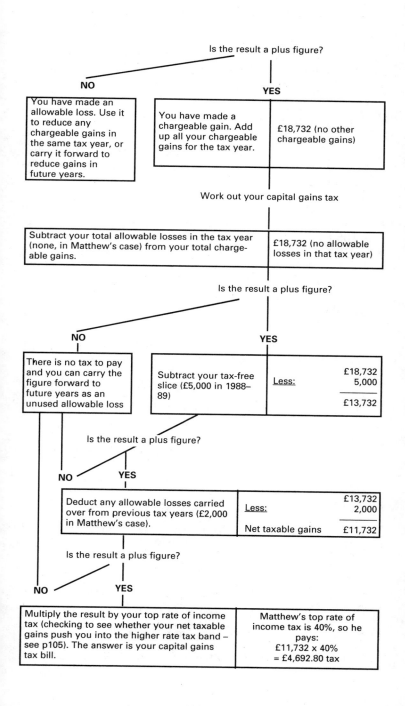

Is the result a plus figure?

NO   **YES**

You have made an allowable loss. Use it to reduce any chargeable gains in the same tax year, or carry it forward to reduce gains in future years.

| You have made a chargeable gain. Add up all your chargeable gains for the tax year. | £18,732 (no other chargeable gains) |

Work out your capital gains tax

| Subtract your total allowable losses in the tax year (none, in Matthew's case) from your total chargeable gains. | £18,732 (no allowable losses in that tax year) |

Is the result a plus figure?

NO   **YES**

There is no tax to pay and you can carry the figure forward to future years as an unused allowable loss

| Subtract your tax-free slice (£5,000 in 1988–89) | _Less:_ | £18,732
5,000
———
£13,732 |

Is the result a plus figure?

NO   **YES**

| Deduct any allowable losses carried over from previous tax years (£2,000 in Matthew's case). | _Less:_ | £13,732
2,000
———— |
| | Net taxable gains | £11,732 |

Is the result a plus figure?

NO   **YES**

| Multiply the result by your top rate of income tax (checking to see whether your net taxable gains push you into the higher rate tax band – see p105). The answer is your capital gains tax bill. | Matthew's top rate of income tax is 40%, so he pays:
£11,732 x 40%
= £4,692.80 tax |

The calculation is as follows: take the RPI for the month of the disposal and subtract the RPI for the month when indexation begins. You then divide the result by the RPI for the month when indexation begins, and work out this figure (called the **indexation factor**) to the nearest 3 decimal places. Or, for the mathematically minded:

$$\frac{A - B}{B} = \text{indexation factor.}$$

The indexation factor, multiplied by the initial value of the asset, or your allowable expense, gives you your indexation allowance.

So before Matthew starts the Route Map he gathers together the RPI figures he needs:

■ A – RPI for month of disposal; for April 1988 this figure was 105.8
■ B – RPI for month of indexation; March 1982 for the house and costs of buying it (79.4), June 1983 for the cost of installing central heating (84.8).

Retail Prices Index
Use these figures for working out your capital gains tax bill. The RPI was rebased (ie went back to 100) in January 1987. We've reworked the figures for previous months so that they are comparable with the rebased figures.

	1982	1983	1984	1985	1986	1987	1988
January	[1]	82.6	86.8	91.2	96.2	100.0	103.3
February	[1]	83.0	87.2	91.9	96.6	100.4	103.7
March	79.4	83.1	87.5	92.8	96.7	100.6	104.1
April	81.0	84.3	88.6	94.8	97.7	101.8	105.8
May	81.6	84.6	89.0	95.2	97.8	101.9	106.2
June	81.9	84.8	89.2	95.4	97.8	101.9	
July	81.9	85.3	89.1	95.2	97.5	101.8	
August	81.9	85.7	89.9	95.5	97.8	102.1	
September	81.9	86.1	90.1	95.4	98.3	102.4	
October	82.3	86.4	90.7	95.6	98.5	102.9	
November	82.7	86.7	91.0	95.9	99.3	103.4	
December	82.5	86.9	90.9	96.0	99.6	103.3	

[1] Indexation allowance only runs from March 1982.

Points to watch

Assets owned on 31 March 1982

Capital gains tax first came into force in 1965, but from 6 April 1988 the law was changed so that only gains made after 31 March 1982 are now taxable. This means that if you dispose of an asset you already owned on 31 March 1982, you are treated as though you actually acquired it on that date. So the initial value of the asset is taken to be its market value at that date (any earlier expenses are ignored), and the indexation allowance runs from March 1982.

However, to stop taxpayers being worse off under the new rules than they would have been under the old, there is an exception to the rules. If the gain from March 1982 to disposal is greater than the overall gain from acquisition to disposal, you take the smaller figure. If the new method produces a gain where the old method would have produced a loss (or vice versa) you will be treated, for tax purposes, as if you had made neither a gain nor a loss on disposal. You *can* choose always to use the March 1982 value, but once you have done so, you can't change your mind.

Gifts

If you give an asset away, or part with it for less than its true worth, your gain is worked out as though you had sold it for its full market value. But there's a special form of relief available when you make a gift on which the tax is due – called **hold-over relief**. The effect of this relief is to avoid a capital gains tax bill at the time of the gift. Tax is put off until the recipient parts with the gift – although it could mean a higher tax bill then.

The recipient is counted as acquiring the asset at its market value when you, the giver, first acquired it, plus any allowable expenses you incurred. He or she gets the benefit of the indexation rules up to the time of the gift, plus any indexation allowance due from the date of the gift until he or she parts with it, plus any more allowable expenses.

You and the person to whom you're giving the asset must apply jointly for hold-over relief, by contacting the taxman.

Don't claim this relief if you know your gains for the year (including the gain on the gift) won't exceed £5,000. You won't save tax, and the recipient might pay more.

Shares and unit trusts

If you own one lot of the same type of shares in the same company (or units in a unit trust), and you acquired them all at the same time, they are treated in the same way for capital gains tax purposes as any other asset. However, if you bought shares or units of the same type, in the same company, at different times, the taxman has special rules for deciding which ones you've sold when you come to sell them. These special rules decide which shares you've disposed of, how much they cost you, and what your indexation allowance is – see Inland Revenue leaflet CGT13, available from local tax and PAYE Enquiry offices. But the rules are very complicated and you may need to get professional advice to sort matters out.

You may get an **equalisation payment** from a unit trust (see p101). The payment itself is not taxable, but it must be subtracted from the purchase price of the units when working out your capital gain or loss. So if you bought some unit trusts for £1,000, and received an equalisation payment of £5, the purchase price of the units for tax purposes is £1,000 – £5 = £995.

With an **accumulation** unit trust, the income for your units is automatically reinvested for you. This affects the purchase price of your units for capital gains tax purposes. However, working out the purchase price is complicated, and depends on exactly how the income is reinvested. Check with the unit trust company.

Capital gains and marriage

A couple who are married before the start of the tax year, or who marry on the first day of the tax year, normally have their gains taxed jointly – ie the husband's losses are set off against the wife's gains and vice versa. They have only one tax-free slice of gains between them.

But a couple can choose to have their capital gains separately assessed – this will make the wife responsible for paying her share of the bill, but won't affect the total amount of the couple's bill. Whether assessed jointly or separately, either of the couple can ask for his or her own losses for any year to be set off against his or her own gains only (present and future). This can save you tax.

If either husband or wife has made net losses during the year while the other has made net taxable gains of £5,000 or less, the one who has made the losses should ask for them to be carried forward and set against his or her own future gains. That way there's no tax to pay this year – and there may be a tax-saving in future years.

All this will change in 1990 when women will be taxed independently from their husbands on any gains they make. This will give husband and wife each an individual yearly tax-free allowance instead of having one allowance split between them.

Example
Paul Porter made a taxable capital gain of £4,600 in the 1988–89 tax year. His wife Shirley made an allowable loss of £1,200. Paul and Shirley talk it over and realise that if they are taxed in the normal way, Shirley's loss will be set off against Paul's gain. They'll have no tax to pay – but will have no losses to carry forward.

If Shirley asks to have her own losses for the year carried forward, however, there will still be no tax to pay (because their joint gains, ignoring Shirley's losses, are less than £5,000). And Shirley will be able to carry her £1,200 loss over to set against her future gains.

How to reduce your capital gains tax bill

■ Be sure to deduct from a gain, or add to a loss, all your allowable expenses.

■ If you have things which have increased in value and on which you will have to pay capital gains tax when you sell them, you'll avoid tax if you can keep the gains you make each year below £5,000. It's worth making use of this £5,000 allowance each year if you can – it can't be carried forward to the next year.

■ If your losses for the year add up to more than your gains, you can carry forward the balance of the losses to set against gains you would have to pay tax on in later years. So keep a careful record of your losses.

■ If either husband or wife has made net losses during the year while the other has made net gains of less than £5,000, the one who made the losses should ask for them to be carried forward and set against future gains. There'll still be no tax to pay that year, and there may be a tax saving in later years.

Inheritance tax

Roughly speaking, inheritance tax is a tax on the value of what you leave when you die, and on some gifts you make during your lifetime. So it's not a tax that affects investments very much. Here we give a brief outline of the rules, and then look at life insurance policies – where a little care can keep inheritance tax at bay.

Who's afraid of inheritance tax?

There may be inheritance tax to pay if:
- you die within seven years of making certain gifts, known as *Potentially Exempt Transfer* (PETs). These include gifts to people other than your spouse (eg gifts from parents to children), and some gifts to trusts
- you make a *chargeable transfer*. These are any gifts which are neither tax-free nor counted as PETs, and include gifts to companies and gifts to discretionary trusts
- you die, and the value of all your possessions plus any PETs and chargeable transfers you've made in the seven years before death is more than a set amount – £110,000 in the 1988–89 tax year.

However, some gifts are tax-free (see below) and ignored by the taxman. For example, gifts between a husband and wife are normally tax-free, no matter when they're made. So if you die worth £150,000, and leave the lot to your wife (or husband), the value of your estate, for IHT purposes, is nil. Or course, when your wife or husband dies, there may be tax to pay on his or her estate.

Most other gifts made by individuals will count as PETs and so only be taxable if you die within seven years of making them. Chargeable transfers are the only type of gift on which you might have to pay tax during your lifetime.

Any gifts which aren't tax-free start to clock up on a running total. When your running total of chargeable transfers goes above a certain level –£110,000 in the 1988–89 tax year – tax is payable at half the rate of tax due on death. At present the tax rate on death is 40 per cent, so the rate would be 20 per cent. The tax-free level will be increased in line with inflation in the Budget each year unless Parliament decides otherwise.

Any gifts made more than seven years ago are knocked off your running total – so your running total can fall as well as rise.

Note: Inheritance tax replaced capital transfer tax in March 1986, but gifts on your running total then are still counted now.

Tax-free gifts

Some gifts are tax-free only if made during your lifetime. Others are tax-free whenever they are made. Gifts that are tax-free during your lifetime include:
- gifts which are part of your normal expenditure out of

income. These must be regular – eg covenant payments – and not reduce your standard of living
■ gifts to people getting married, with a maximum of £5,000 from each parent of the couple, £2,500 from a grandparent, and £1,000 from anybody else
■ maintenance payments to ex-husbands or wives
■ gifts of reasonable amounts needed to support a dependent relative
■ gifts for the education, maintenance or training of your children if they are still in full-time education or training, or not more than 18 years of age
■ small gifts – up to £250 to each recipient each year
■ your **annual exemption** – gifts of up to £3,000 a year. This exemption is in addition to all the tax-free gifts above *except* that you can't give £3,000 plus £250 (the 'small gifts' exemption) to the same person. If you don't use the full £3,000 up in one year you can carry what's left forward for up to one year (ie up to £6,000 in the second year), but you must use up the current year's annual exemption first.

Gifts tax-free whenever they are made include:
■ gifts between husband and wife (provided the recipient is domiciled in the UK)
■ gifts to UK-established charities
■ gifts to political parties
■ gifts to most museums and art galleries, to universities, the National Trust, local authorities, and other similar bodies
■ gifts of property and possessions of outstanding national interest made to various non-profit-making bodies
■ broadly, gifts of shares to a trust which will hold more than half of a company's ordinary shares and which was set up for the employees' benefit, provided the trustees have voting control.

Inheritance tax on life insurance

Regular premium life insurance policies are an excellent way of giving chunks of tax-free capital to your dependants – or indeed to anyone.

The premiums will count as a gift, but there shouldn't be any inheritance tax to pay on them, since they'll normally be in one of the tax-free categories above.

What to avoid

Try to make sure that the proceeds of your policies don't count as part of your estate. If they do, they'll be added on to the rest of what you leave, and your inheritance tax bill could rise.

You can avoid this by getting the policy written in trust so that the proceeds go to someone else. If a policy on your life is for the benefit of your wife (or husband) or children, the Married Women's Property Act provides a simple way of doing this. Otherwise, you'll need to get a declaration of trust written on the policy. Ask the insurance company what to do. Alternatively, you could give away the policy after taking it out, but this could count as a gift for inheritance tax purposes.

Types of policy
■ **endowment policy** (see p311)

what it is: a policy which pays out a lump sum on a fixed date – or when you die, if this is earlier.

useful for: people who want to give tax-free capital away in their lifetime.

■ **whole life insurance** (see p322)

what it is: a policy which pays out on your death.

useful for: paying the inheritance tax bill when you die. A husband and wife who are going to leave everything to each other could take out a last survivor or joint life and last survivor policy, which pays out on the second death (ie when the inheritance tax bill will arrive). The premiums are lower than for a policy on a single life. A joint life first death policy is useful for paying an inheritance tax bill on the first death.

■ **term insurance** (see p315)

what it is: a policy which pays out only if you die before the policy ends (within three years, or ten years, say). If you survive, it pays nothing.

useful for: someone who will be faced with a large inheritance tax bill only if death occurs within a certain time. For example, someone who has received a PET may be caught by a tax bill if the giver dies within seven years.

8

A BIRD'S
EYE VIEW

Before you can put your investment strategy into effect you'll have to get to grips with the nitty-gritty of what different investments offer and what their particular advantages and disadvantages are.

In this chapter we give you a summary of the main types of investment open to you, starting on p120. The most important points about each investment are picked out in the Table (see below for why each row is important).

In the later chapters of the book you'll find much fuller details of each type of investment.

The rows in the Table

Regular saving or lump sum?
Some investments are very flexible. The minimum amount you can invest is fairly low – so they can be used as homes for lump sums, regular savings and odd bits of spare cash.

But some investments are open only to people who have a fair-sized lump sum of money to invest, and others only to people who want to save a regular amount each month or year, say. Of course, if you've a lump sum you can invest it bit by bit on a regular basis, if you like.

Minimum you should invest
This row tells you the minimum sensible amount you can invest. This isn't necessarily the same thing as the minimum amount you're *allowed* to invest. For example, you can invest as little as you like in shares, but the commission you have to pay means that an investment of less than £1,200 or so is less worthwhile.

Does it pay a regular income?
Some investments pay income direct to you at regular inter-

vals. With others, the income is added to the value of what you first invested.

Of course, with some investments which don't pay an income out to you, such as single-premium bonds and National Savings Certificates, you may still be able to give yourself a regular income by cashing part of your investment at regular intervals – indeed, with some investments (such as single-premium bonds) there are often standard schemes to allow you to do this.

With some investments which pay out a regular income, the income is fixed when you take out the investment (for example, guaranteed income bonds). With other investments, such as those offered by building societies, the income can vary after you've invested your money.

If you need to be sure of getting a regular number of £££ from your investment each year, go for one that pays out a fixed income – but see *Keeping up with inflation* on p16.

Note that if you go for a fixed income, you may regret your decision if interest rates in general rise – investments with interest rates which vary may turn out to have been better bets. On the other hand, if interest rates in general fall, you will feel pleased with yourself for putting your money in a fixed income investment.

How long is the investment meant to be for?
This row tells you how long you should expect to have to leave your money invested in order to get the best return.

Can you get your money back quickly?
In some cases, the answer is you can't. So don't put your money in one of these investments unless you're certain you'll be able to leave it there for the agreed period.

With other investments, you may be able to cash in early but not get back (or not be sure of getting back) what you paid in. So, if you want a certain amount of money at a certain time – for example to go on holiday in two years' time – you'd be wise to steer clear of these investments too.

Does the value of your capital fluctuate?
Investments can be divided into two types:
- the value of the capital you invest stays the same (but see *Keeping up with inflation* on p16)
- the value may fluctuate. Unit trusts, single-premium bonds and sovereigns are examples of investments where the value of the capital invested will fluctuate. With investments like these, you stand a chance of making a capital gain, but also run the risk of losing some of your money. And

because the value of the capital fluctuates, the success of your investment depends very much on *when* you invest and *when* you cash in your investment. For more about how to reduce the risk of doing very badly see p19.

Points about tax

This row picks out particular tax points for the various investments. More details on tax are given in Chapter 7, and in the chapters dealing with each investment.

For example, non-taxpayers should beware of investments where composite rate tax (the equivalent of basic rate tax) is deducted before you get the income. You can't reclaim this tax even if you're a non-taxpayer. Other investments, where the return is tax-free, look more attractive the higher the rate of tax you pay. This also applies to investments where you get tax relief on the payments you make – for example, contributions to an employer's pension scheme, payments to a personal pension plan, interest on loans to buy your own home.

Where you can get the investment

This row tells you where to go to put your money in these investments.

Other comments

This gives snippets of information about how some of the investments work, who might find it worthwhile to consider or to avoid a particular investment, and so on.

type of investment (and where to find more details)	Alternative investments (eg stamps, antique furniture, diamonds, gold . . .) . Chapter 25, p403	Annuities Chapter 22, p355
regular saving or lump sum?	lump sum	lump sum
minimum investment [1]	varies	depends on age and income required
does it pay a regular income?	no – in fact you have to pay for insurance etc. But see *other comments*	yes, normally arranged at time you buy the annuity. The older you are at that time, the higher the income
how long is investment meant to be for?	in the main, long-term investment	until you die
can you get your money back quickly?	as quickly as you can find a buyer. But may get back less than you invested	you can't – once you've made investment you can't cash it in
does value of capital fluctuate?	yes	not applicable – can't get capital back
points about tax	no capital gains tax unless value of item at time of disposal more than £3,000 (post-1837 UK gold sovereigns and Britannia coins are free of capital gains tax). If count as trader, may have to pay income tax	income made up of two parts – interest on capital and return of part of capital. Only interest part is taxable – normally paid after deduction of basic rate tax [2]
where can you get investment?	auctions, dealers, other collectors, sometimes investment companies too	life insurance company or adviser
other comments	needs expert knowledge. Watch out for dealer's mark-up	only worth considering for older people (around 70, say). Man gets higher income than woman of same age

[1] Gives an idea of the minimum it's sensible to invest – see p117
[2] Income from annuities you *have* to buy – eg as part of personal pension plan – is all taxed as earned income

type of investment (and where to find more details)	Bank and finance company investments *Chapter 11, p165* – deposit accounts	Bank and finance company investments *Chapter 11, p165* – term and notice accounts
regular saving or lump sum?	either	lump sum
minimum investment [1]	often £1 (£100 to £2,000 for a higher-rate deposit account giving better interest)	normally £1,000 to £10,000
does it pay a regular income?	no – but interest is reinvested and can be withdrawn. Interest varies	yes – if you choose. Interest varies on notice and some term accounts
how long is investment meant to be for?	for emergency funds and a temporary home for other funds (unless interest rate is high)	varies from a few days to a few years
can you get your money back quickly?	in practice, with most banks at once – but may lose some interest	not until end of agreed term or notice period
does value of capital fluctuate?	no	no
points about tax	interest paid after deduction of composite rate tax [2]	see *deposit accounts*
where can you get investment?	High-Street bank, Girobank, finance company	High-Street bank, finance company
other comments	you don't usually need a current account at the bank to open a deposit account	

[1] Gives an idea of the minimum it's sensible to invest – see p117
[2] So basic rate taxpayers don't have to worry about tax; non-taxpayers *can't* reclaim tax; higher rate taxpayers pay extra tax

type of investment (and where to find more details)	Bank and finance company investments *Chapter 11, p165* **– savings accounts**	British Government stocks *Chapter 17, p287* **– conventional stocks**
regular saving or lump sum?	regular saving	lump sum
minimum investment [1]	varies – from £10 a month upwards	none if bought on National Savings Stock Register; otherwise £1,000 sensible minimum
does it pay a regular income?	no – interest is reinvested	yes – income fixed at the time you buy the stock (except with a few stocks)
how long is investment meant to be for?	normally at least one year to get higher interest	until stock due to be redeemed (paid back) by government – but some stocks can also be short-term speculation
can you get your money back quickly?	may be able to cash small amounts once or twice a year	can sell stock at any time. Can take a day or two to get money if sold through stockbroker, a week or so through National Savings Stock Register
does value of capital fluctuate?	no	yes – but if you hold stock until redemption, you know for certain what you'll get back
points about tax	interest paid after deduction of composite rate tax [2]	interest is taxable – paid without deduction of tax if bought through National Savings Stock Register, normally after deduction of basic rate tax if bought through stockbroker. Free of capital gains tax
where can you get investment?	High-Street bank, finance company	stockbroker, post office, High-Street bank or other agent (eg accountant)
other comments	not common nowadays	best stock for you depends to large extent on rate of tax you pay. Get advice on which stock to choose — eg from stockbroker, bank. Buying and selling costs less for small investments if made through National Savings Stock Register

[1] Gives an idea of the minimum it's sensible to invest – see p117
[2] So basic rate taxpayers don't have to worry about tax; non-taxpayers *can't* reclaim tax; higher rate taxpayers pay extra tax

type of investment (and where to find more details)	British Government stocks *Chapter 17, p287* – index-linked stocks	Building societies *Chapter 10, p151* – instant access accounts
regular saving or lump sum?	see *conventional stocks*	either
minimum investment [1]	see *conventional stocks*	anything from £1 upwards
does it pay a regular income?	yes – and income increases in line with Retail Prices Index	you can choose to have income paid out or reinvested. Interest varies
how long is investment meant to be for?	see *conventional stocks*	any period
can you get your money back quickly?	see *conventional stocks*	can cash in at any time (but sometimes only balance over a set amount)
does value of capital fluctuate?	yes – but at redemption, government pays back *nominal value* (see p288) increased in line with Retail Prices Index since time of issue	no
points about tax	see *conventional stocks*	interest paid after deduction of composite rate tax [2]
where can you get investment?	see *conventional stocks*	building society
other comments	see *conventional stocks*	often the more you invest, the higher the interest rate

[1] Gives an idea of the minimum it's sensible to invest – see p117
[2] So basic rate taxpayers don't have to worry about tax; non-taxpayers *can't* reclaim tax; higher rate taxpayers pay extra tax

type of investment (and where to find more details)	Building societies *Chapter 10, p151* – notice accounts	Building societies *Chapter 10, p151* – ordinary shares
regular saving or lump sum?	lump sum	either
minimum investment [1]	normally £500 upwards	normally £1
does it pay a regular income?	you can normally choose to have income paid out or reinvested. Interest varies	you can choose to have interest paid out or reinvested. Interest varies
how long is investment meant to be for?	any period	for emergency funds and a temporary home for other funds
can you get your money back quickly?	often you can either choose to give notice of 1 to 3 months or can cash at once (but lose some interest)	on the spot or in a few days
does value of capital fluctuate?	no	no
points about tax	interest paid after deduction of composite rate tax [2]	interest paid after deduction of composite rate tax [2]
where can you get investment?	building society	building society
other comments	normally pays higher interest rate than ordinary shares. May get higher interest the more you invest	also consider *notice accounts*

[1] Gives an idea of the minimum it's sensible to invest – see p117
[2] So basic rate taxpayers don't have to worry about tax; non-taxpayers *can't* reclaim tax; higher rate taxpayers pay extra tax

type of investment (and where to find more details)	Building societies Chapter 10, p151 – savings accounts	Building societies Chapter 10, p151 – term shares
regular saving or lump sum?	regular saving	lump sum
minimum investment [1]	normally £1 a month	normally £500 to £5,000
does it pay a regular income?	no	you can normally choose to have interest paid out or reinvested. Interest varies
how long is investment meant to be for?	normally any period, but may get higher interest rate if save for more than certain period (eg 1 year)	anything from 6 months upwards
can you get your money back quickly?	varies	with some you can't, until end of term. With others, after 3 months, say – but lose interest
does value of capital fluctuate?	no	no
points about tax	interest paid after deduction of composite rate tax [2]	interest paid after deduction of composite rate tax [2]
where can you get investment?	building society	building society
other comments	may pay more interest than ordinary shares	normally pays higher rate of interest than ordinary shares – say, 1% higher for a 3-year term

[1] Gives an idea of the minimum it's sensible to invest – see p117
[2] So basic rate taxpayers don't have to worry about tax; non-taxpayers *can't* reclaim tax; higher rate taxpayers pay extra tax

type of investment (and where to find more details)	Building society Save-As-You-Earn (SAYE) *Chapter 10, p151*	Commodities *Chapter 23, p367*
regular saving or lump sum?	regular saving	lump sum
minimum investment [1]	£1 a month (maximum £20 a month)	several thousand £££ for direct investment; £1,000 say, for commodity fund or trust
does it pay a regular income?	no	no, with direct investment. Some funds and trusts pay an income – with others you can get income by cashing units
how long is investment meant to be for?	5 or 7 years	long-term investment or short-term speculation
can you get your money back quickly?	can withdraw at any time (but if cashed in before 5 years are up, return is lower). No interest at all on withdrawals in first year	if direct investment, can sell at any time. With fund or trust, a few days or a month
does value of capital fluctuate?	no	yes
points about tax	return tax-free	gain may be taxed as income or as capital gain, depending on circumstances – see *Chapter 23*
where can you get investment?	building society	commodity broker; direct from fund or trust or through intermediary
other comments	at end of 5 years get bonus of extra monthly payments – and a further bonus if invest for another 2 years. Conditions are identical whichever society you go to	investing directly in commodities not sensible for most people. Very risky – consider commodity fund or unit trust instead. For legal and tax reasons, funds may be based offshore – Isle of Man or Channel Islands, say
	[1] Gives an idea of the minimum it's sensible to invest – see p117	

type of investment (and where to find more details)	**Endowment policies** *Chapter 19, p311*	**Home** *Chapter 9, p141*
regular saving or lump sum?	regular saving	either
minimum investment [1]	£15 a month, say	normally at least 10% of price of home
does it pay a regular income?	no	no (unless you let it out)
how long is investment meant to be for?	10 years or more – period usually agreed at outset	any period
can you get your money back quickly?	can cash in policy at any time but what you get back is often at discretion of company (and in first year or two may get little or nothing)	may take several months or longer to sell your home – unless you can raise a loan on it
does value of capital fluctuate?	get at least a guaranteed amount at end of policy (or if you die), usually bonuses too	yes
points about tax	return tax-free so long as pay tax at no more than the basic rate – always tax-free if keep policy going for at least 10 years or three-quarters of its term, whichever is less	get tax relief on interest on up to £30,000 of loans to buy your only or main home – and capital gain is normally tax-free
where can you get investment?	life insurance company or insurance adviser	estate agent, newspaper ads, *For sale* signs
other comments	can be used as a way of repaying a mortgage	proved a very good long-term investment in the past – see p141

[1] Gives an idea of the minimum it's sensible to invest – see p117

type of investment (and where to find more details)	Home income schemes *Chapter 22, p355*	Guaranteed income and growth bonds *Chapter 21, p351*
regular saving or lump sum?	lump sum (raised from mortgaging your home)	lump sum
minimum investment [1]	normally £15,000	often £500
does it pay a regular income?	yes – income (from an annuity) arranged at the time you take out the scheme (depends on age and sex)	income bonds – yes growth bonds – no
how long is investment meant to be for?	until you die	fixed period, varying from 1 to 10 years
can you get your money back quickly?	you can't get your money back at all	with some companies, at the end of agreed period only. With others, can cash in early – but return up to company
does value of capital fluctuate?	[2]	no
points about tax	get tax relief on interest on up to £30,000 to buy a scheme. Part of income tax-free	tax treatment depends on how bonds work – can work in one of several ways. Check with company before investing
where can you get investment?	life insurance company, insurance adviser, building society	life insurance company or insurance adviser
other comments	for how schemes work, see p363. Only worth considering for people over 70	return may be lower if you're over 65 when you cash bond in (see p353), because tax bill could rise

[1] Gives an idea of the minimum it's sensible to invest – see p117
[2] With schemes based on loans, you still benefit in full from increases in value of home. With schemes where you sell part or all of your home to the company ('reversions'), part or all of the increase in value of the home goes to the company – not recommended

type of investment (and where to find more details)	Investment trusts *Chapter 15, p241*	Local authority investments *Chapter 18, p303* **– local authority loans** (often called bonds)
regular saving or lump sum?	either	lump sum
minimum investment [1]	£1,200, say	£100 to £1,000, say
does it pay a regular income?	yes – most companies pay dividends. These can vary	yes – interest fixed at the time you invest
how long is investment meant to be for?	long-term investment or short-term speculation	agreed period – normally between 1 and 7 years
can you get your money back quickly?	can sell and get money back in 2 to 4 weeks – but may get less than you invested	you normally can't get money back till end of agreed period (though your heirs may be able to if you die)
does value of capital fluctuate?	yes	no
points about tax	dividends are taxable – paid after deduction of basic rate tax. Liable for capital gains tax on any gain	interest normally paid after deduction of composite rate tax [2]
where can you get investment?	stockbroker, bank, or other agent (eg accountant)	local authority
other comments	you buy shares in an investment trust company – a company whose sole business is investing in other companies' shares	doesn't have to be your own local authority that you invest in

[1] Gives an idea of the minimum it's sensible to invest – see p117
[2] So basic rate taxpayers don't have to worry about tax; non-taxpayers *can't* reclaim tax; higher rate taxpayers pay extra tax

type of investment (and where to find more details)	Local authority investments *Chapter 18, p303* **– yearling bonds**	National Savings investments *Chapter 12, p171* **– Ordinary Accounts**
regular saving or lump sum?	lump sum	either
minimum investment [1]	£1,000	£1 (maximum £10,000)
does it pay a regular income?	yes – income fixed at time you invest	no – but interest can be withdrawn. Interest can vary
how long is investment meant to be for?	a year or so	for emergency funds and a temporary home for other funds
can you get your money back quickly?	can sell on Stock Exchange. Takes a few days to get your money	£100 at once (about a week to withdraw all money) but see *other comments*
does value of capital fluctuate?	as for British Government stocks	no
points about tax	interest is taxable – paid after deduction of basic rate tax. Free of capital gains tax	first £70 interest each year is tax-free – all interest paid without deduction of tax
where can you get investment?	stockbroker	post office
other comments	alternatives to British Government stocks – but normally give slightly higher return. May be difficult to sell	interest paid only for complete calendar months money is invested. With a Regular Customer Account – see Chapter 12 – can withdraw £250 at once

[1] Gives an idea of the minimum it's sensible to invest – see p117

type of investment (and where to find more details)	National Savings investments Chapter 12, p171 – Investment Accounts	National Savings investments Chapter 12, p171 – National Savings Certificates (33rd issue)
regular saving or lump sum?	either	either
minimum investment [1]	£5 (maximum £100,000)	£25 (maximum £1,000)
does it pay a regular income?	no – but interest can be withdrawn. Interest can vary	no – but can be cashed in to provide income
how long is investment meant to be for?	any period over a month	for best return, 5 years
can you get your money back quickly?	1 month	around a couple of weeks (but return lower if cashed in within first 5 years)
does value of capital fluctuate?	no	no
points about tax	all interest is taxable – paid without deduction of tax	return is tax-free
where can you get investment?	post office	post office, High-Street bank
other comments	worth considering if you don't pay tax	

[1] Gives an idea of the minimum it's sensible to invest – see p117

type of investment (and where to find more details)	National Savings investments *Chapter 12, p171* – index-linked National Savings Certificates (4th issue)	National Savings investments *Chapter 12, p171* – National Savings Deposit Bonds
regular saving or lump sum?	either	either
minimum investment [1]	£25 (maximum £5,000)	£100 (maximum £100,000)
does it pay a regular income?	no – but can cash certificates to get an income	no
how long is investment meant to be for?	initially for 5 years (get overall return of at least 4% at end of 5 years). Can keep money invested longer	any period over a year
can you get your money back quickly?	around a couple of weeks (but certificates not index-linked if cashed in before held for 12 months)	3 months' notice needed (but withdrawal in first year halves return)
does value of capital fluctuate?	yes – but won't get back less than invested	no
points about tax	return tax-free	all interest is taxable – paid without deduction of tax
where can you get investment?	post office, High-Street bank	post office
other comments	value goes up in line with Retail Prices Index – even after initial 5-year term is up	

[1] Gives an idea of the minimum it's sensible to invest – see p117

type of investment (and where to find more details)	National Savings investments *Chapter 12, p171* – National Savings Income Bonds	National Savings investments *Chapter 12, p171* – National Savings Yearly Plan
regular saving or lump sum?	lump sum	regular saving
minimum investment [1]	£2,000 (maximum £100,000)	£20 a month (maximum £200 a month)
does it pay a regular income?	yes – each month	no
how long is investment meant to be for?	any period over a year. Return lower if cashed in first year	for best return, 5 years
can you get your money back quickly?	3 months	around a couple of weeks (but no interest on withdrawals in first year)
does value of capital fluctuate?	no	no
points about tax	all interest is taxable – paid without deduction of tax	return is tax-free
where can you get investment?	post office	post office
other comments		
	[1] Gives an idea of the minimum it's sensible to invest – see p117	

type of investment (and where to find more details)	Pension schemes – employer's schemes *Chapter 13, p187*	Pension schemes – personal pension plans *Chapter 14, p213*
regular saving or lump sum?	regular saving	either
minimum investment [1]	[2]	varies
does it pay a regular income?	yes, from time you retire. Can often choose to have lump sum on retirement instead of part of pension	yes – normally from any age between 50 and 75. Can choose to have lump sum on retirement instead of part of pension
how long is investment meant to be for?	from time you join scheme until you retire or leave job (income carries on for life)	from time you begin payments until income starts (income carries on for life)
can you get your money back quickly?	contributions must stay invested until retirement (unless you leave job within 2 years of joining scheme)	you can't cash investment in, but with some schemes you can get a loan (see p222)
does value of capital fluctuate?	depends on scheme	with some schemes – yes, with others – no
points about tax	get tax relief on payments. Pension taxed as earnings, paid after deduction of basic rate tax. Lump sum taken instead of part of pension is tax-free	get tax relief on payments – see p236. Pension taxed as earnings *not* investment income. Lump sum taken instead of part of pension is tax-free
where can you get investment?	employer	bank, building society, life insurance company, unit trust company, investment adviser
other comments	can choose to make *additional voluntary contributions* (see p203)	

[1] Gives an idea of the minimum it's sensible to invest – see p117
[2] Depends on scheme – some pension schemes are non-contributory (ie employee pays nothing); with others you pay a fixed % of your earnings

type of investment (and where to find more details)	Pension schemes – state scheme *Chapter 13, p187*	Premium bonds *Chapter 12, p171*
regular saving or lump sum?	regular saving (through National Insurance contributions)	either
minimum investment [1]	[2]	£10 (maximum £10,000)
does it pay a regular income?	yes, from retirement age (later if you put off retirement)	no – but might win prizes
how long is investment meant to be for?	you normally make payments until retirement age (income carries on for life)	any period – but can't win prize until bond held for 3 months
can you get your money back quickly?	you can't cash investment in	around a couple of weeks
does value of capital fluctuate?	not applicable – can't get capital back	no
points about tax	don't get tax relief on payments. Pension taxed as earnings, currently paid without deduction of tax	prizes are tax-free
where can you get investment?	payments made through employer, or through taxman if self-employed	post office, High-Street bank
other comments	if you're earning, normally no way you can opt out of the state scheme altogether	prizes worked out to give return of 6$\frac{1}{2}$% on all bonds held for 3 months or more.

[1] Gives an idea of the
minimum it's sensible to invest
– see p117
[2] You have to pay a
percentage of earnings (up to
certain limit) if employed and
earning over certain amount;
flat amount (and sometimes
percentage of profits) if self-
employed

type of investment (and where to find more details)	Save-As-You-Earn share option scheme *Chapter 15, p241*	Shares *Chapter 15, p241*
regular saving or lump sum?	regular saving	lump sum
minimum investment [1]	£10 a month (maximum £100 a month)	£1,200, say, in each company
does it pay a regular income?	no	yes – most companies pay dividends. Amount can vary
how long is investment meant to be for?	5 or 7 years of saving	in the main, long-term investment. But can also be short-term speculation
can you get your money back quickly?	around a couple of weeks (but if cashed in before 5 years are up, get lower return). No interest at all on withdrawal in first year	can sell shares and get money in 2 to 4 weeks – but may get less than you invested
does value of capital fluctuate?	value of shares you can buy does – but there is a minimum guaranteed amount	yes
points about tax	return tax-free (but see p262)	dividends are taxable – paid after deduction of basic rate tax. Liable for capital gains tax on any gain
where can you get investment?	your employer (but not all employers run these schemes)	stockbroker, bank or other agent (eg accountant)
other comments	at end of 5 years get bonus of extra monthly payments – and a further bonus if invest for another 2 years. Can use money to buy shares in your firm at price agreed at start of investment (see p262)	buying shares of just one or two companies is very risky (see p243)
	[1] Gives an idea of the minimum it's sensible to invest – see p117	

type of investment (and where to find more details)	Single-premium investment bonds *Chapter 20, p327*	Unit-linked regular premium plans *Chapter 20, p327*
regular saving or lump sum?	lump sum	regular saving
minimum investment [1]	varies – but often £1,000	varies – £10 a month upwards
does it pay a regular income?	not usually – but most companies have schemes which let you cash in part of investment (can cash up to 5% a year without paying tax at the time)	normally no
how long is investment meant to be for?	in the main, long-term investment	at least 10 years
can you get your money back quickly?	varies – can be straightaway, sometimes up to a week or month. May get back less than invested	can cash at any time – but may get back less than you invested (and in first year or two, may get little or nothing)
does value of capital fluctuate?	yes	yes
points about tax	when you cash in bond, may have to pay tax on the gain you've made (including any amounts you got earlier on, not taxed at the time) if you pay tax at higher rates. Fund pays capital gains tax on gains	return tax-free so long as pay tax at no more than the basic rate – always tax-free if keep policy going for at least 10 years, or three-quarters of its term, whichever is less. Fund pays capital gains tax on gains
where can you get investment?	life insurance company or insurance adviser	life insurance company or insurance adviser
other comments	value of investment depends on performance of fund of investments normally run by insurance company – eg property fund, equity fund, managed fund. Can switch between funds. Limited appeal except to higher-rate taxpayers or people who want to switch funds frequently	money invested in unit trust or insurance company fund (as for *single-premium investment bonds*). Limited appeal except to higher-rate taxpayers or people who want to switch funds frequently

[1] Gives an idea of the minimum it's sensible to invest – see p117

type of investment (and where to find more details)	Unit trusts *Chapter 16, p267*
regular saving or lump sum?	either
minimum investment [1]	for lump sum, often £250 to £1,500; for regular saving often £25 a month
does it pay a regular income?	yes, with many trusts – amount can vary
how long is investment meant to be for?	in the main, long-term investment. But can also be short-term speculation
can you get your money back quickly?	varies between trusts – can normally sell each day (but may get back less than you invested)
does value of capital fluctuate?	yes
points about tax	income is taxable – paid after deduction of basic rate tax. Liable for capital gains tax on any gain
where can you get investment?	direct from unit trust company or via insurance adviser, stockbroker, bank
other comments	value of investment depends on performance of fund of investments

[1] Gives an idea of the minimum it's sensible to invest – see p117

SECTION II

Where to Put Your Money First

9

YOUR HOME

A house is first and foremost somewhere to live. But it can be looked on as the largest single investment most people make.

The Diagram on p142 shows that house prices have, on average, increased more than 15 times over the past 25 years. On the Diagram we've also shown the Retail Prices Index (RPI), which measures increases in prices in general. You can see that for most of the period, house prices increased more quickly than the RPI. This means that the real value of a home in terms of the buying-power of what it's worth has, on average, gone up over this period. Of course, part of the increase in house prices is due to better standards of housing – eg more houses now have central heating than 25 years ago, many dilapidated properties have been brought up to scratch. And there were times – particularly after boom periods – when house prices increases haven't matched inflation – eg in 1980 and 1981.

Of course, not all houses have gone up by the amounts shown in the Diagram. Some types of home and some areas will have risen more than average, others less. The map on p144 shows how prices varied in the UK in 1987 – and the rate at which they'd gone up over the previous five years. For each region, we've shown prices for three different types of property – detached, semi-detached and terraced.

Within the regions prices vary considerably – because of things like size, number of rooms, how big the garden is and whether there's a garage, central heating and so on. But other things like the age of the house and its condition, architectural style, the area it's in may also affect prices and the rate at which they change.

For example, in rural areas houses in a pretty village may become expensive because people increasingly want to buy them as second homes. But houses in a less attractive village a few miles away may be cheaper-than-average for the

House prices and inflation over the past 25 years

Sources: Nationwide Anglia Building Society
and Department of Employment

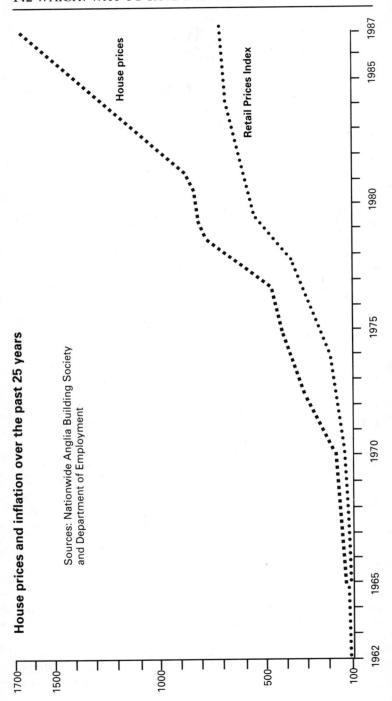

region because there are few jobs for the locals and people want to move away.

Local redevelopment could cause the price of your home to plummet. And if you have to sell your house quickly (because your job moves, say) you may also have to accept a cut in price.

What makes house prices change?

House prices are influenced by several factors – both in the long-term and the short-term.

Long-term factors include:
■ people's earnings – particularly in terms of buying-power
■ the availability of homes to buy
■ trading-up (ie the tendency for owner-occupiers to move on to more expensive homes).

In the short-term, relatively sudden increases in earnings (compared with prices in general) and in the numbers of first-time buyers, temporary shortages of houses to buy (eg not enough new houses being built), and speculation about house prices can fuel short, sharp booms of perhaps a few years' duration. Also the availability – or otherwise – of loan finance (mortgages from building societies, banks etc) can play a part.

A house as an investment

In the Diagram on p147 we've shown the rate of return you could have got by investing in a house over two different time periods. We've shown three yearly rates of return (allowing for buying and selling costs in each case):
■ investing in your only or main home with an 80 per cent mortgage, allowing for mortgage repayments (after basic rate tax relief on the interest)
■ investing in your only or main home bought outright with cash
■ investing in a second home bought outright with cash, and allowing for capital gains tax on the gain you make.

The Diagram also gives the rate of return you would have needed to keep pace with inflation.

It's clear from the Diagram that you'd have done better to buy a home with a mortgage than for cash. This is because of the effect of gearing (see p148) and the tax relief you get on mortgage interest (see p146).

For how investing in a house has compared with other

House prices in the UK

Average house prices in fourth quarter 1987 and average yearly rates of increase since fourth quarter 1982 [1]

Key: rate of increase since 1982

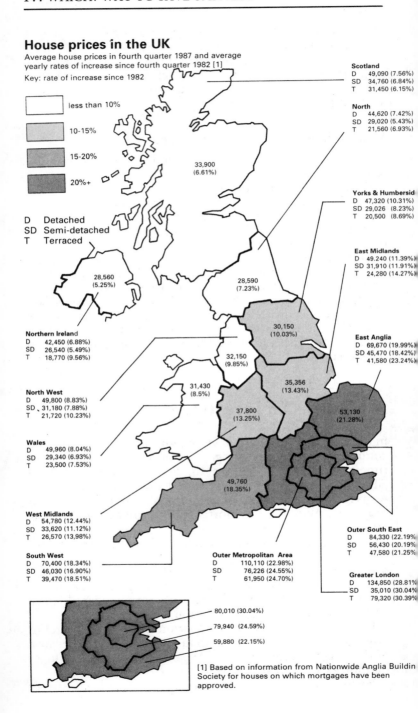

less than 10%

10-15%

15-20%

20%+

D   Detached
SD   Semi-detached
T   Terraced

Scotland
D   49,090 (7.56%)
SD   34,760 (6.84%)
T   31,450 (6.15%)

North
D   44,620 (7.42%)
SD   29,020 (5.43%)
T   21,560 (6.93%)

Yorks & Humbersid
D   47,320 (10.31%)
SD   29,026 (8.23%)
T   20,500 (8.69%)

East Midlands
D   49.240 (11.39%)
SD   31,910 (11.91%)
T   24,280 (14.27%)

East Anglia
D   69,670 (19.99%)
SD   45,470 (18.42%)
T   41,580 (23.24%)

Northern Ireland
D   42,450 (6.88%)
SD   26,540 (5.49%)
T   18,770 (9.56%)

North West
D   49,800 (8.83%)
SD   31,180 (7.88%)
T   21,720 (10.23%)

Wales
D   49,960 (8.04%)
SD   29,340 (6.93%)
T   23,500 (7.53%)

West Midlands
D   54,780 (12.44%)
SD   33,620 (11.12%)
T   26,570 (13.98%)

South West
D   70,400 (18.34%)
SD   46,030 (16.90%)
T   39,470 (18.51%)

Outer Metropolitan Area
D   110,110 (22.98%)
SD   76,226 (24.55%)
T   61,950 (24.70%)

Outer South East
D   84,330 (22.19%)
SD   56,430 (20.19%)
T   47,580 (21.25%)

Greater London
D   134,850 (28.81%)
SD   35,010 (30.04%)
T   79,320 (30.39%)

33,900 (6.61%)

28,560 (5.25%)

28,590 (7.23%)

30,150 (10.03%)

32,150 (9.85%)

31,430 (8.5%)

35,356 (13.43%)

53,130 (21.28%)

37,800 (13.25%)

49,760 (18.35%)

80,010 (30.04%)

79,940 (24.59%)

59,880 (22.15%)

[1] Based on information from Nationwide Anglia Buildin Society for houses on which mortgages have been approved.

investments, see the Diagram on pp20–21. Bear in mind that, over the periods we've looked at, houses have improved in quality which artificially increases the return somewhat. And, of course, the gain on a house is not easy to get at – you may have to sell and rent, or trade down to see your money. On the other hand, it's likely to be quite easy to realise the value of a second home.

With a house, you have to pay various running costs – eg decorating, repairs, rates etc. If you weren't buying your own home, but renting one instead, you would be paying some of these costs anyway (perhaps indirectly in your rent). But with a second home, these running costs are additional ones (unless you can rent the home out to cover them).

For the periods we've looked at, you can see from pp20–21 that when compared with some conventional homes for your money, such as building society ordinary share accounts, buying your main home with a mortgage has proved a very good investment. When compared with less conventional investments – eg gold sovereigns, antique furniture – the picture is less clear. You might have done better with these investments or worse.

A hedge against inflation?

There is a traditional belief that investing in property – including private houses – offers protection against the ravages of inflation, as property tends to hold its value in real terms. The Diagram on p147 supports this belief. Of course, when you invest and when you sell are crucially important. If, for example, you'd bought a house in 1979 (when prices were booming) and sold again in 1982, the return you'd have got could well have been below the increase in the RPI – especially after allowing for hefty buying and selling costs.

Why have houses done so well?

The main reason is that house prices have gone up by more than prices in general. But a number of other factors help to make housing an attractive investment. These include:

■ tax relief on mortgage interest
■ exemption from capital gains tax on your only or main home
■ the effects of gearing.

Tax relief on mortgage interest

In general, you can get tax relief on the interest you pay on up to £30,000 of loans to buy your only or main home (normally the one you live in most of the time).

To get tax relief on a loan you must, in general, be buying an interest in the home – eg the whole of it, a half share, or buying out someone else. The home must also be in the UK or Ireland.

What tax relief is worth

Tax relief reduces the amount you have to pay for your mortgage. If you're a basic rate taxpayer, tax relief reduces the amount of interest you pay by 25p in each £ (in the 1988–89 tax year). If, say, you pay higher-rate tax at 40% tax relief reduces the cost of your mortgage by 40p in each £. This means that borrowing can be much cheaper than it seems at first sight. For example, tax relief means that a basic rate taxpayer who borrows money at 10.5% is, in effect, paying interest of only three-quarters of 10.5% (ie 7.875%). And a 40% taxpayer, in effect, pays interest of only 6.3%.

Note that there are some loans you can't get tax relief on even if they are used for buying your only or main home. These include overdrafts and borrowing on credit cards.

The £30,000 rule

The £30,000 limit applies to the total amount you and any other person buying with you owe on one property. If you have more than one mortgage which qualifies for tax relief you get relief on the earliest loan first. If taking out a further loan takes you over the £30,000 limit, you get tax relief on only part of the interest you pay on the new loan – check with the taxman.

If you are 65 or over, you can also get tax relief on the interest on up to a further £30,000 of loans to buy an annuity, if the loan is secured on your only or main home – see p363 for more details.

Moving home

You may be faced with paying out on two loans at once – one on your new home, and one on your (unsold) old home. Under the normal rules, you get tax relief on £30,000 of loans on your new home. But for a year (longer in deserving cases) you carry on getting tax relief as before on your old home too.

Different ways of investing in a home

Average yearly rate of increase in value

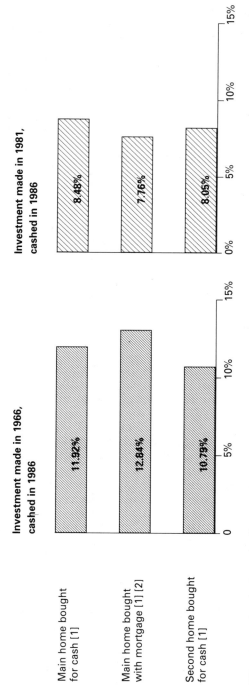

Investment made in 1966, cashed in 1986

Main home bought for cash [1] — 11.92%

Main home bought with mortgage [1] [2] — 12.84%

Second home bought for cash [1] — 10.79%

Investment made in 1981, cashed in 1986

8.48%

7.76%

8.05%

Where appropriate, buying and selling costs, income tax and capital gains tax have been taken into account.

[1] Based on average house prices. Costs such as insurance, maintenance and rates not included.
[2] Assumes 25-year, 80 per cent repayment mortgage taken out by a basic rate taxpayer.

Information supplied by: The Bristol & West Building Society, Nationwide Anglia Building Society.

Capital gains tax

Unlike many other forms of investment, your only or main home is, in most cases, exempt from capital gains tax when you sell. This helps existing owner-occupiers to trade up – ie to move to a better house. The non-taxable profit from the first home can be ploughed back into the next home together with a bigger mortgage, in the hopes of reaping a higher capital gain. For more details, see *Gearing* below.

If you (or you and your husband or wife) have two or more homes, you can choose which one should count as your main home for capital gains tax purposes. Make your choice within two years of acquiring the second home – otherwise the taxman can choose for you. You can alter the choice at any time, simply by telling the taxman (your new choice can be back-dated by up to two years).

In addition, one home owned by you or your husband or wife and occupied rent-free by a dependent relative may be exempt from capital gains tax (but, normally, not if the relative gave you the home in the first place).

But you may not get full exemption from capital gains tax if any of the following apply:
- you let all or part of your home
- you use part exclusively for work
- the home wasn't your main one for capital gains tax purposes for all the time you owned it
- you were away from the home because of your work for periods totalling over four years (though you get full exemption for any period in which you were an employee working entirely abroad)
- you were away from the home for reasons unconnected with your work for periods totalling over three years
- you were away from the home for more than two years while you were trying to sell it
- your home is one of a series of homes you bought, or spent money on, in order to make a profit
- your garden is bigger than one acre.

For more details, see Inland Revenue leaflet CGT4 and CGT8 plus supplement – available free from your tax office. For how capital gains tax works, see p104.

Gearing

In the investment world, borrowing money to buy an asset, and only putting down a small part of the money yourself, is called **gearing**. This is a shrewd move, if the asset increases in value at a greater rate than the rate of interest you have to pay on your loan. If house prices go up by more than the after-tax relief interest on the mortgage, you'll get a relatively high return for your money.

You can see the effects of gearing from the Diagram on p147 – by comparing the rate of return for a main home bought with a mortgage with the return on a main home bought for cash.

Suppose, for example, that you had bought a home in December 1966 for £3,820 and sold it in December 1986 for £41,150. With an 80 per cent mortgage, your initial investment would have been 20 per cent of £3,820 – ie £764. Your gain in 1986 (after buying and selling costs) would be £35,677 and the return on your investment (initial investment plus mortgage repayments, allowing for tax relief at the basic rate) works out at about 12.84 per cent a year. If you'd bought a home for cash, your investment would have been £3,896, and your rate of return 11.92 per cent a year. If you'd had a 90 per cent mortgage instead of an 80 per cent one, gearing would have been even more profitable.

If you sell your home at a profit and use that profit to buy another home, the size of your mortgage relative to the cost of your home is likely to decrease. So a first-time buyer might get 90 per cent mortgage, then sell his or her home and get a 70 per cent mortgage on the new home. This lessens the effect of gearing, and means that the return on the investment will be smaller (of course, if house prices were to fall, the loss would also be smaller).

But, be warned, your investment may come adrift if the after-tax relief mortgage interest rate exceeds the rate of increase in the price of your house. And if your house should fall in value, you'd feel the loss on your stake as dramatically as you'd feel any gain.

House prices in the future

If you've owned a house over the last 20 years, the chances are you'll have seen its value increase. Indeed, you may well have seen it do better than many other forms of investment. Is this trend likely to continue?

It's impossible to say for certain. Some people take the view that the rise must eventually slow down. First-time buyers, the argument is, will soon not be able to borrow enough money to get on the bottom rung of the housing ladder. This will have a knock-on effect as it will become more difficult to sell houses and flats at the bottom of the market, so there will be less money available to spend on more expensive properties.

While it has certainly become more difficult for first-time buyers to get into the housing market in London and the South-East, there is no sign as yet that this is depressing house prices. First-time buyers are clubbing together to buy houses or flats, or looking further afield (pushing up prices in the suburbs and dormitory towns), or in areas previously thought unattractive.

Some people hold a more gloomy view: that house prices must eventually fall sharply, as did the Stock Exchange in 1987. They argue that, as house prices have gone up, people have been forced to borrow so much more, that many are now living beyond their means – borrowing more than they can afford to repay.

Between 1979 and 1987, the number of houses repossessed each year by building societies has increased more than tenfold, and the number of people in mortgage arrears of 6 months or more has gone up from about 8,500 to 50,000. If the number of people unable to keep up their mortgage repayments continues to rise, house prices could fall as a result. This has happened in other European countries. Could it happen here?

Probably not. At the moment, in the UK, there's very little alternative to buying. In some other European countries there is a strong rented market, so people can wait until they can afford to enter the property market. Furthermore, some European countries have fixed rate mortgages – you pay the same rate of interest for the whole period or for five years, say. So when interest rates are high, sellers are likely to have to cut their prices to attract buyers, whereas, in the UK, buyers may be prepared to go ahead in the hope that interest rates will fall.

10

BUILDING SOCIETIES

Building societies are a very popular home for people's savings – about 65 per cent of the adult population has at least one building society savings account and together they add up to investments of £130 billion, 50 per cent of short-term personal savings. Building societies' main business is to borrow money – often in small amounts – from individuals, and lend it to other individuals who want to buy their own homes. But to make sure they could cope with a rush of withdrawals, about 15 per cent of their funds is held in investments they can cash readily, such as British Government stocks.

How safe are building societies?

Building societies have traditionally been very safe places to invest – they rarely run into difficulties and those that have were quietly bailed out by others.

This safety is partly because societies' traditional business has been restricted to lending on mortgage securities. But societies – particularly the large ones – are now diversifying into many different financial products, and some observers worry that this might in time shake their tradition of security. But there are limits on what proportion of 'riskier' business societies can undertake, and your investment is protected by law to the same degree, no matter how large or small the society you invest with.

If a society gets into difficulties, you are guaranteed to get back 90 per cent of up to the first £20,000 of your savings in that society; with a joint account each account holder is separately protected up to £20,000.

Building society, plc

Building societies are 'mutual' organisations, owned by their investor members. But the largest ones can, if they and their members wish, become limited companies like banks, and regulated by company and banking legislation rather than the Building Societies Act. However, protection for money deposited with banks is similar to that invested with building societies.

What building societies offer

Building societies offer a wide range of different investment schemes, varying from society to society and from time to time. Though many accounts have descriptive names these can be a very misleading guide to the actual terms and conditions of the account. And a single account may have a number of 'variations' which can quite change it.

So it is more useful to look at the features available on building society accounts: most 'new' account types are composed of different selections of these basic features. Armed with this knowledge, you can go on to see how these features are applied in practice to the account types currently available, and then decide how to go about choosing an account for your particular needs.

Basic features of building society accounts

Although schemes vary they are all based on variations of three main factors:
- how you intend to **pay money in**, when and in what form
- how easily and quickly you want to be able to make **withdrawals**
- arrangements for paying **interest.**

Paying money in

Some schemes have no restrictions on how you pay your money in – you can open the account with a modest pound or two, and pay in what you like, when you like. But many do have some restrictions:
- the minimum investment to open an account can vary from £1 up to tens of thousands of £££

■ you may not be allowed to make any additions to the account once it's opened
■ you may be allowed to make additions only in certain multiples, for example in lumps of £100
■ you may have to make regular additions, usually every month
■ you may be restricted to a maximum investment level (though rarely less than, say, £20,000 except perhaps for children's accounts).

There are also practical aspects to making investments. All societies will accept money over the counter at their branches and through their agents (people like solicitors, insurance brokers and estate agents); most will accept money (preferably cheques) through the post; and many are linked to a network of cash machines which allow you to make deposits outside opening hours.

There is no formal limit on how much you can invest in any one society, but there are guidelines based on how large a society's assets are. Individual societies set their own limits based on these guidelines and other factors; their limits can sometimes vary from account to account. A few societies have no maximum investment; most have a limit of between £100,000 and £250,000.

Withdrawals

Some accounts let you get at your savings instantly, on demand; others require you to give some notice; still others lock your money away for a period (or 'term') of time.

To make these **notice accounts** and **term shares** more attractive, many have one or two concessions:
■ they may offer easy access to the balance over a certain amount in your account. The 'balance-over' figure is often £10,000 and the access usually instant: that is, if you have £12,000 invested you can withdraw up to £2,000 on demand whatever the normal conditions for withdrawals. But the balance-over figure may be as low as £2,000; and you may be able to withdraw your money only by giving a few days' notice
■ instant access, in spite of the normal withdrawal conditions, if you pay a penalty charge (of three months' interest, say).

There may be other restrictions on withdrawals:
■ withdrawing only part of your savings may not be allowed; you may have to close the account if you want any money out

■ you may have to withdraw in fixed multiples of, say, £100 or even £1,000.

And there are the same practical points to consider as for paying in money.

Interest

How often is interest paid?

Accounts are available which pay interest yearly (occasionally even less frequently), half-yearly, quarterly or monthly. For how the frequency of interest affects the true rate of interest you get, see p25.

In most cases you can choose to have the interest:
■ paid out to you, or directly into, say, a bank account
■ paid into another account with the same society
■ kept in the same account to roll up (so that you get compound interest). This option is not often available where the interest is paid monthly.

Some accounts offer a choice of interest payment frequencies, for example, half-yearly or monthly. If they do, there may be penalties such as lower interest rates or higher minimum investments if you choose to have your interest paid more frequently.

How are interest rates quoted?

Building societies (and banks) have a code of conduct they should follow. It allows them to quote rates in any of a number of different ways:
■ **net** – the rate before taking into account how often interest is paid, but after allowing for the tax deducted before you get it (see below). This must be quoted in any advertisement, at least as prominently as any other rate
■ **gross equivalent** – the net rate grossed up (see p27)
■ **Compounded Annual Rate (CAR)** – a true rate of return, taking into account how often interest is compounded within the account – see p27. It is usually the net CAR (ie the compounded net rate), but societies can also quote:
■ **gross equivalent CAR**.

For more information on how to compare the different ways of expressing interest rates, see p25.

Variable or fixed interest?

Almost all building societies accounts are **variable** – a society can change interest rates (up or down) on any of its accounts whenever it likes, without giving any notice, and without making any special concessions to its existing account holders. However, there is an informal base rate structure in which the rate on 'ordinary shares' tends to be the same for most societies (an ordinary share account is one with no restrictions: no-notice withdrawals, minimum investment of £1 and rarely any frills).

An overall increase or decrease in rates is usually signalled by one of the largest societies (and usually linked with a change in mortgage rates and a sustained change in bank base rates). Over the next month or two almost all other societies will move their ordinary share rate in line with the signallers. Some small societies pay higher ordinary share rates, and a very few have paid less, but even these will tend to move by the same percentage points as the others.

Some accounts offer a **guaranteed premium** (or differential) – they guarantee to pay at least a set amount above the ordinary share rate, whatever happens to rates generally (though perhaps only for a year or two after you take up the offer). In practice, almost all accounts act as though they had a guaranteed premium, so this is not something you need look out for especially.

How is interest taxed?
Interest from building societies is almost always paid with what's called composite rate tax already deducted from it. Because, of this, you don't have to pay basic rate tax on it. The result is that:
- **basic rate taxpayers** don't have any further tax to pay on their interest
- **non-taxpayers** cannot reclaim the tax deducted
- **higher rate taxpayers** will have to pay extra tax. For more on tax, see p99.

Building societies *are* allowed to pay interest without deducting tax to charities and people classed as expatriates. But this does not mean that these people simply get a grossed-up rate on any building society account. They have to open special accounts on which the societies fix their rates according to commercial factors: so their rates may be higher or lower than the grossed-up rates on equivalent accounts. Most, but not all, societies run gross-paying accounts for expatriates; rather fewer have them for charities.

How much interest?
As a rule of thumb, the longer your money is tied up for, and the larger the investment required, the higher the interest rate you get.

Tiered interest accounts stick to this rule: the larger your investment the higher the interest. Usually you get the higher interest automatically if your balance grows enough to tip you into a higher tier (the rate is cut automatically if it falls) but watch out for accounts that do not do so. You usually get the highest rate your investment level entitles you to on the *whole* of your balance, but watch out for accounts that pay you the higher rates only on the amount of your money in each tier (which results in a lower average rate overall).

A tiered interest account can be linked to notice periods rather than investment levels. For example, some years ago there were very complicated accounts in which your interest rate depended both on how long you *intended* to leave your money invested, and how long you *actually did* leave it invested.

Some accounts pay a bonus if you satisfy particular conditions, such as not making any withdrawals for a year.

Types of building society account

Term shares

These are accounts which lock your money up for a period of time, which can be anything from six months to perhaps five years. The term is usually fixed at the time you open the account. There are few of them around: most accounts that are called 'term shares' or similar names are actually notice accounts.

Normally you will not be allowed to withdraw until the account 'matures' at the end of its term; if you are allowed withdrawals, then you will have to pay a **penalty charge** and, perhaps give some months' notice as well, or be restricted to withdrawing only the **balance over** a certain amount. You may not be allowed to add to the account, though normally you can start another one.

The minimum investment is usually low; £500 to around £5,000 is the main range. There is little in the way of tiered interest term shares.

Check what happens to your investment at the end of the term. It may be:
■ automatically cashed in, and you're sent a cheque
■ automatically transferred to another account, paying a different rate
■ left where it is, paying the same rate, and converted into a notice account (in which case check whether you can give the required notice *before* the end of the term, otherwise the

term will be longer than you originally thought – for example, if you have to give three months' notice at the end of a one year term share you've effectively got a 15-month term share).

Notice accounts

Accounts allowing you access to your money at three months' notice are very popular, but there are many others with shorter notice periods (down to one week) and a few with longer (four or six months).

Most notice accounts allow instant access if you pay a **penalty charge** of, usually, the same number of months' interest as the notice period. For example, on a three-month account you can give either three months' notice, or have instant access and lose the equivalent of three months' interest on the money you're withdrawing. These are useful in an emergency, but can drastically reduce the effective interest rate you get.

You may have access to the balance over a certain amount in a notice account without notice or penalty. And some are **tiered interest** accounts with minimum investment levels and tiers ranging anywhere from £1 (though £500 is more common) to tens of thousands of £££s.

Mandatory penalty charges

Watch out for accounts that operate a penalty charge in addition to requiring a notice period. Some of these are term shares, so you don't suffer the penalty if you leave your money invested for the full term. But some are not, and you'll *always* suffer the penalty charge, whenever you withdraw. With these accounts you'll never get as high an interest rate as that quoted, taken over the whole period of your investment.

Instant access accounts

Many instant access accounts are **tiered interest**, with minimum investments levels and tiers ranging anywhere from £1 to tens of thousands of £££s. Even though instant withdrawals are allowed, there may still be some restrictions: often you can draw no more than £250 in cash, perhaps as little as £5,000 as a cheque; larger cash sums or cheques take up to three days to arrange.

Beware of accounts that give you instant access, but only

if you pay a penalty charge. Beware, too, of accounts which give you instant access only to the balance over a certain amount (though if this amount is low, these accounts can still be useful if you have a large amount to invest).

Fixed rate bonds

Accounts that offer a fixed rate of interest for a period of, usually, a year (occasionally six-month fixed rate bonds are available) are a gamble. If rates fall during the term of the bond you may do well; if they rise you might have been better off with a variable rate account.

Fixed rate bonds are only available now and then; only a handful of societies ever offer them; and often the issues are open for investment for only a short time. Minimum investments are not usually large – £500 or £1,000 is typical.

There are, once in a blue moon, variations on the theme – such as an account with a *minimum* interest rate, which will rise if rates generally increase.

Monthly income accounts

These are accounts which pay out interest monthly, to help you boost your income. They come in all sorts of minimum investment levels and notice periods. Though your capital is as safe as in any other building society account (see p151) your monthly income will fluctuate up and down as rates vary.

Monthly income accounts are often variations of other accounts, but with a poorer interest rate and a higher minimum investment – so make sure that you are looking at the right version of the account.

Regular savings accounts

Once the only high-interest account available from building societies, regular savings accounts (sometimes called subscription accounts) are now few and far between. They are not available from all societies, and they have not recently paid particularly high rates. But they could be useful if you really have only a few £££ a month to invest, and you need to discipline yourself to save it regularly.

Regular savings offer perhaps the most complicated conditions of any account type, so check carefully that what you are being offered suits your needs. Ask:
■ what are the minimum and maximum amounts I can save each month?

- can I vary the amount I save? As I wish each month, or only by agreement with the society?
- can I miss payments? How many, and how often?
- can I withdraw part of my savings? How much, and how often?
- are there any restrictions (such as a notice period) for closing the account?

In general, the more restrictive the conditions you accept, the higher the interest rate.

Building society Save-As-You-Earn (SAYE)

SAYE is also a regular savings scheme, offered by some societies. The conditions are identical no matter which society you go to, and you can invest in only one scheme.

You make a fixed investment of £1 to £20 a month for five years. Interest is added as a tax-free bonus of 14 months' savings at the end of the term (equal to a fixed rate of 8.30 per cent). Leave your money and the bonus invested for two more years, and you get a bonus of another 14 months' savings, boosting the return to 8.62 per cent.

You can stop payments and withdraw at any time, but do this in the first year and you'll get no interest at all. After the first year you'll earn interest of 6 per cent a year (8 per cent if the reason for stopping is the saver's death). You can miss up to six payments over the five years provided you make them up in the months directly following the end of your five year term.

Current accounts

Building societies are increasingly used not only for savings but also for handling day to day finances. Many instant access accounts have a range of additional features, the best of which enable you to run a building society account as a direct replacement for a bank current account with cheque book and guarantee card; your salary paid directly in; cash machines; access to overdrafts – and at least some interest on your balance.

These features don't necessarily come free – you could be sacrificing higher interest from an account not offering all the frills.

Children's accounts

Many societies have an account aimed at children. This may be little more than a colourful passbook with a cartoon character; others offer a wide range of extras, such as free gifts, membership to zoos and clubs, magazines and so on.

Interest rates vary from among the lowest of any building society account to the very highest; usually the highest payers offer the least extras. But high interest might not be the most important aspect for a child in deciding where to save. In particular, remember that children (like everyone else) cannot reclaim the tax deducted from the interest, even if they are non-taxpayers. See Chapter 4 for more on investing for children.

Combination accounts

A few societies offer building society accounts combined with other investments such as unit trusts or life insurance. They are also available from time to time as 'special offers' from financial advisers. The money you invest can be split in various ways – for example half going into a building society account, half into, say, an insurance company investment bond; or all your money going into a building society account, but with the interest used to buy unit trusts.

Often, the building society investment will sport a very high rate (usually because the society has split its commission on the other investment with you), but this rate may apply for only a relatively short period. There is nothing magical about the other investment, which will be as good or as bad a buy as any other investment of its particular type, despite its building society connection.

Don't got for a combination account purely on the strength of a high initial building society rate; check that both parts of the account look like good buys over the investment period (which is likely to be relatively long compared with most building society accounts).

Combination accounts may be less popular with societies in the future, as they are now able to offer a wide range of investments, eg from life insurance companies, themselves.

Friendly society bonds

Some (very few) building society accounts are linked with friendly societies who are allowed to offer a very restricted tax-free regular savings scheme. You pay a *maximum* of £9 a month (or £100 a year) for ten years which the friendly society invests with the building society. Because the scheme is tax-free, you make a little more interest than you would by investing directly in the building society – but not as much as you might think (only one to two per cent or so extra) because of the friendly societies' management charges. The scheme is free of higher rate tax, too, so is more appealing to higher rate taxpayers (but the actual £££ involved is small because the savings limits are so restricted).

If you cash in within the first $7^1/_2$ years, you get back, at most, only your gross premiums; between $7^1/_2$ and 10 years you may get a little more.

A version allowing you to pay in a lump sum (maximum £1,000) is also available: the money goes into a building society account from which the regular premiums are automatically paid. Because you have to pay tax in the normal way on the interest on this pool of money, the lump sum scheme has a lower effective rate of interest. To a basic rate taxpayer it could be little better than the best normal building society account, which should offer better access and fewer restrictions.

Other friendly society investments

Friendly societies don't invest only through building societies. The regular savings scheme described above may also be available investing in, say, unit trusts – with the same tax advantages (and same restrictions). And there are some funds which are taxable, investing, say, half in equities and half in safer investments such as British Government stocks or building societies. Some of these plans (whether involving building society investments or not) may be available through building societies.

Making your choice

Too little income to pay tax?
You *may* get a better return from investments that don't deduct composite rate tax, which you then can't reclaim – for example, National Savings.

Investing for the long term?
Building society investments are safe but, over the long term, may not make as much as more risky forms of investment. If you have a very large sum to invest for a long period, think about putting some of it into other investments – see Chapters 1 and 2.

Don't need your money for a year or so?
Term shares look tempting, but you may get as good or

better rates (especially on large sums) from a **notice account** – and easier access to your money.

Think interest rates will fall?
Check if any **fixed rate bonds** are currently available. For a wider choice of fixed rate investments, consider British Government stocks, local authority loans, income bonds.

Prepared to wait a while for your money?
A **notice account** may give higher interest than one offering instant access – often, the longer the notice period, the higher the interest. But don't tie up money you think you may need to get out quickly.

Can't wait, won't wait?
Try an **instant access account**. If you have a large investment and need instant access to only part of your money, look at a notice account which gives you instant access to money above a certain amount. Or can you make do with a short notice account (say up to a month)?

Want a regular income?
You can draw a monthly income from any account, but it is easiest to do so from an account offering **monthly interest** – many different types do. But your income will vary as rates change; if you want a fixed income, think about other investments like British Government stocks, local authority loans or income bonds.

Want to save regularly?
A **regular savings account** is a possibility, if you need to be disciplined. But, especially if you have a few hundred £££ to start you off, you could make more interest and have better access to your money from any other type of account (except those that don't allow you to add to your original investment). The building society **SAYE** scheme sometimes compares well if you can save for five years (especially if you are a higher-rate taxpayer). Consider also the National Savings Yearly Plan, a with-profits endowment policy or unit-linked savings plan, using the money to improve your pension, or (if you're prepared to take some risk) a unit trust savings scheme.

Expect your savings to fluctuate?
Think about an account with a **tiered interest rate** structure. But even so, keep an eye on your balance and what it is earning.

Choosing a society

With over 1,500 accounts and variations on accounts on offer, from over 110 building societies, picking the best buy is not easy. Consider first **convenience**: if you want to withdraw *and* deposit money quickly and frequently (and especially if you want current account facilities) then you will need a branch or a cash machine close to your home or place of work: this will restrict you to the larger 'national' societies, and whichever local societies are in your area.

For larger, more infrequent, transactions you can deal by post. This gives you a wider range of societies to choose from. When comparing rates:

■ note that slight differences in interest rate are important only with large investments. For example, on an investment of £1,000 1 per cent extra on a rate will make you only between £10.00 and £10.47 extra in a full year

■ make sure you are comparing the right rate. The CAR or 'true' rate applies strictly only to money that is invested for a full year or more. If you are investing for much shorter than a year, the net rate is a better comparative guide.

You can find information on the best buys from several sources, including *Which?* from time to time; the financial pages in newspapers (the *Daily Telegraph* carries a small selection each Saturday); and *Building Society Choice* which publishes monthly lists of the highest-paying accounts in various categories (£10.95 a year from Riverside House, Rattlesden, Bury St Edmunds IP30 0SF).

11

BANK AND FINANCE COMPANY ACCOUNTS

If you're looking for a way of investing your money so that its value in £££ can't fall, you could consider an account with a bank, finance company or other company authorised by the Bank of England to take deposits from the public – see *Safety*, below.

Interest is paid on your money and the rate may be fixed when you invest or it may vary, depending on the type of account you choose. In lots of ways, these accounts are very similar to the range of accounts offered by building societies (see Chapter 10). As with all investments, you should keep an eye on how the rates compare with those offered elsewhere. The financial pages of daily newspapers can help keep you up-to-date.

Interest on bank and finance company accounts is paid after composite rate tax (effectively, basic rate income tax) has been deducted. So:

- if you're a non-taxpayer, you won't be able to reclaim the tax that has been paid on your behalf
- if you're a basic rate taxpayer, you won't have to pay any extra tax on the interest you get
- if you're a higher rate taxpayer, you'll owe extra tax. For more details of how this works, see p99.

Safety

Under the Banking Act 1987, organisations which can take deposits from the public have to be authorised by the Bank of England and have to meet certain conditions.

The Banking Act also provided for a deposit protection fund to be set up. The fund will pay out 75 per cent of the first £20,000 in your account if your bank or finance company goes bust.

Note that not all organisations are covered by these particular rules – for example, local authorities, among others, are excluded. Insurance companies and building societies are regulated in different ways. And the deposit protection fund does not cover deposits placed in the Isle of Man or the Channel Islands.

Banks

Nearly all the banks have several ways in which you can invest your money. There are six main types, but not every High-Street bank offers them all. Note that if you've got a large lump sum, say £25,000 or £50,000, you may be able to arrange some sort of special deal with a bank – so ask around.

Deposit account

All the High-Street banks offer deposit accounts in which you can save small sums – often a minimum of £1. You don't have to have a current account at the bank to open a deposit account. When you invest, you'll be given an account number, and a paying-in book or cash card. You can withdraw money at the branch of the bank which has your account, or you can arrange for the money to be transferred to your current account, or you may be able to go to another branch if you make special arrangements. You don't get a cheque book.

In theory, with most of these accounts you have to give seven days' notice if you want to get your money out. In practice, the banks will pay out on the spot, but will deduct seven days' interest. But some deposit accounts which offer cash cards allow withdrawals through a cash dispenser without deducting interest.

Interest is usually worked out every day and added to your account twice a year. With Scottish banks, the interest is worked out on the minimum amount you have in the account during each month. The interest will vary with interest rates in general but tends to be very low – in April 1988 a typical interest rate was 2.5%. You can invest as much money as you like for as long as you like – but it's best to use a bank deposit account as a home for an emergency fund or as a temporary home for other money. And you should certainly consider the alternatives very seriously before putting your money in such a low-paying account.

Higher-rate deposit accounts

Some banks and finance companies now offer instant access accounts paying a higher interest rate than on basic deposit accounts – up to 3 per cent or so higher. The minimum investment required can be anything from £100 to £2,000. Some of these accounts offer a cheque book facility – though there may be restrictions on the use of the account, such as a minimum withdrawal of £100. Interest may be paid only once a year or four times a year. Because there are so many variations, it is worth seeing what several banks and finance companies have to offer before choosing. And make sure you know all the terms and conditions of the account before investing.

Regular savings schemes

Some of these are fairly similar to ordinary deposit accounts. Others may be linked to the promise of being able to borrow money from the bank after a certain period of saving. There's usually a minimum amount you have to save (£10 a month, say) and you have to save for a certain time (one year, say) to get a higher rate of interest than on a straight-forward deposit account. With some schemes, you can withdraw part of the money during the year; with others you have to leave it untouched for a whole year. The rate of interest paid could be, for example, one or two per cent higher than the deposit account rate.

Fixed term; variable rate of interest

If you've got a lump sum to invest (£1,000 to £10,000 or more) and you can invest for an agreed period of time, you can get a higher rate of interest than on a deposit account. The rate will vary during the period. The periods offered vary from scheme to scheme, and can be as short as 6 months or as long as 7 years. Usually the rate of interest is guaranteed to be a certain amount higher than the deposit account rate (or equivalent), or lower than the base rate – eg $2\frac{1}{2}$ per cent higher than the deposit account for a six-month period, or $\frac{1}{2}$ per cent below base rate for a four-year period.

Fixed term; fixed rate of interest

You lock your money away for between one month and five years at a fixed rate of interest – you can't withdraw any of your money within the period you've agreed.

If you agree to invest for a fixed period you would normally expect that the longer the period you agreed to invest for, the higher the rate of interest you would get. This doesn't always happen. If the banks think interest rates will fall, you might get a lower rate of interest the longer you invest for.

With some schemes, the rate of interest offered for the period is closely linked to what's happening in the money market and so the rate of interest offered on new accounts can change every day – check carefully before you invest. And ask all the banks offering this type of account – rates of interest vary from bank to bank. The minimum deposit ranges from £1,000 to £10,000.

Notice accounts

You invest a lump sum and have to give an agreed period of notice before you can withdraw your money. The period of notice varies from scheme to scheme – say 1, 3 or 6 months. These schemes offer a higher rate of interest than a deposit account – two to four per cent more, say – the longer the notice you are prepared to give, the higher the rate will be. Rates vary and interest may be paid monthly, or at less frequent intervals, for example, twice a year. Most minimum investments are in the £1,000 to £10,000 range.

Finance company accounts

To be allowed to take deposits from the public, a company must be authorised (and supervised) by the Bank of England. The rates offered by finance companies vary, so check as many companies as you can before investing.

These investments are, in general, for people with lump sums to invest and there are two main types. A few deposit-taking institutions also offer other forms of account – for example, savings schemes, money funds (where the fund is managed and invested in the money market) and high interest deposit accounts, like those offered by banks, some with a cheque book facility – see p167.

Fixed term; fixed rate of interest

You agree to invest for a certain period – say 1, 2 or 3 years, but it could be only weeks or it could be up to 10 years. In return, you get a fixed rate of interest. Normally you would expect that the longer you agree to invest for, the higher rate of interest you'll get added or paid. But this may not always be so. If the company thinks interest rates will fall, you might find the longer you invest the lower the rate of interest added or paid.

Interest is usually added twice a year and you can often choose to have the interest paid out to you if you want. With a few accounts, interest can be added once a month or paid out to you as an income. Minimum investments needed for this sort of account range from £500 to £5,000. There's often a maximum too, say £25,000 or £50,000. You can't normally get your money out until the end of the period you agreed, although a few companies allow you to get out a small amount each year.

Notice accounts

You invest your money and agree to give a certain period of notice to withdraw it – 1, 3 or 6 months, or a year, say. If you choose this sort of account, the interest rate paid on it will normally vary with interest rates in general. The minimum amount you have to invest is around £100, but can be as high as £5,000 or as low as £1.

Verdict

If you're looking for a home for your emergency fund, you could consider a bank deposit account. But check up on interest rates offered by other suitable alternatives – you'll generally do better with, say, a building society account, though non-taxpayers may find a National Savings account offers them a better rate of return (see Chapter 12). Note that many banks and finance companies now pay interest on some of their current accounts too. For lump sum investments shop around the banks and finance companies to see if there's a scheme which suits your needs and offers you a good rate of return.

12

NATIONAL SAVINGS INVESTMENTS

One way in which the Government raises money is to borrow it from the public. It offers various forms of investment in the hope that people will put their money in them. One such investment is the wide range of British Government stocks – dealt with in Chapter 17. Here we look at National Savings investments.

National Savings Certificates

The first national Savings Certificates – then called War Savings Certificates – were issued in 1916. Since then, Governments have brought out a new issue whenever the rate of interest on the old issue seemed too high, or too low, in the prevailing circumstances. Normally, you can buy only one issue – the current one – at any one time. In all, various governments have brought out 33 issues of National Savings Certificates (by May 1988). Once you've bought a certificate you can in practice hold it indefinitely. Moreover, you don't have to have been alive and investing in 1916 in order to own some of the first issue – because certificates can be inherited. So you could hold quite a wide range of certificates. Here we tell you about conventional National Savings Certificates – see p176 for index-linked certificates.

How interest is paid

With the early issues – up to and including the 6th – interest is added ad infinitum to the value of your certificates at a fixed rate of $5/12$ a month (or, with some of these issues, $1^1/2$p or $1^1/4$p every three months). Because the amount of interest is fixed, it follows that the rate of interest – expressed as a yearly percentage return on the value of your investment – is going down, year by year. These now offer a miserly rate of return – well under two per cent a year.

For issues after the 6th, the interest paid used to vary depending on the issue and the year – the exact rates were fixed for a certain number of years at a time – five or seven years, for example. But in 1982, the Government announced that when a particular certificate got to the end of the period for which interest rates had been set, a common rate of interest called the **general extension rate** – would be paid. The general extension rate was 5.01 per cent in May 1988.

Note that with all National Savings Certificates, interest is not paid out to you – it's added on to the value of your certificate, and you get it when you cash in the certificate. The interest is free of income tax, and capital gains tax doesn't apply.

Below we give details of the 33rd issue, the one available when this book went to press. And then we look in detail at whether you should cash in any old certificates you have.

Investing in National Savings Certificates (33rd issue)

Anyone can invest, irrespective of their age. You can invest anything between £25 and £1,000, in units of £25 – so they are suitable for both lump sums and savings. A husband and wife can invest up to £1,000 each. If the certificates are in their joint names, however, they can invest only £1,000 between them.

If you are cashing in earlier issues of National Savings Certificates which you've held for at least five years you can invest up to £5,000 in **Reinvestment Certificates** on top of the ordinary £1,000 limit. The terms are the same as for other 33rd issue certificates, except that if you cash reinvestment certificates within one year of having invested you will get interest equivalent to 5.5% a year for each complete three months of investment.

How to invest
Fill in an application form available from most post offices and banks. Your certificate showing how many units of £25 you have bought will be sent to you later.

How much interest?
Interest is added to the value of your certificate over the period of its life (which is five years at the outset). The amount of interest added increases as time goes by – giving an added incentive to hanging on to your certificates. Table 1 opposite gives the details, and shows the rate of interest for

each year. Within any year, it's the rate of interest in the right-hand column which you should compare with say, the after-tax rate of interest on building society accounts. If you hold the certificate for the full five years, the overall yearly rate of return works out at 7.0 per cent.

Table 1 How a £25 unit of the 33rd issue grows

during year	£25 certificate increases by	for each complete	value at end of year	rate of interest for year
1	£1.38	12 months	£26.38	5.52%
2	£0.39½	3 months	£27.96	5.99%
3	£0.45½	3 months	£29.78	6.51%
4	£0.59½	3 months	£32.16	7.99%
5	£0.72½	3 months	£35.06	9.02%

How do you cash your certificates?

Get form DNS502MA from a post office. You shouldn't have to wait more than a couple of weeks for your money. You can cash in any number of units – for example, if you hold 100 units each bought for £25, you can cash in 50 of them.

What happens to your certificates should you die?

Your heirs can either cash in the certificates or transfer them into their own name. Form DNS904 from most post offices will set things in operation.

What about your old certificates?

Because interest is not paid out, but added on to the value of your certificates, working out what return you are actually getting from your investment isn't an easy matter. Moreover, besides needing to know the rate of interest you are getting now, you need to know what interest will be paid on them in the next year or two – in case the interest, though low this year, will get better later on.

First, find your Savings Certificates. Next, check which issue (or issues) your certificates are. This is printed on the certificates – eg *'sixth issue'*, *'decimal issue'*. Next, look at the date stamp on each certificate to find out when it was bought.

If you are still holding certificates from one of the very earliest issues – from the 1st to the 6th (on sale from 1916 until November 1939) the interest rate you are getting on these is between 1.1 and 1.8 per cent a year.

For later issues you should look at the Table opposite. If there isn't an entry which matches the age and issue of certificates you hold, you are earning interest at the *general extension rate* (see p172). For the last few years this has tended to be around one or two per cent higher than the rate paid by big building societies on their ordinary share accounts (see p155).

If there is an entry which relates to a certificate you hold, then column 3 gives you the value of each certificate in 1988 on the anniversary of the date it was bought. For example, a 9th issue certificate bought on 16 November 1955 will be worth £3.26 on 16 November 1988. This value, incidentally, is that for a single unit. The certificate documents you have may in fact say that they are for multiples of 2,3,4 or more units – in which case the value is the figure in column 3 multiplied by 2,3,4 and so on, as the case may be.

British Savings Bonds

These are no longer earning any interest. If you still have bonds you should surrender them for repayment as soon as you can. Write to the Bonds and Stock Office, Blackpool, FY3 9YP.

Interest
■ **Column 4** tells you the rate of interest paid for the year ending during 1988 – on the anniversary of the date the certificates were bought. If this anniversary fell before the date you are reading this, this information is now of historical interest only. If the anniversary is yet to come, the figure tells you the rate of interest you will get if you hold on to your certificates until that date. Because the interest is tax-free, this is, in effect, the after-tax rate of return.
■ **Column 5** tells you the rate of interest due to be paid next year – that is, for the year ending during 1989 on the anniversary of the date the certificates were bought.
■ **Column 6** tells you the rate of interest for the year ending during 1990.

Value for money
As we have said, all the early issues from the 1st to the 6th give a deplorably low return – it varies between 1.1 and 1.8 per cent. Other investments can give a much better return. So if you've any of these early issues, cash them in at once and reinvest elsewhere.

With certificates of the later issues, you'll have to compare the rate of return you're getting with that available on other investments (taking your rate of tax into account). Don't forget to look at the rate of return next year, and the year after next, before coming to a decision. For example, with 30th Issue bought in 1985, although the rate of return this year is 8.6 per cent, next year you'd get 10.0 per cent, and the year after 11.4 per cent. So it may be worth hanging on to them.

Table 2 National Savings Certificates

1 name of issue (and issue price)	2 year bought	3 value in 1988 (at anniversary of date bought)	4 interest now	5 interest next year	6 interest year after next
			rate of interest for year ending at anniversary of date bought, in:		
			1988	**1989**	**1990**
		£	%	%	%
7th (15s)	1944	4.19	9.97		
	1945	3.81	9.80	9.97	
	1946	3.47	7.26	9.80	9.97
	1947	3.23$\frac{1}{2}$	6.94	7.26	9.80
£1 (£)	1947	3.61$\frac{1}{2}$	10.05		
8th (10s)	1951	2.32	8.41		
9th (15s)	1955	3.26	9.95		
	1956	2.96$\frac{1}{2}$	9.81	9.95	
10th (15s)	1961	2.86	8.54		
	1962	2.63$\frac{1}{2}$	9.79	8.54	
	1963	2.40	7.38	9.79	8.54
25th (£25)	1983	35.90	9.65		
26th (£25)	1983	37.17	10.59		
	1984	33.61	9.37	10.59	
27th (£25)	1984	32.44	8.28	9.37	
28th (£25)	1984	34.43	10.25	11.73	
29th (£25)	1984	33.34	9.03	10.20	
	1985	30.58	7.90	9.03	10.20
30th (£25)	1985	31.17	8.64	10.01	11.43
31st (£25)	1985	30.40	7.80	8.95	10.14
	1986	28.20	6.66	7.80	8.95
32nd (£25)	1986	28.63	7.51	8.66	9.90
	1987	26.63	6.52	7.51	8.66

Index-linked National Savings Certificates (4th issue)

These certificates are worth considering if you're worried about inflation. They guarantee that the buying-power of the money you invest will keep pace with rising prices. For how they compare with index-linked British Government stocks, see p296.

How much can you invest?

You can invest anything between £25 and £5,000, in units of £25 – so they are suitable for both lump sums or savings (regular or a bit at a time). A husband and wife can each invest up to £5,000 (ie up to £10,000 in all). If the certificates are in their joint names, however, they can invest only £5,000 between them.

How to invest

Go to a post office or bank and fill in an application form. You'll get a receipt and your certificate, showing how much you've invested, will be sent on to you by post.

How index-linked certificates work

You can hold each certificate for up to five years. If you cash it in within a year of buying it, you get back only the money you invested in the first place. But after a year, its value is increased in line with the change in the Retail Prices Index (RPI) since you bought it, plus extra interest for each complete month from the day you invest. If you hold your certificate for the full five years, your overall return is 4.04 per cent a year on top of inflation. The certificate then continues to be revalued each month, and you get this increased value back if you cash it in. See Table 3 below.

Table 3 How a £25 unit of the 4th index-linked issue grows

during year	index-linked increase [1]	interest	Value at end of year
	£		£
1	1.25	3% of purchase price	27.00
2	1.35	3.25% of value end year 1	29.23
3	1.46	3.5% of value end year 2	31.71
4	1.59	4.5% of value end year 3	34.73
5	1.74	6% of value end year 4	38.54

[1] Inflation assumed to run at 5 per cent a year.

Which month's index applies?

The level of the RPI for the previous month is announced on the second or third Friday of each month – and reported in the newspapers the following day. When you buy a certificate or cash one in, the RPI figure that applies is the one announced in the previous month – which, in turn, refers to the cost of living in the month before that. See p110 for a list of RPI figures since March 1982.

Working out how much you'd get if you cashed in now

The easiest way to find out the present value of your holding in 4th index-linked issue certificates is to look at the chart on display at post offices. But to decide whether or not your return is worthwhile compared with other risk-free investments, you should also consider the rate of return you are getting. Each year, your return is the interest rate applicable to your holding (see Table 3, opposite) plus the rate of inflation.

Is there any tax to pay on the gain?

No. The gain is free of both income tax and capital gains tax. This makes these certificates particularly attractive to people paying higher rate income tax, or who have used up their yearly tax-free slice for capital gains tax.

What happens to your certificate if you die?

The certificate can be transferred into your heir's name – even if he or she has already the maximum holding of certificates.

How to cash in certificates

Get form DNS502MA from a Post Office. Fill it in and send it off in the pre-paid envelope provided with the form. You shouldn't have to wait longer than a couple of weeks for your money.

Can you cash in only part of your money?

Yes. When you bought your certificate you bought a number of £25 units. You can cash in any number of units you wish.

Any old National Savings Stamps?

Remember them – 10p each (or 6d and 1/- in pre-decimal days)? They were withdrawn on 31 December 1976, but you can still cash in any you've got knocking around. Send them to NSB Boydstone Road, Glasgow, G58 1SB and ask for their value to be refunded.

What happens if the Retail Prices Index goes down?

The value of your certificate goes down in line with the fall in the Retail Prices Index though interest is still added. But it is guaranteed that when you cash your units in, you'll get back at least as much as you originally invested (plus the extra supplements).

What happens if the rate of inflation goes down?

Your certificate will continue to increase in value, but at a slower rate than before. A fall in the rate of inflation does *not* mean that the value of your certificate will fall. What's important from the point of view of your investment is how the rate of inflation, plus the interest, compares with the rate of return you could get on other comparatively safe investments (eg building society accounts).

Should you cash in old index-linked certificates?

You don't have to. You can keep your money where it is, and your investment will continue to be index-linked. In addition, you'll get tax-free interest. For example, if you have money invested in the Retirement Issue (on sale between 1975 and 1980) or the 2nd index-linked issue (sold between 1980 and 1985), on 1 August 1988 you'll have received a bonus of 3 per cent of the value of your investment at 31 July 1987. Assuming that inflation is running at around 5 per cent a year, your rate of interest for the year will be around 8% tax-free. This compares favourably with building society interest rates, but if you withdrew your money and invested in the 4th issue (details above), you'd get the same rate (3 per cent) at the end of the first year, but then a higher guaranteed rate for the next four years.

But if your investment in these issues is coming up to its fifth or tenth anniversary, you have an added incentive to hang on to your certificates until that date is past. That's because a bonus of 4 per cent of the amount you originally invested will be added to the value on the fifth anniversary of your purchase – you'll get this in 1989 if you bought 2nd index-linked issue certificates in 1984. On the tenth anniversary of your purchase you'll get a bonus of 4 per cent of the value of your investment on the fifth anniversary.

If you have certificates of the 3rd or 4th index-linked issues, Table 4 opposite shows what interest to expect on top of index-linking. It is calculated monthly and added on the anniversary of purchase. Your overall return will depend on the rate of inflation over the year. The higher the rate, the higher your return. So when you're deciding whether to cash in your investment, you have to consider what you think is going to happen to inflation. If you think it is on the increase, you should be less keen to cash in your investment and vice versa. However, you should look at the return being offered by the current issue of index-linked certificates to see whether it betters what you are getting.

Table 4 Index-linked National Savings Certificates

Name of issue	Year bought	Interest added at end of year to value at start of year (on top of index-linking)		
		This year 1988 %	Next year 1989 %	Year after next 1990 %
3rd	1985	3.25	4.00	5.25
	1986	2.75	3.25	4.0
4th	1986	3.25	3.5	4.5
	1987	3.0	3.25	3.5

Other National Savings investments

National Savings Ordinary Accounts

Who can invest?
Anyone aged 7 or over can open an account. If aged under 7, the account can be opened by a relative or friend.

How much can you invest?
You must invest a minimum of £1 to open an account, while the maximum is £10,000, no matter how many Ordinary Accounts you have.

How to invest
You can open an account at most post offices – you'll be sent a bank book where a record is kept of all your transactions.

How much interest?
The rate of interest can vary, though it tends to be fixed for at least one year at a time. For 1988, if your account has been kept open from 31/12/87 to 1/1/89, you'll get interest at a rate of 5 per cent for each calendar month in which the balance is £500 or more. Otherwise you'll get the standard rate of interest – 2.5 per cent. Interest is worked out on each complete £1 in the account for a full calendar month. Money in your account doesn't start earning interest until

the start of the month following the one in which it is deposited. And it stops getting interest from the start of the month in which it is withdrawn. So you'll get most interest if you put your money in on the last day of a month, and take it out on the first day of a month.

Interest is added to your account on 31 December. The first £70 of interest is tax-free (see p101 for more on tax).

Getting your money out

You can withdraw up to £100 at once by taking your bank book to most post offices. If you want more than £100, you have to apply in writing on an application form available from most post offices – getting your money could take about a week. If you withdraw more than £50, your bank book has to be sent to the Savings Bank headquarters (the limit is £250 if you have a *Regular Customer Account* – check at your post office).

What happens if you die?

The money in your account can be cashed in or transferred to your heir's account. Form DNS904 gives all the details. ·

National Savings Investment Accounts

Who can invest?

The same people as for Ordinary Accounts.

How much can you invest?

You must invest a minimum of £5 to open an account. The maximum is £100,000, no matter how many Investment Accounts you have.

How to invest?

As for Ordinary Accounts.

How much interest?

The rate of interest varies (in April 1988, it was 8.5 per cent a year).

Interest is added to your account on 31 December. All interest is taxable, but is paid without tax having been deducted – which makes the account particularly suitable for non-taxpayers.

Getting your money out

You have to give one month's notice to withdraw your money. You can get an application form from most post offices. You'll have to send your bank book in with your application form.

What happens if you die?
As for Ordinary Accounts.

National Savings Income Bonds

Who can invest?
Anyone irrespective of age. They may be particularly suitable for non-taxpayers who want a regular income from their savings.

How much can you invest?
Income bonds cost £1,000 each. The minimum number you can buy is two, and the maximum holding is £100,000 (100 bonds). So they are suitable only for lump sum investment.

How to invest
You can get an application form from the post office which you send to the *Bonds and Stock Office*. A certificate showing the value of the bonds you have bought will be sent to you.

How much interest?
The rate of interest varies, depending on how much the Government feels it needs to offer to attract investors (in May 1988, the rate was 9 per cent a year). Interest is paid out to you monthly (on the fifth day of each month). When you first invest, you will have to wait at least six weeks for your first payment. All interest is taxable, but is paid without tax having been deducted.

Getting your money out
You have to give three months' notice if you want to cash one of your bonds. If you cash a bond within a year of purchasing it, you'll get only half the normal rate of interest on it. After a year, there is no penalty and your bond will be repaid in full. Get form DNS201 from a post office if you want to cash a bond.

What happens if you die?
Your heirs can cash the bonds without notice and with no loss of interest. Form DNS904 gives details of what to do.

National Savings Deposit Bonds

Who can invest?
Anyone, irrespective of their age. Non-taxpayers, in particular, might find them useful as tax is not deducted from the interest before you get it.

How much can you invest?
A minimum of £100 with a maximum of £100,000 in multiples of £50. They are suitable for lump sum investments or occasional savings.

How to invest
If you invest at a post office, you will get a receipt, and a certificate showing how much you have invested will be sent by post from the Deposit Bond Office later. Otherwise you can get an application form from the post office and apply direct by post.

How much interest?
The interest rate varies depending on how much the government feels it needs to offer to get the amount of money it wants from investors (in May 1988 the rate was 9 per cent a year). Interest is added to the value of your bond each year on the anniversary of your investment. This interest is taxable, but it is paid without tax having been deducted.

Getting your money out
You can withdraw any amount above £50 as long as at least £100 of your original investment remains. You have to give three months' notice and if you want to cash all or part of your investment within a year of investing it you'll get only half the normal rate of interest on the amount withdrawn. After a year there is no penalty. Forms for withdrawals are available at post offices.

What happens if you die?
Your heirs can withdraw your investment without notice and with no loss of interest. Form DNS904 gives the details of what to do.

National Savings Yearly Plan

Who can invest?
Anyone, irrespective of age, who wants to save regularly.

How much can you invest?

You have to save a regular monthly amount of between £20 and £200 in units of £5 by standing order for one year. After the first year you can either continue paying the same amount on the same date each month for another year, or start a new plan if you want to alter the amount and/or the date of payment.

How to invest

Get an application form from the post office and send it to the *Savings Certificate Office, Yearly Plan.*

How does Yearly Plan work?

At the end of the year you get a Yearly Plan Certificate showing a value equal to your twelve monthly payments plus interest on each – in April 1988 this was paid at a rate of 5.25 per cent a year. If you hold this Certificate for a further four years you get a higher rate of interest (7.25 per cent a year in April 1988). If you keep the Certificate for the full four years, the overall rate of return works out at 7 per cent. If you hold your certificate for more than four years it will earn interest at the general extension rate (see p172). The interest is free of income tax and your gain is not liable to capital gains tax.

Getting your money out

If you want to stop saving before having made your twelve monthly payments you get back only what you have paid in. Once you have your Certificate, the interest you get depends on how long you hold it before cashing-in. With the rates as they were in April 1988 you'd get interest at a rate of 5.75 per cent a year if you had held the Certificate for at least one month but less than two years. If you cashed it in when you'd had it for more than two years, but less than four, you'd get a higher rate – 6.5 per cent.

What happens if you die?

Your heirs can cash in your Yearly Plan or, if a certificate has been issued, they can transfer it to their own name. Get form DNS904 from a post office.

Index-linked Save-As-You-Earn (3rd Issue)

You can't now start an index-linked SAYE plan. However, if you started investing before May 1984 you can continue with this regular savings plan. Under the scheme, savers who made a regular monthly payment for five years had the value of each payment increased in line with the change in the RPI between the time it was made and the end of the five-year period. The accumulated value could then be withdrawn or left invested for a further two years, during which time the index-linking continued. At the end of the two years a bonus of two monthly contributions was added.

Is it worth cashing in your investment?

The answer to this is rather complicated as it depends on when you started your contract as well as other factors.

If you have not yet made regular monthly payments for five years but want to cash in your investment, your savings will not be index-linked. Instead you will get interest at a rate of 6 per cent a year. If you have missed any payments the whole SAYE contract is lengthened by one month for each payment missed, so you have the chance to make up the 60 payments.

If your SAYE contract is coming up to its seventh anniversary it is probably worth leaving your savings untouched until it has passed its seventh anniversary.

Once your SAYE contract qualifies for index-linking, you will also get supplements added to your investment. For example, on 1 September 1988 a supplement of 3 per cent of the SAYE scheme value at 31 August 1987 was added. This gives a rate of return of 3 per cent on top of inflation. Another supplement will be paid on 1 September 1989, but the amount of this is not yet known.

There is no tax to pay on the returns from index-linked SAYE. To cash in your savings you should get form DNS699MA from a post office.

Premium Bonds

Who can invest?

Anyone aged 16 or over can buy premium bonds. And they

National Savings and premium bond gift tokens

You can get gift tokens worth £5, or in multiples of £5 up to £60, from most post offices. These can be deposited in National Savings accounts as if they were money, or can be used to buy premium bonds or National Savings Certificates.

can be bought in the name of someone under 16 by parents, grandparents or legal guardians.

How much can you invest?
Premium bonds cost £1 each, but you have to buy a minimum of £10 worth. You can hold up to £10,000 of bonds in multiples of £5.

How to invest
You can get an application form from most post offices and banks. Your bonds will be sent to you by the *Bonds and Stock Office* (which keeps all the records).

How do you know if you've won a prize?
You'll be contacted by post at the last address the Bonds and Stock office has. So make sure you let them know if you move – get change-of-address forms from a post office. There's over £4 million in unclaimed prizes because the winners can't be traced.

How do you cash your bonds?
Get a form (DNS303) from a post office or bank. For each £1 invested you'll get £1 back (but, of course, if you've had your money invested for some time, inflation will have eaten away at its buying power).

What happens if you die?
Your bonds will remain eligible for prizes for 12 months after your death. To cash in the bonds, your heirs should get form DNS904 from a post office.

How do premium bonds work?
You don't get interest on your money as such. Instead you get a chance of winning prizes. The total value of the prize money is equal to interest on all bonds that have been held for at least three months (over 2,060 million of them) calculated – in July 1988 – at a rate of $6^1/_2$ per cent a year.

Once you've held a bond for three clear months it has a chance of winning one of the monthly prizes, ranging from £50 to £250,000 and the once-a-week prizes of £100,000, £50,000 and £25,000. All prizes are free of both income tax and capital gains tax.

There are rules about how the total prize money is divided into prizes of different amounts. For example, in March

1988, the prize money for premium bonds was split up as shown in the Box below:

Premium bond prizes in March 1988	
1 prize of	£250,000
4 prizes of	£100,000
4 prizes of	£50,000
4 prizes of	£25,000
5 prizes of	£10,000
25 prizes of	£5,000
355 prizes of	£1,000
1,065 prizes of	£500
11,195 prizes of	£100
167,919 prizes of	£50

13

PENSIONS FROM EMPLOYERS AND STATE

Your pension is probably one of the most important ways of saving for the future. Understanding how state pensions work is particularly important. Unless you know roughly what you are going to receive from the state, you'll be ill-prepared to sort out the rest of your savings and investments.

The Government has recently made changes to the state pension scheme, and created new choices which you must make between the state system, a pension from your employer, and a personal pension plan. In this chapter we explain the choices facing you to do with the state and employers' schemes; for your personal pension plan choices see Chapter 14. For how pensions in general tie in to planning your savings and investments for retirement, see Chapter 3.

The state pension system

There are three main parts to the state system. Your state pension may be made up of:
- a flat rate basic pension
- a graduated pension based on your earnings from 1961 to 1975
- an additional pension based on your earnings since April 1978, usually known as the **State Earnings Related Pension Scheme (SERPS).**

The amount of these pensions is increased each year in line with changes in the Retail Prices Index.

Basic pension

Anyone who has paid enough full Class 1, Class 2 or Class 3 National Insurance contributions, or has been given cred-

187

its, qualifies for this pension. There are complicated rules to work out whether you have paid enough in contributions. But you are pretty certain to qualify if you have paid full-rate contributions for nine-tenths of your 'working life' (broadly, between ages 16 and 64 for a man, or between ages 16 and 59 for a woman). If there were periods when you were not working, but were receiving a National Insurance benefit such as Unemployment Benefit, Sickness or Invalidity Benefit, Maternity Allowance, or Invalid Care Allowance, you would have been credited with contributions for these years.

Since April 1978, if you've stayed at home to look after children, or an elderly or sick person, the number of years needed to qualify are reduced. This is called 'home responsibilities protection'. Even if you don't qualify for the full pension, you may qualify for a reduced one, if you have contributed for a quarter of the years in your working life or more.

You can write and ask the DHSS about your contribution record; the address of the local office will be in the telephone directory under 'Health and Social Security, Department Of'. Quote your name, any previous name (for instance, a maiden name if you are now married), your date of birth, and your National Insurance number.

It is possible, in some cases, to make up gaps in your contribution record, by paying voluntary (Class 3) contributions yourself. Ask the DHSS whether this applies in your case and, if so, how much it would cost.

Graduated pension

People who were employed in a job between 1961 and 1975 and had reached 18 before 1975, are likely to have a small amount of graduated pension payable on top of the basic pension.

Between April 1961 and April 1975, there were two kinds of National Insurance contribution; a flat rate one paid by almost everyone in employment, and a graduated one paid by people who earned more than £9 in any one week.

For each £7.50 he contributed during those years, a man gets a unit of pension, which is now worth just under 5.4p a week (in the year 1988–9). If you're a woman, it will have taken £9 of contributions to earn that 5.4p a week. The rules were set in this way because women have an earlier state pension age than men, and live longer on average.

The graduated pension has been increased in step with rising prices since April 1978. But it's never going to be very large. In 1987–88, the maximum graduated pension was £3.88 a week for a woman and £4.63 a week for a man.

The DHSS keeps records of how many *units* of pension each person has earned. You can check with them about your own position.

Many people were *contracted out* of the old graduated scheme because their employers ran their own pension schemes. But when the scheme was wound up, many employers paid the money back into the state scheme in order to get rid of their liabilities. Again, you can ask the DHSS about this. If it turns out that your employer did not buy you back into the state scheme, ask the employer instead for details of how much is owing to you.

State Earnings Related Pension Scheme (SERPS)

This is a supplement to the basic pension for employed people paying the full National Insurance contribution. It started in 1978, but the Government has now decided to cut back on it for people retiring after April 1999.

What you get, and what you pay, depends on your earnings. We tell you how the scheme works on p191 onwards. If you are *contracted out* of SERPS, the benefits from your contracted out scheme replace SERPS. We explain the different methods of contracting out on p194.

Married women

If you pay the full rate National Insurance contribution, you are treated in exactly the same way as a man or a single woman. If you have had to spend time at home caring for children, or elderly relatives, you can qualify for a basic pension with a shorter contribution record, under 'home responsibilities protection' (see opposite).

However, there are still many married women paying the reduced rate contribution, which used to be called the 'small stamp'. No-one has been able to *start* doing so since 1977. Reduced rate contributors only qualify for a state pension on their husband's record, and they have to wait until their *husbands* start getting their pensions. They don't qualify for SERPS. The pension for a dependent wife is 60 per cent – three-fifths – of the rate the husband is getting.

If the man has retired, and his wife is under 60, he can draw a dependant's allowance for her too, *provided* she is not earning, or drawing an occupational pension of, more than £32.75 a week. If she is over 60, then the pension is the same amount (three-fifths of his pension) but it is paid directly to her. Occupational pension is not taken into account once she is over 60, and her benefit is only cut back once she is earning over £75 a week.

Widows

If your husband paid enough National Insurance contributions, you qualify for a number of benefits, including state retirement pension when you reach retirement age. For details, get leaflets NP35 and NP36 from your local social security office. All widows' benefits, except the state retirement pension, stop when you remarry or live with a man as his wife.

Widows' benefits increase in the same way as the basic retirement pension.

If you're over 60 when your husband dies, you'll normally get the basic retirement pension. If you were under 60 and your husband was not getting the retirement pension when he died, you will also get a tax-free lump sum 'widow's payment' of £1,000. You will also be entitled to an additional pension based on your husband's SERPS record.

Earning extra state pension

You can earn extra state pension by putting off drawing your state retirement pension, for up to five years after retirement age.

For each six days, excluding Sundays, you postpone drawing the pension, your total state pension is increased by $1/7$ per cent. But you have to put off your retirement for at least 42 days (excluding Sundays) before the pension is increased, because the minimum increase is 1 per cent. For each *year* that you postpone your retirement, the pension is increased by 7.5 per cent.

Once you are 65 if a woman, 70 if a man (ie five years over state retirement age), you have to start taking your state pension, and continuing to work won't increase it any further. You won't get any increases in the state pension for any weeks when you are drawing other state benefits such as unemployment benefit.

Any graduated pension, and any SERPS benefits (see p188 and p192) will be increased in the same way.

A wife can't claim a pension on her husband's contributions until he starts drawing the state pension. If he puts it off, her part of the pension will be postponed too, and increased by the same percentage as her husband's.

If you've already started drawing your state pension, you

can cancel your retirement *once*, and earn increases in your pension from then on.

The earnings rule

During the first five years after you reach state retirement age, the *earnings rule* applies, to both employed and self employed people. This rule says that you can earn up to £75 a week, in the 1988–89 tax year, without your pension being reduced. But for every £ above that, up to £79, it is reduced by 50p, and for every £ above £79, it is reduced by £1.

So if your earnings are likely to affect your pension, it may be better to put off taking it for a few years, and build up a bigger pension instead.

How SERPS works

If you earn more than a certain amount, called the Lower Earnings Limit (£41 a week in the 1988–89 tax year), you pay National Insurance contributions on the whole of your earnings up to a given ceiling, the Upper Earnings Limit, which is £305 in 1988–89. These contributions qualify you for a SERPS pension.

The DHSS have a record of your PAYE earnings for each year since 1978–79. Your SERPS pension is related to the earnings recorded for all those years, *revalued* in line with the way average earnings have increased between the date when they were earned, and the date you retire. So it is largely protected against inflation.

Who's not in SERPS

There are several groups of people who are outside the SERPS framework. These are:
■ the low paid – people earning less than the Lower Earnings Limit (£41 in the 1988–89 tax year). They don't pay any National Insurance contributions, and so will not qualify for any basic pension either
■ the self-employed – their National Insurance contributions only qualify them for the basic state pension
■ people paying voluntary contributions
■ people whose earnings aren't taxed under the Pay As You Earn (PAYE) system. If you are in the 'black economy' and not declaring your income to the taxman, you will not qualify for a SERPS pension either

■ people who are unemployed. If you are unemployed, you receive credits for the *basic* state pension only. But for SERPS purposes, for a year of unemployment you would have an earnings record of zero, which will reduce your pension at retirement

■ people who are at home looking after children or dependant relatives. If they are covered by 'home responsibilities protection' (see p188) those years are not counted in their SERPS record at all, and so don't reduce their pension at retirement.

How much pension will SERPS give you?

Contributions on earnings up to the Lower Earnings Limit count towards the basic pension, but not towards SERPS. So an amount equal to the Lower Earnings Limit for the tax year in which you are 64 (59 if you are a woman) is knocked off each of the revalued figures. What's left is the amount of earnings counted towards your SERPS pension. The original idea was that after the scheme had been running for more than 20 years, the best 20 years would be picked out and averaged together, but this has now been dropped. Nowadays, the pension is based on the *average* of all your revalued earnings, minus the Lower Earnings Limit. This will include years of unemployment and part-time work – so, for many people, this new formula will significantly reduce their SERPS pension. If you are earning more than the Upper Earnings Limit (£305 in 1988–89) these higher earnings are ignored.

How fast the SERPS pension builds up depends on when you are due to retire.

For anyone retiring before, or in, April 1999, the SERPS pension builds up at 1/80th (1.25 per cent) of your revalued earnings for each year) since 1978. So the maximum available is 20/80ths, or 25 per cent. But after April 1999 SERPS will be gradually reduced. The pension earned before 1988 is always 'safeguarded' by being worked out on the 1/80th basis, though as time goes on it will be a smaller and smaller fraction of your total SERPS pension.

For anyone retiring after April 2008, the SERPS pension will be 20 per cent of earnings between the Lower and Upper Limits for the years after 1988. During the transitional years, 1998–2008, the SERPS pension earned after 1988 drops by 0.5 per cent a year, for those retiring in that year. So someone retiring in 2000–01 gets 24 per cent, someone retiring in 2001–02 gets 23.5 per cent and so on. (It's always state retirement age that matters, not the age at which you choose to retire.)

Working out your SERPS pension

It's not possible to work out your own SERPS pension accurately, because you don't know what your earnings pattern is going to be over the future. A few bad years, or a few good ones, would change the average over your working lifetime considerably. The safeguarding for the years between 1978 and 1988 also complicates the arithmetic.

But you can get a *rough* idea, in today's money, by ignoring the safeguarding and assuming that your current earnings are what you will always earn, in real terms. This means you are ignoring the effects of inflation or changes in your earnings pattern. What it will give you is an idea of what *proportion* of your earnings you can expect from SERPS.

■ **Step One** Decide on the figure for your total weekly earnings before tax in the current tax year (1988–89). Deduct the Lower Earnings Limit (£41). If your earnings figure is above the Upper Earnings Limit (£305) then ignore the extra earnings as well. For example, Fred Hurst's earnings are £201 a week. So he deducts £41, leaving £160 as the slice of earnings used for calculating SERPS. Mary Henson, however, is earning £320. She ignores the last £15, and assumes that her earnings are £305 (the Upper Earnings Limit). So she deducts £41 from £305, leaving earnings of £264 a week.

■ **Step Two** Work out what tax year you will reach state retirement age. If it's the 1998–99 tax year or earlier, go to **Step Three**. If it's the 2008–09 tax year or later, go to **Step Four**. If it is between 1998–99 and 2008–09 (the transitional years) go to **Step Five**.

■ **Step Three** Work out how many full tax years there are between 1978–79 and your retirement date. If you are a man who reaches 65 in May 1993, for instance, there will be 14 full tax years. For each year since 1978–79, you get 1/80th of your earnings. So someone retiring in May 1993 would get 14/80ths. This means that you divide the earnings figure you worked out in **Step One** by 80 and multiply by 14.

■ **Step Four** If you will reach state retirement age in 2008–09 or later, you get 20 per cent, or a fifth, of your earnings. So this means that you divide the earnings figure you worked out in **Step One** by 5.

■ **Step Five** This is for the people reaching state retirement age during the transitional years, who have the most complicated sum. You need first to work out how many full tax years it is between 1998–89 and state retirement age. Then you take the 25 per cent figure (the amount of SERPS pension you would have had if you'd been retiring in 1998–99) and deduct 0.5 per cent for each year after 1998–99. So if you'll retire in 2003–04, you deduct 2.5 per cent. This leaves you with 22.5 per cent, and you now work out 22.5 per cent of the earnings figure already calculated in **Step One**.

The Chart on p44 shows what SERPS pension a person on average earnings can expect, depending on their retirement date.

The DHSS always start by working out your SERPS pension as if you have been contracted in to SERPS since it began in 1978. But if in fact you have been contracted *out*, they will assume that part of it is coming from other sources.

Remember, what you have worked out is an *approximate* figure, based on some fairly crude assumptions, and in today's money values. See p227 for some points on how inflation will affect the calculations.

The steps above are a simplified version of the (very complicated) SERPS calculations. For a more complex version, taking account of all the factors including the safeguarding arrangements, look at DHSS leaflet NP32.

If you ask, the DHSS will also provide you with an additional pensions statement which will be more accurate about the SERPS entitlement based on your past earnings, but still based on guesswork about the future. To obtain this statement, get leaflet NP38 from your local DHSS office. This includes a form to be posted back to the main DHSS office in Newcastle. They will send a statement showing:
■ the amount of SERPS pension earned up until the end of the last tax year, at today's values
■ an estimate of what your SERPS pension will be if you carry on working up to state retirement age; and
■ an estimate of the SERPS pension at that date if future earnings increase faster than prices.

Contracting out of SERPS

When SERPS started in 1978, employers who ran pension schemes for their employees could choose whether their employees should belong to it or not. If they chose not to, they could 'contract out'. This meant that the employer's scheme took over the job of providing the equivalent of SERPS, and had to guarantee to do so. In 1988, two new forms of contracting out were introduced, without the same guarantees.

If you are contracted out, then a lower percentage of your National Insurance contribution goes towards the state pension scheme. The remainder, called the 'rebate', is intended to be used for the contracted out pension. At present (1988) the rebate is 2 per cent of the employee's contribution, on his or her earnings above the Lower Earnings Limit (explained on p191); 3.8 per cent of the employer's contribution, on the same slice of earnings, is rebated. This makes a total of 5.8 per cent which is expected to go towards the replacement pension.

The size of the rebate is being reduced in five-yearly stages. It was originally 7 per cent, and is now down to 5.8 per cent. By 1998 it's expected to be round about 4 per cent, jointly between employer and employee.

Contracting out with a pensions guarantee

This was the original way of contracting out. Broadly, a contracted out scheme must guarantee that the pension it pays (including the deferred pensions of early leavers) is at least equivalent to the SERPS pensions that you would have had from the state, if your employer's scheme had not been contracted out. This is called the *guaranteed minimum pension* or GMP for short. In return for giving these guarantees, both employer and employee pay lower National Insurance contributions.

The GMP will go up to take account of inflation both before and after your retirement. Before retirement, this is the responsibility of the employer's scheme; after retirement, the first 3 per cent increase each year (on pension earned after April 1988) will be provided by the scheme, and the state will provide the rest. For deferred pensioners, increases in the GMP are provided partly or wholly by the scheme, and any extra that is necessary is added by the state.

Contracting out with a Contracted Out Money Purchase scheme (COMP)

Since April 1988, employers have been allowed to contract out their workers in a new way, with what's called a **Contracted Out Money Purchase (COMP)** scheme. Here they guarantee only the amount of money going *in*, as contributions.

This money is used to create *protected rights* to a money purchase pension (explained on p206) payable at state retirement age, and to a spouse's pension, based on the fund that has built up so far, when you die. If only the minimum contribution is going in, no other benefits are possible. There are special restrictions on how the money is invested to cover your protected rights, and each person must have an individual account which can be identified. You *give up* your SERPS rights for those years, and the COMP pension could be greater than what you would have had from SERPS – or it could be less. The DHSS calculates the pension you would have had from SERPS, and then deducts a theoretical amount for each year you were in a COMP scheme. If the COMP in fact provides less than the theoretical amount, you bear the shortfall.

The employer and employee both pay lower National Insurance contributions than if the scheme was contracted into SERPS. But at least as much as the rebate (see p195) *must* go into the COMP scheme, plus, in some cases, a 2 per cent incentive (see Box opposite). The employer makes the payments, and can (but need not) recover the 2 per cent from the employee. It is the employer who chooses whether to run a COMP scheme or not, and what contributions to charge the employee. But nowadays you don't *have* to join an employer's scheme if you don't want to.

Contracting out with an Appropriate Personal Pension (APP)

These were introduced in July 1988, and allow you to contract out of SERPS, outside your employer's scheme. You can take out an APP if:
- your employer doesn't have a contracted out pension scheme *or*
- your employer has a contracted out scheme, but you don't belong to it *or*
- your employer has a contracted in scheme, whether or not you are a member of it.

If you take out an APP, your National Insurance rebate of 5.8 per cent, plus the 2 per cent incentive in many cases, goes into the scheme and buys you *protected rights*, on a money purchase basis (explained on page 206). These entitle you to a pension at state retirement age (no earlier), and a spouse's pension on your death. If you want extra pension or a different pattern of benefits, you must pay extra. You *give up* your SERPS rights entirely for the years you are in an APP. The APP may be bigger than what you would have got under SERPS, if the APP you choose has done well – or it may be less. As for COMP schemes, the DHSS calculates the pension you would have had from SERPS, and then deducts a theoretical amount for each year you were in an APP scheme. If the APP in fact provides less than the theoretical amount, the individual bears the shortfall.

If you have an APP, you pay *full rate* National Insurance

contributions. You (and whoever you take out the APP policy with) notify the DHSS that you have taken out an APP. At the end of each tax year the DHSS calculates what your rebate is, and pays it over to the 'provider' (ie the organisation running the APP for you). But if anything is wrong with the DHSS records, or the provider's records, there will be a delay while it's sorted out, and the rebate will not reach your account (and so start earning interest or dividends) until then.

The 2 per cent incentive

The Government wants to give the new arrangements a good start, and so up until 1993 it is paying an extra 2 per cent of people's earnings, above the Lower Earnings Limit, towards the pensions of people who have not been contracted out before. The conditions differ slightly for employer's schemes and APPs.

■ For an employer's scheme, the incentive is paid if it was contracted out after 1 January 1986, there has been no contracted out pension scheme covering that employment before, and no scheme that the individuals could have joined but did not. So if there was only a scheme for managerial staff, shop floor employees are eligible for the 2 per cent. The incentive is paid for the five years between 1988 and 1993.

■ If a person takes out an APP the DHSS will pay the 2 per cent incentive so long as he or she was not contracted out, in their present job, for two years or more before leaving to take the APP. The 2 per cent is payable for *six* years at the most, because for those who take out an APP before April 1989 it can be backdated to April 1987 (as can the National Insurance rebate).

Is contracting out a good idea?

If your employer is contracting you out and replacing SERPS with a *Guaranteed Minimum Pension*, you cannot lose – you are guaranteed to get at least the pension you would have had from SERPS. But the wisdom of contracting out via a COMP or an APP depends very much on your age and circumstances.

Since SERPS is going to be reduced for people retiring after 1998, it may seem that anyone retiring after that date would be better out of it. But this is not so. The National Insurance rebate is the same percentage of your earnings – 5.8 per cent – whatever age you are, and it is likely to be reduced in the future. But a *money purchase* pension (ie a COMP or an APP) builds up much faster for a younger person than for an older one. This is because the contributions made in the early stages have far longer to build up compound interest, so are much more valuable.

So what matters is firstly, the age at which you put the contributions in – and it's a case of the younger, the better – and secondly, how fast you think your contribution will grow. If you are optimistic about how investments generally will do in the future, the 5.8 per cent contribution of a man under 43, and a woman under 35, should be enough at least to equal the SERPS pension that would build up during that year. If you are not too optimistic about investment returns, then the age at which you believe SERPS will beat an APP or COMP will be lower; if you are very optimistic, it will be higher. However optimistic you are, it is highly unlikely that anyone in their fifties will see their 5.8 per cent beating SERPS. If you're going to receive the 2 per cent incentive (explained on p197) the relevant ages are pushed up by a few years.

The Diagrams opposite show how investment returns affect the latest age at which contracting-out will beat SERPS. So Diagram 1 assumes that your investment grows by 0.5 per cent, after inflation and taking salary increases in to account; Diagram 2 is more optimistic and assumes a growth rate of 2.5 per cent. By contracting out for a particular tax year (1988–89 in this Example), you are giving up that year's Guaranteed Minimum Pension (GMP) – what you would have had in an employer's contracted out pension scheme linked to earnings. So each diagram compares the amount of GMP that would build up in that year (the broken line), with the amount that would build up in an APP or COMP to which you make the minimum contribution (ie the contracted-out rebate and tax relief on your rebate) both with and without the two per cent incentive. The figures shown are for a man, but the same principles apply for women.

As you get older, the balance between the amount of APP or COMP you've built up *in that year*, and the SERPS for that year, changes. So if you already have an APP or COMP, you need to reassess your decision as you reach these ages. And in 1993 when the 2 per cent incentive ends and the National Insurance rebate changes, everyone needs to think again.

For example, if you are 38 in 1988, you might want to contract out now via an APP. But in 1993 you should review your decision, and unless your particular APP had done very well, or you were optimistic that it would do well in the future, you'd be wise to contract back in. However, it is always possible that the Government could make contracting

SERPS or an Appropriate Personal Pension?

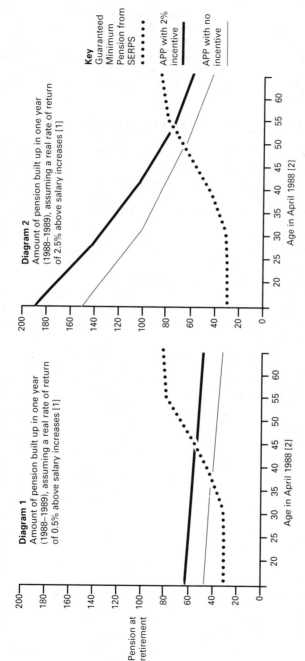

Diagram 1
Amount of pension built up in one year (1988–1989), assuming a real rate of return of 0.5% above salary increases [1]

Pension at retirement

Age in April 1988 [2]

Diagram 2
Amount of pension built up in one year (1988–1989), assuming a real rate of return of 2.5% above salary increases [1]

Age in April 1988 [2]

Key

Guaranteed Minimum Pension from SERPS

APP with 2% incentive

APP with no incentive

[1] Assuming that employee earns £10,000 and his contribution is 5% of his gross earnings, including the employee's share of the National Insurance rebate. Take-home pay would be the same whichever option was chosen. It is assumed that 0.6% of earnings above the Lower Earnings Limit (see p191) is going towards life insurance providing a lump sum of once times earnings. The figures don't make any assumptions about pay increases between now and retirement.
[2] Graphs show figures for men, but the same principles aply for women.
Source: Bacon and Woodrow

out a 'one-way street' – so that you could contract out but never contract back in again.

So if you want to take no risks at all, SERPS is the place for you. If you are willing to take some risks, then if you are young enough, contract out. But don't regard it as a once-for-all decision. Think again at least every five years.

A pension from your employer

Since April 1988, all employers' pension schemes have had to become voluntary. So if you are starting a new job, you now have a choice whether to join or not. Even if you are already in a pension scheme, you always have the option to leave your scheme and make your own provision. But if the employer provides a scheme which is any good, then your best bet will be to stay within it, and receive the benefits of the employer's contributions as well as your own.

An employer's pension scheme may be contributory, which means you pay in a proportion of your salary to the scheme each week or month. Four or five per cent are common contribution rates (normally your employer will be paying the same, or more). Or the scheme may be non-contributory. In either case, the employer makes contributions into the scheme on your behalf. Provided the scheme meets certain conditions laid down by the Inland Revenue, it gets very favourable tax treatment (as do personal pension plans — see Chapter 14). You get tax relief on any contributions you make, you pay no tax on any contributions made by your employer, and the pension fund itself pays no income tax or capital gains tax.

To work out how much you will get from your pension scheme, you need to know what kind it is. There are five main kinds. The type covering most people is a **final pay** scheme, explained below. The other sorts are summarised on p206 onwards.

Final pay scheme

With a final pay scheme, the number of years you've been a member of the scheme, and the yearly amount you're earning at the time you retire or averaged over the few years before then, decide the size of your pension. Many schemes pay 1/60th of your final pay for each year of membership. Others pay, for example, 1/80th of final pay.

Under the Inland Revenue's rules, the maximum pension you can get at normal retirement age is 2/3rds of your final pay. In what's known as a 'fact accrual' scheme, you can get this maximum after only ten years' service, if you were in the scheme before 17 March 1987. But if you changed employer after that date, this maximum can only be reached after 20 years. It is only senior executives, and people in a few unusual industries, who have one of these 'fast accrual' schemes. For most people, the benefits are assumed to build up over 40 years.

So if you reach normal retirement age after 40 years' membership of a scheme which pays 1/60th of your final pay for each year, you can retire on 2/3rds final pay. But even if you retire after 45 years in the scheme, you can still only have a 2/3rds pension.

In a scheme which works on 80ths, you would only have a pension of half final pay (ie 40/80ths), after 40 or more years of membership.

The higher your final yearly pay, the higher your pension from the scheme. There are different definitions, though, of what 'pay' is. Sometimes the rules define it to include bonus, commission, overtime, and such items as London Weighting, or some of these and not others; sometimes it does not. The Inland Revenue no longer allows income from *share option* schemes to be counted.

There are also differences in the way 'final' is defined. Common methods are:

■ average pay in the best 3 consecutive years out of the last 13

■ basic salary in the last year before you retire (or the last but one year), plus the average of your 'fluctuating emoluments' such as bonus or commission over the last few years

■ average yearly pay over the last few years (most often three or five).

Check in your scheme booklet exactly how the scheme works. You have a legal right to *up-to-date* details of your scheme.

Taking account of the state pension

Some final pay schemes make a deduction *either* from the final pay used to work out your pension, or from the pension itself, to allow for the fact that you'll be getting some money from the state. Often the way this is done is to take away an amount equivalent to the Lower Earnings Limit (explained on p191) or more or less than that level, from your pay before the pension and contribution are calculated. But schemes vary so check what yours does. If the normal retirement age in your job is earlier than state retirement age, the deduction for the state pension ought not to be applied until you reach the official retirement age for the state pension. It's particularly important that it does not apply if you're forced to retire early because of ill-health.

Inflation proofing

Retirement can last a long time, particularly for women. On average, men retiring at 65 can expect 13 years of retirement; women retiring at 60 have 20 years. You want an adequate pension not just at the time you retire, but later in your retirement too. A pension of, for example, only half your final pay but with inflation proofing, will soon overtake an apparently better pension of two-thirds of your final pay with no protection against rising prices.

In public sector jobs, such as the Civil Service, most pensions increase in line with the rise in the Retail Prices Index. In the private sector, not many do. Many, though, do promise to increase pensions by a certain percentage each year. Often this is 3 per cent or 4 per cent, or the increase in the Retail Prices Index if less. While this doesn't look too bad at today's rate of inflation, this low level may not last.

Some schemes – particularly those run by large companies – have in practice given increases which don't fall far short of inflation. In the last few years, when pension schemes have been flush with money, many have done a 'catching up exercise', for older pensioners, increasing their pensions to the real level they were at when they retired. But how far pension funds can continue to do this, especially if inflation rises again or the funds do not grow fast enough, is uncertain.

So when you retire, unless your pension is guaranteed to be inflation-proof, you should make some allowance for a fall in its buying power when you retire.

Tax-free lump sums

When you retire, you can normally exchange part of your pension for a tax-free lump sum. With some schemes, especially in the public sector, you automatically get a rather smaller pension and a lump sum – which you may be able to exchange for a pension. You can have up to one and a half times your earnings as a lump sum.

If you have a choice, should you go for a tax-free lump sum or more pension? If the pension is inflation-proofed, be wary of exchanging any of it for a lump sum. But if you don't expect any worthwhile increases in your pension after retirement, it might pay you to exchange as much as possible of your pension for a lump sum, and then buy an annuity (explained in Chapter 22). Your after-tax income from the annuity may be worth more than the pension you are giving up. It would be worth checking, close to the time you retire, what income you'd get from an annuity. The size of the annuity available to you will depend on interest rates at the time. If they are high, you could do very well. If they are low, you could do badly.

The maximum lump sum available, under the Inland Revenue's rules, is now £150,000. While this may sound a lot, it may not be increased in the future, and so it will gradually lose its real value as it is eroded by inflation. In doing your retirement planning, you ought not to assume a lump sum greater than this, whatever you think your earnings at retirement will be.

Additional Voluntary Contributions (AVCs)

All employers' pension schemes allow members to make additional voluntary contributions (AVCs), over and above those they have to make to belong to the scheme, in order to build up extra pension. Some employers offer a range of AVC schemes, and some – but not many – will match the members' extra contributions with some of their own. The most you can put into an employer's pension scheme and AVC scheme altogether is 15 per cent of your total earnings in any one tax year. However much you put in, you cannot have more than the final 2/3rds pension allowed by the Inland Revenue.

You are also entitled to make contributions to another scheme run by a commercial pension provider such as an insurance company, *outside* your employer's scheme. These schemes are called Free Standing AVCs, or FSAVCs for short. The provider must check with your employer that you are not contributing too much (ie more than 15 per cent altogether), and you are still not allowed to go over the 2/3rds limit on pension. You can also use an FSAVC for contracting out of the State scheme, if your employer's scheme is contracted in. This is an alternative to an APP (see p196), but it is less tax efficient because you do not receive tax relief on the 2 per cent National Insurance rebate, if you do it this way.

Anyone who starts an AVC or FSAVC scheme now can use it to provide only a pension, not a lump sum. The rules on this changed in April 1987, and so anyone who was already paying in at that date still has a right to take a lump sum. The rules also changed then to say that *if your scheme allows it*, you can start and stop contributions as you like, reduce the amount or pay in windfall amounts in odd years (before that, once you'd started you were not allowed to stop or reduce the amount). Check whether the rules of your own scheme have been made flexible in this way.

Before deciding whether to make AVCs to your employer's scheme, check what will happen to them. Will they build up solely on your behalf (for instance, via an account in your name with a building society) or will they go into the general pension fund, which might mean that you don't get the full benefit from them? Next find out what benefits you'd get from the AVCs. It could be only a fixed amount of pension at retirement age, which won't go up as time passes. But with some schemes, you may be able to use your extra contributions to buy extra years on your main pension, or add to the rate at which the pension increases, or to provide a pension for your spouse.

Your extra contributions are normally treated in the same way as ordinary ones for tax purposes. That is, you get tax relief on them at your top rate of tax, and they go into a fund which pays no tax on its income or capital gains. But you can't get them out until you draw your main pension, though in many cases you will be able to transfer them, along with your main pension, to another provider. AVCs can be a very good way of saving, particularly for higher rate taxpayers and those close to retirement age. But they are less flexible than other forms of saving.

With an employer's AVC scheme, the employer almost always pays the setting up and administrative costs. In an FSAVC scheme, you do so – and the commission to the broker. But you may still feel you want to take this route. An FSAVC is like a personal pension (described in Chapter 14), but goes on top of your employer's scheme rather than replacing it.

Other benefits from your employer's scheme

An employer's pension scheme may provide other benefits besides a retirement pension, such as:
■ a pension if you are forced to retire early because of ill health; this is usually more generous than the pension if you retire early of your own accord. Or there may be a permanent health insurance scheme, which provides a long term benefit for anyone who is off sick for a long spell, even right up to retirement

- a pension for your husband or wife if you die first
- pensions for children or other dependants you leave on death
- life insurance – which can be as much as four times your earnings – if you die before leaving or retiring.

In some cases, the permanent health insurance and the life assurance will be paid to all employees whether they are a member of the pension scheme or not. More often, employers provide these benefits only for those who are actually in the scheme, although they may provide a reduced rate of life insurance for everyone.

Changing jobs

People who left a final pay pension scheme before retirement used to get a very raw deal. It's now been improved by a change in the law, though it is still a final pay scheme's weak spot, compared to a money purchase scheme (see p206). The position now is:

- if you leave the scheme (whether or not you leave the job) within *two* years of joining, you can have a refund of your contributions. But if you were contracted out of SERPS, part of your contributions will be used to buy you back into SERPS. You'll also pay 20 per cent tax on what's left
- if you leave after longer than that, you can have a **preserved pension**. Your Guaranteed Minimum Pension (explained on p195) is increased either at a fixed rate or in line with inflation, and the state picks up any shortfall. Any pension above that, which you earned before January 1985, does not have to be increased at all – though some schemes do so. Any pension you earned after January 1985 has to be increased by 5 per cent (compound), or the increase in the Retail Prices Index, whichever is less, between the date of leaving and the date of retirement. Your scheme *may* do better than this – for instance by giving 5 per cent even if that is more than the increase in prices
- alternatively, you can take a **transfer value**, worked out according to standard tables, to a new employer's scheme, a Personal Pension, or a 'Section 32' policy. A Section 32 policy is a special type of deferred annuity (roughly, another type of pension) which you buy with a single premium. Other names for it are 'buyout plans' or 'transfer plans'. You have the right to contact any employer whose scheme you left after January 1986, and with which you have a preserved pension, at any date up to a year before retirement, and say that you now want a transfer. You lose the right to a transfer if the employer's scheme is wound up, in which case

the administrators must buy an annuity for you.

A transfer between two public sector jobs is governed by special rules, which mean you are unlikely to lose out. With a transfer to a private sector employer, your new employer will either:
■ agree to pay you extra pension in your retirement; this is normally fixed in £££ and not increased in line with future pay increases; *or*
■ give you a credit of so many years' membership of his scheme. This may not be the full number of years that you had been in the old employer's scheme, because the benefit you get from it may be different. If you are offered credited years, try to negotiate a guarantee of the minimum pension in £££ from the transfer payment. This should not be less than the preserved benefits you're giving up, but will help if you change jobs again.

If you are transferring a pension that has been contracted out of SERPS, then there are special rules. If you are transferring a preserved Guaranteed Minimum Pension (see p195) into a Section 32 policy, it must guarantee to pay at least as much. On the other hand, if you are transferring it into a personal pension plan, then its *money value* is turned into a 'protected right' (see p196) within the personal pension plan. This means that it can only be used in certain ways, and you are giving up the guaranteed benefits the Guaranteed Minimum Pension gave you.

Other sorts of scheme

Money purchase schemes
Few large employers used to run this type of scheme, but now, with the new way of contracting out via a COMP (see p195), a number of new schemes have begun. They operate on the same basis as the personal pension plans covered in Chapter 14.

To summarise, you and your employer pay contributions which are fixed as a percentage of your pay. The bulk of these contributions is invested for you (the rest goes to pay the expenses of the people running the scheme). On retirement, the proceeds are used to buy a pension. How much pension you get depends on how the investments have done, and what level the interest rates are at when you retire.

The Inland Revenue have special rules for 'simplified' money purchase schemes, such as COMPs (see p195). For example, if a scheme limits the total contribution to 17.5

per cent of earnings, on top of the National Insurance rebate, there need be no limit on the amount of benefit. So, in theory, if a simplified scheme did exceptionally well, you might end up with a pension bigger than your earnings (not normally allowed). Only a quarter of the total pension fund accumulated for you, however, may be taken as cash – the rest must be pension. There are also various restrictions on the way a scheme like this is run, and when the benefits may be taken.

With a money purchase scheme, you don't lose out on leaving your job; the fund simply continues to receive interest and dividends on the amount already in there, though no more will be paid in. You could transfer it to a new employer's scheme or a personal pension plan, if you felt that they were going to produce a better return on your investment than the current managers. But you would need to look carefully to see how much you would lose by leaving the existing scheme, especially if you have been in it for only a few years.

Though they have existed for many years, more employers are now introducing 'hybrid' schemes, which are either final pay schemes with a guarantee that you will not do worse than on a money purchase basis with a given level of contributions, or money purchase with a guarantee of at least a certain growth rate on the final pay basis. If the guarantees are at a reasonable level, these hybrid schemes can give you the best of both worlds. They protect the pensions of early leavers (still the weak spot for final pay schemes), and provide protection against inflation, in line with increases in earnings, for those who stay to claim their pensions.

Average pay schemes

With these, your pension is based on your pay in each year you belong to the scheme. There is usually a graded scale of earnings. For each year that your pay is in a particular earnings band, you get a fixed amount of pension. As you move up the earnings scale, the amount earned in pension will rise, as will any contributions you pay. The yearly pension you're eventually paid will be the total of all the little bits of yearly pension you've earned in each band, so there is no protection against inflation in these schemes.

For example, for each year your earnings are between £3,000 and £4,000, you may get £50 in pension a year. For each year your earnings are £4,000 a year, you may get £60 a year.

Revalued average schemes

These work in the same way that SERPS does (explained on p191). Your earnings are revalued to take account of the rise in earnings (or sometimes only prices) between the date when you earned them and the date when you retire. Then they are averaged and a fraction given, depending on the rate at which the pension builds up, for each year you are in the scheme.

Flat rate schemes

Flat rate schemes provide a fixed amount of pension – perhaps £5 a year – for each year's membership of the scheme.

Verdict: employer's scheme or personal pension plan?

If you are in a good employer's scheme that is based on final pay and *contracted out* of SERPS, you should think very seriously before deciding to leave and go it alone with a personal pension plan. It would mean that you were giving up the guarantees made by your employer about the level of retirement benefits. Your pension will be less certain, because it is not based on final pay, and it will depend instead on two other uncertain things; how well your money has been invested up to your retirement date, and interest rates at that time. A sudden change in the fortunes of the stock market – like the crash in share values in October 1987 – or a drop in the interest rates which dictate annuity rates, could mean a big change in your pension. (Of course all this applies also to money purchase schemes – the new COMPs – as well as to personal pension plans.)

It's likely that if you go outside the scheme, your employer will say that you must also provide death in service benefits and disability benefits for yourself. Find out about this before taking any decision, and shop around to compare the costs; if you are over a certain age, you may well find that replacing them costs more than your contribution to the employer's scheme as a whole.

Before taking any decision, also find out whether the employer will allow you to rejoin the pension scheme if you change your mind. In many cases, they allow you 'one mistake' but say that if you leave again, you stay out. Others put an upper limit on the ages at which people will be allowed to join, say, age 45. Still others say that if you leave, you will be out for good.

It's very unlikely that an employer will contribute to a personal pension plan, unless you are in a sufficiently senior position to bargain for special treatment. As many employers contribute twice as much as the members to their pension scheme, this means that only the very young or very lucky will have more pension from a personal pension plan than from an employer's scheme.

For a personal pension plan, there will be administrative and commission charges, which the employer normally pays for his or her own scheme. In any case, the administrative charges are likely to be higher for a personal pension plan than for an employer's scheme, because there won't be the same 'economies of scale' in running the scheme. All this means that if you are in a personal pension plan for only a short time, it is likely to be poor value, because the administrative charges will be deducted at the beginning of the policy.

If the pension plan is (or includes) a contracted out APP, the DHSS 'clearing house' system, explained on p197, may mean that there is considerable delay in passing on your contributions – whereas with an employer's scheme the money goes in immediately.

On the other hand, the attraction of a personal pension plan is that there is no loss on changing jobs. There is also no limit on benefits, only on contributions (as explained in the next chapter). So full advantage can be gained from favourable investment conditions. In an employer's pension scheme, the employer tends to reap the benefit in terms of lower contributions. You also have the freedom to choose who will provide the pension – though you will not have any influence over the investments they put your money in.

Overall, unless you are under 30 or so, intend to move jobs rapidly, *and* have no dependants, a reasonable employer's scheme, based on final earnings, is likely to be the best for you. If you take out a personal pension plan in the early years of your working life, you ought to aim to move back into an employer's scheme in your 30s, or when you get married. If you want to have your own visible pension 'pot' you can do this by setting up a FSAVC scheme (explained on p203) in addition – so taking out a two-way bet.

If your employer's scheme is *contracted in*, then as a younger person you may want to contract out of SERPS. Again, you can do this with an FSAVC or an APP (see p196), without needing to leave the employer's scheme.

If the employer runs a money purchase scheme, you may feel that you could do better with your own money purchase personal pension plan. But find out how much the employer himself is putting in to the scheme, and what administrative charges (if any) are being deducted. Doing your own

Employer's scheme or personal pension (or COMP)?

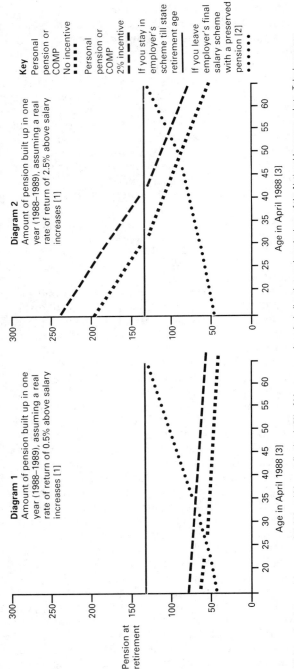

Key

Personal pension or COMP
No incentive ▪▪▪▪▪

Personal pension or COMP
2% incentive ▬ ▬ ▬

If you stay in employer's scheme till state retirement age ———

If you leave employer's final salary scheme with a preserved pension [2] •••••••

Diagram 1
Amount of pension built up in one year (1988–1989), assuming a real rate of return of 0.5% above salary increases [1]

Age in April 1988 [3]

Pension at retirement

Diagram 2
Amount of pension built up in one year (1988–1989), assuming a real rate of return of 2.5% above salary increases [1]

Age in April 1988 [3]

[1] Assuming that employee earns £10,000 and his contribution is 5% of his gross earnings, including the employee's share of the National Insurance rebate. Take-home pay would be the same whichever option was chosen. It is assumed that 0.6% of earnings above the Lower Earnings Limit (see p191) is going towards life insurance providing a lump sum out of once times earnings. The figures don't make any assumptions about pay increases between now and retirement.
[2] Assuming that you leave in April 1989, with a preserved pension increasing by 5% for each year it is preserved.
[3] Graphs show figures for men, but same principles apply for women.
Source: Bacon and Woodrow

thing is likely to mean paying your own charges as well. And with an employer's COMP scheme, the money goes straight in each month when the payroll calculations are done. With a personal pension, the National Insurance rebate is held back by the DHSS until after the end of the tax year. It does not start earning interest or dividends until it reaches the personal pension plan provider.

The Diagrams opposite show how the amount of pension you would get at retirement is affected by staying in an employer's final salary scheme or leaving to take a personal plan. It compares the amount of pension that would build up in one year (1988–89), depending on your age and which option you choose. Once again, it shows figures for a man – but the same principles apply for women.

14

PERSONAL PENSION PLANS

Personal pension plans are a type of pension scheme for individuals, provided by banks, building societies, unit trusts, and insurance companies for anyone – employed or self-employed – who is not in an employer's contracted out pension scheme. A special type, the Appropriate Personal Pension (APP) allows you to contract out of the State Earnings Related Pension Scheme (SERPS), as explained in Chapter 13.

If you have been in an employer's scheme in the past, you can transfer the money already built up in that scheme into a personal pension plan. Alternatively, you can set up a 'Section 32' policy when you change jobs, as explained on p205. Although transfers and 'Section 32' policies come under different rules from personal pension plans, the investment methods, and the sort of points to look out for, will be much the same. So although this chapter does not refer to transfers or 'Section 32' policies as such, read it if you are thinking of taking one out.

You take out a personal pension plan by paying a premium (or agreeing to pay a series of premiums) to whichever pension provider you've chosen. They invest the money and, when you retire, they pay you a tax-free lump sum and/or a pension for life – see Diagram overleaf.

For example, if you started paying £1,000 a year into a scheme at age 40, you might build up a fund of around £208,000 from age 65. Out of this you could have a pension of £23,000 a year. Or you could take a lump sum of a quarter of the fund, £52,000 and a pension of around £15,000 a year.

What are the advantages?

Pension schemes get much more generous tax treatment than any other investment. You get tax relief on your premiums, provided you keep within certain limits, at the

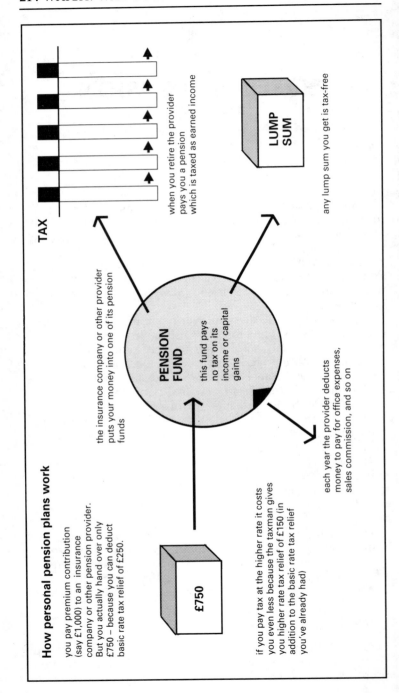

How personal pension plans work

you pay premium contribution (say £1,000) to an insurance company or other pension provider. But you actually hand over only £750 – because you can deduct basic rate tax relief of £250.

if you pay tax at the higher rate it costs you even less because the taxman gives you higher rate tax relief of £150 (in addition to the basic rate tax relief you've already had)

£750

the insurance company or other provider puts your money into one of its pension funds

PENSION FUND

this fund pays no tax on its income or capital gains

each year the provider deducts money to pay for office expenses, sales commission, and so on

TAX

when you retire the provider pays you a pension which is taxed as earned income

LUMP SUM

any lump sum you get is tax-free

highest rate of tax you pay. So if you paid tax at the basic rate of 25 per cent, the £1,000 premiums in the example above would cost you only £750, or £600 if you paid tax at 40 per cent. The provider does not pay tax on the profits from investing your money and any lump sum you get is tax-free. This means that you are likely to get a higher income, after tax, from a pension scheme than from a comparable investment in , say, an investment-type life insurance policy with which you buy an immediate annuity at age 65.

Whether any pension scheme turns out to be a good investment *for you* depends mainly on how long you live. If you live to a ripe old age you get much better value than if you die shortly after retiring. But what you're paying for is the certainty of having a regular income as long as you live.

What are the disadvantages?

Once you've handed your money over you can't normally start to get it back until the retirement age written into your plan – which can't be younger than 50. Even when you reach retirement age, you can take only a limited amount as a lump sum (the rest has to be paid as pension). So if you decide later that another form of investment would give you a better return, you won't normally be able to switch. However you can stop your payments, and you can often borrow money from the provider on the strength of the money already in your plan.

All this means that you shouldn't put money that you are likely to need in an emergency into any sort of pension scheme. But you should start paying in as young as possible, because the contributions you make when young have much longer to build up compound interest.

Another disadvantage is inflation. Personal pensions are all based on the *money purchase* principle, which means that the size of your pension depends on the investment returns available over the whole time when you put in the contributions, and the time you convert the total invest-ment into a pension. A few years of high inflation can cut into this very substantially.

Suppose you're aged 40 now, planning to retire at 65, and the pension provider predicts that your contributions will grow enough to provide a pension of £15,000 a year for you. This may sound substantial as a pension today, but if inflation averaged even 3 per cent over the 25 years you had been saving, your pension would be worth only about £7,170 (in today's buying power) in the year you retired.

With 9 per cent inflation, it would be down to £1,740 – and by the time you reached 75, it would be worth only £735. So if you are some way from retirement, the pension you'll need is going to be much higher than would seem sufficient now. We tell you how you can allow for inflation on p227.

Finally, a *money purchase* policy will give a lower pension to a woman, for the same level of contribution, than to a man retiring at the same age. This is because she can expect to live longer than he can, so the same amount of money has to be spread over a larger number of payments.

The exception here is the *Appropriate* Personal Pension (explained on p223), where the annuity rates which determine how much pension you get have to be 'unisex' at the same age – that is, the same for men and women.

Who qualifies?

Since 1 July 1988, anyone has been able to buy a personal pension plan, so long as they are not in an employer's contracted out pension scheme. This includes the self-employed, those whose employer has no pension scheme, and those whose employer has a scheme which they have decided not to join, or to leave. You are also eligible for a personal pension if your employer runs a scheme which gives simply death and dependant's benefits, without a pension for you. Even if you *are* in an employer's pension scheme which is not contracted out you can now take out what's called an Appropriate Personal Pension (explained in Chapter 13), though the payments put in for you are limited to those from the DHSS (see p224).

People in an employer's contracted out pension scheme are not eligible for a personal pension plan as such – but they can buy very similar polices under the arrangements for Free-Standing Additional Voluntary Contributions (FSAVCS) explained in Chapter 13. These go on top of the employer's scheme, and have different contribution and benefit limits, but are in fact much the same policies wrapped in a different package. FSAVCs can also be used for contracting out independently, if your employer's scheme is contracted in.

Finally, if you are in an employer's scheme for your main employment, but have some freelance earnings, or a second job from which you don't get a retirement pension, you can have a personal pension based on the earnings from these *non-pensionable* employments, while still remaining in your main employer's scheme.

What happened to the old system?

Until July 1988, only self-employed people and those not in an employer's scheme could buy personal pensions, in the form of policies called 'Section 226' schemes or 'Self-Employed Retirement Annuities'. No more of these policies have been sold since 1 July 1988, but if you already have such a scheme, you are allowed to keep it in force and increase your payments to it, until you retire or decide you want to change it.

With the old types of policy, the pension limits were less flexible than with new personal pension plans – in particular, you could not normally have a retirement age of below 60 – but on the other hand the lump sum available was probably larger than under the new arrangements. So if you already have one or more of these policies, it is worth maintaining it in its present form, and switching only at or near retirement date, if it looks then as if it is worthwhile.

When to start paying for a personal pension

The younger you are when you make contributions to a money purchase scheme, the longer they have to gather interest and dividends. If you paid the same amount in premiums each year, starting just one year earlier could increase the pension you get by over 10 per cent.

When can you start receiving the pension?

Generally, at any time between the ages of 50 and 75, depending on the age which you specify when you take out the plan. People in certain occupations can retire earlier, and you may also be able to do so if you become too ill to carry on working – though the pension payable will be at a very much reduced rate. If you have several plans, you can start receiving the benefits from each at different times. You don't have to stop working to do so. (We use the word *retire* in this chapter as shorthand for *start receiving the benefits of the plan* regardless of whether or not you actually stop work at the time.)

The types of plan

There are several hundred different personal pension plans available, but hardly any two are the same. The main

variations are in:
- who is providing the scheme
- how the pension you're entitled to is worked out
- how often you pay premiums.

Who is providing the scheme?

Pensions business was, until July 1988, strictly the province of the insurance companies. Even if you thought you were buying a policy from someone else like a building society, the small print would have revealed that they were either in partnership with an insurance company, or running the scheme through an insurance subsidiary.

But in July 1988 this changed and banks, building societies, unit trusts, and the larger friendly societies were all allowed in on the act. When the pension starts to be paid, however, the business must revert to an insurance company, because only they are legally allowed to provide the annuities which are used to provide the pension payments.

So if you have a plan with one of the other providers, you will be asked to choose an insurance company from which to buy the pension. This is called the 'open market option'. (If you have an Appropriate Personal Pension, you will always have the right to do this in any case.)

How your pension is worked out

The various pension providers offer benefits calculated in different ways, depending on how your pension plan is worded.

A **deferred annuity** plan talks in terms of the pension you will get from a certain age. This will be based on the amount you've paid into the scheme. Taking the example on p213, if you pay in £1,000 for 25 years from age 40, the provider might quote you a pension of £23,000 a year if you retire at 65.

A **cash-funded** plan (much more common) talks in terms of the amount of money that accumulates for you to buy your pension with. For example, the plan may say that if you paid in the same amounts as in the example above, a cash fund of £208,000 would have accumulated for you by the age of 65.

When you retire, the cash is used to buy an immediate annuity which would pay you an income for life. The income you get will depend on the company's annuity rate for your age and sex when you retire. This will specify how much pension you get for each £ in your fund. So for example, if annuity rates at the time you retired were at the level which applied in March 1988, your pension would be, say, 14 per cent for a 65 year old man. So your pension might be 14 per cent of your cash fund of £208,000, which is £29,120. But if annuity rates were lower, your pension – for the rest of your life – would be correspondingly lower.

Your choice of investment

Below are the details of four main types of plan. For which type to choose, see p225.

Non-profit

Your premiums go into the provider's pension fund, to be invested as they see fit. It will be invested mainly in shares, British Government stocks, loans and property. Whatever happens to these investments, the amount of pension you get is guaranteed by the company at the outset. It won't be more or less.

These guaranteed pensions are low, because the providers must feel certain they can pay out the agreed amounts, whatever happens to the investments and interest rates in the meantime.

With-profits

The premiums are invested in the provider's fund in the same way as for a non-profit plan. They guarantee from the outset the minimum pension it will pay you (if the policy is a deferred annuity one) or the minimum amount of money you'll have with which to buy an annuity (if it is cash funded). These minimum amounts are at first even lower than those from non-profit policies. But as the provider makes profits on its investments, it announces increases in the minimum pension (or fund) you're guaranteed at retirement. These are called **reversionary bonuses**, and once they've been announced – usually every year – they cannot be taken away.

With most policies, a one-off **terminal bonus** can be added at the time you retire. You have no idea how much this will be until that time arrives. As a result of these bonuses, you're likely to end up with a pension or cash fund which is considerably higher than you'd have got from a non-profit policy.

Unit-linked

Your premiums buy units in one or more of a number of funds offered by the insurance company. The most common types of fund are:

■ property funds – which invest in office blocks, factories, shops and so on

■ equity funds – which invest in shares, directly or through unit trusts

■ fixed-interest funds – which invest in British Government stocks, company loan stocks, and other things which pay out a fixed income

■ cash funds, which invest in bank deposit accounts, short term loans to local authorities and other investments which pay out rates of return which vary along with interest rates in general

■ managed funds – which invest in a mixture of the things listed above, in proportions decided by the investment managers.

Each fund is divided into a number of units. The price of each is, approximately, the value of the investments in the fund divided by the number of units that have been issued. So the unit price goes up and down as the value of the investments in the fund fluctuates. With *cash* funds, most companies guarantee that the price of units won't go down.

With most providers there's a choice of funds to invest in, and you can switch from one to another. This could prove useful if you want to move your money around in the hope of getting the best return. But if you time things wrongly, you could end up doing rather badly. There's often a charge for switching — perhaps 0.5 per cent of the amount you're moving – if you switch more often than, say, once a year.

Nearly all unit-linked policies are cash funded, so the amount of pension also depends on annuity rates at the time you start taking the benefits. If both the value of your units and annuity rates themselves are low at the time you retire – as they were for instance after the stock market crash in October 1987 – you could find yourself having to make do with a low income, or putting off your retirement in the hope that things will improve.

A few unit-linked policies guarantee a minimum cash fund or a minimum annuity rate, but these guarantees tend to be at a pretty low level.

Deposit administration
These are provided particularly by the banks and building societies, though the other providers also offer them in some cases.

They work rather like a bank deposit account. Your premiums are put into an account with the provider, and interest is added from time to time. The interest rate will vary with the general level of interest rates, but there may be a guaranteed minimum amount, sometimes linked to the mortgage rate. The value of your fund, in £££, can't go down. With some providers you can switch between deposit administration and unit-linked policies. It is often sensible to switch your pension savings into this type of fund as you near retirement, if you think that your unit-linked fund might go down in value.

All deposit administration schemes are cash-funded, and a few guarantee a minimum amount of cash fund you'll have at retirement. The amount of pension will depend on annuity rates at the time you retire – though many policies do guarantee a minimum annuity rate at retirement.

How often you pay premiums

Most companies offer both regular- and single-premium policies. With a regular-premium policy you agree to make payments every month, quarter, half-year or year. With most providers, the terms you get are decided when you first take out the plan, and apply to all your regular premiums. So if you take out a policy that is cash funded, and with a certain level of charges, this will apply for as long as the plan lasts.

With a single-premium policy, you pay in a lump sum which remains invested until you retire. The terms depend on when you pay the premium. So they could be worse, or better, than for a regular premium policy running at the same time. The distinction between single- and regular-premium policies is not always clear cut. For example, having paid in your first premium, a scheme may allow you to make any number of payments of almost any amount, at any time in the future. And with all schemes you can stop paying altogether at any time – as explained on p228.

Single premium policies allow you to decide with no constraints what you want to pay, and when. You also have the chance to shop around each time for the company offering the best terms.

There is little point in going for a regular-premium policy that does *not* guarantee that the terms you get each year are the ones laid down at the outset – you'd be better off with single-premium policies. But regular premiums do provide the discipline of asking you to pay money over regularly.

You may do best to go for a mixture of single premium and regular premium policies. At retirement you can use the open market option (see p218) to transfer the value of all your policies to the company offering the best annuity rates.

Borrowing back from the provider

Many schemes include what's called a *loan-back* facility, so that you can borrow from the provider up to the amount you've got in the pension fund. There is a minimum amount – usually £5,000 – and you need to be able to offer security such as your house, business premises, or shares. With some providers you have to be paying a minimum regular premium.

When you take a loan, part of the pension fund equal to the amount you've borrowed ceases to be unit-linked or have bonuses added to it. Instead you pay interest on the loan to the provider, which deducts its charges and passes on the balance to the pension fund. So you are effectively paying interest to yourself. You can repay the loan when you like – perhaps from selling your business when you retire, or out of the tax-free lump sum you get on retirement if this is large enough.

There may be little advantage in borrowing in this way rather than, say, getting a loan from a bank. The bank's interest rates may be more competitive than those charged by the provider. But the facility could be useful if you wanted to borrow at a time when credit was difficult to obtain (though it you are turned down by a bank because you are not creditworthy, you are also quite likely to be turned down by the pension provider).

Pension mortgages

It is also possible to arrange to link your pension and your mortgage. Legally, there is no link, because you are not allowed to 'assign' your pension benefit – that is, use it as security for a loan. Instead, what happens is that you take out an interest-only mortgage, and receive tax relief on the repayments as normal. You also pay your pension scheme contributions, receiving tax relief on them. At retirement date, you use your tax-free lump sum to pay off the capital on the mortgage. A legal link is unnecessary – as the bank or building society holding the mortgage can foreclose on your house if you do not pay them back.

Pension mortgages like this are now increasingly available on the strength of employers' schemes as well. A number of them have linked up with banks and building societies to enable them to offer them. So although the offer of a pension mortgage will often be made to tempt people into a personal pension plan, this is not a sufficient reason for leaving any employer's scheme for a personal pension.

Pension mortgages also have some disadvantages. They can tie you to one provider, who may not in fact offer the best rates or the best returns. They can mean that you *have* to take the pension at a fixed date, though it may be inconvenient to do so for other reasons. You commit yourself many years ahead to a particular use for your tax-free lump sum, though when it comes to it there may be other things you would prefer to spend the money on.

You may find that having a pension mortgage creates problems if later on you join an employer who has a good pension scheme. You will only be able to join that if you stop paying in to the personal pension plan. It should usually be possible to make a new arrangement for paying off the mortgage, however, so you are not locked in to the personal pension altogether.

There will also be difficulties in keeping up payments to the pension scheme if you become unemployed, and so have no earnings from which to pay. You can buy insurance to cover this, though at extra cost. With a mortgage linked to the employer's scheme, there is the added problem of re-arranging the scheme if you leave that employment – though again, this will become easier if pension mortgages become more common.

Above all, taking a pension mortgage could reduce your income in retirement. If you're using part of your pension fund to repay a mortgage, there will be less available to provide a pension for you.

So, although the tax advantages are considerable, they *don't* necessarily outweigh the disadvantages. Think about these carefully before deciding to take out a pension mortgage.

Appropriate Personal Pensions

These are the pension policies, approved by the Occupational Pensions Board, which are contracted out of the State Earnings Related Pension Scheme (SERPS) and therefore *replace* the SERPS benefit for the years in which they run. How they work was explained on p196. Only employees can take these out – the self-employed are not in SERPS to start with.

You cannot have more than one Appropriate Personal Pension (APP) in any one tax year, but you can pay additional contributions to it and add as many ordinary personal pension plans on top as you like. In practice, if you took out only an APP policy you would get a very poor and inflexible pension – so it is not recommended, however young you are.

You would also forego the chance of a lump sum at retirement, or of retiring at any age earlier than state retirement age. In most cases, the providers will sell an APP with the option of paying extra contributions as one package, and will be reluctant to let you buy only the most basic APP on its own.

The contributions to an APP are made up of:

■ the National Insurance rebate – 5.8 per cent on your earnings between the lower and upper earnings limits (see p191) for the years up to 1993, then probably a lower figure. Of this 5.8 per cent, 2 per cent comes from your National Insurance contributions, and 3.8 per cent from your employer's contributions

■ the 2 per cent 'incentive' for the years up to 1993, for people who have not already been in their current employer's contracted out scheme for at least two years before they took out the personal pension plan; and

■ tax relief on your rebate (2 per cent) which comes to another 0.67 per cent of your earnings.

These contributions are paid over by the DHSS after the end of the tax year, when they have sorted out the paperwork. They come to just over 8 per cent in all, and are not counted by the Inland Revenue against their limits for tax relief, explained on p236.

For whether or not an APP would be a sensible choice for you, see p197.

What contributions to an Additional Personal Pension buy you

You can choose to contribute:
Extra payments, up to 17.5% of earnings
(more if aged over 50)

Other benefits (death in service, lump sum on retirement, chance to retire earlier than state retirement age)

Protected rights to pension and spouse's pension

DHSS contributes:
5.8% National Insurance rebate +
2% incentive + tax relief

Planning your pension

Which type of policy?

Non-profit policies are the only ones where you know from the start how much pension (or cash fund) you'll get. We don't recommend them, except possibly if you are very close to retirement and want to know exactly where you stand.

Deposit administration policies and the cash funds of unit-linked policies are very dependent on levels of interest rates. So they look good when interest rates are high, but less good when they are lower. Because the value of your fund or the price of your units (in £££) can't go down, these policies are also useful for people nearing retirement who want to make sure they don't lose any money. If you have a unit-linked policy, switching into the cash fund or a deposit administration scheme can be useful if you're worried about units going down in value. But the pension will still be dependent on annuity rates when you retire.

For the longer term, the choice is between with-profits and unit-linked policies. With-profits schemes are the less risky. Although the guaranteed pension or cash fund is initially low, it is reasonably certain to be increased steadily over the period to retirement. But many insurance companies have been piling a large proportion of the 'profits' into the terminal bonus, which is not guaranteed and can be held static or cut, and even future rates of reversionary bonus can be reduced if a company falls on hard times.

If you go for a deferred annuity scheme, your pension will not suffer if annuity rates are low at the time you retire (though some companies will increase your pension if annuity rates are high). With unit-linked policies (apart from the small number of index-linked ones available), the return is much more dependent on *when* you make your payments and *when* you start taking the benefits. While you may do very well with a unit-linked policy, you could do rather badly.

One good compromise would be to take out a regular-premium with-profits policy for an amount you can fairly easily afford, at as young an age as possible – say, age 30. It is probably worth going for a policy which allows you to increase the premiums on guaranteed terms in future years. But in years in which you can afford to pay a substantial extra amount, take out a single-premium policy, perhaps a unit-linked one. As time passes, in order to protect your pension from inflation you would need to take out further policies, which would help spread the risks, or to pay more into your existing policies.

This strategy should make sure that you have enough pension from with-profits policies whenever you want to retire. So you'll then be in a better position to choose a good time for taking the benefits of the unit-linked policies, when the prices of the units or annuity rates (or both) are high. Alternatively, in the few years before you intend to retire, switch into a cash fund or a deposit administration fund. You could do this when the price of the units reach high levels or you think they are going to go down.

How much to pay in

With regular premium policies, most companies set a minimum regular premium of say, £250 a year or £25 a month. The minimum for a single-premium policy could be £500 or £1,000, but can be a good deal higher for a scheme set up and specially tailored for senior people on high salaries. These are called 'executive plans'.

The maximum you can pay is the maximum amount you can get tax relief on, explained on p236.

Organisations selling pension plans give very accurate looking and impressive figures showing the pension you'd get from each £ you pay from a certain age. But these quotations are only estimates, based on set assumptions about future investment returns laid down under the Financial Services Act. The estimates take no account of inflation, which can be devastating over long periods of time.

For example, if you started paying £500 a year into a regular premium policy at age 35, you might imagine yourself living in comfort on the £17,000 a year the insurance company quotes you. But if inflation averaged 5 per cent over the rest of your working life, the buying power of this pension at age 65 would be under £4,000 a year. Ten years after retirement it would be worth only about £2,400 a year, if inflation continued at 5 per cent.

This makes it extremely difficult to know how much you should be paying in to your pension. But you should consider the following points:

■ how much income you'll have after retirement from other sources, such as state retirement pension, from selling your business, or from part-time work

■ the age you intend to retire at – the older this is, the more pension you'll get for each £ you've paid in

■ inflation after retirement. If you live to age 65, you can expect to live to age 78 on average if you're a man, 82 on average if you're a woman. You'll still want your pension to have reasonable purchasing power in your old age, so your pension in the first year of retirement will need to be much higher in £££ than you'd think. Alternatively you could give up some pension in the early years of retirement in order to have a pension which increases each year – see p234

■ inflation between now and retirement. Over such a long period of time, inflation can make mincemeat of your pension.

You can use the Table below to work out how many £ pension you'll need for various rates of inflation. For example, if you think you'll need a pension of £10,000 a year in today's money, in 30 years' time, and you reckon inflation will average 5 per cent over that time, you'll need to get £10,000 x 4.3 = £43,000 a year from the scheme to achieve this.

yearly rate of inflation	£££ you'd need to get, for each £ (in today's buying power) of pension you want:				
	in 10yrs	in 20yrs	in 30yrs	in 40yrs	in 50yrs
5%	1.6	2.7	4.3	7	11
10%	2.6	6.7	17	45	117
15%	4.0	16	66	268	1,084
20%	6.2	38	237	1,470	9,100

To take account of inflation both before and after retirement, use the number of years up to your 70th or 75th birthday, say, even if you intend to retire younger than that.

You may well find that you cannot possibly afford the premiums for a pension of the amount you've worked out. Your best approach may be to pay up to your limit for tax relief each year (see p236) – or, if you are an employee, to try to persuade your employer to put something in also. But if you're close to retirement, it may be impossible to achieve anything like enough pension, even if you do this.

When to start

If you are aiming at a pension at age 65 of two-thirds of your final pay (which is the most that someone in an employer's scheme would be allowed to have) you'll need to pay the full percentage of earnings allowed by the Inland Revenue each year from about age 37 onwards to achieve this.

But you'd be unwise to leave starting a scheme as late as this. There may be years when you can afford to pay only a small amount in premiums; you may decide to use some of the premiums qualifying for tax relief to get life insurance or a pension for your dependants; you may need to retire before 65, perhaps because of ill-health; inflation may be very high in the first few years of your retirement. So, unless you are confident you would have substantial income from elsewhere, you should certainly start paying for your pension by your early 30s.

If you stop paying

You may need to stop paying into a regular-premium policy, perhaps because you have no qualifying earnings in a tax year, or find yourself short of cash. Most providers will let you miss one or two payments, but there is usually a limit at which the policy has to be made 'paid up'. This means that your money remains invested in the fund, and you'll get a pension when you retire, though it will be smaller than if you had kept paying. Check with the provider how they'd work out the pension.

You can often reinstate a policy within a year or so of it's being made paid up. With with-profits policies, you'll normally have to pay all the premiums you've missed and perhaps a fee as well. But this could be worth doing if the guarantees on your old policies are better than they would be on a new one, or if the old policy is a Section 226 scheme with the higher level of lump sum available. Make sure you'll qualify for tax relief on the made-up premiums – see p237.

When you plan to retire

You must start to take the benefits from a personal pension plan some time between your 50th and 75th birthday, unless your job is recognised as having a lower retirement age. There are now only a few of these, such as various groups of sportsmen and athletes with retirement ages of 35 or 40. Under the older, Section 226 policies, the minimum retirement age was 60, so there was a far longer list of exceptions.

If you have Section 226 policies and want to retire at an age between 50 and 60, it will be possible to alter them into personal pension plans, but you will lose the right to the greater lump sum if you do so.

There's no need to stop working in order to draw your pension and lump sum.

If you become too ill to work before the lowest age at which you can retire, you can start taking the benefits then, but the amount will be much reduced. This is because you'll have been paying in for a shorter period and will expect to draw out for longer.

With some policies, you have to say at the outset when you intend to retire, though you can change your mind later. Other policies have a standard retirement age, but you can still retire when you like within the age range allowed. If you don't know when you'll want to retire, check that you won't lose out by retiring earlier or later than the date you name.

Phasing your retirement

You may not want to stop work suddenly but would rather slide out gradually over a period of years. If so, you may want to supplement your earnings over a number of years by drawing a small amount of pension, increasing year by year until you draw your full pension when you've stopped working altogether.

You could do this by having several policies and taking the benefits from each at a different time. Or you could invest with companies which write their policies as a series of separate units, each of which can start paying out at a different time. But check that this doesn't mean you are paying too much in administration charges.

If you die before retirement

With most policies, a lump sum will be paid to your heirs if you die before you have started taking the policy benefits. With some policies you have a choice about how much will be paid out – for example, whether they just give you back the premiums you've paid, or add interest to them.

The more you want paid out on your death, the less pension you'll get. It could be better to get the biggest pension you can and arrange extra life insurance separately (see Box overleaf) – though you no longer get tax relief on life insurance premiums unless they are paid as part of your pension contributions. To weigh up which is best for you, ask the insurance company (or other provider) to give you illustrations of the costs of both options.

A few providers will pay out a pension for a dependant instead of a lump sum. But the dependant might be able to get a better income by getting the lump sum and investing it.

See p235 for how personal pensions can be used to provide for dependants if you die after retirement.

Additional life insurance

If you qualify for a personal pension plan, you'll be able to use part of your contributions – up to 5 per cent – to buy life insurance. This is particularly valuable now that the premium subsidy has been abolished on ordinary life insurance policies.

You don't have to get the life assurance from the same provider whose personal pension plan you are paying into — though they may give you a discount. Shop around for a discount, or get a broker to do so for you.

For more on the important subject of life insurance for your family, see p315.

Choosing a policy

With so many different types of organisation now selling pensions, there are likely to be several hundred personal pension plans to choose from. Choosing among them isn't easy and, if this is going to be your main way of saving for retirement, it might be sensible to spread your investment over more than one plan – though each extra scheme you take out means an extra administration charge. Use the Checklist in the Box opposite to sort out the features you want in each plan.

To find out for yourself which policies offer which features, get hold of the most recent edition of the *Personal Pensions Handbook* published by FTBI (ask if your library has a copy). This gives useful comparative details on most plans. There are other guides and magazines available too.

You'll then want to try to find a company which will give you a better-than-average return on your investment. For policies other than non-profit ones, there's no sure way of knowing how each company will perform in the future.

With *with-profits* policies you could check on what pension you'd get from different companies if their current bonus rates were maintained, and on how they've done in the past. However, there's no guarantee that companies that have done well in the past will continue to do well in the future. The book mentioned above provides these figures in a broadly comparable way.

With unit-linked and deposit administration schemes, the past is, again, little guide to the future, and neither are current growth rates. The assumptions about future growth have been standardised to some extent by the regulatory

Pension Checklist

THE POLICY   **YOUR CHOICE**
deferred annuity or cash funded

non-profit, with-profits, unit-linked or
deposit administration

loan-back facility

pension mortgage

single-premium or regular-premium

if regular-premium:
■ do you want terms for future
premiums guaranteed at the outset?
■ do you want to be able to vary the
premiums?
■ do you need a policy that is flexible
if you stop paying?

YOUR PREMIUMS
if single-premium, amount (before tax
relief) you'd like to pay in

if regular-premium, yearly amount
(before tax relief) you can
commit yourself to

RETIREMENT
age at which you expect to retire

do you want to be able to phase retirement but still take out just one policy?

do you want to contract out via an APP?

IN CASE YOU DIE BEFORE RETIREMENT
be sure to find out what would be paid, and consider taking out
extra protection-only life assurance

authorities, but probably the most important question is the
charges made. These are worked out in complicated and
varying ways. It may be best to go for a company that keeps
its charges down – though you can't be sure that it will
continue to do so in the future. The *Personal Pensions*

Handbook gives more-or-less comparable figures for the different plans with standard assumptions about future growth.

If you get an insurance adviser to do the work for you, bear in mind that he or she is unlikely to steer you towards a policy which pays no commission. So check what commission is being given. The rule is that they must give you details of any commission they get if it is not in line with an industry agreement (see p75). If it is in line with the industry agreement, they can tell you this, and you can get details by writing to the Life Assurance and Unit Trust Regulatory Organisation (LAUTRO) – their address is on p80. However, from 1 January 1990 advisers must tell you the amount of commission automatically.

The clearer your own ideas of what you want, before you visit an adviser, the less likely you are to be persuaded by sales talk to buy something you don't want. You may also increase your chances of getting good advice if you go to more than one adviser.

The security of your policy

Insurance companies are covered by the Policyholders' Protection Act. If the company fails, then the Policyholders' Protection Board – set up by the Government to administer the Act – has to try to get another company to take on the policy. Provided you carry on paying the premiums due, the Act guarantees that you'll get at least 90 per cent of the amounts guaranteed at the time the company went bust – unless the Board considers these amounts to be excessive.

But you get no guarantees of future bonuses from the new company that takes over your policy. So you could lose quite a lot if your company goes bust, and it's prudent to stick with a large, well-established company.

Very few insurance companies do go bust. Sometimes they get taken over instead, and sometimes if they get into financial trouble they have to cut their bonus rates. In those cases, you won't lose the guarantees – but the rate of growth on the policies will be slower than you had expected.

Other pension providers are covered by compensation funds (though in some cases these cover smaller amounts than the Policyholders' Protection Act), and they have to abide by rules laid down by the Financial Services Act and the laws for banks and building societies – see Chapter 5. In every case, therefore, you won't lose the minimum guaranteed amounts – but you could lose the rest.

Your choices at retirement

When to retire

Once you reach an age at which you can start taking the benefits under your plan (between 50 and 75 for a new personal pension plan, or between 60 and 75 for a Section 226 scheme), you can write to the provider at any time and tell them you want to start taking the benefits of your policy.

Shopping around for a higher pension

With all appropriate personal pensions and nearly all personal pension plans, you don't have to take your pension from the providers you have been saving with. When you retire, you can shop around to see if you can get a better deal for the money that's built up for you. This is called the *open market option*.

If you want to do this, you first have to find out the value of your cash fund. If the policy is a deferred annuity, the provider will have to work out (using what is called its *commutation* rate) the number of £££ of fund you're allocated for the pension you're entitled to. You then compare the benefits you would have got from this provider with the benefits you could get if you switched this amount to someone else. If, over the years, you've taken out a number of different plans, you could transfer them all at retirement to the insurance company offering the best package of benefits.

With some providers, the cash fund you can transfer is slightly lower than the one the original provider would have credited you with.

To choose an insurance company yourself, get an up-to-date copy of one of the main pensions magazines such as *Pensions Management* (price £1.95 from FTBI – see p280 for address), or ask an adviser to check on the most recent figures via the Quotel computer system.

Lump sum

When you retire, you can normally choose to have a reduced pension, and a tax-free lump sum. You may be glad to have a lump sum to spend at the start of your retirement. Or you could invest the money and draw on it later. Even if you used the money to buy an immediate annuity, you could end up with a higher after-tax income than the pension you've given up. For more on immediate annuities, see Chapter 22.

The Inland Revenue rules on the size of the lump sum depend on whether you have a Section 226 policy (bought before, 1 July 1988) or a personal pension policy (bought after 1 July 1988).

The Section 226 rules say that the maximum lump sum you can buy is three times the biggest remaining pension the company could pay you. The personal pension rules, on the other hand, say that you can take only a quarter of your fund as a lump sum. If you have an *Appropriate* Personal Pension as part of the scheme, the value of this can be included in working out the total value of the fund, but you must *not* take any part of that as lump sum – it must be paid as pension.

In most cases, the Section 226 rules give a larger lump sum. Exactly how much larger depends on your age, whether you are male or female, and what the annuity rates are at the time. But a typical insurance company quote is for a lump sum of about 29 per cent of the fund for a man at 65. So if you already have a Section 226 policy, and want to take a large lump sum, it's unwise to transfer it into a personal pension plan. If you exercise the open market option you automatically get caught by the 25 per cent limit for personal pensions. The most you can have from either type of scheme is £150,000 – though you can have this from each scheme you take out.

Level or increasing pension?

The buying power of a level pension will quickly be eaten away by inflation. You could instead choose a pension which increases each year. It will, though, be smaller to start off with. For example, a pension which increases by 5 per cent compound each year will start off at around three-quarters of the amount of a level pension. Although the increasing pension would catch the level pension up in about six years, it would take about 12 years before you'd actually received the same *total* number of £££ in pension. If inflation averaged 5 per cent over your total retirement, it would take 14 years before you received the same amount in buying power from the increasing pension.

A few providers offer pensions which are linked to an index – often the Retail Prices Index. But a pension which is increased in line with such an index will start off much lower than a level pension. If it started off at half as much when you retired at 65, it would have to increase by an average of 20 per cent a year if you were to have received the same total buying power by the time you were 75, or 12.5 per cent a year if you were to have received the same total buying power by the time you were 80.

With many unit-linked policies you can choose to have the pension unit-linked as well. This means it will go up and down in line with the price of units in the fund. This could be a good idea for part of your pension, but it would be unwise to link too much of your pension in this way, in case the fund hits bad times.

If you have an *Appropriate* Personal Pension as part of your policy, that must be increased by 3 per cent a year compound. The smaller SERPS pension you are being paid will have its increases tailored (in a rather complicated way) to take this in to account.

A pension for a dependant after you die

There are two ways in which you can provide an income for your husband or wife (or other person you name) if you die after you start drawing the pension. The first is to choose to have a pension paid as long as you or someone else is alive (called a joint life, last survivor annuity). The pension may continue at the same level, or you can normally arrange for the pension to be higher while you are both alive. A joint-life pension (if you're both 65 and the pension stays level) might be around 15 per cent lower than a pension payable on one life only.

Alternative, you can choose to have the pension paid for a certain period (often five or ten years) whether you live that long or not. As this removes the risk of getting virtually nothing back if you die soon after retirement, the pension you get at age 65 will be around 4 per cent less if it's guaranteed for five years, or 10 per cent less if it's guaranteed for 10. If you died, your dependant would be left with nothing from the plan after the end of the guarantee period – so don't look on this as adequate protection.

With an *Appropriate* Personal Pension, the policy must provide for a pension of half of what you would get, for your widow or widower after your death (even if you are not married at the time when you retire).

The tax rules

The main rules about how much you can pay into personal pension plans each year are given below. More details can be obtained from the Inland Revenue Superannuation Funds Office, Lynwood Road, Thames Ditton, Surrey, KT7 0DP.

If you pay in more than the maximum you are allowed in any one year to a personal pension plan, the excess must be returned to you – but you get no interest on it.

How much tax relief

You get tax relief at your highest rate of tax on premiums of up to 17.5 per cent of your *net relevant earnings* for that year, if you are 50 or under at the beginning of the tax year. If you are older, the limits are:

51–55	20 per cent
56–60	22.5 per cent
61–74	27.5 per cent

Husband and wife each have their own 17.5 per cent (or higher) limit worked out on their net relevant earnings.

If your own contributions are below these limits, your employer is allowed to make contributions up to the balance (though they don't have to do so).

Contributions are now dealt within the same way as most mortgage interest which qualifies for tax relief: that is, you just pay the after-tax relief amount and the provider reclaims the tax from the Inland Revenue. So if you wanted to pay a total premium of £10, you would actually pay in £7.50, and the provider would reclaim £2.50 (with tax at 25 per cent) from the Inland Revenue. If you're a higher rate taxpayer, you reclaim the higher rate relief at the end of the tax year.

Your net relevant earnings

These will depend on the income used to work out your tax bill for that year. If you are in a job, your tax bill is worked out for the current year. That is, your tax bill for, say, the 1988–89 tax year is worked out on your pay during that tax year. This normally also applies if you have small freelance earnings.

But if you are self-employed on a large scale, and your business has been going for some years, you will be taxed on a preceding year basis. That means that your tax bill for the 1988–89 tax year will be based on the taxable profit your business makes in your accounting year that ends in the 1988–89 tax year.

Your taxable profit from being self-employed is your takings (less certain debts to you) less certain costs you incur and deductions you can make. These are:

- business expenses
- capital allowances – for the cost of machinery and plant (including a car) used in your business
- any business losses for earlier years which haven't been set against other income.

In the first two and last three years of a business, there are special rules about what income your tax is based on. Your net relevant earnings are your taxable profits, *minus* certain payments, such as patent royalties and annuities paid out from a business.

For more details, see the section on *Tax if you're Self-Employed* in the most recent *Which? Tax-Saving Guide*.

For employees, net relevant earnings will usually be any earnings you pay tax on under the Pay As You Earn system.

Unused relief for the last six years

You can get tax relief on premiums you pay on top of the normal limit, and up to the whole of your net relevant earnings in that tax year, if you didn't pay the maximum premiums allowed in any of the previous tax years. You have to use up the earliest unused relief first. You then receive the relief at the rate at which tax was payable in that year. So anyone now paying 40 per cent tax, who was on a higher rate in earlier years, can get relief at those higher rates on unused premiums before 1988–89.

Unused tax relief from longer ago

If an assessment becomes final for a tax year more than six years in the past, you *may* be able to claim some unused relief from that year. The rules are very complicated – check with your tax inspector.

Looking over your shoulder

You can ask in any tax year to have all or part of the premiums you pay in that year treated as if you'd paid them in the previous tax year. And, if you didn't have *any* net relevant earnings in the previous tax year, you'll be able to get the premiums treated as if you'd paid them in the year before that.

SECTION III

Other Ways of Investing

15

SHARES

The number of private shareholders declined steadily from the early 1960s until the early 1980s. Then came the Government's programme of selling off public institutions like British Gas and British Telecom. Largely as a result of privatisation, the number of private shareholders has grown quite dramatically. Even after the 1987 stock market crash there are now nine million private shareholders in Britain.

Investing directly in shares is a risky business, as was demonstrated in the October 1987 stock market crash, when shares lost 20 per cent of their value in a few days. To reduce the risk, you need to be able to spread your money around a number of different shares – something you're unlikely to be able to do if you invest directly, unless you've got a lot of money to spare.

If you haven't got enough money to be able to spread your investment, and you don't fancy the risks of direct investment in shares, there are various ways of investing indirectly in shares. By investing indirectly and pooling your money with that of other investors, you can spread your risk, because your money will be invested in a wide range of companies. One way of indirect share investment is to put your money in unit trusts, dealt with in Chapter 16. For other ways of investing in shares, see p262 onwards.

Investing directly in shares is a way of investing in the performance of a company. You can expect two sorts of return:

■ income – the company will pay out an income (called dividends) to its shareholders. The hope is that this income will increase over the years as the profits of the company rise

■ capital gain – the hope is that the share price of the company will rise over the years. This may happen if, for example, the company's prospects improve. But you shouldn't expect the share price to rise steadily.

An investment in shares: 1968–1987

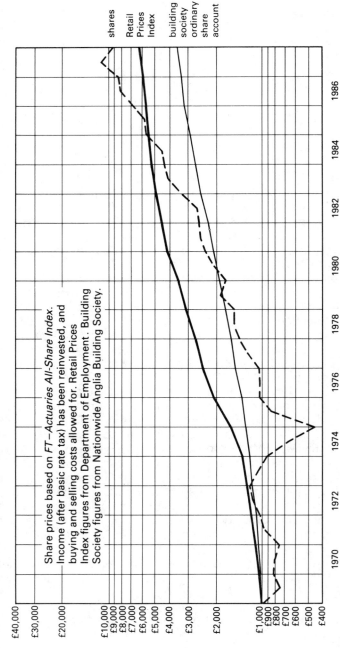

Share prices based on *FT–Actuaries All-Share Index*. Income (after basic rate tax) has been reinvested, and buying and selling costs allowed for. Retail Prices Index figures from Department of Employment. Building Society figures from Nationwide Anglia Building Society.

shares

Retail Prices Index

building society ordinary share account

Looking at what's happened in the past gives some sort of idea of the ups and downs of investing in shares. The Chart opposite shows how the value of an investment in shares has varied between 1968 and 1987. As you can see it's been a bumpy ride. The success of your investment depends crucially on when you buy the shares and when you sell. And no one has a cast-iron method of forecasting the right moment to buy and sell.

But over the years the return on shares has, on average, been higher than with safer investments – for example, look at an investment in building societies. Unfortunately, the past is not a guide to the future. The average investor should assume that investing in shares is a long term business.

Spreading your investment

If you invest heavily in just one company's shares, or in those of a very few companies, you could do very badly, or very well indeed. But if you invest in a wide spread of different shares, the results you'd get from your investment are unlikely to be far removed from the results for shares on average.

What are your chances of losing most of your money? Or of making your fortune? A few years ago, *Which?* did some research to find out what might have happened if you'd invested in a different number of shares over a sample period of time – from the beginning of June 1969 to the beginning of June 1973. Note that even though the research was done for this particular period, its message applies to other periods too.

It was assumed that you had picked your shares from among those of the British companies whose names and prices were then listed in the back pages of the *Financial Times*. The shares of rubber, tea and mining companies (which are untypical, because they can involve extra risks) were excluded, as were the shares of investment trust companies (also untypical, in that they don't themselves run a business, but invest in a spread of different companies' shares – see p265). This left a list of 1,700 shares.

The value of £1,000 invested in each of these 1,700 shares was worked out four years after 'buying' them. To keep things simple, the expenses of buying and selling shares (eg stockbroker's commission and stamp duty) were not taken into account, nor was capital gains tax or the dividends paid on the shares.

The Table on p245 shows what your chances would have been of ending up with a particular result – say from £1,500 to £2,499 – depending on how many companies' shares you spread money over. The first column of the Table lists the range of possible values which an investment of £1,000 in June 1969 might have risen to – or sunk to – by June 1973. The second column – headed *comparative rating* – gives you a guide to how these results compare with the average for the period (close to £2,000).

Look, first, at the chances of ending up with a really handsome sum of money. You can see that someone investing in only one share had 0.4 chances in 100 of ending up with £10,000 or more. At the other end of the scale, the investor in one share would have had almost 3 chances in 100 of ending up with under £400 (ie less than one-fifth of the average result for the period).

By contrast, investors who spread their money over four or more shares had negligible chances of finding that their investment finished up in the top two or bottom two categories.

Now have a look at the results which fell in the range £1,500 to £2,499 – ie within about 25 per cent of the average for the period. You will see that an investor owning one share had about 33 chances in 100 of coming within this range. An investor with eight shares, on the other hand, had 72 chances in 100; and an investor with 32 shares was almost certain to do so (95 chances in 100).

Generally, the results suggest that going from an investment in one share to an investment in two makes a fairly big difference to your likely result. Thereafter, each additional share you include in your collection makes proportionately less difference to your chances than the previous share. Since spreading your money over the shares of 16 or so companies reduces the risk of a much-below average result to an acceptably low level – as the Table shows – there is little to be gained from buying more than this number.

The results show that the number of shares over which you spread your money can have a large effect on the outcome.

If you buy the shares of just one company, there's a small chance, but not a negligible one, that you might achieve either a much above-average return, or lose most or even all of your money. If you buy the shares of more than one company, your chances of an extreme result become much smaller.

If you spread your money over the shares of as many as 16 or so companies you'll be taking a very different sort of risk from that of an investment in shares of just one company. The chances of all of them doing much worse than average

Table: Results of a four-year investment of £1,000

value in June 1973	comparative rating	chances in 100 of £1,000 invested in June 1969 reaching the values shown — number of companies' shares held					
£10,000 or more	jackpot! more than *five times* average	0.4	0.1	—	—	—	—
£8,000 to £9,999	riches! from *four times* to *five times* average	0.4	0.2	—	—	—	—
£6,000 to £7,999	from *three times* to *four times* average	0.6	0.6	0.3	—	—	—
£4,000 to £5,999	from *twice* to *three times* average	5.0	2.6	1.3	0.1	—	—
£2,500 to £3,999	from *25% better than* average to *twice* average	16.4	16.9	14.2	10.4	6.0	1.7
£1,500 to £2,499	*within 25% of average* for period (taken as £2,000)	32.7	44.2	56.4	72.2	85.0	95.4
£1,000 to £1,499	from *half* of average to *25% below* average	23.7	25.7	24.3	15.7	8.9	2.9
£700 to £999	from *one-third* to *half* of average	11.7	7.5	3.1	1.4	0.1	—
£500 to £699	from *one-quarter* to *one-third* of average	4.3	1.7	0.3	0.2	—	—
£400 to £499	near-disaster! from *one-fifth* to *one-quarter* of average	1.6	0.3	—	—	—	—
Under £400	disaster! less than *one-fifth* of average	2.9	0.2	—	—	—	—

are remotely small, as the Table shows. Unfortunately, the chances of a much above-average return are also extremely small.

It would be best to choose the shares of companies in different industries, because there's also the risk that a whole industry – and the shares of most of the companies in it – may hit the doldrums for a while. Similarly, it might be wise to spread your investments over different countries (see Chapter 24), so that the outcome of your investment doesn't depend entirely on the UK stockmarket.

But remember, share prices fluctuate ñ both individually and on average. So, even if you invest in a wide spread of shares, you can't be sure that the value of your share investment won't fall – particularly in the short or even medium term.

Because of buying and selling costs it doesn't make sense to invest small amounts in shares – less than about £1,200, say. So to get a good spread – of, say, 5 to 10 shares – you'd need about £6,000 to £10,000 available for this type of investment.

Ways of choosing shares

If you've made the decision to buy shares, you are still faced with the problem of choosing which ones.

Often, the amateur investor won't do the choosing entirely on his or her own, but will get professional advice (see Chapter 6) from a stockbroker, for example, or from the business pages of a newspaper. But in order to understand this advice, and to assess its worth, it would be helpful to know something about the different methods of choosing shares which may be used by advisers. There are four main ways of choosing shares:
- technical analysis
- fundamental analysis
- beta analysis
- hunch and inside knowledge.

Technical analysis ('chartism')

Technical analysis is concerned with the behaviour of the stockmarket – ie the rises and falls in share prices – rather than the details of a company's management, earnings, and so on. The method normally includes the study of charts (hence 'chartism').

A typical chart

share price (p)

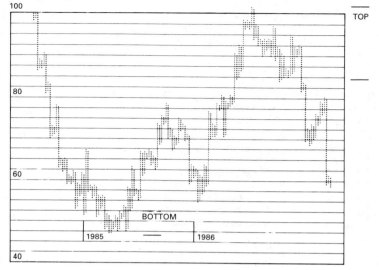

The underlying assumption is that investors, collectively, are in possession of all the available facts about companies, and that movements of share prices accurately – and quickly – reflect this knowledge. But technical analysts believe that share prices may not move instantly to take account of the information. And so analysts believe they can predict movements in price.

The method involves studying charts or graphs showing the range of prices at which each company's shares are bought and sold. The share price record of a company can indicate periods when investors have displayed confidence (or lack of it) in the company, and have built up (or sold) large holdings of its shares. Chartists argue that their graphs can tell them when such periods are about to recur – and they look for *trendlines*, and for significant shapes like *tops* and *bottoms*. If the chart of the share price of a company has completed a top formation (see Chart above), a chartist would say this was the time to sell that share. And vice-versa for a bottom formation (see Chart) – a signal to buy.

Fundamental analysis

The basic assumption here is that, at any given time, a company's shares have an intrinsic value. This value depends normally on the earning capacity of the company,

---

A few examples of common terms and ratios

Net working capital
First the value of what is owed by the company to suppliers, the taxman, shareholders (in the form of dividends), the bank (eg in the form of an overdraft) and so on is worked out. This value is then deducted from the sum of what is owed to the company by customers, cash held by the company or which the company can get at straight away and the value of items held as stock. This gives net working capital. A company needs to have sufficient working capital to keep going.

Profit margin
This is worked out by finding what the profit of the company is as a percentage of its sales.

Return on capital employed
This is worked out by finding what the profit of the company is as a percentage of its assets – ie the sum of the value of its property, its stock, what it is owed by its customers and so on.

---

which in turn depends on such things as the quality of management, and the outlook for the industry and for the economy as a whole. If the current market price of the shares is lower than what you suppose the intrinsic value to be, the share is one to consider buying.

Fundamental analysis will sometimes calculate a precise intrinsic value for a share, based on detailed estimates of the company's future earnings.

The analysis will use any information that can be obtained – in particular, by visiting companies, talking to the management and analysing the company report and accounts. Companies are obliged by law to publish the accounts of their business at least once a year, and to provide certain information. These accounts may reveal some important facts about the company's performance during the period covered by the accounts.

So specialists called investment analysts study and analyse these accounts with the idea of discovering how well the company is really doing. By working out the relationships between various factors (the P/E ratio described on p257 is probably the most commonly used; see Box above for some other examples) they try to build up a picture of the company's financial position. This can be compared with other companies in the same industry to assess the company's performance and the performance of its management. In addition, by studying the economic background, this method is used to make predictions about how well, or badly, particular industries (eg heavy engineering) or even whole countries are going to fare.

But there are problems. The information available is far from comprehensive and not sufficiently standardised. And information in accounts is out of date. For example, after the most skilful reading of a company's account, one may still not know whether one part of the company's business is making losses and is being subsidised by more profitable parts.

Beta analysis

This is a method of share analysis which concentrates on the riskiness of a share. It doesn't look at the risk of investing your money in the shares of only one company which does badly or even goes bust – the section on *Spreading your investment* on p243 shows how you can reduce this risk. Beta analysis looks at the *market risk* of a share. This occurs because the stock market goes up and down, roughly speaking, as the prospect for the economy goes up and down.

A share which has moved exactly in line with the FT-Actuaries All-Share Index is said to have a beta of one. But some shares and unit trusts go up and down more than the average. These are called *aggressive* – ie when the index goes up, the share or unit trust goes up relatively more, and when the index goes down, it goes down relatively more. The value of beta for aggressive shares or unit trusts is more than one. Some shares and unit trusts are *defensive* – ie they go up and down less than the average (and the value of beta is less than one). Other shares and unit trusts fall somewhere between the extremes. The beta of a share is a measure of how much the rate of return on that share is likely to be affected by general stock market movements. It's normally worked out from the past performance of the share – which, or course, is not necessarily a good guide to the future.

Some people use this analysis so that, if they think the general level of prices in the stock market is going to rise, they can invest in shares with high betas – because their prices will (hopefully) go up correspondingly more. And if they think share prices in general are going to fall, they will switch to shares with low betas, whose prices should fall less than average. Another way of using this analysis is to find the right investment for people – taking into account the amount of risk they want to take.

Hunch and inside knowledge

Of course, you could choose your shares by hunch – ie you have a feeling that things are going to go well for a particular company. Fortunes can be made or lost this way.

Investing as a result of a tip from an insider is a dodgy business. And if *you* are the insider and you use your knowledge to invest and make yourself or someone else some money, then it's probably against the law and you could be convicted.

Verdict

There is no effective, reliable, proven, and generally usable method of picking out which shares are going to be winners. Apart from hunch and inside knowledge, all the methods we've described depend, to some extent at least, on looking at how shares have fared in the past. But past performance is no guide to the future. A share can perform well for many months, then fall in value unexpectedly overnight.

This does not mean, however, that you cannot make a sensible choice of shares. A collection of shares which a person holds is called a portfolio; and a portfolio chosen to match *your* objectives and circumstances and preferred level of risk should certainly give you better results than one which hasn't been so chosen. In broad outline, choose your shares as follows:

■ decide what your objectives are – because different shares are likely to suit different objectives. For example, you may (or may not) attach importance to drawing an income from your investment. Or you may be speculating with your money – in the hope of maximum gain, but accepting the possibility of a big loss

■ choose shares which carry the degree of risk you are willing to accept. If you want to speculate, you could put all your money into a collection of very risky shares. Alternatively, see p262 for other ways of speculating in shares – in particular, *warrants*, *options* and *traded options*. On the other hand, if you are investing for the long term, divide your money among the shares of a fair number of companies and spread your investment over a number of carefully selected different industries

■ consider reducing the influence of the stock market on your investments by investing some of your money in other investments, which are less risky – eg building society, British Government stock or company loan stock (see p261). And look at the possibilities of investing some of your money overseas and giving yourself a spread of geographical areas and currencies – see Chapter 24

■ in general, the best policy is likely to be *buy and hold*. Don't buy and sell shares too frequently. The costs of doing this will eat into any profits that you make.

Buying and selling shares

You can buy or sell shares by going to a stockbroker. Alternatively you could go to a bank or building society, many of whom own or have agreements with stockbroking firms. For more details, see Chapter 6. Whichever you choose, the procedure is more or less the same.

There are a number of market places for buying and selling shares. Novice investors should probably stick to shares which are quoted on the main market place – ie those with a full listing on the Stock Exchange. However, the Stock Exchange also runs two markets for shares in younger (often more risky) companies – the Unlisted Securities Market and the Third Market. The procedure for buying and selling shares quoted on these markets may alter slightly from that described below – a stockbroker should be able to advise you

Buying shares

Suppose that you have found a broker to deal for you, and that you decide you would like to buy 500 Slagthorpe Jam shares. You look at the share price lists in the morning paper and see that they are quoted at 300p.

There are two points which must be made at once about this price. Firstly, it is normally yesterday afternoon's price – the price being quoted towards the close of Stock Exchange business. Secondly, the price quoted in most of the newspapers is normally a 'middle' price. If the newspaper says that Slagthorpe Jam PLC was 300p it probably means that, yesterday afternoon, the offer price (the price at which you could have bought Slagthorpe) was 303p, while the bid price (the price at which you could have sold) was 297p. The difference between the two figures is called the *spread*.

You can give your order to your broker in either of two ways. One is simply to ring him or her up and say, 'Buy me 500 Slagthorpe Jam'. The broker will take this as an order to buy this number of shares at the best (ie cheapest) available price *now*.

The other way of giving a buying order is to give the broker a *limit*. Suppose that you decide that the shares would be a good buy at 295p but not a penny more. You ring up your broker and say, 'Buy me 500 Slagthorpe, at not more than 295p'.

So you lose nothing by setting a limit, and you protect yourself from the risk of buying at a higher price than you expected. However, it is no use setting too low a limit; you won't get your shares, and will have wasted your time, and the broker's. And make sure your broker knows how long you want your limit to stand (there may be a standard time limit – eg one month).

Once you've placed your order, it's too late to change your mind – you've made a verbal contract. For most shares, the broker can call up SEAQ (Stock Exchange Automated Quotation System) on a computer screen. This gives up-to-the-minute information on the prices that a number of market-makers (share wholesalers) are prepared to buy and sell shares at. The broker buys the shares on your behalf from the market-maker offering the best price. This is likely to be done automatically, by computer, in the future.

At the broker's office, a contract note will be made out for the shares you have bought. You should get this on the following day, or soon after, and should check it at once to see that the details of what you have bought are correct. Keep this contract note carefully, as evidence of what you have paid for the shares. It will look something like the example opposite.

Selling shares

As with buying, so with selling. There are two kinds of order that you can give to your broker. You can simply ring up your broker and say 'Sell 500 Slagthorpe Jam'. Or you can set a limit – eg sell 500 Slagthorpe Jam if the price reaches 320p.

The contract note for a sale looks much like the contract note for a purchase. There's VAT to pay on the commission. Minimum commission rates used to be fixed, but now brokers can charge what they like and rates and minimum charges vary widely. In April 1988, charges varied between 1 per cent and 1.65 per cent on a deal of up to, say, £7,000. The typical minimum commission was £20 or £25. The contract levy is the same amount as it would be on a purchase of this size. But with a sale, there is no stamp duty.

When the contract note for your sale has been made out, the broker will send it to you. He or she will also send you a transfer form. All you will have to do is sign it at the place

CONTRACT NOTE

| UNIQUE CODE NO.
6405/97Z | F. MURRAY | DATE & TAX POINT
22 JUN 88 | EXECUTED AT 12.00 |

YOU HAVE BOUGHT, SUBJECT TO THE RULES AND REGULATIONS
* * * * * *

OF THE STOCK EXCHANGE, FOR SETTLEMENT ON 11 JUL 88

| 500
.... | SLAGTHORPE JAM ORD £1
BARGAIN OF PREVIOUS EVENING
** TALISMAN SECURITY ** | 295P | **1** | £1,475.00
.... |
| 500 | | | | £1,475.00 |

	CONTRACT LEVY (O)	0.80	**2**	
	TRANSFER STAMP (O)	7.50	**3**	
	COMMISSION (T)	24.34	**4**	
	VALUE ADDED TAX AT 15% ON £24.34	3.65		
	TOTAL CHARGES			£36.29
	DUE TO US			.... £1,511.29

COMMISSION DETAILS
£1,475 AT 1.65%

(O) – OUTSIDE SCOPE OF V.A.T.
(T) – LIABLE TO V.A.T.

WE HAVE ACTED AS AGENT IN THIS TRANSACTION

U.K. RESIDENTS SHOULD RETAIN THIS CONTRACT NOTE AS THEY MAY REQUIRE IT FOR
CAPITAL GAINS TAX AND VALUE ADDED TAX PURPOSES

| BGN NO.
0928 | REFERENCE
NO.01435 |

1 Consideration The name sometimes given to the amount you pay for the shares (or get for them if you're selling) before the various deductions are made. In our example, the consideration is £1,475.

2 Contract levy If the consideration is over £1,000, an additional charge of 80p is made – this is a levy for the Panel on Takeovers and Mergers and the Securities and Investments Board (see Chapter 5).

3 Stamp duty This is the main government duty on the deal. It is 1/2% of what you pay for the shares (rounded up to the nearest £50). In our example, the stamp duty is 1/2% of £1,500 (ie £1,475 to the nearest £50 upwards).

4 Commission The rate of commission varies depending on what you pay for the shares. For more details, see opposite. VAT at 15% will be charged on the stockbroker's commission.

indicated, and send it back to your broker, with your share certificate. Don't date this transfer form – the broker will do this for you. You should keep the contract note as evidence of how much you have sold the shares for.

Provided you have sent in the transfer form properly signed, together with your share certificate, you should get the balance due to you from your broker on settlement day (see below).

Settling up

All share deals on the Stock Exchange are done within a period called an account, usually lasting 10 working days. An account normally starts on a Monday, and ends on the Friday of the following week. Settlement day, or account day, is normally on the sixth working day after the final day of the account (ie on a Monday). On settlement day, the broker pays the market-maker (or the reverse, for sellers) for all deals done during the account in question – and so the broker must have your money by that day.

So, following the end of an account in which you have done business with him, your broker will probably send you a statement. The statement will set out the totals from all the contract notes which have been sent to you during the account. If the statement shows that, taking purchases and sales together, you owe money to your broker, you should send him a cheque to arrive in time to be cleared by settlement day. If you are owed money, you should get it on settlement day or the day after, provided that you have sent the share certificate and signed transfer deed to the broker.

When you buy shares, anything from 10 to 21 days can elapse before you have to pay for them (but, of course, when you sell you may have to wait a corresponding length of time for your money).

The broker and market-maker settle most of their purchases and sales through a system known as *Talisman*. The broker who was sold shares will deliver a transfer form and share certificate to the Talisman office and Talisman gives the company registrar details of the new holder of shares. The registrar will send a new share certificate to your broker who sends it on to you.

How soon you get the share certificate depends on the company – it can be six weeks, or longer. But your contract note is evidence that you have bought the shares. Should you want to sell them again before you have received the certificate, there should be no problem with shares in British companies. But you may have to wait until you can supply your broker with the certificate before you are paid since the market-maker will not pay the broker without this document.

Shares in detail

What is a share?

When you buy ordinary shares you are literally buying a share in the company, and a right to benefit from its earnings (if any). You can go to general meetings and vote on matters to do with the company.

Some companies issue ordinary shares only. The net (ie after tax) profits of such a company all count as earnings available to the ordinary shareholders. This does not mean, however, that all such earnings will actually be paid to the ordinary shareholders – see *Dividends*, on p256.

Many companies, by contrast, raise their capital in other ways – eg occasionally by issuing 'preference shares', more commonly by issuing loan stock or debentures (see p261). The company's first commitment is to pay the fixed income to its lenders and preference shareholders, which is why all such payments are commonly called prior charges. With such companies, the earnings available to the ordinary shareholders are the profits after deducting the prior charges and tax.

What the papers say

The shares page of a daily newspaper can be puzzling. But if you know how to work out what it says, it contains a lot of useful information.

Let's suppose you wanted to find out about Slagthorpe Jam. The relevant section of the newspaper would look something like this:

FOOD, GROCERIES, ETC

183	161	ASDA Group.........α	174	.....	†3.5	3.3	2.7	14.9
506	438	Acatos & Hutcheson 50p y	485	.....	8.5	2.9	2.3	19.5
62	33	Alpine Soft D 10p.. y	41	+2	–	–	–	–
185	140	Appletree Hldgs. 10p.y	165	.....	3.0	1.8	2.4	26.8
212	182	Argyll Group.........α	207	+1	†h4.55	2.2	2.9	20.4
314	280	Ass. Brit. Foods 5p...α	295	+5	†7.3	3.9	3.3	9.6
190	151	Ass. Fisheries........y	165	+2	5.0	2.9	4.0	9.2
£439	£356	BSN Fr 100............	£383	+5¾	vQ85%	φ	2.2	φ
220	185	Banks (Sidney C.)...y	190	.....	†h6.63	4.6	4.6	6.3
153	133	Barker & Dbsn 10p...β	148	+1½	ua5.0	φ	4.6	φ
609	543	Barr (A.G.)............y	598	.....	13.0	4.4	2.9	10.5
216	195	Bassett Foods.......y	216	+10	†7.24	2.1	4.5	14.3
93	81	Batleys ....y	83	....	2.3	?	3.7	9.7
1⁹	⁷⁶	Bejam ....β	¹69	+⁷	75		7	1³

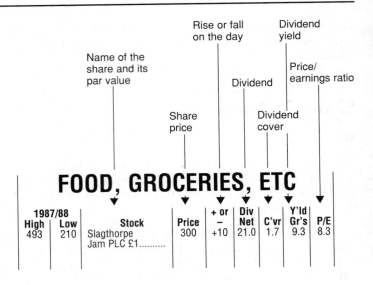

	1987/88				+ or	Div		Y'ld	
High	Low	Stock	Price	−	Net	C'vr	Gr's	P/E
493	210	Slagthorpe Jam PLC £1..........	300	+10	21.0	1.7	9.3	8.3

Here's what the papers tell you

The name of the share and its par value
The par, or nominal, value is a requirement of company law and of use to the company's accountants. But it is irrelevant to the ordinary investor.

The share price
This is usually the previous day's middle market (ie halfway between offer and bid) closing price.

Dividends
Shareholders receive their share of the company profits as dividends. Dividends will be sent to you at the address which your broker puts on the transfer form. Dividends come in the form of dividend warrants. These are in effect cheques, which can be paid into your bank account. Slagthorpe Jam last year declared dividends of 21p per share. Basic rate tax has already been deducted (in other words, it is a *net dividend*) – so it is equivalent to 28p per share before basic rate tax. For more details of how dividends are taxed, see p97.

Companies usually pay dividends twice a year (so long as they have earnings to distribute). About six to eight weeks before each dividend is paid, the company declares a dividend – ie announces what the next dividend will be. A week or two later, the company's shares go *ex-dividend* (and the share price is marked xd) and the register of shareholders is temporarily closed. The coming dividend will be paid only to those people who are on the register of shareholders on the day it was closed. Anyone who buys shares in the company after they have gone ex-dividend will not get the coming dividend.

A company normally keeps back part of its net profits (in our Example on p258, £1,800,000 – £1,050,000 = £750,000) to finance expansion of its business, or to build up cash balances, or both. Amounts kept back are called retained profits or earnings, or retentions.

Dividend cover
How many times the company could have paid its dividend out of the profit for that year.

Dividend yield
The current market price of Slagthorpe Jam Company shares is 300p each. The dividend for each share is 21p. So you will have paid 300p to get a yearly income of 21p (provided future dividends are the same as last year's) – basic rate tax has already been deducted.

Now, 21p is 7% of 300p. Therefore the yield on your money would be 7% a year (with no basic rate tax to pay). This yield on your money is called the dividend yield. In practice, the dividend yield is usually quoted before-tax ñ and works out at 9.3% a year in this Example.

Note that the dividend yield makes up only part of the return you hope to get from investing in shares – you also hope to get a capital gain.

When you see the dividend yield of a share published in a newspaper, there are two important points to be aware of. It applies to buying the share at the price indicated, and it is usually worked out on the basis of the last dividend ñ so has meaning only if the future dividend rate remains more or less unchanged.

Price earnings ratio
A common way of looking at share prices is to say that in buying a share what you are really doing is buying a right to benefit from a corresponding share in the company's yearly stream of earnings. The price earnings ratio (or P/E ratio for short) is a way of saying how expensive (or how cheaply) you're buying that stream of earnings.

To work out a P/E ratio, first work out how much earnings there are for each share – ie divide the total after-tax earnings of the company by the number of shares. The P/E ratio is

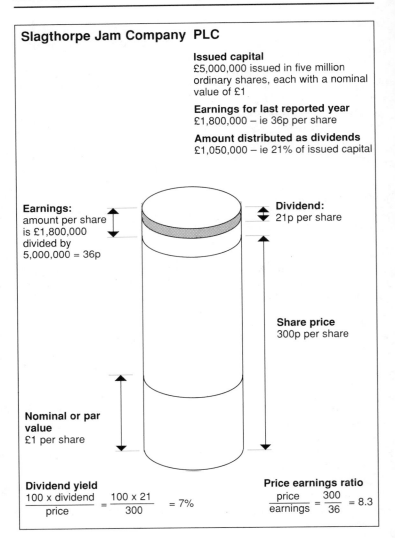

Slagthorpe Jam Company PLC

Issued capital
£5,000,000 issued in five million ordinary shares, each with a nominal value of £1

Earnings for last reported year
£1,800,000 – ie 36p per share

Amount distributed as dividends
£1,050,000 – ie 21% of issued capital

Earnings:
amount per share is £1,800,000 divided by 5,000,000 = 36p

Dividend:
21p per share

Share price
300p per share

Nominal or par value
£1 per share

Dividend yield
$$\frac{100 \times \text{dividend}}{\text{price}} = \frac{100 \times 21}{300} = 7\%$$

Price earnings ratio
$$\frac{\text{price}}{\text{earnings}} = \frac{300}{36} = 8.3$$

found by dividing the current market price by the earnings per share.

Take our Slagthorpe Jam Example. Suppose the company's earnings in the last reported year were £1,800,000, which – since the company has five million ordinary shares (see above) – works out at 36p for each share. Each share actually costs 300p at current prices, so to buy earnings of 36p a year, you have to pay 300p. So Slagthorpe Jam would be said to have a P/E ratio of 300 divided by 36 = 8.3.

New issues

If a company is not quoted on the Stock Exchange, it may be difficult to buy or sell its shares. You have to find an individual or an organisation who is prepared to deal with you. When the company decides it wants to make a better market in its shares, it may offer its shares to the public and become quoted on the Stock Exchange. Two well-known companies which have done this in recent years are Laura Ashley and Virgin.

The most usual method for marketing a new issue is an *offer for sale* by an issuing house – often a merchant bank. The issuing house puts advertisements in newspapers giving details of the company and offering a stated number of shares at a stated price (the prospectus). The advertisements normally include an application form. If you want to buy some of the shares, fill in the form saying how many you want, and send it with a cheque for the value of the shares you want to buy.

If the terms on which a new issue is made look attractive to the investing public, the issue may be over-subscribed – that is, more shares may be asked for than are on offer. In that case, the shares will be allocated by the issuing house (there is a variety of methods for doing this).

Scrip (or bonus) issue

As a company grows, its share price may increase so much that it becomes too unwieldy to trade easily. So the company may make an extra issue of free shares to its existing shareholders. This is called a scrip or bonus issue. If, for example, you have 500 shares in Slagthorpe Jam and the share price is 300p each, your shareholding is worth £1,500. If the company makes a 1 for 1 scrip issue, you will get another 500 shares, making 1,000 in total. But the share price will instantly fall to 150p each, so your shareholding is still worth £1,500.

After a time, the share price will go ex-scrip, marked xc – this works in much the same way as ex-dividend, see opposite.

Rights issue

Occasionally, a company may decide it needs to raise more money from its shareholders – perhaps to finance some new investment. It usually makes a rights issue to its existing shareholders. This means the company offers you the right to invest more money in exchange for new shares it will issue.

You will know about this rights issue because the company will send you a document, telling you what it is raising money for and enclosing a form so that you can apply to take up some new shares. Do not ignore this document – it is valuable. If you don't understand what it is, ask a professional adviser.

There are four choices facing you as shareholder:
■ you can do nothing
■ you can pay up
■ you can sell your rights to the new shares on the Stock Exchange
■ you can sell part of your rights and take up part, so keeping your investment in the company at the same level.

What you do depends on whether you have the cash available and whether you want to increase your investment in the company.

Suppose, for example, you have 500 shares in Battendown Foods, the share price is 400p each and the company makes a one-for-one rights issue at 200p each. If the company has 3 million shares already issued, it is raising £6 million by the rights issue (issuing another 3 million shares for 200p each). The market value of the company before the rights issue is £12 million; afterwards it is £18 million. The share price after the rights issue will be:

$$£18 \text{ million} – 6 \text{ million} = £3 \text{ each.}$$

If you do nothing, your 500 shares are now worth only £1,500, so on the face of it, you might have lost £500. However, all UK companies will sell rights which haven't been taken up and send you the proceeds. If you take up your rights, your investment is now worth £3,000 – but you've had to hand over another £1,000 to the company. Or you can sell your rights to the new shares on the Stock Exchange – in theory, for £500. This is worked out by taking the new share price from the old one – ie £4 – £3 = £1 per share.

Your fourth choice is to sell part of your rights and use the proceeds to buy the rest of the new shares.

After a while, the share price will go ex-rights (marked xr) – this works much the same as ex-dividend (see p256).

Mergers and takeovers

One company may decide it would like to acquire another company and it therefore offers to buy the shares from the company's shareholders. For example, suppose Battendown Foods decides to take over Slagthorpe Jam. Battendown will

send you a document offering to buy your shares. This
document will contain a lot of information, including:

■ what Battendown will pay for your shares. It may offer you
cash, or some of its own shares in exchange, or a mixture of
loan stock and shares and possibly cash
■ why Battendown wants to buy Slagthorpe
■ a profit forecast for Battendown
■ the date on which its offer closes.

If Slagthorpe decides it doesn't want to be taken over, it
will also send you a document telling you why you
shouldn't accept Battendown's offer, probably giving a
profit forecast for Slagthorpe, and so on.

Things can get very complicated after this, if, for example,
a second company decides it would like to acquire
Slagthorpe, or Battendown decides its first offer will not be
accepted by the majority of shareholders and so increases its
offer. You might end up with quite a few documents. Don't
ignore them. You have to decide which is better – sticking
with Slagthorpe or accepting one of the offers. If you have a
professional adviser, ask his or her advice.

Other ways of investing in companies

Companies can raise money by issuing *company loan stock*
or *debentures*. They work like British Government stocks –
they normally pay a fixed rate of interest and the loan will
be repaid some time in the future. Because they are riskier
than British Government stocks, you can expect the return
to be higher. And if the company is in financial difficulties,
the return – and the risk – may be very high indeed.

A variation is a *convertible loan stock*. This starts out as
a loan when the company first gets the money. But the
person holding the loan stock has the right to convert it or
part of it into an agreed number of shares on a fixed date (or
between certain dates). If the share price of the company
rises this may make the price of a convertible rise substantially too. If the share price falls, then it may not be worth
converting the loan.

Some companies have *preference* shareholders, though
these are getting less common. A fixed rate of dividend is
usually paid on them. There are different types of preference
shares, but this is a highly specialised market ñ not usually
for the average investor.

There are some very risky types of investments you can
buy and sell on the stockmarket – *warrants, options* and

traded options. A warrant is issued by the company, and is often tacked on to a loan stock – it can be detached and sold by the loan stockholder if he or she wants. A warrant gives you the right to buy shares in the company, usually during a fixed period and at a fixed price. If the shares of the company never reach that price, the warrant is worthless. But if the share price does rise, the price of a warrant will rise substantially.

An option is similar but is not issued by the company. Instead you pay a market-maker (see p252) for the right to buy or sell shares in a company at a fixed price within a three-month period. Once you've got the option you can't sell it – you can buy and sell only the shares of the company.

A traded option is a slightly different investment – and can itself be bought and sold. It lasts for a period of up to nine months and you can use the option to buy or sell shares at predetermined prices. Traded options exist for about 50 companies.

Other ways of investing in shares

Employee share schemes

Some employers encourage their employees to invest in the company that they work for through employee share schemes. There are three types:

■ **approved profit-sharing schemes.** Open to all employees who have been with the company at least five years. The company sets aside some of its profits to buy shares which are then allocated to employees. Not everybody gets the same amount – it depends on things like age, seniority and length of service. The maximum one employee can get is shares with an initial value of £1,250 (or 10 per cent of earnings if higher), with an overall limit of £5,000 worth of shares. There is no tax to pay when the shares are allocated. You have to keep the shares for two years. If you keep them for five years, there is no income tax to pay on the money you make from selling them. However, you will have to pay income tax on dividends and any profit you make on the sale could be liable to capital gains tax. These schemes are common in the USA, and gradually becoming more common in the UK.

■ **SAYE share option schemes.** Again, open to all employees who have been with the company five years or more. The employee agrees to pay a fixed monthly sum between £10 and £100 into a building society or National Savings Save-As-You-Earn (SAYE) plan, for five (or sometimes seven) years. At the end of the period there is a bonus. You can use the money in your plan to buy shares in your company at a discount – but you don't have to. There's no income tax to pay, but you could be liable for capital gains tax, when you sell any shares you're bought.

■ **approved share option schemes.** Such a scheme doesn't have to be offered to all employees. You are given the option to buy shares in your company. If you use your option between three and ten years after it is granted, and only at three-yearly intervals, you pay no income tax. Again though, you may be liable to capital gains tax.

Verdict

Share option schemes can be a very good deal indeed, but don't be tempted to buy shares in your company if, for example, it's in difficulties. And look carefully at the whole offer – some companies offer share option schemes as an alternative to a portion of your salary. Make sure that the extra risk is really what you want.

The Business Expansion Scheme

The Business Expansion Scheme (BES) was set up to encourage investment in new companies. When you buy shares in a company that qualifies under the BES rules, you get tax relief at your highest rate of tax on the money you invest. To qualify, your shares must be in a UK company that has been in business for at least four years.

It must *not:*

■ be quoted on the Stock Exchange or the Unlisted Securities Market

■ deal in land or shares, provide financial or legal services, or hold collectable goods (eg antiques, wines) for investment

■ be a company owned by you, or one in which you (or your family or business partners) own more than 30 per cent of the business

■ be a company of which you are a paid director or employee.

How to invest in BES

You have a choice. You can invest either directly in companies or through a fund. If you opt for the direct route, the minimum investment is £500 per company. You should take advice before investing directly, eg from a stockbroker or accountant.

A novice investor would probably do better to invest

through a fund. Your money is pooled with that of other investors and spread around several BES companies – which helps to reduce the risk. The minimum investment through a fund is usually £2,000 and there's likely to be an initial fee of, say, 7 per cent of your investment.

Tax

You can get tax relief at your top rate on up to £40,000 invested in BES in one tax year. Married couples get up to £40,000 between them. You have to hold the shares for at least five years. If you sell before that time, or the company ceases to qualify within three years (eg by changing its business, or getting quoted on the Unlisted Securities Market), the Inland Revenue can claim back some or all of the tax relief.

Higher-rate taxpayers will benefit most from BES, but should only invest if they're prepared to take the risks. Basic rate taxpayers have less to gain from BES. Non-taxpayers obviously won't benefit from BES tax relief at all and should definitely not invest in BES.

Shares in BES companies issued after 18 March 1986 are free of capital gains tax on their first disposal.

Verdict

Because BES companies tend to be new and small, they're likely to be risky. You shouldn't invest money in a BES unless you're prepared for the possibility that you might lose the lot.

Personal Equity Plans

Personal Equity Plans (PEPs) were introduced in 1987 to encourage direct investment in UK companies. The attractions of PEPs are that you get tax relief on money that you invest and someone else takes care of the day-to-day detail of share-ownership – buying and selling, dealing with paperwork. However, PEPs can be expensive.

How to invest in a PEP

You can invest up to £3,000 a year in shares, including up to £450 (or 25 per cent of the total invested) in unit trusts and investment trusts. You must invest through a 'plan manager' – a bank, building society or other investment adviser. The plan manager deals with all the administration – buying the shares, registering your name with the company, collecting dividends and reclaiming tax. You have a choice of schemes:

■ **discretionary PEPs** – your money is pooled with that of

other investors. The plan manager chooses investments for you
■ **non-discretionary PEPs** – you choose your investment yourself and tell the plan manager to buy and sell on your behalf.

Of course, you have to pay for the services of a plan manager. Costs vary, but on an investment of £3,000 in a PEP, you could find yourself paying £100 in the first year.

Tax
You have to keep your money in your PEP for at least a full calendar year after the year in which the investment is made. Otherwise you'll pay tax. But providing you obey the rules, there are two tax benefits:
■ you pay no income tax on any interest you may get on money within a plan waiting to be invested. Dividends are usually paid with the equivalent of basic rate income tax already deducted. During the minimum holding period the plan manager will claim this back for you
■ you pay no capital gains tax on profits that you make when you sell your shares. This is in addition to your normal capital gains tax exemption (£5,000 in the 1988–89 tax year).

Verdict
You'll benefit from a PEP only if you pay tax. If you've already used up your £5,000 capital gains tax exemption, a PEP is likely to be worth considering. But look at the charges made by the plan manager – they may outweigh the tax exemptions.

Investment trust companies

Investment trust companies are companies quoted on the Stock Exchange. You buy and sell their shares just like those of any other company. Their business is investing in the shares of other companies. So, by investing in an investment trust company, you are buying a share of all the shares that the company owns (known as the underlying investments). Like investing in a unit trust (see Chapter 16), this lets you spread your risk. However, there are important differences between investment trusts and unit trusts.
■ Investment trusts usually have a fixed number of shares. The number of units in a unit trust automatically increases or decreases as units are bought or sold by investors.
■ The price of units in a unit trust reflects the value of the underlying investments. If the value of the shares that the unit trust managers have bought goes up, so does the price

of the units in the unit trust. But the price of shares in an investment trust company is not directly linked to the value of the underlying investments. Shares in investment trusts are bought and sold on the stock market and so rise or fall according to the trust's popularity with investors. So the total value of the shares in an investment trust company may not always be the same as the total value of the underlying investments (known as the Net Asset Value, or NAV). Usually the market value of the shares is less than the NAV, in which case the share price is said to stand 'at a discount'. If the share price is higher than the NAV, it stands 'at a premium'. Clearly, if you buy at a discount, you'll get more investments for your money.

■ An investment trust can borrow money to invest in shares. This is known as 'gearing' and has the effect of exaggerating the ups and downs of the share price. So, when shares are doing well, investment trusts can perform particularly well. But in bad times for shares, investment trusts may fare very badly.

Tax
Like any other company, investment trusts deduct the equivalent of basic rate income tax from all dividends before paying them to their shareholders. If you pay no tax, you can claim it back; if you pay tax at a higher rate, you'll have to pay extra. If, when you sell your shares, you make a profit, you may be liable for capital gains tax.

Verdict
Investment trusts are worth considering as a way of spreading the risk of share investment. But remember that, when the stock market is not performing well, investment trusts may perform particularly poorly.

16

UNIT TRUSTS

Most unit trusts are a way of investing in shares. However, some unit trusts invest in British Government stock and other loans and a few invest in other unit trusts. In the future, a unit trust will also be a way of investing in:

- property
- deposits and short-term loans
- futures, options and commodities and
- a mixture of all these investments.

For many investors, investing in a unit trust is less risky and more convenient than investing directly in shares, for example. If you invested directly, and put all your money in one company, say, you'd lose it all if that company went bust. But a unit trust invests in the shares of a lot of companies (around 60 or 70, say – though it varies widely). So if one company goes bust you lose only a bit of your money. Of course, you can invest direct in a lot of companies' shares but this involves more money and more work. For more details on investing in shares, see Chapter 15.

The return you get back from a unit trust comes in two parts:

- **income** – this is made up of dividends from the shares the unit trust invests in. It can normally be paid out to you
- **capital growth** – the hope is that the prices of shares which the unit trust has invested in will rise.

In practice, you can always reinvest your income to give more capital growth or cash in part of your investment to use capital growth as income – see p284.

This Chapter looks at the points to consider before investing in unit trusts, and the choices that are open to you if you decide to invest. Then, on p281, it moves on to look at the nitty gritty of unit trust investment, including how prices are calculated, how to buy and sell, and what charges you can expect to pay.

Timing your investment

Investing in unit trusts is riskier than many types of investment – for example, building society accounts. But although there is a chance of you losing money with a unit trust, the hope is that you get a better return. You can see from the Diagrams in this chapter that investors in unit trusts have had a bumpy ride over the years – doing very well in some periods, very badly in others. So the success of an investment depends very much on when you invest and when you cash your investment. If you'd invested in a typical general unit trust – see Diagram on p270 – at the beginning of 1987 and cashed in a year later, you'd have lost about 20% of your money. But over the 15-year period you'd have done very well – an investment in this unit trust of £1,000 at the start of 1973 would have been worth more than six times as much by the end of 1987. Sadly, there's no foolproof way of forecasting when share prices are going to rise or fall.

For the long-term or short-term?

There are two schools of thought about how long you should invest in a unit trust for. Either:

■ you invest for a long time (at least seven years or so) and stick pretty well to the same trust (or trusts),
or
■ you invest for a shorter time and move your money in and out of unit trusts or from trust to trust as the prospects alter.

For most small investors, the former is most probably the better strategy. Switching your money in, out or between trusts, could be expensive in charges – see p282 – and unless you're lucky or very knowledgeable you might time it badly. For example, suppose you'd switched a £1,000 investment between the general trust in the Diagram on p270 and building societies, and got it wrong every time (ie sold your units just as shares were about to rise and bought them back just as shares began to fall). You'd have around £700 after 15 years compared with around £6,000 if you'd stuck with the trust throughout. Of course, if you'd got your timing right, you'd have over £30,000. But unless you're prepared to do the work and take the chance of getting it all wrong, you should think of unit trusts as a long-term investment.

Size of investment

The minimum you can invest varies, but with most unit trusts it's in the £250 to £1,000 range – or, for regular saving, often £20, £25 or £50 a month. Regular saving means less worry about timing your investment – see p285.

How unit trusts compare

The Diagram on p270 shows the outcome of a number of imaginary investments made at the start of 1973 and cashed at the end of 1987. £1,000 has been invested in each of:
■ a typical general unit trust
■ building society term shares (ordinary shares for the first couple of years)
■ the longest running property bond.

From the Diagram you can see that the unit trust investment is worth more after 10 years than, say, the building society, but has gone up and down a lot over the years. So you should only put your money in unit trusts if you are prepared to take the risk of losing money for the chance of greater gain.

From the Diagram on p271, you can see how the outcome of an investment in unit trusts could have varied depending on the trust you'd chosen. It shows what has happened to an investment of £1,000 in three different unit trusts made in January 1973. The middle line is an investment in a typical general unit trust, the others are typical specialist unit trusts in one of the best-performing and worst-performing sectors (for what a specialist unit trust is, see p273).

Choosing a unit trust

There's no magic formula to tell you which trust will do best – we've tested several theories on p274 onwards. And you can't automatically expect that an investment adviser or newspaper will pick a trust which is going to perform. But the step-by-step guide on p278 should help you narrow down the choices.

A general unit trust compared with other investments [1]

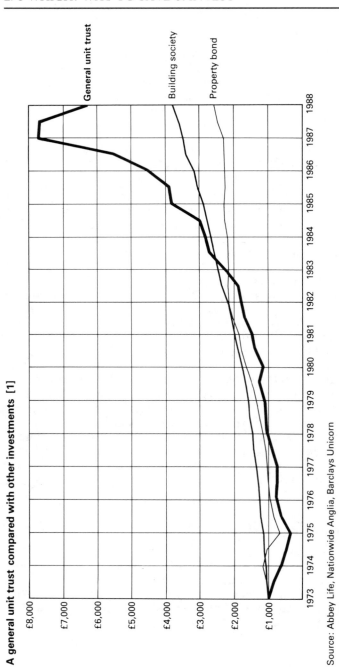

Source: Abbey Life, Nationwide Anglia, Barclays Unicorn

[1] Figures for building society and unit trust include income reinvested after deduction of basic rate tax. Includes buying and selling costs

A general unit trust compared with two specialist trusts [1]

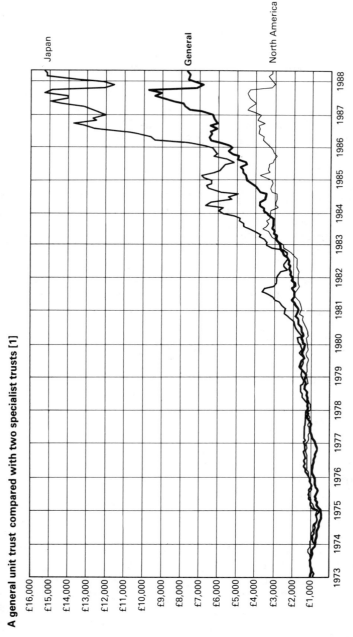

Source: Micropal   [1] Figures do not allow for buying and selling costs. Net income is reinvested

Types of unit trust

Unit trusts vary in their aims and the kind of shares they invest in. One way of grouping them is:

- general funds
- income funds
- capital growth funds
- specialist sector funds (eg commodities, energy)
- specialist regional funds (eg Japan, US)
- managed funds (which invest in other unit trusts).

General funds (or balanced funds)

The longest-running unit trust of most unit trust groups is likely to be a general fund. The aim of the fund, as described in company literature, might be something like:
'The fund's objective is to produce steady growth of both income and capital.'

Most general funds invest mainly in the UK, but in several different industries. You should expect the value of your investment to go up and down as the UK stock market goes up and down.

But some general funds (often called *international funds*) invest in several different stock markets around the world – so the fortune of your investment is not so tightly tied to the fortune of the UK stock market. However, international funds are subject to an additional risk – currencies can fluctuate as well as share prices.

Income funds

These funds are often called *High Yield, Extra Income* and so on. The objective of the fund might be described by the company as:
'Designed for investors whose primary requirement is an above average and increasing income. The fund's objective is to provide a return about 60% higher than that of the FT-Actuaries All-Share Index.'

We looked at the size of the income for funds which have words like *Extra Income* or *High Yield* in the name. And we found that funds with this sort of name did pay out a higher-than-average income (ie the fund was achieving what its name suggested). Many of these income funds invest in British Government stocks, preference shares or loan stocks as well as shares giving a high income.

Capital growth funds

The aim of these funds is to concentrate on getting increases in the unit price, rather than pay out a high income. Many funds with names like *Capital Growth, Special Situations, Smaller Companies,* and so on, come into this category.

The aim of this type of fund might be described as:
'The investment aim is maximum capital growth through the active management of a small portfolio of shares . . . Yield (ie income) *is not normally taken into account.'*

With *active management* the shares in the fund may be changed more frequently than with other types of funds – so incurring a higher level of costs, due to buying and selling shares.

Specialist sector funds

These funds invest in particular industries (eg financial, energy). We looked at the shares held by these funds and compared the type of shareholdings with the name of the fund. In most cases, the name of the fund did give a clue to its content.

The aim of a specialist fund might be described as:
. . . 'The Fund's main objective is long-term capital growth, but there may be wider than average day-to-day price fluctuations . . . .'

In other words, the managers are warning you that you could be in for a bumpy ride. This is because if a unit trust invests its money in one UK industry and the industry does particularly badly or well the unit trust will do badly or well, too.

Specialist regional funds

These unit trusts invest in certain overseas stock markets. A typical fund might have an objective like:
'This fund aims to achieve growth of capital through investment in the Far East covering countries such as Japan, Hong Kong, Australia, Singapore . . .' In the main, these funds concentrate on getting increases in unit prices rather than income. Typically there are funds specialising in Europe, Japan, US, Far East, Australia.

You should not expect specialist funds to move in line with the UK stock market. This is why specialist regional funds and commodity funds often appear at the top — and the bottom — of tables showing unit trust performance. The

Table on p275 shows specialist funds appearing frequently at the top and bottom of unit trust performance. The exception is the top performers of 1987, when stock markets throughout the world fell, and the best performers were funds investing for income.

Note that funds which invest overseas are also affected by the caprices of the currency market – the unit price of an overseas trust will tend to rise if the exchange rate of the £ goes down, fall if the exchange rate of the £ goes up.

Managed funds

These have appeared on the scene fairly recently. The idea is that one unit trust invests in other unit trusts, with the aim of providing a managed investment for more cautious investors. These unit trusts are also known as 'funds of funds'. There are rules about how such unit trusts can be invested. For example, they cannot invest in another managed fund and must invest in at least five unit trusts. Limits are also put on what management charges can be made. A managed fund cannot make an initial charge, but you will still have to pay this when it invests in other unit trusts. However, the managers of managed funds are allowed to make a yearly charge.

As such a fund is designed for investors wanting lower risk, the return is also likely to be a bit pedestrian

Verdict: which type of fund?

If you want to invest in a unit trust and hang on to it for a while, it's probably best to choose a general or income unit trust. If you have enough money, spread it between two or more unit trusts, perhaps one general and one other – the other could be a growth or specialist fund. If you want to invest with the idea of shifting from fund to fund, you can choose from the full range, according to your educated guess.

How to choose a unit trust

There is no magic recipe for choosing a unit trust. Below we look at some well-known systems for picking a winner – and put them to the test. Although we used details of unit trusts for the period 1 January 1973 to 30 October 1980, we expect the results to hold true today. Note that our verdicts on the

Best and worst performing unit trusts

1986
TOP 5

Legal and General Far East	112.2
County Japan Growth	104.7
Sun Life Far East Growth	100.0
Eagle Star Far Eastern	99.1
Wardley Japan	89.4

BOTTOM 5

MIM Britannia Universal Energy	11.1
LAS North American Equity	12.4
3i's Smaller Companies	12.8
Canada Growth	14.0
Target Australian	20.6

1987
TOP 5

Guinness Mahon High Income	59.8
ManuLife UK Smaller Companies	56.9
Wellington Income	42.3
Key Income	42.1
Royal Trust Preference	40.0

BOTTOM 5

Dumenil French Growth	48.2
Royal Trust Prestige Hong Kong	50.4
MIM Britannia Hong Kong	51.7
MIM Britannia Australian	61.9
Target Australian	38.1

Note: includes net income reinvested; valued on an offer to bid basis.
Source: Money Management

theories are general ones – there are always exceptions to any rule.

More recent research done by other organisations shows results broadly in line with our earlier research: none of the systems below would prove a useful strategy to pick winners. There may be slight evidence to support one or other of the theories, but for a limited period or a limited gain, which would mean you couldn't profitably take advantage of it because of your buying and selling costs.

Theory 1: small funds do best

It's argued that the managers of small funds can buy and sell investments more easily and so get the best return.

We divided funds up by size. Our results showed that, over the period, funds in the smallest size group (less than £2 million) had performed slightly worse than bigger ones. But over one year (1979) small funds did much better. So size doesn't seem to be a useful guide to picking a unit trust.

We also looked to see if small unit trusts were riskier than big ones – but there was no evidence for this.

Verdict: size is not a particularly useful criterion for picking a unit trust.

Theory 2: the past is a guide to the future

This theory claims that trusts which have done well in the past will do well in the future.

We looked at the performance of unit trusts for the first half of the period (ie four years) compared with the second half.

We found that, in general, unit trusts which did worst in the first period did best in the next and vice versa. But this result could be because in the first period the UK stock market was plummeting down most of the time, while in the second period it was shooting up. So, for example, unit trusts invested overseas might do much better in the first period but those invested in the UK come out top in the second period.

We had a closer look at past performance by comparing the results of a fund in one year with its results in the next year for every year of the period we looked at. This time we found that the results gave no support to the theory.

Verdict: past performance is not a good guide for picking a unit trust.

Theory 3: new is best

Because the managers will be giving a new unit trust lots of expert attention, it's claimed they'll do better than with old unit trusts.

We worked out the average return for new funds for the year after they were started and compared these returns with the average return on all unit trusts. We then compared the average return on new funds with the average return on existing funds of the same type. There was no evidence that new trusts performed better than old ones.

Verdict: no reason to believe that new unit trusts will perform better than old ones.

Theory 4: winners turn to losers

Is it true that last year's winners are likely to be this year's losers, and vice versa?

We looked at what would have happened if, at the beginning of 1974, we had invested money in the six worst-performing unit trusts for the previous year, then sold at the end of 1974 and reinvested in the six worst-performing trusts for 1974 and so on until 30 October 1980. We then repeated this exercise six times, starting with 1975 and then 1976 and so on.

Then we turned to the six best-performing unit trusts and did the whole thing again.

The results are in the Table below. As you can see the winner – ie whether investing in the best, or worst, performing funds was the best idea – depended on the year you started in.

Verdict: not a good guide for picking a unit trust.

Results of investing £1,000 in six worst-performing and six best-performing funds each year

Period of Investment	Six worst	Six best	THE WINNER
1974–1980	£1,003	£1,133	BEST
1975–1980	£1,769	£1,412	WORST
1976–1980	£1,454	£1,195	WORST
1977–1980	£1,609	£1,413	WORST
1978–1980	£1,368	£1,757	BEST
1979–1980	£1,312	£1,662	BEST
1980	£1,140	£1,812	BEST

Theory 5: pick a management company

It's claimed that some management companies do better than others.

We compared the average return of the different management companies' trusts for the first half of the period compared with what happened in the second half of the period.

We couldn't find any evidence that good performance in one period would mean good performance in the next. But this result has to be treated with caution as so many companies merged in the first four years.

Verdict: evidence too slight to say that management company is good way to pick a unit trust.

A step-by-step guide to choosing a unit trust

Although there's no sure-fire way of choosing the unit trusts which will perform best, you can narrow down your choice amongst the bewildering number available by following the steps below. But be warned – it's a long job. You could ask advisers to do it for you – see p280.

Step 1 Make sure a unit trust really is a suitable investment for you – see Chapters 1 and 2. Don't feel that you have to invest **now** just because you've got the cash available now – bear in mind that the success of your investment will depend very much on when you buy and when you sell.

Step 2 Decide how many trusts to invest in. If you have enough £££ (minimum investment is usually in the £250 to £1,000 range), invest in more than one unit trust.

Step 3 Decide which types of fund to go for – see p272.

Step 4 Do you want to invest a lump sum or a regular amount each month? If you want to save a certain amount each month, only around a third of all unit trusts offer a savings plan. You could consider investing via a life insurance policy instead (see Chapter 20).

Step 5 Find out when you can deal. With a few unit trusts you can't deal daily, and this may be inconvenient.

Step 6 Still left with lots of unit trusts to choose from? Look at the investments the fund holds, whether they've been changed a lot (which can be costly) and so on. Ask the company to send you manager's reports and the scheme particulars (see opposite).

Step 7 Finally, choosing between these unit trusts will have to be based on your own hunches.

Example: choosing a unit trust

Jack and Jill Gander are in their late 40's with two children – one about to go to college and one about to take the GCSE.

Step 1 They've already got a big enough emergency fund plus some other investments. Jack has just inherited £6,000. From reading newspapers and talking to people, they discover that the stock market has seen recent falls but is still well above levels existing a few years ago. They hum and haa, because they don't want to do what some small investors do – invest all their money in unit trusts just when share prices are about to fall further. Finally, they decide to put only a bit of their money (£2,000, say) in unit trusts.

Step 2 £2,000 is enough money to split between two unit trusts.

Step 3 As they're looking for a long-term investment, they decide to go for a general unit trust in the UK and for an overseas fund (Far Eastern one).

Step 4 They want to invest a lump sum, so there's no narrowing down here.

Step 5 They want to be able to sell their units within the same day – however since most funds now offer this it doesn't restrict their choice much.

Step 6 Jack and Jill decide to go for a general fund with some overseas investments. They visit their local library to look at the brief details of each trust published in the Unit Trust Year Book, and find there are funds which match these needs. They get in touch with the companies and ask to see the latest scheme particulars and latest managers' report on the particular unit trust and a current list of what investments are in the trust. Then they:

■ look at what the investments are

■ check that none of them are big holdings that the unit trust managers would find it difficult to sell

■ try to find how often investments are bought and sold – they'd prefer to go for one that's not too active

■ look at the charges made.

They do a similar exercise with the Far Eastern funds, mainly looking at where the fund is invested and how much in any one region.

Step 7 Finally, they plump for the two unit trusts they're going to invest in.

Getting information

From the company

If you want information about a unit trust, ask to see the latest **manager's report** and the **scheme particulars**. What goes in each of these documents is laid down by the Securities and Investments Board (see Chapter 5). The scheme particulars have to be revised once a year or more frequently if a major change occurs in the unit trust. The managers of the unit trust have to produce a report every six months. From these two documents you should be able to find most of what you want to know about the unit trust.

The manager's report should, among other things, tell you what the objectives of the fund are and how the fund has done over the last six months, how much income will be paid out, what changes have occurred in the investments, information about the highest buying and lowest selling prices since the fund began (or for the last ten years, if less).

The scheme particulars will give the names and addresses of the manager, the trustee, the investment adviser for the fund (if there is one), the auditor and the registrar (if there is one). There should be a statement saying what the investment policy of the fund will be and giving details about its valuation, the charges and expenses of the fund.

From newspapers and magazines
Details of most unit trusts are listed in several newspapers. An entry might look like this:

Westover income 494.8   523.2   470.2 – 0.3   3.83

This tells you the name of the unit trust and (in the order above) the price you could sell your units for yesterday, the price at which you could buy them yesterday, the cancellation price (the lowest bid price worked out using the DTI formula – see opposite), how much the price has changed since the previous day, and the yield (see p284). Once a week the initial charge will be shown as a percentage of price.

Magazines, such as *Money Management*, *Planned Savings* and *Unit Trust Management* give other details – for example, what £1,000 invested five years ago would be worth now.

The Unit Trust Year Book gives lots of information about each unit trust and each management group. It is available from FTBI, the Marketing Department, Financial Times, 7th Floor, 50–64 Broadway, London SW1H 0DB, price £25 (1988). Or try a library.

From investment advisers
In Chapter 6 we looked at the various sources of professional advice – many of whom will help in choosing unit trusts. But remember that it's up to *you* to evaluate the advice you get.

Both independent advisers and unit trust company representatives can sell you unit trusts. Independent advisers generally get a commission of up to 3 per cent of the value of unit trusts they buy for you. Company representatives could get more or less, depending on the company.

If you buy from one of these groups as a result of an unsolicited sales call (see p76), in certain circumstances you have the right to cancel the investment within fourteen days of receiving a notice of your rights. What you will get back will be the price you would have paid if you had bought on the day you decided to cancel.

Investing in unit trusts

Units

When you invest in a unit trust you buy units in the trust from the management company. When you cash your investments, you sell units back to the management company (it *has* to buy them from you). The management company puts the cash you pay for units into the fund and it's used to buy investments, such as shares.

Prices

A unit has two prices. These prices are based on the value of the investments in the trust fund. The higher price (the offer price) is what you pay to buy units. The lower price (the bid price) is what you get if you sell units. You buy or sell at the price worked out when the fund is next valued – which means that, as with shares, you won't know the exact price until the deal is done. But the fund can, in certain circumstances, let you deal at the price which was worked out when the fund was last valued. Generally speaking, the fund is valued once a day, but a few are valued less frequently.

The prices are worked out using a method laid down by the Department of Trade and Industry (DTI). To get the offer price the company finds out the lowest price it would have to pay to buy the investments currently in the unit trust fund. It then adds various costs to this – eg management charges. The value it has after doing this sum is divided by the number of units the company has issued – and this gives the maximum offer price the company can charge you to buy units.

The lowest bid price (ie the price the company has to pay you for your units) is worked out in a similar way. But this time the company has to find out what is the highest price it could get if it sold the investments currently in the unit trust fund.

The difference between these two prices is called the spread. The average spread quoted in the newspapers is around 7%. If you want to sell a large number of units, (£15,000 plus) the management company does not necessarily have to buy at the bid price it is quoting other sellers of units. Instead, it could offer to buy your units at a price nearer or equal to the minimum bid price or make you wait until it has worked out what the price will be at the next valuation.

In fact, it's possible for the unit price for any size purchase to rise or fall without the share prices of the investments in the unit trust rising or falling. This is because the spread the management company quotes is usually less than the spread it could quote under the DTI rules. So, for example, if lots of unit holders are selling, the management company can shift the unit prices downwards to discourage selling and attract buyers. However, if it wants to alter where its prices are in the permitted range, the company cannot do so and carry on using the price from the last valuation. It can only let you deal at the price worked out at the next valuation.

Buying and selling

You can buy or sell in several ways, for example, over the telephone, by letter or through a company representative or independent adviser. Note that an order over the telephone is just as binding as one made in writing. If the fund is dealing only at the prices worked out at the next valuation, you can, of course, set a limit on the price you're prepared to pay for units or accept if you sell them – eg only sell at 65p or more. In this way, you should get no surprises.

Once the unit trust manager has received your unit trust certificate, if you are selling, you should get the money in five days.

Charges

There are two different sorts of charges. These are:
■ **initial charge**. This is often 5% and is included in the spread between the bid and offer prices
■ **regular charge**. This is often in the range $^3/_4$% to $1^1/_4$% a year, but can be as much as $1^1/_2$ or 2% (all plus VAT). This charge is usually taken from the income of the fund.

Management of the unit trust

There may be three groups of people involved. First, a management company which does the administration and advertising. Secondly, there is an investment adviser. Generally, this is the same company as the management company. But some have advisers such as stockbrokers deciding how the fund should be invested. Thirdly, there is the trustee (see opposite).

Under the Financial Services Act (see Chapter 5), there will be a procedure for handling complaints about unit trusts. Contact the unit trust company first, and they will tell you which of these three groups will deal with an unresolved complaint. If this doesn't work, contact LAUTRO (see p80).

Trustee

There are over a dozen companies – mainly banks – acting as trustees to over 1,200 unit trusts. Trustees have several jobs. First, the trustee keeps all the cash and investments of the fund in its name.

Secondly, the trustee makes sure that the managers stick to the terms of the trust deed and the scheme particulars (see p279). The trust deed will have the following information among other things:
- name of the fund and its investment aim
- the currency of the fund
- when income of the fund will be paid out.

Thirdly, the trustee checks that the unit price calculation has been done correctly and cancels and issues units.

Exactly how much the trustee does can vary, depending on how the trustee interprets the trust deed.

Income

The investments which are held in the unit trust fund get income in the form of share dividends, interest from British Government stocks and so on. The management company takes its regular charge from the income and will usually pay out what's left to unit holders in the form of **distributions**. There are usually two distributions a year – but some trusts, which concentrate on producing income, pay out distributions once a quarter.

As the income comes into the fund, the unit price rises to take account of this, until it finally includes the whole of the distribution. On a certain day, the price will be marked *xd* (ie *ex distribution*) and will fall by the amount of the distribution. After that time, if you buy units, you will not get the next distribution to be paid; if you sell units, you still get the next distribution.

There are four different types of trust:
- accumulation trusts
- distribution trusts
- trusts with both accumulation and distribution units
- trusts where you can automatically reinvest income.

With accumulation trusts, the income of the unit trust fund is not paid to you in £££ – instead the unit price is simply increased to reflect the income. There are only a few accumulation trusts.

With distribution trusts, the income of the unit trust fund must be paid out in £££ to each investor.

With many unit trusts, you can buy either accumulation units (where the income of the fund is used to increase the unit price) or distribution units (where the income of the fund is paid out to you).

With the rest of the funds, you can choose to have the income automatically reinvested (rather than paid out). This means the income is used to buy more units – and you have to pay an initial charge on these.

Tax

Distributions from a unit trust come with a **tax credit**. The effect of this is that if you're a basic rate taxpayer, there's no income tax to pay on the distribution. If you pay tax at the higher rate, you'll have to pay more tax. If you're a non-taxpayer, you'll be able to claim tax back. For more details, see p97.

The normal capital gains tax rules apply to unit trust investments. See p104 for details.

Size of income

If you are buying a unit trust as a way of getting an income, look at the **yield** of the fund. The higher the yield, the higher the income is compared to the £££ you invest.

To get the yield, the amount of the distribution per unit is divided by the unit price. This is then multiplied by 100 to give a percentage. For example, if the distribution per unit is two pence and the unit price is 40p, the yield is $2 \div 40$ x $100 = 5\%$.

Of course, if you bought units when the price was lower, say 30p, the yield on your investment would be $2 \div 30$ x $100 = 6\,{}^2/_3\%$.

Note that the yield usually quoted is the gross yield – ie based on the distribution *plus* tax credit (see above).

Another way of getting an income from unit trusts

The disadvantage of using the distribution from a unit trust to provide you with an income is that it can go up and down – because the dividends paid by shares held by the unit trust fund can also go up and down. It also alters because managers of the fund will buy and sell the investments of the fund. So around 10 unit trust companies have **withdrawal**

schemes. With these you can choose to have as your income either:

■ a percentage, say 5 per cent, of the original amount of £££ you invest. So you can be certain you get the same income each year. Or,

■ a percentage, say 5 per cent, of the current value of your investment. In this case, the income would still go up and down each year.

If the distributions of the unit trust are not high enough to meet this amount of income, then some of your units are sold. But more units will have to be sold to make up your income when unit prices are low than when they are high – the opposite of what you want. And selling units can lead to you using up your capital increasingly quickly – the more units you sell, the lower your income from distributions in the future, so the more units will have to be sold in the future.

If you decide a withdrawal scheme could be useful, you'll need to check the minimum investment the company will take – it varies, but can be as high as £15,000.

Around 20 unit trust groups organise regular income schemes. In these, you invest in three or more unit trusts, each with a different month for paying income. In this way, you can get a regular if varying income.

Size of investment

For lump sum investments, all unit trusts ask for a minimum investment when you first invest – eg £250 or £1,000. If you want to increase your investment you can usually do so by smaller amounts.

Over a third of unit trust companies will let you invest a regular amount, often £25 a month – but it can be as little as £10 a month. This is known as a **savings plan**. For how this can be linked to a life insurance policy see p340.

One advantage of a savings plan is that you don't have to worry so much about when you should invest as you would with a lump sum. **Pound-cost averaging** is sometimes cited as being an advantage of a regular savings plan. What this seems to show is that you can get a bargain by investing regularly. This is because, if the unit price goes up and down, the average cost of your units will be less than the average of unit prices – when the unit price is low your fixed sum of money buys more units than when it is high. But there's nothing magic about this – it just shows the advantage of not having to worry about timing your investment correctly. Don't let this sort of advertising for savings plans persuade you that you are getting a bargain. You still have to worry about when you should cash in your investment.

If you already hold shares, you could swap these for units – through a **share exchange scheme**. The unit trust company will usually do one of two things with your shares:

■ put them in one of its funds, if the fund already holds that company's shares. In this case, in exchange for the shares, the company will often give you units equal in value to the price that it would have to pay in the Stock Exchange to buy the shares. As this is higher than you could get by selling the shares yourself through the Stock Exchange, this seems a good saving

■ sell them for you if the company does not want to put them in a fund. In this case, the company often pays the selling costs – eg stockbroker's commission.

Most unit trust companies have a share exchange scheme – the details about minimum value of shares, number of shares and so on vary from company to company.

But don't let quite small savings push you into poor investment decisions.

Cost of switching

With the growth of more and more specialist funds and specialist advisers, there has been an increase in the number of companies which will let you switch your investment from one of their unit trusts to another for a lower-than-normal initial charge. Most unit trust companies will normally give you a discount of between 1 and 4% off the price of units in the trust you are switching to.

17

BRITISH GOVERNMENT STOCKS

The Government issues British Government stocks as a way of borrowing money. They can prove good investments. But they can also turn out to be poor investments, for example if interest rates and inflation rise, as they did in the 1960s and 70s.

British Government stocks could suit four quite different categories of people:

■ those who want a regular (normally fixed) income and who are confident that they won't want their money back in a hurry

■ those who want to invest for a specific time period and want a fixed return over that period – and may not be too bothered how much of that return comes as income, how much as capital gain

■ those who want to gamble that interest rates, in general, will fall (stock prices are then likely to rise, leading to a capital gain)

■ those who want to protect some of their money against inflation – they could choose index-linked British Government stocks.

Below we describe how conventional stocks work. For more details on index-linked stocks, and on their pros and cons, see p294.

How conventional stocks work

Most British Government stocks (commonly called gilt-edged securities or just gilts) pay a fixed amount of income each year. In the late 1970s, there were also three issues of stocks whose income could vary. The last of these came to an end in 1983 and so far no more of these *variable rate* stocks have been issued.

With stocks which are *dated*, the Government also promises to pay the holder of the stock a fixed number of £££ in a lump sum at the time the stock comes to an end. With *undated* stocks, no final date is specified – so the Government need never pay off its debt.

Like shares, stocks are bought and sold on the Stock Exchange. And, as with shares, the prices of stocks fluctuate – so once you've bought some stock, the value of your investment can vary widely.

The Diagram opposite shows what has happened to the price of an undated stock since 1975. You can see, for example, that if you'd bought in August 1979 and sold two years later you'd have done badly. You'd have got a before-tax income of 10.5 per cent a year on your original investment, but when you sold you would have got back only three-quarters of the money you originally invested – an overall loss of around 4.5 per cent a year for a basic rate taxpayer.

If, on the other hand, you'd been lucky (or shrewd) enough to invest in October 1981 and sell four and a half years after that, you'd have done very much better. You'd have got a before-tax income of 14.2 per cent a year on your original investment and your investment would have increased in value by 66 per cent by the time you sold – an overall return to a basic rate taxpayer of around 19.7 per cent a year.

So when you buy and when you sell is crucial to the success or failure of your investment. Of course, if you buy a dated stock and hold it until it comes to an end, you'll know from the outset what you'll get – both in income and capital gain (or loss).

Getting to know the different stocks

Nominal value

British Government stocks are bought and sold in amounts which have a nominal value (sometimes called face value) of so many £ and pence. For each £100 nominal of stock you hold, the Government promises to pay you £100 in cash at an agreed time in the future – see *redemption date*.

But you don't have to buy stocks in multiples of £100 nominal. You could, for example, invest £125 in a stock costing £80 for each £100 nominal. You would then get: £100 x 125 ÷ 80 = £156.25 nominal of stock.

Name

Each stock has a name, like Exchequer, Treasury or War Loan. This is of no particular significance to investors but

How the price of undated stock [1] has changed

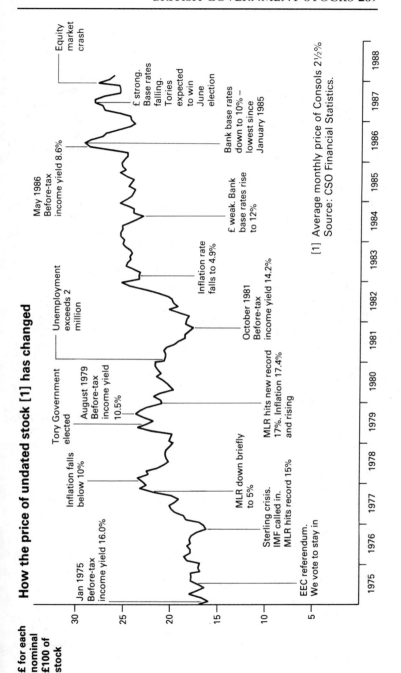

£ for each nominal £100 of stock

Equity market crash

£ strong. Base rates falling. Tories expected to win June election

May 1986 Before-tax income yield 8.6%

Bank base rates down to 10% – lowest since January 1985

£ weak. Bank base rates rise to 12%

Unemployment exceeds 2 million

Inflation rate falls to 4.9%

October 1981 Before-tax income yield 14.2%

Tory Government elected

August 1979 Before-tax income yield 10.5%

MLR hits new record 17%. Inflation 17.4% and rising

Inflation falls below 10%

MLR down briefly to 5%

Sterling crisis. IMF called in. MLR hits record 15%

Jan 1975 Before-tax income yield 16.0%

EEC referendum. We vote to stay in

[1] Average monthly price of Consols 2½%
Source: CSO Financial Statistics.

helps to distinguish one stock from another.

Coupon
The percentage immediately after the name of each stock, for example 10% in Exchequer 10% 1989, is called the coupon. It tells you the before-tax income the stock pays out each year, expressed as a percentage of the nominal value – in the case of Exchequer 10% 1989 the stock pays out £10 for every £100 nominal. Interest on nearly all stocks is paid twice yearly in two equal instalments.

Redemption date
Following the name and the coupon is a year – 1989 in the example above. The date on which the Government has promised to redeem the stock – ie to pay out the nominal value of the stock – falls in this year.

The date may be a range of years, for example 1995–98. In this case, the Government (but not the investor) can choose in which year out of this range to redeem the stock.

With a few stocks, the coupon is followed by a year and the words *or after*, for example 1923 *or after*. This means that the Government can choose 1923 or any later year which suits it in which to redeem the stock. These, and a few other stocks which have no year quoted at all, are called undated and need never be redeemed.

The life of a stock
Stocks are generally split into four groups according to the length of their remaining life – ie the time left until redemption. The precise splits vary somewhat depending on their use, but these are what the groups are called:
■ short-dated if the stocks must be redeemed in the next five (or sometimes seven) years
■ medium-dated if their latest redemption date is more than five (or seven) years but not more than fifteen years away
■ long-dated if over fifteen years
■ undated if no latest redemption date is given.

What makes stock prices change?

In general, changes in interest rates in the economy as a whole. If interest rates rise, the price of stocks is likely to fall. If interest rates fall, stock prices are likely to rise. Why?

Suppose you invest £100 in an undated British Government stock which pays out an income of £10 a year. The yearly return is then roughly 10 per cent. But now suppose that interest rates in the economy as a whole rise. New investors could then get a higher return on their money by investing elsewhere – so they'll hold off buying British Government stock. This means that the price of Government stock is likely to fall until the yearly return it offers is comparable to the return investors could get elsewhere. For example, if interest rates double, the price of the undated stock which pays out £10 a year may have to halve to £50 – so that the yearly return it then offers is roughly 20 per cent.

Similarly, if interest rates as a whole fall, the price of British Government stock is likely to rise.

But it's not quite as simple as that with dated stocks, because there are other factors at work. The main ones are:

■ **how long to go until the stock comes to an end.** In general, the shorter the period left to run, the smaller the fluctuations in price. Take the example above of an undated stock paying interest of £10 a year and halving in price from £100 to £50. Suppose this stock was due to end in a year's time when the Government would pay the holder £100. If the price was £50, someone buying it now would get back £100 in a year's time plus £10 in income in the meantime – a return of around 120 per cent a year. The price needs to fall from £100 to only £90 or so to give a return of around 20 per cent

■ **the stock's coupon** (see opposite). In general, the higher the coupon, the smaller the fluctuations in price. Take a stock with a coupon of 10 per cent, for example, and five years to go before it comes to an end. If it is currently selling for its nominal value (see p288) of £100, the yearly return will be 10 per cent. For the return (taking account of both income and capital growth over the next five years) to rise to 20 per cent, the price of the stock would have to fall by about 28 per cent to £72. But if the coupon was only 2 per cent, the stock would have to be selling for around £71 to give a yearly return of 10 per cent. For this return to rise to 20 per cent the price would have to fall by around 32 per cent to £48 or so.

What makes interest rates change?

A whole host of reasons. To take just two examples, the Government may increase interest rates to discourage people from borrowing, or to attract investors' money from abroad. An important influence will be the gap – if any – between the Government's income and its spending, which will determine how much the Government needs to borrow (by issuing Government stocks and by other methods). See Diagram on p289 for some of the events of the past thirteen years.

The price you pay

The price of British Government stocks is quoted as the price for each £100 nominal of stock. Prices are normally quoted in £££ and fractions of a £, and shown to the nearest £^{1}/$_{32}$ (just over 3p) for short-dated stocks, and to the nearest £^{1}/$_{16}$ (just over 6p) for others.

Buyers pay more than the quoted price, sellers pay less, for example buyers might pay £^{1}/$_8$ more and sellers £^{1}/$_8$ less. The difference between these two prices – the **spread** – will vary according to how actively the particular stock is traded and the size of your transaction. Spreads will tend to be larger with inactive stocks and small deals.

The price at which you buy or sell will be adjusted for something called accrued interest (see below).

Cum-dividend and ex-dividend

Most of the time, when you buy a stock, you buy it cum-dividend. This means that you are entitled to a full half-year's interest when it next becomes due, even if you haven't held the stock for that long.

However, some five weeks before the interest is due to be paid, the stock is declared ex-dividend. If you buy a stock ex-dividend, you are not entitled to the next interest payment – and therefore have a longer-than-normal wait for your first interest payment. The quoted price for an ex-dividend stock has *xd* after it.

For stocks with more than five years to redemption, except War Loan 3^1/$_2$%, there's an additional period of three weeks before the stock is declared ex-dividend, during which you can choose to buy or sell the stock either cum-dividend or ex-dividend; during this time, the ex-dividend version is called special ex-dividend. Because the cum-dividend version of the stock entitles you to the next interest payment, it costs more than the ex-dividend version. You'll find only the cum-dividend price quoted in the newspapers during this three week period.

Accrued interest

This is the interest that a cum-dividend buyer gets for the period when he didn't own the stock, or which an ex-dividend buyer forfeits by getting his first interest payment late.

Since 28 February 1986, the quoted prices for all stocks have not included the accrued interest. This means that you have to pay a bit more than the quoted price when you buy cum-dividend, a bit less when you buy ex-dividend.

Similarly, you receive a bit more than the quoted price if you sell cum-dividend, and you receive a bit less if you sell ex-dividend. (Before 28 February 1986, only short-dated stocks were quoted in this way.)

Working out accrued interest
Since the quoted price of a stock does not include the accrued interest, you'll need to work out the amount of interest accrued so far in order to find out the total price you'll have to pay.

Correctly, accrued interest is worked out in a way that takes each day's interest into account. But you won't go far wrong if you do the sums in weeks.

For a cum-dividend stock, count the number of weeks between the last date interest was paid and the date for which you want the accrued interest. For an ex-dividend stock, count the number of weeks still to go before the next interest date. Ignore odd days. The approximate accrued interest in pence is then:

coupon x weeks just counted x 2

For a cum-dividend stock, you need to *add* the answer you get to the quoted price to give you the total price you'll pay. For an ex-dividend stock, you need to *subtract* the answer from the quoted price to get the total price you'll pay.

Example
What was the accrued interest on Treasury 10% 1992 on 20 March 1988?

This stock was cum-dividend on 20 March 1988. The previous interest date was 21 February. Count the weeks from 21 February to 20 March – four weeks.

The approximate accrued interest is:
10% (ie coupon) x 4 (ie weeks you've just counted) x 2 = 10 x 4 x 2 = 80p.

The return you get

In income
A stock's coupon (see p290) tells you the before-tax income paid on each £100 nominal of stock. But it won't tell you how much income you'll get – because you are unlikely to pay £100 for each £100 nominal of stock. To work out the income you'll get (as a percentage of the amount invested), do this sum:

coupon x 100 ÷ quoted price for each £100 nominal of stock.

This is known as the income yield (or interest yield).

Capital gain (or loss)

If you hold the stock until it comes to an end, you know you'll be paid its nominal value so you can work out the capital gain (or loss) you'll make. But with undated stocks or stocks sold before they come to an end, you don't know in advance what price you'll get, so you can't be sure of what capital gain (or loss) you'll make.

The total return

With a dated stock, you can get some idea of the average yearly return on the stock if you hold it until it is redeemed by looking at what's known as the redemption yield. This takes account of both income paid out and the capital gain (or loss) you make in redemption. But it doesn't normally take account of buying and selling costs and it assumes that the income paid out is reinvested at a rate of return equal to the redemption yield – for higher coupon stocks this over-states the return you're likely to get in practice. Before-tax redemption yields are printed daily in the newspapers mentioned on p299.

Working out the after-tax redemption yield for any stock is not easy. It depends not only on the rate of tax you pay but also on how much of the return comes as taxable income and how much as tax-free capital gain.

In general:

■ stocks vary widely in redemption yields – in March 1988, before-tax redemption yields varied from 5.2 per cent to 9.6 per cent

■ for stocks with about the same period of time left to run, people who pay the higher rate of tax tend to get the best after-tax redemption yields from relatively low coupon stocks. By contrast, people who pay no tax tend to get the best redemption yields from high coupon stocks

■ when it is possible to buy the same stock in the special ex-dividend period, taxpayers normally get better redemption yields if they buy ex-dividend.

Index-linked stocks

Here we look at index-linked British Government stocks and how they compare with other British Government stocks. We also look at how they compare with index-linked National Savings Certificates (4th Issue) – another invest-ment suitable for a lump sum, which offers index-linking (see p176 for details of this investment).

How they work

There were twelve index-linked stocks when this book went to press – each with a different lifetime. The stock with the shortest life ends in 1990; and the stock with the longest life ends in 2024. When the life of a stock comes to an end, the person then owning it will be paid the nominal value (see p288) of the stock *increased in line with inflation over the lifetime of the stock.* So, for example, someone owning £100 nominal value of 1996 stock, issued in 1981, would get just under £210 if inflation averaged out at a constant five per cent over the life of the stock.

All the stocks also pay out a small income – their coupon (see p290) is 2% or $2^1/2$% depending on the stock. The income is guaranteed to increase each year in line with inflation.

For technical reasons, inflation is measured by the twelve-month change in the Retail Prices Index (RPI) recorded eight months before the dividend dates.

What happens to the buying and selling prices of the stocks?

Over the long term, the prices of the stocks will tend to rise roughly in line with inflation. If the price is £100 and the RPI goes up by 5 per cent a year, the price after a year might well be £105. But the price will also be affected by people's views on the future rate of inflation and interest rates, and by the return they can get on other investments.

The price of stocks with a longer life may well fluctuate more than the price of those with a short life.

Will your investment keep pace with inflation?

This depends entirely on the price at which you buy (or sell) the stock and whether or not you hold the stock until redemption. If you bought £100 nominal value of stock for £100 when the stock was issued, and if you then kept it throughout the lifetime of the stock, the increase in capital would exactly match the increase in inflation.

But suppose you had bought your £100 nominal value of stock for £90. Since it's the £100 nominal value which is index-linked, your capital gain at the end of the stock's lifetime would be more than the rate of inflation. If you'd bought at £110, your capital gain would be less.

If you want to buy stocks some time after they are first issued, you should compare the current market price with the nominal value *adjusted for the increase in the RPI between the issue date and the time at which you want to buy*. If the RPI has increased by 5 per cent, say, you should compare the market price with £105. If the price is higher, then your capital gain if you hold the stock to redemption will be less than inflation; if the price is lower, your capital gain will be more than inflation.

If you can't hold on to the stock until redemption, your gain will depend on the price you can sell at – see p290.

How do they compare with other British Government stocks?

■ **pro**: If you buy at the right price (see above) and hold them until redemption, you're guaranteed that the money you invest will at least keep pace with inflation.
■ **con**: The coupon for all index-linked stocks is low. And it could be costly to sell small amounts of stock to boost the income. So if you're after income, a high coupon stock may suit you better.

How do they compare with index-linked National Savings Certificates (4th Issue)?

■ **pro**: You can choose from a range of stocks with different redemption dates up to 2024. National Savings Certificates are designed to last five years – and give the best return if you hold them for the full five years.
■ **con**: Assuming 5 per cent inflation, stocks were offering a real (ie on top of inflation-proofing) return of up to 3.8 per cent a year before tax when this book went to press; Certificates were offering 4 per cent a year as well as the index-linking – and this return was completely tax-free. As there would also be buying and selling costs with the stocks, the Certificates looked the better investment over a five year period. And because the price of stocks can fluctuate, you have to be careful about the prices you buy and sell at – you can eliminate the second of these risks by holding the stocks until the end of their lives.

Worth buying?

If you're a higher-rate taxpayer not looking for a large increase in income, you should consider putting some of your money into these stocks. And they're definitely worth considering for anyone who wants to keep a nest-egg on ice for a fairly long time.

If you need to sell stocks, the price should roughly match inflation over the time you've owned it – though fluctuations in price may work against you.

New issues of stocks

When the Government issues stock it usually advertises in the newspapers and includes in the advertisement a form for you to cut out and send in as your application for stock (along with your cheque).

Stocks used commonly to be issued for sale at a fixed price, but this method has now been replaced by issues *by tender*. With a tender issue, it's usual for only a minimum price to be quoted. You can offer to buy stock at whatever price you like at or above the minimum.

If the whole issue (of, say, £800 million) is able to be sold at or above the minimum price, the issue is closed. But you don't need to worry about bidding too high – everyone who bids pays the price paid by the lowest successful bidder, rather than the price they themselves bid. And issues don't normally sell out on the first day – so usually everyone who applies gets stock at the minimum price. After the initial offer, the stock that's left over is sold on the Stock Exchange by the Gilt-Edged Division of the Bank of England over a period of time – and not necessarily at the issue price.

During this period, the stock is commonly called a tap stock (because the supply of the stock is turned on and off like a tap, depending on the demand for it). When all this extra stock is sold, the tap is said to be exhausted. New short-dated stocks are called short taps; new medium-dated stocks, medium taps; and so on.

Since May 1987, the Government has also experimented with another method of issuing stock – the *bid price auction* – which will continue alongside tender issues. In an auction, you also choose the price at which you bid for stock. The main differences between a tender and an auction are that at auction all the stock is usually sold and all the bidders pay the price they bid – so bidding too high could turn out to be costly. However, 'small' investors – making bids up to £100,000 – do not have to join the main auction. They can put in non-competitive bids, in which case they will be sure of getting stock at the *average* price of the issue.

Buying stock direct from the Bank of England when it's first issued has the advantage that you don't have to pay any stockbroker's commission (and there's no price spread – see p292). Nowadays, most newly-issued stocks can eventually be registered on the National Savings Stock Register (see p302) which may keep your eventual selling costs down too.

New issues of stock are often partly-paid. This means that you don't have to pay the full cost of the stock when you first buy it – for example, you may have to pay 15 per cent with your application and the remainder a month later.

How stocks are taxed

Since 2 July 1986, Government stocks have been completely free of capital gains tax. You have to pay income tax on the income you get from the stocks at your highest rate of tax – see p97.

If you buy stocks on the National Savings Stock Register (see p302), income is paid without any tax deducted – though, if you're a taxpayer, you will have to pay the tax eventually. See p302 for details. If you buy through a stockbroker or an advertisement, your interest is normally paid after deduction of basic rate tax. However, if your interest payment is £5 or less, or if you buy War Loan 3 $\frac{1}{2}$%, tax won't be deducted regardless of how you bought the stock. But the £5 limit doesn't apply to *Gas* stock – with this, tax is always deducted.

The price you pay for, or get from, stocks equals the quoted price with accrued interest either added or deducted (see p292). The amount of this accrued interest used to be treated as part of your capital gain or loss and was subject to the capital gains tax rules – which often meant no tax to pay at all. But since 28 February 1986, accrued interest has been treated as income and is subject to income tax rules. There are a few exceptions: the main one for private investors is that, if the total nominal value of *all* the stocks you hold is no more than £5,000, the accrued income scheme does not apply; in that case, there is no income tax (and no tax relief) on accrued interest.

The contract note that you get when you buy or sell stock will show how much accrued interest is involved in the deal. How it is treated for income tax depends on whether you are a buyer or a seller:

■ if you sell cum-dividend, you are taxed on the accrued interest included in the price you get

■ if you sell ex-dividend, you get tax relief on the accrued interest that has been deducted from the quoted price

■ if you buy cum-dividend, you get tax relief on the accrued interest included in the price you pay

■ if you buy ex-dividend, you are taxed on the accrued interest which has been deducted from the quoted price.

For more details about the way accrued interest is taxed, see Inland Revenue leaflet IR68 (from tax and PAYE offices).

Choosing a stock

Which stock to choose depends on what you want from your investment.

A high fixed income?
Go for a high coupon stock. But beware of going for a stock which has a long time to go before it has to be redeemed – if you're forced to sell before then, you may lose heavily if the price of the stock has fallen meanwhile.

A known total return over a fixed period?
Go for a stock which lasts for the period you're interested in. If there's a choice, go for one which gives the best after-tax redemption yield (see p294) for someone in your tax position. In general, a higher rate taxpayer should go for a low coupon stock, a non-taxpayer for a high coupon stock.

Want to gamble on interest rates falling?
Go for a stock with a long time to run, or for an undated stock. And choose one with a low coupon. But bear in mind that if interest rates rise, you may end up losing heavily.

Protection against inflation?
Index-linked stocks might suit you. But bear in mind that you have to buy stock at the right price and hold it until redemption to be certain that the full index-linking will apply; the extent to which your investment will be protected against inflation will depend on the price you buy at. The stocks currently available are low coupon ones so may suit higher rate taxpayers best.

Where to get information and advice

Several newspapers give some information each day about British Government stock prices. But the most comprehensive information is given in the *Financial Times* and *The Times*.

Buying and selling British Government stocks

	Through a stockbroker, High-Street bank or agent for a stockbroker	Through the National Savings Stock Register

How much can you buy or sell?

no limits – but minimum charges make it expensive to buy or sell small amounts	you're not allowed to invest more than £10,000 in any particular stock on any one day. No limits on sales

– at what price?

You can usually set a price limit – eg you won't pay more than £92 for £100 nominal value of stock – but such 'limit orders' may be possible only if you meet certain conditions (eg you are buying or selling at least £2,000 of stock, the limit lasts only for the day).	you can't set a price limit

– can you buy cum-dividend or ex-dividend if the choice applies?

yes, usually (not possible with a few bank stockbroking services) – you can choose which you want in the special ex-dividend period (see p292).	no, you have to buy cum-dividend in special ex-dividend period

What are the buying and selling costs?

usually a minimum charge in the range of, say, £10 to £30 – often £20. Thereafter, the rate of commission depends on the amount you invest or sell for. Typical charges might be:	commission (which includes VAT) based on the amount you invest (or sell for):

value of stock	commission (as % of value of stock)		value of stock	commission
up to £5,000	0.75% or 1.0%		up to £250	£1 (but for *selling* stock worth £100 or less, commission only 10p for every £10 or part)
next £15,000	0.25%			
thereafter	0.125%		over £250	£1 plus 50p for every extra £125 (or part)

VAT (currently 15%) is extra. There is no stamp duty to pay on purchases or sales of British Government stock, but there is a **contract levy** of 80p if the value of the stock is over £1,000 (see p253). Some examples of the commission (including VAT and contract levy) that you might pay are:

No stamp duty

		Some examples of charges for different amounts invested (or sold)	
value of stock	commission (assumes minimum commission of £20)	value of stock	commission
£500	£23	£500	£2
£1,000	£23	£1,000	£4
£5,000	£58.30	£5,000	£20

How convenient?

a phone call or letter to your stockbroker or bank, say, is all that's needed; with banks you may be able to give instructions over the counter at your branch. You may also be able to give instructions by telex or fax	you get special form from Post Office and post it off in the envelope provided (no stamp needed)

How quick?

stock should be bought or sold within minutes of your order reaching the stockbroker (if in working hours)	stock normally bought or sold on day application received (probably day after posting)

Can you get after-tax redemption yields?

yes, with most brokers and banks	no

If buying, when must you pay?

on working day after one on which you buy, unless you've arranged otherwise – but in that case it may cost you a bit more	send payment with order (or can be taken from National Savings Ordinary Account)

If selling, when do you get cash?

as for buying – but first you have to give the stockbroker or bank your stock certificate with signed stock transfer form	you should get it within a week

To find the after-tax redemption yield for someone paying tax at the rate you pay it, and to get advice on which stock would suit your needs best, contact a stockbroker, bank or one of the increasing number of other organisations offering a similar service.

How to buy and sell

You can buy and sell British Government stocks through a stockbroker, High-Street bank (many now have their own stockbroking arm rather than just acting as agents for other stockbrokers), or through some building societies and solicitors or accountants, say, who act as an agent for a stockbroker. Nearly half the stocks are also listed on the National Savings Stock Register – you get forms for buying and selling these at Post Offices. There are important differences between buying and selling through a stockbroker on the one hand, or via the National Savings Stock Register on the other. In particular, except for large amounts of stock, buying through the National Savings Stock Register is cheaper. On the previous pages we summarise the main differences.

Investing via a unit trust

There are now around 60 unit trusts specialising in British Government stocks and other fixed income investments.

Investing via a unit trust is generally more expensive than investing in stocks direct. The difference between the buying and selling prices of units is often around five per cent – and there's a yearly charge.

From the income tax point of view, there's not a lot of difference between investing in a unit trust or investing direct. British Government stocks are not liable for capital gains tax, but gains on trusts are – though of course the first £5,000 of gains made by selling assets in the 1988–89 tax year is exempt.

Another problem with unit trust investment is that you have to accept the spread of stocks that the trust chooses to invest in. By investing directly you can choose the particular stock which is best for your particular tax rate and investment needs.

18

LOCAL AUTHORITY INVESTMENTS

If you've got a lump sum to invest, and you don't mind locking it away for a time, putting it into an investment issued by a local authority could make sense. With these investments, the interest rate and value of your capital are usually fixed – so you can be sure of the number of £££ income you'll get each year and of how much you'll get back when the investment comes to an end.

But most local authority investments aren't suitable for money you're likely to need at short notice. And there's no guarantee either that your savings will keep pace with inflation.

There are two main ways in which you can invest in local authorities:

■ by lending money direct to a local authority for a fixed period, usually a year or more. We call this type of investment a local authority loan. It's this type which you may have seen advertised in newspapers, and often referred to as a bond – eg City of Bristol Bonds

■ by buying local authority yearling bonds or local authority stocks on the Stock Exchange. Of these two types, yearling bonds are more common; there haven't been any new issues of local authority stocks for some time.

Other local authority investments

You may come across two kinds of local authority investments not covered in this chapter – mortgage loans and local authority bills.

Mortgage loans are similar to – and to a large extent have now been replaced by – local authority loans.

Local authority bills aren't really suitable for small investors. They are issued in units which might be for a minimum of, say, £25,000 but are often for considerably more, and are for fixed periods of three months.

How safe is your money?

Money lent to local authorities is not guaranteed by the Government – but the Government has laid down rules which strictly control how much a local authority can borrow, and what it can use the money for, with the result that money lent to a local authority is pretty secure. Broadly, a local authority can borrow money for periods of a year or more only to pay for capital expenditure – such as building council houses. It can borrow money to pay for day-to-day expenses (such as the wages and salaries of its employees) only on a temporary basis – and only to cover a temporary shortage of cash which will be made good when it has collected all the year's rates, Government grants and so on. Except with Government approval, a local authority isn't allowed to borrow on the strength of *next* year's rates to cover *this* year's spending. And this includes interest due on existing loans.

The Government also funds the Public Works Loans Board which, in recent years, has replaced local authority investments as the source of much of local authorities' borrowing.

Local authority loans

How long for?

You have to agree to lend your money for a fixed period – commonly between one and seven years. Some authorities offer to take money for longer – perhaps ten years.

Cashing in early

In general, local authority loans are not designed to be cashed in early. If you want to do this, you may have to convince the local authority that your circumstances have changed – for example if you've lost your job, and can't afford to live off the income you're now getting. If the authority agrees to your request it may make a charge. These loans can be transferred to someone else – but you may have difficulty in finding a buyer. They are not quoted on the Stock Exchange, but can be sold through a broker.

What happens if you die depends on the local authority. Some automatically repay the money, others insist on the loan being transferred – for example to your heirs.

Minimum investments?
This depends on the local authority – it is often £500 or £1,000 but possibly as low as £100 or £200.

What rate of interest?
Rates vary frequently – in March 1988, most local authorities were offering interest rates of between 6 and 9 per cent. The rate you get depends on:

■ **when you invest.** Rates of interest offered by local authorities go up and down from time to time, in line with general movements in interest rates in the economy. But once you've invested your money, the rate of interest is fixed for the period of the loan – even if the rate to new investors soars or plummets

■ **the amount you invest.** You may get a higher rate of interest if you invest at least £2,000, say, than you would if you invested only £500

■ **how long you invest for.** If interest rates, in general, are expected to rise you might get a higher rate of interest the longer the period you invest for – for example, you might get $1/2$ per cent extra if you invest your money for four years rather than two. But at times when interest rates in general are expected to fall, local authorities may well offer a lower rate of interest, the longer you want to invest for.

When is the interest paid out?
Normally half-yearly. A few loans pay all the interest at the end of the period of the loan. For this type of loan to be worth getting, it would have to pay you a higher advertised rate of interest to compensate for the delay in paying the interest out — at least $1/4$ per cent higher for a one-year loan, $3/4$ per cent higher for a two-year loan. For more details see p26.

Tax treatment
Since 6 April 1986, interest on loans made after 18 November 1984 has been paid with composite rate tax (the equivalent of basic rate tax) already deducted. Non-taxpayers can't reclaim this tax, and so should think twice before investing in local authority loans. Higher rate taxpayers have extra tax to pay. The same tax rules apply to interest from banks and building societies – see p99 for more details.

How to invest
You will need to scan the newspapers. Local authorities wanting to borrow money from the public often advertise in newspapers, giving details of the rate of interest paid, the minimum amount accepted, and the length of time they

want your money for. Note that if you have a lot to invest (over £25,000, say) you may be able to get special terms.

There's normally no financial advantage to be gained from investing in your own local authority – though there's nothing to be lost by asking. If you decide to invest, contact the local authority direct. You can ask for an application form, fill it in, and return it with your cheque.

The number of local authorities accepting loans has dropped in recent years.

Temporary loans

You may also come across what are known as **temporary loans**. A temporary loan is for a period of less than a year. Some local authorities won't accept temporary loans unless you invest at least £5,000 or more. But others will take smaller amounts – perhaps £500 or £1,000.

Some temporary loans are, in fact, for periods of 364 days – ie virtually a year. But others are for shorter periods – for example, three months. Interest is quite often paid at the time the loan is repaid, rather than half-yearly.

Some temporary loans are arranged so that you can withdraw your money by giving an agreed period of notice – commonly seven days. With these, the interest rate can change – but the local authority must give you seven days' notice of any change.

Verdict

The main advantages of local authority loans are:
- your money is relatively safe (see p304)
- you know exactly how much income you are going to get, when you are going to get it, and how much you'll get back at the end of the period you invest for. Even if interest rates in general fall, your income will stay the same
- you need to invest a minimum of only £100 or so.

The main disadvantages are:
- you usually have to keep your money invested for an agreed period
- the return is fixed at the time you invest your money – so if interest rates in general rise, you may find that you could have done better by investing in, for example, a building society (where the rate of return you get can vary after you've invested your money)
- non-taxpayers can't reclaim the tax deducted, so need to compare the return they could get elsewhere.

Buying a stock or a bond on the Stock Exchange

There are two main types of local authority investments which you can buy and sell on the Stock Exchange.

Local authority negotiable bonds are often called yearling bonds because they commonly last for a year or so. They work in a similar way to British Government stocks (see Chapter 17). Unlike most stocks they are issued at their *nominal value* (see p288 for what this means). Local authority stocks (often called corporation loans or corporation stocks) are generally issued for fixed periods of six or more years. Again, they work in the same way as most British Government stocks. However, very few new stocks have been issued in recent years, and there are no new issues currently available.

Yearling bonds

How they work
Bonds are issued once a week. On the day they are issued, all bonds lasting the same length of time pay the same rate of return. There is no difference between the rate paid by different local authorities. The rate of return is fixed for as long as the bond lasts.

How long for?
Most yearling bonds are issued for a fixed period of a year and six days. Larger ones may be issued for up to five years, but are very rare now.

Cashing in early
You can cash in your stock at any time by selling it on the Stock Exchange, but there's no guarantee of what you'll get. There'll also be commission to pay if you sell early, which will reduce the return on your investment. A fixed return investment will be most in demand with buyers when interest rates in general are falling. The reverse will be the case when interest rates generally are rising.

Minimum investment?
£1,000. And you have to invest in multiples of £1,000 – so you can't invest £1,500, for example.

What rate of return?
To give an example, the bonds issued on Tuesday 8 March

1988 will give a before-tax return of $9^7/_{16}$ per cent (paid with basic rate tax deducted) and will be redeemed on 15 March 1989.

When is the income paid out?
Normally half-yearly, on fixed dates which vary from stock to stock.

Tax treatment
Interest is paid with basic rate tax deducted. Non-taxpayers can reclaim the tax but higher rate taxpayers will have extra tax to pay.

There is no capital gains tax to pay on gains made from disposing of a bond after 1 July 1986.

It used to be possible for higher rate taxpayers to avoid paying higher rates of income tax on the interest from these bonds by converting the income to a capital gain taxed at 30 per cent. The introduction of the 'accrued income scheme' (see p292) from 28 February 1986 meant that this was no longer possible.

How to invest
You can't choose a local authority. You put in your order with a stockbroker and take what comes. You have to buy through a stockbroker – you can contact one direct, or go through a bank, solicitor or accountant. There are no fixed rules about how much commission you'll be charged (though it is quite likely to be in line with the commission on short-term gilts – see p300). Watch out for a minimum commission. Commissions may be lower if you have a minimum of say, £10,000 to invest. There's no commission to pay when the bond comes to an end and the local authority pays back your investment.

Local authority stocks
How they work
Local authority stocks work very like British Government stocks. As with British Government stocks, the rate of return you get from your investment is a mixture of the income you get each year and the capital gain (or loss) you make when you sell the stock (or when it is 'redeemed').

As most new stocks were issued for a fixed period of six or more years and no new ones were being issued when this book went to press, the overall number of stocks is declining as old stocks are redeemed. A few stocks were, however, issued undated, ie with no latest redemption date.

Minimum investment
No fixed minimum. But the minimum commission charged by the stockbroker might make investing small amounts – less than £500 or £1,000 say – not worthwhile.

Tax treatment
As for yearling bonds.

How to invest
No new local authority stocks were being issued when this book went to press.

Verdict

Broadly, the advantages and disadvantages are the same as for local authority loans. However, you can cash in your investment early — though you can't be sure of just how many £££ you'll get if you do.

Changes in the tax rules for yearling bonds (see opposite) meant that they lost popularity after February 1986. A minimum investment of £1,000 for yearling bonds also means they are not suitable for smaller investors.

The Table overleaf gives you an idea of how the returns from different types of available local authority investment – together with British Government stocks — compared in March 1988. You'll see that local authority investments generally gave a somewhat higher return than British Government stocks if held until they come to an end. This may be because local authorities do not have quite such a good credit rating as the British Government, and also because local authority investments are regarded as less marketable than British Government stocks.

Rate of return from local authority investments and British Government stocks

rates correct in March 1988 [1]

	return for someone paying			minimum investment needed to get this return
	no tax %	25% tax %	40% tax %	
Local authority loans for two to five years, say	5.06–9.43	5.06–9.43	3.96–7.37	commonly between £100 and £1,000
Local authority temporary loans	6.62–10.2	6.62–10.2	5.18–7.97	can vary from as little as £500 to as much as £25,000
Local authority yearling bonds held to redemption [2] for one year	9.69	7.27	5.81	£1,000
British Government stocks examples of stocks held to redemption [3]				
best short-dated (up to 5 years)	8.76	6.73	5.51	no fixed minimum
medium-dated (between 5 and 10 years)	9.06	6.84	5.52	
long-dated (over 10 years)	8.87	6.68	5.38	

[1] But using tax rates applying from 6.4.88

[2] But you normally have to pay commission when you invest, which reduces return somewhat

[3] As for footnote [2] — but return reduced by less if you buy through the National Savings Stock Register

19

ENDOWMENT POLICIES

An endowment policy is basically a long-term investment with life insurance tacked on. It's a way of investing in a mixture of shares, British Government stocks, company loans, property and so on – but you invest via a life insurance company.

How an endowment policy works

You agree to save for a certain period, which must normally be for 10 years or more. With a **with-profits endowment policy**, at the outset you are guaranteed that if you save until the end of the period you will get a guaranteed lump sum in return. But you hope that you will get much more than the guaranteed sum when your policy comes to an end. In the past, with-profits policies have paid out perhaps three to six times as much as the sum you have been guaranteed at the outset (of course, you can't be certain that they will do as well in future).

What happens is that the guaranteed sum grows over the years as the life insurance company adds **bonuses** to it – see p314. If you had started saving 10 years ago in a 10-year with-profits endowment policy you would find that when the policy pays out you would be getting an average return of 11 to 12 per cent, without allowing for any tax relief you might have got on the premiums. With one of the best-performing companies, the return for a 10-year policy ending now would be 15 per cent, say; for a 25-year policy the return is slightly less – around 11 per cent for one of the best performing ones.

How endowment policies work [1]

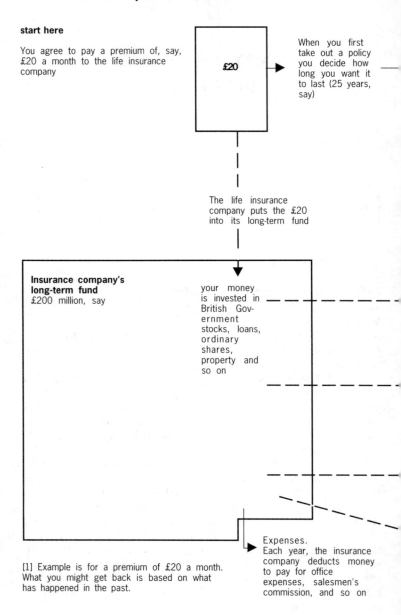

start here

You agree to pay a premium of, say, £20 a month to the life insurance company

£20

When you first take out a policy you decide how long you want it to last (25 years, say)

The life insurance company puts the £20 into its long-term fund

Insurance company's long-term fund
£200 million, say

your money is invested in British Government stocks, loans, ordinary shares, property and so on

Expenses.
Each year, the insurance company deducts money to pay for office expenses, salesmen's commission, and so on

[1] Example is for a premium of £20 a month. What you might get back is based on what has happened in the past.

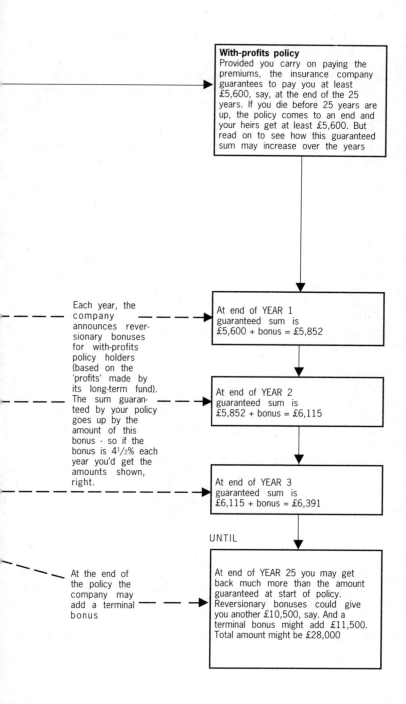

With-profits policy
Provided you carry on paying the premiums, the insurance company guarantees to pay you at least £5,600, say, at the end of the 25 years. If you die before 25 years are up, the policy comes to an end and your heirs get at least £5,600. But read on to see how this guaranteed sum may increase over the years

Each year, the company announces reversionary bonuses for with-profits policy holders (based on the 'profits' made by its long-term fund). The sum guaranteed by your policy goes up by the amount of this bonus - so if the bonus is 4½% each year you'd get the amounts shown, right.

At end of YEAR 1 guaranteed sum is £5,600 + bonus = £5,852

At end of YEAR 2 guaranteed sum is £5,852 + bonus = £6,115

At end of YEAR 3 guaranteed sum is £6,115 + bonus = £6,391

UNTIL

At the end of the policy the company may add a terminal bonus

At end of YEAR 25 you may get back much more than the amount guaranteed at start of policy. Reversionary bonuses could give you another £10,500, say. And a terminal bonus might add £11,500. Total amount might be £28,000

Bonuses

There are two sorts of bonuses. **Regular** bonuses (usually called **reversionary** bonuses by the insurance companies) are added to your with-profits policy. Once a reversionary bonus has been added to your policy, this new figure becomes your new guaranteed sum – it cannot be taken away once it has been added. For how these bonuses are decided, see p316.

If the company announces a compound bonus of 4 per cent, say, it works out what this would be on the guaranteed sum. If, for example, your original guaranteed sum is £6,000, the amount of the bonus at the end of the first year would be £240, and the new guaranteed sum would be £6,240. At the end of the second year, the bonus would be 4 per cent of £6,240, which is £250, and the new guaranteed sum would become £6,490.

Some companies add different rates to the original guaranteed sum and to the reversionary bonuses already added to the policy. For example, a bonus of 4 per cent might be added to the original guaranteed sum and a bonus of 6 per cent to the reversionary bonuses already announced.

It's important to realise that there's no guarantee that a bonus will be added each year. In the past, it has been rare for a company to reduce its rate of bonus, let alone not pay one. But, in the last year or so, one or two life insurance companies have slightly reduced their reversionary bonus rates.

Life insurance companies usually also pay a *terminal* bonus as well as reversionary ones. This is a one-off bonus added at the end of the policy. So, for example, in a 25-year policy, it is added at the end of the 25 years when your policy matures. In the last few years, the amount of the terminal bonus has gone up a lot. With 25-year policies maturing in 1988, the amount of the terminal bonus could make up as much as 40 per cent, or even more, of the amount policy-holders get back. If you cash in your policy early (see p319), you normally get no share of the terminal bonus.

These terminal bonuses can vary widely, depending on the current market value of the insurance company's investments – for example, the shares it owns. After the fall in share prices at the end of 1987, some companies have cut their terminal bonuses.

Comparing bonus rates with other rates of return

You can't compare them directly. First, you have to work

out what a given bonus rate means in terms of the cash you get back at the end of the policy. Then you have to work out what rate of return this represents on the amount you save each month. Only then can you compare the rate of return you might get on a with-profits endowment policy with the rate currently offered by, say, a building society.

Is a with-profits endowment policy life insurance or investment?

It's an investment. If what you want is life cover to protect your family from financial hardship in the event of your early death, you should take out *term insurance*. With this sort of insurance, you insure for an agreed period. If you die within that period, the insurance pays out. If you survive, the policy pays nothing.

For a given amount of cover, term insurance is very much cheaper than other types of insurance. For example, a 30-year-old man insuring his life for £30,000 for 15 years might pay £4 or so a month for term insurance, £170 a month, say, for with-profits endowment insurance. However, the cost of term insurance, particularly for men, is likely to rise over the short-term as life insurance companies need to allow for the greater chance of early death due to AIDS.

You can also take out term insurance policies which pay out a tax-free income if you die within the term. These are known as family income benefit policies.

For more details, see *Your money for your life*, Which? 1987, p430.

What sort of return do you get from a with-profits endowment policy?

If you had chosen one of the best-performing companies whose policies were coming to an end in 1987, you could have got a return of, say, 11 per cent or so on a 25-year policy, 13 per cent or so on a 15-year policy and 15 per cent or so on a 10-year one.

The returns you can get depend on your age, your sex and your health. So, a younger person would get a slightly better return than an older person, a woman a slightly better return than a man and a healthy person a better return than someone in poor health. This is because there is life insurance tacked onto the investment and the life insurance company deducts some money from what you invest to pay for the life insurance.

The returns you could have got in the past vary widely from company to company. So, for example, the best-performing company could be paying out almost twice as much as the worst-performing company for the same amount of savings. Sadly, you can't be sure in advance which is going to be the best-performing policy.

Where your money is invested

Your money goes into the life insurance company's long-term fund. The long-term fund is invested in a spread of different types of investment. For example, a company might have:

- 50 per cent of its long-term fund in ordinary shares
- 15 per cent in property
- 30 per cent in British and foreign government stocks, company loan stocks, local authority loans, mortgages, etc
- 5 per cent in cash or other investments.

The idea of spreading the money around in this way is that it reduces the risk of the fund doing very badly. If all the money was invested in shares, for example, the value of the fund would plummet if shares as a whole plummeted. At the same time, of course, spreading the money around reduces the chances of the fund doing extraordinarily well. This, together with the way that the fund is valued (see below), means that an endowment policy should be regarded as providing a relatively safe, steady return on your money.

How reversionary bonuses are worked out

By law, an insurance company has to keep the money concerned with its *long-term business* in a *long-term fund* – separate from the rest of its money. Long-term business includes life insurance, permanent health insurance, annuities and pension schemes. The company has to get an actuary to value the assets and liabilities of its long-term business at least once a year. The Government lays down rules about the valuation.

Assets
Some examples of the maximum values that can be given to assets are:

- land and property: its market value, estimated by a professional surveyor or valuer not more than three years before
- debts due to be collected in more than a year's time: what the company could expect to get if it sold the right to collect the debt

■ ordinary shares, debentures, British Government stock and other investments quoted on a stock exchange: the closing middle market price.

In addition, there are rules which limit the value that can be put on one particular investment – eg shares in one particular company. This is to prevent the fund becoming too dependent on that investment.

Liabilities

The liabilities are the benefits that the insurance company will have to pay out in the future – eg when policyholders die or their policies come to an end. The actuary estimates how much the insurance company will have to pay out in each of the next 35 years, or more.

But he also has to take account of the fact that £1 which has to be paid out next year is of greater concern to the company than £1 to be paid out in 10 years' time, say. This is because the company can earn interest on the assets of its long-term fund – so that less than £1 needs to be set aside now, to meet the debt in 10 years' time.

The value the actuary puts on future liabilities depends on the assumptions he makes about the future return on the assets. The higher the return he assumes, the lower the value he puts on the liabilities. In practice, the actuary tends to assume a much lower rate of return than the one currently being earned.

The actuary then values the premiums the company is going to receive in the same sort of way – allowing for office expenses, commission and so on. By taking away the value of the premiums from the liabilities, he gets a figure for net liabilities.

Surplus (or excess)

This is simply the amount by which the assets of the long-term fund exceed the net liabilities. Having worked out the surplus, the actuary decides how much of it should be paid out to the company's shareholders, and what rate of bonus should be paid on each type of with-profits policy – eg endowment and whole life.

Note that once a bonus has been announced, it becomes part of the liabilities of the company, and cannot be taken away from the value of your policy (unless you cash the policy in early).

Does the company have to pay a bonus?

The Secretary of State for Trade and Industry has considerable powers to intervene in an insurance company's affairs – if, for example, he thinks that policyholders' *reasonable* expectations won't be met. If a company wasn't going to pay a bonus, it would probably be in a poor state of health and would be closely supervised by the Department of Trade and Industry.

In practice, companies normally do add bonuses to with-profits policies each year.

How endowment policies are taxed

There's normally no tax to pay on the money you get back from an endowment policy provided you don't cash it in (or make it paid-up, see opposite) within its first 10 years — or within the first three-quarters of the period you insured for, if this is shorter. But if you do cash it in, and you pay tax at the higher rate or would do if the gain on your policy is added to your income, there may be some tax to pay. The amount of the gain is normally the amount you get less the total of the premiums paid. There is no basic rate tax to pay on the gain, because the life insurance fund has already paid tax.

Any gain on cashing a policy counts as part of your 'total income', which is used to work out how much age allowance you can get. So, if you are 65 or over during the tax year, be careful about cashing in an endowment policy before the end of the agreed saving period. It may mean a reduction in your age allowance and more tax to pay.

Before 14 March 1984, when you took out an endowment policy you also got tax relief (really a premium subsidy) on what you paid for the policy. Policies taken out after midnight on 13 March 1984 do not qualify for this premium subsidy. However, you can carry on getting the premium subsidy on a policy which you took out before that date, as long as you have not changed the policy to give you more benefits – for example, by extending its term or increasing its cover.

The amount of the subsidy is currently 15 per cent. But from 6 April 1989 it falls to $12^{1}/_{2}$ per cent, so what you pay for your policy will rise from that date.

For more information on tax, see Chapter 7.

Ending a policy early

To get the best return on a with-profits endowment policy, you have to keep it going for the period you originally agreed

– often 10, 15, or 25 years. But your financial life could be drastically altered during this time (through marriage, divorce, having children, moving home, being made redundant, starting your own business, for example). So you may find yourself wanting to end the policy early.

There's no doubt that a substantial number of endowment policies are cashed in early (or simply allowed to lapse) – though there are no reliable figures showing how many. If you find that you need your savings back early, or you can no longer afford the premiums, what are the alternatives?

Cashing in your policy

The cash-in value (also called the 'surrender value') of an endowment policy is usually entirely at the discretion of the insurance company.

If a 29-year-old man cashed in a 25-year policy with premiums of £30 a month, he would get back around £450 if it had been going for two years, around £4,500 if it had been going for 10 years. This means a loss of around £270 for the two-year period and a return of around 4.4 per cent a year over 10 years. Not very impressive.

Note that with most companies you get nothing back if you cash your policy within its first two years.

Making it paid-up

You stop paying the premiums and the insurance company reduces the guaranteed sum for which you are insured. This new guaranteed sum – called the paid-up value – is paid out at the end of the period you originally insured for (or when you die, if this is earlier).

Most insurance companies continue to add bonuses to the paid-up value of a with-profits policy.

Getting a loan on it

Nearly all insurance companies will consider lending you money, using your policy as security for the loan. Generally the maximum loan is between 80 per cent and 90 per cent of the cash-in value. Some companies will not make a loan of less than a certain amount – usually £100 to £250. Interest charged is currently around 11 per cent to 13 per cent a year, depending on the company.

What should you do?

If you need the cash, you'll have to choose between cashing in your policy and getting a loan on it. If you don't need the cash – but can no longer afford the premiums – you could also consider making your policy paid-up.

Which is the best choice for you will depend on the particular circumstances of your own case. The first thing to do is to ask the insurance company for:

■ the policy's cash-in value
■ details of any loan you can use your policy to get (eg rate of interest charged, how much you can borrow)
■ the current sum guaranteed by the policy
■ the current rate of bonus *and*, if you don't need the cash
■ the paid-up value and whether bonuses will continue to be added to this value.

Then you'll have to work out for yourself what the best course of action is. The Example below will give you an idea of how to do this.

Example: deciding what to do

Simon Smart has a 25-year with-profits endowment policy – for which he has been paying premiums of £30 a month for the last 15 years. In April 1988 he finds he can't afford to carry on paying his premiums. He writes to his insurance company and finds:

■ the cash-in value is £11,414
■ he can borrow up to £10,272 on his policy. The rate of interest would be 12% at present, but could vary
■ the current sum guaranteed by the policy is £20,645 (the original £7,946 plus £12,699 in bonuses)
■ the current rate of bonus is 5% compound plus 2% on the bonuses
■ the paid-up value is £16,369 and bonuses will continue to be added.

Cashing-in

Simon doesn't need the cash. So if he cashed his policy in, he'd invest the £11,414. He finds that if he invested the money in a 10-year British Government stock, for example, he might (at that time) get a return of around 9.5% a year before tax. He'd get a total of around £30,970 in 10 years' time (assuming he could reinvest the interest at 9.5% too – which of course, may not be possible).

Selling your policy

Unless you took on the policy very recently, you may be able to get more than its cash-in value by selling it in an auction.

What happens is that whoever buys the policy carries on paying the premiums – and collects the money paid out when the policy comes to an end.

The name and address of a firm which auctions policies is: H.E. Foster & Cranfield, 20 Britton Street, London EC1M 5NQ. Tel: 01-608 1941. They currently charge a fee of £50 plus a commission of one-third of the difference between what the policy sells for and its cash-in value. (You don't have to sell the policy if the highest bid is below the cash-in value.)

Making the policy paid-up

The paid-up value is £16,369. The company would add bonuses to this amount for the remaining 10 years of the policy. So, if the current 5% bonus rate plus 2% extra on bonuses continues, he'd get back around £31,671 in 10 years' time. The company may add a terminal bonus to this – say £7,918. This would make a total of £39,589.

Getting a loan

Though Simon doesn't need the cash at the moment, it might still make sense for him to get a loan on his policy and use this to help pay his premiums.

The amount his policy is likely to pay out if he continues to pay the premiums, and if the current rate of bonus continues, is £39,044 (ie the current guaranteed sum *plus* bonuses of 5% compound a year and 2% extra on the bonuses). And the company may add a terminal bonus to this. At current rates, it would be £9,761, making a total of £48,805. As he took out the policy before 13 March 1984, he gets the premium subsidy of 15% (12$\frac{1}{2}$% from 6 April 1989) and his £30 a month premium actually costs him £25.50 (£26.25 from 6 April 1989). So he'd need to borrow around £3,141 over the 10 years.

When his policy came to an end he could expect to get back £48,805 *less* the £3,141 loan – ie £45,664.

Of course, he'd also have to pay interest on the loan. This could be kept to a minimum if he borrowed the money in instalments, rather than borrowing the full £3,141 straight-away. In this case, the interest might work out at about £2,100 over the 10 years – rather than the £3,770 or so if he borrowed the full £3,141 now.

Deducting £2,100 interest from the £45,664 he'd get back from the policy, leaves a net amount of £43,564.

What Simon decides to do

Simon sees that, in this particular case, the best thing to do would appear to be to get a loan from the company to pay his premiums. If he can, he'll get a loan each year; if not, he'll get a loan now to pay all the premiums, and invest the money in a building society until it's needed.

The worst thing he could do at the moment is to cash in the policy. He realises, however, that he can only make an estimate of the outcome. Things could alter in the next 10 years – interest rates could go up and bonus rates could go down, for example.

Other types of policy

There are a number of variations and similar policies. These are:

■ **non-profit** endowment policies. These were common ten or twenty years ago, but are rare today. With a non-profit policy you agree to save for a certain period, which must be ten years or more. The policy gives a poor, but guaranteed, return. You get the amount guaranteed if you save to the end of the agreed period; your heirs get the same amount if you die within the period. You get no bonuses on the guaranteed amount

■ **flexible** endowment policies. There are a few of these policies around today, but they may be phased out over the next few years. They are similar to a with-profits policy; bonuses are added to the original guaranteed sum. But there is some flexibility built in because you have guaranteed cash-in values after a certain time, 10 years, say. Because of this flexibility, the return is not as good as with a straightforward with-profits endowment policy

■ **low cost** endowment policies. These are sold linked to mortgages for buying a home and are a special type of insurance package. The package is a combination of a with-profits endowment policy (which has bonuses added on over the years) and term insurance

■ **unitised with-profits** endowment policy. These are a fairly new type of policy, somewhat similar to a unit-linked policy, see Chapter 20. With a unitised with-profits policy, what you pay buys units in a fund, but each year bonuses are declared. Once a bonus has been announced, it cannot be taken away

■ **whole life** policies. With these, you agree to pay premiums for the rest of your life or up to a certain age, 65 or 85, say. The policy pays out only when you die, not at the end of the premium-paying period. The insurance company agrees to pay out a fixed sum (plus bonuses if the policy is a with-profits one). You can cash in your policy at any time, but in the first few years the cash-in value is likely to be little or nothing. Even after a very long time, the cash-in value is likely to be fairly low.

In general, this type of policy is unlikely to match your needs. If you want protection for your dependants, it would be better to go for *term insurance* (see p315) which is cheaper, unless you are getting on in years. If you're looking for an investment you're likely to get a better return elsewhere – without being tied to such a long savings period.

But a whole life policy may be useful to pay an inheritance tax bill on your death (see p114). The policy should be made out so the proceeds go to your heirs, not to you (otherwise the proceeds could form part of your estate and become liable for inheritance tax themselves). If you go for a whole life policy, *don't* take out a non-profit one (see opposite), which will give a poor return.

Is an endowment policy suitable for you?

With-profits endowment policies with their wide mix of investments (shares, property, fixed-interest investments), provide a safer home for your money than, say, unit trusts alone. The way that endowment policies work mean that the ups and downs in performance which can be experienced from year to year are smoothed out by the actuary, and so there will not be a huge difference between the payment for a policy maturing in one year compared to the payment for another policy maturing in the next. In return for this lower risk you have to expect that you may experience a lower return than other investments.

Of course, it is possible for you to spread your own savings among a number of different types of investments and to avoid cashing your investment all at the same time. If you do it yourself, you do not incur the expenses of the life insurance company, mainly its costs of marketing and selling policies. However, you may not want to undertake it yourself, prefer saving regularly or simply not have enough money to get a reasonable spread of investments. If so, you could consider a with-profits endowment policy as a relatively safe home for part of your savings.

However, you should think carefully before committing

yourself to such a long-term savings plan, as cashing in a policy before the agreed saving period is up means a lower return – and in the first couple of years or so, not even getting your money back.

How to choose a company

If you're taking out a with-profits policy, you'll be planning to pay money to a company for at least 10 years. So it makes sense to choose the company carefully. In the past, you have been able to get almost twice the return with the best-performing company compared to the worst-performing company.

The return from a with-profits policy depends on several things such as how successfully the management invests the long-term fund, how much of your premium goes in commission and expenses, how the actuary values the long-term fund, whether the company has any shareholders to share in the surplus made by the long-term fund, how many with-profits policyholders the surplus has to be split between.

So you can see that success at investing money (which is unpredictable) is only one of the important factors. A company's past performance may give some guide to the future, although there are a number of reasons why it might not. Actuaries, for example, can move jobs or fall under a bus just like ordinary mortals. A change in actuary can mean a change in policy and hence in the trend in adding bonuses to a policy. Actuaries are also subject to changes in company policy, eg different marketing strategies which can mean more emphasis being put on one product rather than another (and so influencing the amount of bonuses added).

The other factors which affect return are the amount of expenses (including representatives' and independent sales people's commission) and the amount of the reserves put aside over the years in the long-term fund. Unfortunately, life insurance companies as yet do not have to give any information on these factors. However, it's possible that in future companies might have to give information about some of these items, which would enable consumers to make more informed and rational decisions as to which life insurance company to choose.

Buying a policy

Under the new investor protection regime (see Chapter 5), if anyone tries to sell you a with-profits endowment policy, the person should either be a company representative or a completely independent intermediary. They are normally paid by commission on the policies they sell. Under the Financial Services Act, a commission agreement has been set up which lays down scales of commission for intermediaries. If what is paid to an intermediary is in line with these scales, the intermediary doesn't, at present, have to tell you how much the commission is, unless you ask.

For example, for a 25-year with-profits endowment policy an intermediary would receive 25 per cent of what you pay for the first 38 months plus $2^1/_2$ per cent of what you pay for the rest of the policy. However, if an intermediary sells a policy from a company which pays more than the set scales of commission, he or she will have to disclose the amount automatically. And from 1 January 1990, intermediaries will have to disclose the amount of commission received on *all* sales.

Life insurance companies which pay commission to their company representatives have to keep their commission scales roughly in the same ratio between products as the scale for independent intermediaries. But the amount does not have to be the same, so a representative could receive twice as much or half as much as an intermediary, for example.

There are also a number of rules about how endowment policies can be sold to you by representatives and intermediaries, see p76.

Company safety

Insurance companies are closely supervised by the Department of Trade and Industry. The Secretary of State for Trade can intervene in the affairs of an insurance company if he thinks it's getting into difficulties. He can, for example, prevent it taking on any new business. Friendly societies are supervised in much the same way – but by the Chief Registrar of Friendly Societies (the head of a different Government department).

Insurance companies, but not friendly societies, are covered by the Policyholders Protection Act. If your company fails, the Policyholders Protection Board has to try to get another company to take over the policy. In this case, provided you carry on paying your premiums, the Act guarantees that at the end of the policy you'll get at least 90 per cent of the sum guaranteed at the time your company went bust – unless the Board considers this amount to be *excessive*. You get no guarantee of what bonuses the new company will add.

So you may lose out on quite a lot of money if your company goes bust – it makes sense to be cautious when choosing a company. It would be prudent to avoid relatively new or small companies.

A dispute with a life insurance company?

Take it up with the insurance company first. If the complaint is unresolved by the end of three months, the company must tell you what the complaints procedure is (which may be to contact the Life Assurance and Unit Trust Regulatory Organisation or the Insurance Ombudsman Bureau). For more details and addresses, see p80 and p88.

20

UNIT-LINKED LIFE INSURANCE

Unit-linking has become increasingly common over the past few years and life insurance companies have found ways to unit-link different types of policies. They can be used for investing a lump sum, saving regularly or even repaying a mortgage.

In the past, unit-linked insurance was attractive partly because of favourable tax rules. The tax rules have become steadily less favourable, although some investors may still find that unit-linked life insurance suits their tax situation better than other forms of investment, as we shall explain in this chapter. Anyone who took out a life insurance policy before the rules changed, however, can still benefit from the old tax rules.

To invest you buy either a single-premium bond (eg an equity, property, managed bond) or a unit-linked regular premium plan. Both are technically life insurance policies – though with many policies you get only a small amount of cover.

In general, when you invest, your money buys you units in a fund of investments run by the insurance company. The price of each unit you buy is, approximately, the value of the investments in the fund divided by the number of units issued. The unit price goes up and down as the value of the investments in the fund (eg property, shares and so on) fluctuates.

When you sell your units, what you get back depends on the price of the units at the time. If the fund has been performing badly, you could make a loss. On the other hand, you stand the chance of making a large profit, if the fund is doing well when you sell.

The first part of this chapter deals with things which apply in general, whether you've got a lump sum to invest or want to save something each month. The second part of the chapter looks at particular types of policy. Information about single-premium bonds starts on p332, and about unit-linked regular premium plans on p340.

How unit-linking works

Where your money is invested

Your money goes into a fund of investments, usually run by the insurance company. Most insurance companies run a number of funds. The main types are:
■ property funds – which invest in office blocks, factories, shops and so on
■ UK equity funds – which invest in shares of British companies
■ fixed-interest funds – which invest in things which pay out a fixed income (eg British Government stocks, company loan stocks)
■ managed funds – which invest in a mixture of things such as property, shares, and fixed-interest investments
■ cash or money funds – which invest in bank deposit accounts, short-term loans to local authorities and other investments which pay out rates of return which vary along with interest rates in general.

A number of more specialist funds have become available in recent years. These are:
■ international equity funds – which invest in a mixture of shares all over the world
■ North American funds – which invest in North American securities
■ Far East funds – which invest in the stock markets of countries such as Japan, Hong Kong, Australia or even South Korea
■ European funds – which invest in European stocks
■ index-linked funds – which invest in British Government stocks increasing in value with the Retail Prices Index
■ unitised with-profits funds – (for regular premium plans only) you buy units in the normal way, but the value of the units is worked out by allocating **bonuses**, in the same way as for with-profits policies (see Chapter 19). This means that the value of the units can't fall.

A number of equity funds are invested through a unit trust and managed funds may be invested in a selection of unit trusts. On p346 we help you decide whether unit trusts or unit-linked insurance funds are the best type of investment for you.

What should you expect if you invest?

Funds investing in property and equities all aim at long term growth. Traditionally, property and shares have been seen as more suitable long term investments than things which pay interest, like building society and bank accounts.

This is because by investing in property and shares you are investing in real things. Your money should grow as the value of these assets increases, giving you better protection against inflation.

The diagrams below and overleaf give an indication of how the value of £1,000 invested in a property, UK equity or managed bond has varied over seven years. The solid lines show the value of your investment in terms of £££, the other lines in terms of buying power (taking account of rising prices).

The success of your investment, particularly with bonds, can depend very much on when you invest and when you cash your investment. Investing on a regular basis instead of putting a lump sum into a bond removes the danger of investing all your money at the wrong time. On the other hand, it also removes the chance of doing extremely well by investing all your money when unit prices are low. And the success of your investment will still depend very much on the price of units at the time you cash them. Whether you invest a lump sum or through a regular premium policy will depend on your personal circumstances.

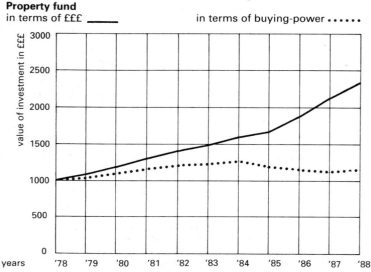

How your investment might have done

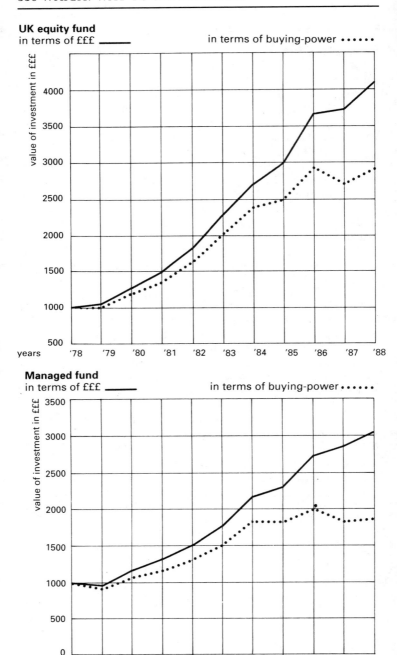

UK equity fund
in terms of £££ ———   in terms of buying-power ••••••

Managed fund
in terms of £££ ———   in terms of buying-power ••••••

Figures are shown on an offer to bid basis with net income reinvested. They show the average of all insurance funds in each of the three sectors.

Source: Money Management

Reducing the risks

Unit values can go down as well as up and the unit values of funds in different geographical or industrial sectors can rise and fall at different times. In general, the more specialised a fund is, the more you should avoid putting *all* or most of your money into it.

A fund specialising in Japanese stocks, for example, may show spectacular returns for a period, but may then slow down and be overtaken by another sector. To minimise the risk of having your money in the wrong sector at the wrong time and to maximise your chances of being ready to take advantage of a rising sector, you should spread your money across different types of investment.

The easiest way to do this is by investing in a managed fund. Alternatively, if you have a large sum to invest, try to invest in two or more different types of fund.

If stock markets crash

Towards the end of 1987, share prices suddenly fell very sharply all over the world. At a time such as this, the best thing to do if you have a lump sum is to sit tight and wait for prices to go up again, rather than take a loss.

If you are paying regular premiums and prices have dropped you at least get the consolation of picking up more units for your money than when prices are high. This is known as 'pound cost averaging'. Of course, pound cost averaging won't leave you better off unless the price recovers before you sell your units.

If your regular premium policy reaches maturity just after equity prices have fallen, your policy proceeds may be disappointing. You are still more than likely to have got back far more than you put in. But this is a disadvantage of unit-linked as compared to with-profits insurance (see Chapter 19), where gains, once made, cannot be taken away.

Keeping track of your investment

You can follow the fortunes of your investment by looking up the unit price in a newspaper (the Financial Times lists most companies' unit prices – look under the section headed *Insurances* in the *Unit Trust Information Service section*).

Buying and selling

You can buy or sell your units at any time at the going price.

Buying and selling units in a unit-linked insurance fund is the same as buying and selling units in a unit trust.

Each unit normally has two prices. What you pay for the units (the offer price) is usually 5% more than what you can sell your units for (the bid price). Details of buying and selling units are on p281.

Single-premium bonds

With these policies, you hand over a lump sum to the insurance company. The company takes part of the money to cover its expenses and to provide you with a little life insurance. The rest of the money buys units in whichever fund you choose.

The Table opposite shows how the after-tax returns from a building society account, British Government stocks held until the end of their term and typical property, equity and managed bonds have compared over 10 years, 5 years and 1 year. You can see that none of the investments emerged as a clear 'best buy' over all three periods. For example, British Government stocks or a property bond would have been the winner over the twelve month period, the equity bond over five or ten years.

Who should consider investing in these bonds?

You should *not* invest in bonds if:

■ you are likely to want your money back at short notice (because the property or share market may be in a slump when you find you need to cash your bond)

■ you object to the value of your investment fluctuating.

However, even if neither of the points above applies to you, a single-premium bond may still not be the most suitable investment for you unless you're in one of two groups of investors. The tax rules mean they're particularly useful for higher rate taxpayers who've used up their capital gains tax allowance. They are also suitable for people who will want to switch from one type of fund to another from time to time in the hope of putting their money where it will increase in value quickest.

If you aren't in one of these groups, but still want an investment where you lock a lump sum away for several years in the hope that it will increase in value in the long-term, a unit trust is an alternative worth considering.

How approximate after-tax returns have compared

	yearly return [2] for someone paying basic tax rate at 25%, over:			yearly return [2] for someone paying tax at 40%, over:		
	10 years	5 years	1 year	10 years	5 years	1 year
	%	%	%	%	%	%
British Government stocks [1]	6.9	6.6	6.5	5.5	5.3	5.2
building society ordinary share account	7.4	6.3	4.6	5.9	5.0	3.7
property fund	8.8	7.8	6.3	7.8	6.8	5.4
managed fund	12.4	9.3	−8.4	11.2	8.1	−8.4
equity fund	15.9	16.0	−8.4	14.5	14.1	−8.4

[1] held until redemption   [2] to April 1988

Bonds or unit trusts?

Investing in a single-premium bond is very similar to investing a lump sum in a unit trust. In fact, many insurance funds are invested in unit trusts. The advantages or disadvantages of either investment depend largely on taxation.

Life insurance companies and unit trust companies pay income tax on the dividends they receive on shares in their portfolios. If you are a non-taxpayer, you can reclaim this tax from the Inland Revenue for a unit trust investment, but not for a bond investment.

When shares in an insurance fund are sold at a profit, insurance funds have to pay capital gains tax. Insurance companies set aside an amount to meet this tax which is indirectly passed on to the policyholder in lower unit values.

Unit trust investors pay capital gains tax according to their own personal liability when they cash in their units. Since you are allowed to make a certain amount of gains (£5,000 in the 1988–89 tax year) before having to pay capital gains tax, you should invest in a unit trust if you are not likely to use up this allowance.

If you want to withdraw money from a unit trust to provide an income you could face a capital gains tax bill. But special rules let you take some income from a bond without paying tax or you can put off paying tax on your income until a future date. See *Taking an income* below for details. On finally cashing in the bond, only higher rate tax payers have to pay income tax on the gains they have made and only at the higher rate. This is explained in greater detail in Chapter 7.

Single-premium bonds are more suitable for investors who want a spread of investments and like to change from fund to fund. You pay higher charges for taking your money out of one unit trust and putting it into another and you will either use up some of your capital gains tax allowance or face a capital gains tax liability every time you do this. See *Switching* on p337.

Taking an income

With most insurance company funds, you don't get an income in the conventional sense of having interest paid to you. This is because you don't directly own the things the fund invests in. The income earned by the fund's investments is generally put back into the fund to buy more shares, property or whatever.

Taking an income from your bond

Special rules mean that you can take an income from your bond but put off paying any tax until you eventually cash in the bond. Then there's only higher rate tax to pay – no basic rate tax – and only at the rates that apply at the time you cash in the bond.

The maximum income you can take under these rules is one-twentieth of your original investment (ie ignoring any growth) for each year, up to a maximum of 20 years – eg if you invest £1,000, you can withdraw up to £50 a year.

Original investment
each year you can take as income 1/20 of original investment

YEARS
1 2 3 4 5 6 7 8 9 10 11 12 13 14 15 16 17 18 19 20

If you take less than one-twentieth any year, you can carry the unused portion forward indefinitely to add to the amount you can withdraw in future years — eg if you invest £1,000 and take nothing for the first two years, you could withdraw up to £150 in year three, and so on. If you take more income than the rules allow in any year, you may have to pay higher rate tax at that time.

YEARS
1 2 3 4 5 6 7 8 9 10 11 12 13 14 15 16 17 18 19 20

Instead, you can normally arrange to cash in part of your investment from time-to-time – on either a regular basis (under a withdrawal scheme) or an irregular basis. If you're a higher-rate taxpayer, cashing in part of your bond could possibly lead to a bill for income tax (see p101 in Chapter 7), but in general paying tax on the gain you make can be avoided if you withdraw no more than five per cent (or one-twentieth) of your original investment in any one year. The Table on p335 shows how this works.

To make getting an income easier, bonds are often sold as a cluster or series of identical mini-policies so that you can cash in a whole policy – or several – at a time, according to your needs. The tax rules are simpler, too, if you cash in a whole policy rather than part of one. Of course, cashing units to get an income will start eating into the value of your investment if the unit price is increasing at a lower rate than the rate at which you are cashing units.

You can normally choose for the income to be either:
■ a percentage of the number of units you hold (in which case your income will go up and down with the price of units)
or
■ a percentage of the amount of your original investment (in which case your income in £££ will be fixed, but the number of units cashed in will go up when the unit price falls, down when the unit price rises)
or
■ the income the fund earns can be paid straight to you (in proportion to your unit-holding), rather than being rein-vested in the fund.

Charges

The insurance companies normally make:
■ an initial charge of around 5% of the amount you invest. This is usually included in the spread between the buying and selling prices
■ a regular charge. The insurance company deducts a charge from the fund at regular intervals to cover the costs of managing the fund. This charge might add up to be-tween $1/2$ and $1 1/2$ per cent of the value of the fund each year. Brokers charge between $3/4$% and 1% on top of these charges for investment in a broker managed fund.

Not all companies spell out in their policy documents the maximum charges they can make – so check up on charges before investing.

Switching

The majority of the insurance companies allow you to switch your money from one fund to another (eg from the equity fund to the property fund) without paying their initial charge again. This could prove a useful facility for investors who want to move their money around between different types of investment from time to time in the hope of keeping it in the type of investment which will increase in value quickest. But if you're tempted to use the switching facility, bear in mind that if you time your switches wrongly, you could end up doing very badly.

Note that switching your investment between funds doesn't count as cashing in your bond for tax purposes – so does not affect your tax position at all.

Most companies make some charge when you switch – typically £15 each time you move. But some companies allow you one free switch a year. The minimum amount you can switch is usually £500 or £1,000.

Policy wording

The policy document is the contract between you and the insurance company, so it makes sense to see a copy before you invest. Check that most of the following points are spelled out:

■ how the fund is valued. For example it might show that stocks and shares are valued at the market prices quoted on the Stock Exchange

■ that property in the fund is valued by an independent valuer, such as a surveyor

■ the maximum period between valuations

■ how unit prices are worked out

■ the charges the company makes – and the other costs it can deduct from the fund

■ that you won't be double-charged if your fund invests in other funds run by the company

■ what happens to the fund's income. See *Choosing a company* on p340.

Tax

When you cash your bond, the gain you make is added to your investment income for the tax year. The gain is the amount you get (including any amounts you got earlier on which weren't taxed at the time) *less* the amount you paid for the bond in the first place. You don't pay basic rate tax on the gain (the insurance company has already paid tax on the income and capital gains of the fund), but you do have to pay any higher rate tax that is due – though your tax bill may be reduced by *top-slicing relief*. The tax rules are complicated (especially if you cash in only part of your bond), but can be used to your advantage, if you are careful over *when* you cash your units in. For more details, see p102.

How to invest in single-premium bonds

Minimum investment
All the companies set a minimum amount you can invest – usually £1,000. Note that if you invest a substantial amount in one go, over £25,000, say, or invest in a newly launched fund, some companies give you extra units, eg one per cent more.

Age limits
Many insurance companies set minimum age limits for bondholders – 18, say. And a few set maximum age limits for new bondholders – 80, say.

Life insurance

Single-premium bonds normally pay out only slightly more than the value of the investment if the investor dies, say 101 per cent of the value of the units. For a young man under 30, however, the death benefit could be $2\frac{1}{2}$ times the value of the bond. The death benefits are limited to reduce the costs. A large amount of life cover would be expensive for an older person. If what you want is greater protection for your dependants, see p315.

Adding to your investment
As the term implies, a single-premium bond is bought with one lump sum payment. With an **additional premium facility** you have the option of buying more units at any one time by paying an additional premium. (This is subject to a minimum amount which varies from £250 to £1,000 depending on the company.) These units are added to the original policy you took out. The advantage in doing this is that if you *are* liable to tax on the gain when you cash the policy in, top-slicing relief relating to the additional premium can be spread over all the years since you originally invested – and not just from the date you paid the additional premium. This could reduce your tax bill.

Cashing in part of your investment

Most companies allow you to cash (ie sell) part of your bond. But you often have to cash a minimum amount, and leave a minimum amount. The minimum amount you can cash is commonly £50 or £100 – and the minimum amount you must leave varies between £100 and £1,000. There may be a maximum on the amount you can cash in, say, 10% of the value of your investment.

If you already have shares

Most companies are prepared to give you units in their funds in exchange for your holdings of stocks and shares through their **share exchange schemes** – though different companies have different rules about the size of the holdings they'll accept and the value they'll place on them.

Commonly, if the company is happy to put your shares into one of its funds, it will value them at the price it would have to pay to buy them on the open market. This benefits you because if you sold them, you'd normally get a somewhat lower price and would have to pay commission to a stockbroker.

If the company doesn't want to put your holdings of stocks and shares in a fund, it will usually sell them for you (and with many companies, you pay no commission on the sale).

Note that exchanging your shareholding counts as a disposal for capital gains tax purposes – ie you may have to pay capital gains tax on any gain you've made. But there are ways in which the tax can be kept to a minimum, so get professional advice – particularly, if you are exchanging substantial shareholdings.

Where to buy bonds

Bonds are sold by a variety of methods – through newspaper advertisements, by insurance brokers, by company salesmen, and by agents such as accountants and solicitors. Brokers, agents and so on normally get commission from the insurance company for selling bonds – the rate varies between 3 and 5 per cent or so of what you pay for the bond.

Some brokers offer their own 'broker managed bonds'. An insurance company provides the life cover while the broker chooses from that company's range of funds to make up what he thinks is the best mix in his own fund.

Some of these bonds do considerably better than the insurance company's funds, but not all do, and of course there's no guarantee that a high-performing broker bond will continue to do as well in the future. Sometimes the broker is able to choose from a number of companies' funds. Many broker bond funds are listed in the *Financial Times* under the insurance company's funds.

Choosing a company
For details about the insurance companies and their funds, the following magazines do regular surveys (including details of past performance) – *Planned Savings, Money Management*. Remember, though, that past performance is *not* a reliable guide to the future. Try asking a financial adviser (or perhaps several) for advice, but make sure he or she knows what it is *you* expect to get from your investment. At the end of this chapter is a list of things to check when deciding which company to go for.

Unit-linked regular premium plans

With a unit-linked regular premium plan you agree to pay premiums at regular intervals (monthly, quarterly, half-yearly or annually). In return the insurance company uses some of your money to pay for life cover and expenses. The rest is invested in the funds of your choice (see p328).

You can select a plan which lasts for between 10 years and the rest of your life (a few plans are available which last for less than 10 years, but they are not common). Within certain limits, you can choose the amount you think your dependants would need if you were to die before the end of the policy.

Types of plan

Unit-linked plans fall into three main categories:
■ maximum investment plans – for minimum life cover and high investment
■ endowment plans – for higher life cover and longer term investment
■ flexible cover plans – designed to adapt to your changing circumstances throughout your life.

Look at the Table opposite for how three typical plans might compare.

How typical plans might compare

For a 29-year-old man (non-smoker) paying premiums of £30 per month

	maximum investment plan	endowment plan	flexible cover plan
length of plan	10 years	between 10 and 25 years	whole life
amount of life cover	£3,645 for 10 years	£35,000 for 25 years	£105,340 for whole life
minimum monthly premium	£15	£20	£15

If you die

If you die during the period of your plan, the life insurance company guarantees to pay out a set amount of life cover or death benefit. But your dependants would receive the full value of your units if this is more than the death benefit.

The amount of death benefit payable under your policy depends on the length of your plan and the premiums you pay as well as your age and state of health when you take out your plan.

The end of your plan

When your plan comes to an end you should be entitled to a lump sum on which you do not have to pay tax. This is because most unit-linked policies are set up as 'qualifying policies' under the Inland Revenue rules (see p101). However, although the lump sum is tax-free in your hands, the insurance company will already have paid tax on the money in its funds. With some plans, a *capital gains tax deduction* is shown on the statement you get when the plan matures. This is tax on the company's gains, not yours — you can't claim it back, even if it is below your annual capital gains tax-free slice.

Insurance companies will give you an illustration of what a plan will provide, often based on a growth rate of $7\frac{1}{2}$ per cent each year. Companies are also allowed to show illustrations for a growth rate of up to $10\frac{1}{2}$ per cent a year. Remember though, the final payout is not guaranteed and neither are these growth rates. Only the death benefit is guaranteed. (The only exception to this is if you are using a unit-linked plan to repay a mortgage. In this case, some companies may guarantee to provide a sum equal to your mortgage at the end of your plan if your investment falls below the expected level of growth.)

At the end of some plans you may have the option of continuing your plan – normally with a higher proportion of future premiums being invested for you.

How the plans work

Maximum investment plans

These plans may be known as high investment plans or capital accumulation plans. They usually last for 10 years and the minimum premium can be as little as £10 per month or as much as £50 per month. There is no maximum investment.

These plans usually provide the minimum life cover under the 'qualifying' rules – currently three-quarters of the premiums payable during the term. This low level of life cover means that the maximum amount of your premiums can be invested.

Unit-linked endowment plans

Endowment plans may also be known as standard plans. They can last for up to 25 or even 30 years and provide a higher level of life cover. Minimum premiums for these policies vary from £20 per month to £50 per month.

During the 1980s these plans have become accepted by many lenders as a way of repaying a mortgage. With an endowment plan you only pay the interest on your mortgage every month and your endowment plan should provide enough to repay the amount you have borrowed when your mortgage ends and perhaps leave something over for you. The death benefit with an endowment mortgage plan is equal to the amount you have borrowed. When you move you can usually take your policy with you. If you increase your mortgage you may also be able to increase your level of cover without giving proof of your state of health. However, when choosing an endowment mortgage, you should bear in mind that the bonuses allocated to a with-profits policy cannot be taken away once they have been allocated, while the value of a unit-linked plan may fluctuate.

Flexible cover plans

Sometimes called flexible whole life plans, these plans last throughout your life or until a given age, say, 85. Given the size of the premium and your age and state of health at the

How a unit-linked regular premium plan works

You take out a policy running for a set length of time – 10 years in this example – and agree to pay premiums of £300 a year, say. The insurance company takes a cut to cover the cost of life insurance and other expenses – in this example, 40 per cent in the first year and 3.3 per cent thereafter (charges vary considerably from company to company).

What's left is used to buy units in a fund. The number you can buy depends on the offer price of the units when the money is invested – so the same amount buys different numbers of units from year to year.

The number of units you have increases month by month. But their value depends on what the insurance company will buy them back at (the bid price) – normally around five per cent lower than the offer price.

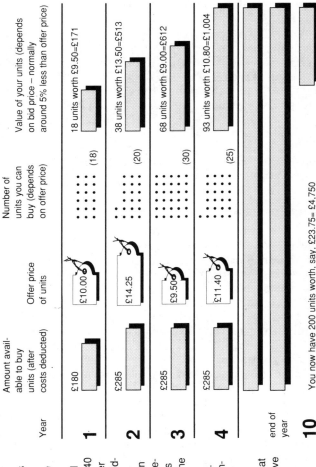

Year	Amount available to buy units (after costs deducted)	Offer price of units	Number of units you can buy (depends on offer price)	Value of your units (depends on bid price – normally around 5% less than offer price)
1	£180	£10.00	(18)	18 units worth £9.50=£171
2	£285	£14.25	(20)	38 units worth £13.50=£513
3	£285	£9.50	(30)	68 units worth £9.00=£612
4	£285	£11.40	(25)	93 units worth £10.80=£1,004
end of year				
10			You now have 200 units worth, say, £23.75=£4,750	

start of the plan, you can choose the amount of cover you want.

After, say, 10 years, you may need the lump sum you have accumulated. You can then take a lump sum but continue to pay premiums to build up another sum for the future. Once you have retired, you may wish to stop paying premiums and make the policy 'paid up' — the money already invested continues to grow.

You can alter the level of cover and premiums to suit your needs during the various stages of your life. Some plans include a variety of benefits and insurances you can add on to the plan as and when you need them. These are often called 'universal' plans.

Monitoring your investment

With longer term policies, life insurance companies keep an eye on your investment to make sure its value will be sufficient to provide the expected payouts. This is done by reviewing your policy, usually after 10 years and then every five years.

During the last five years your policy may be reviewed once a year. Some companies suggest you invest in a cash fund during the last five years so as not to lose any of the money you have made if share prices fall suddenly near the end of your plan.

If the growth of your investments has fallen below the expected rate you will probably have to pay higher premiums or accept reduced benefits.

On the other hand, if the growth of your investment is greater than the expected rate, you may be able to reduce your premiums or build up a larger sum. If you have an endowment mortgage, you may be able to repay your mortgage early (with the lender's agreement).

If you stop your plan early

You should look on most unit-linked life insurance plans as a long term commitment. The way that most companies arrange their charges means that their expenses such as administration and commission to brokers or salesmen as well as life cover are deducted from the premiums in the first few years.

If you cashed in your policy (often called 'surrendering' it) in the first two years, say, you may not get anything back and you would be unlikely to get back as much as you had paid in. The amount you would get varies from company to company, depending on how they calculate the cash-in value.

If you don't need to cash in your plan but want to stop investing, you could make your plan 'paid up.' This means you stop paying your premiums but the money you've already paid in is invested in the fund. Even so, you may only be allocated the number of units which you could buy with the money you'd get if you actually cashed in your plan.

Alternatively, go for a plan which is broken up into a series of mini-policies. Then, if your circumstances change later, you have the option of cashing just some of your units, keeping your plan going and paying a reduced premium.

Provided you have kept the policy going for 10 years or three-quarters of the premium-paying term if this is less, you should not have to pay tax on any gains you make from cashing in your policy. Only higher rate taxpayers may pay tax if a gain has been made during this period and they will receive 'top-slicing relief' (see p102 for details).

You can also get cash from your policy by taking out a **policy loan** (which you could then use to pay the premiums). Normally you can borrow up to 90 per cent of the cash-in value of your plan, and the interest rate will often be lower than that for other forms of borrowing. The loan repayments and interest payments are usually paid annually in addition to your normal premiums.

See p320 for guidance on how to work out the best way of stopping your plan early.

Charges

As we've already said, the costs of administration and life insurance are met by deductions from your premiums in the first few years. Some companies make these deductions by investing your premiums in what's called **capital** or **initial** units. These are not worth as much as the ordinary units and they hide the amount of charges. Other companies use a more straightforward system of unit allocations so you can see exactly how much you are paying.

For example, with an endowment plan, you might get a unit allocation of 55 per cent in the first year. In other words, just under half of your premiums are going towards administration costs and life cover in the first year. Your unit allocations depend on the length of your plan, the amount of life cover and the premiums you pay.

Don't forget, there is also a difference between the price at which you buy units and the price at which you sell them

Life insurance or unit trusts?

	Unit-linked regular premium plan	Unit trust savings plan
Income tax	Paid by the life insurance company and *cannot* be claimed back by non-taxpayers	Paid by the unit trust company and *can* be claimed back by non-taxpayers
Capital gains tax	Paid by the insurance company and reflected in lower unit values	Not paid by the unit trust company
At the end of a plan	No tax is payable on qualifying policies (tax has already been paid on the insurance company's funds)	Capital gains tax is charged according to personal liability – you get a tax-free allowance (£5,000 in the 1988–89 tax year)
Cashing in a plan early	If policy has been going less than 10 years or ³/₄ of the policy term, whichever is less, higher rate tax-payers may pay the difference between the higher and lower rate of income tax on any gains	
Switching from one fund to another	No tax is payable and charges are generally lower	You could use up some of your allowance or face a capital gains tax bill. Charges are generally higher

– usually 5 per cent (see p331). In addition a management fee is deducted from the fund, usually between $1/2$ and $1^1/2$ per cent a year.

Should you invest?

Keeping insurance and investment separate
Unit-linked life insurance policies can lock away your money for a long time. If you might want your money back early but you still need protection for your dependants, it is best to keep your insurance and your investment separate.

If all you want is life cover to protect your dependants from financial hardship, term insurance is probably the cheapest way to buy life cover (see p315). It can often be converted into an investment-type policy during its term without you having to give proof of continued good health.

If you are considering a unit-linked insurance plan, compare the costs and the benefits with a separate term insurance policy and a savings plan suited to your tax position (for example a unit trust savings plan). Chapter 8 gives a bird's-eye view of the main investments available.

Provided none of the points above apply to you, a unit-linked regular premium plan may be suitable if:

■ you are a higher rate taxpayer and you expect to have used up your annual capital gains tax allowance when you take the proceeds of your plan

■ you want to switch between funds.

If you want to invest in a fund, the main differences between the taxation of unit trust savings plans and unit-linked life insurance plans are set out in the Table opposite.

Special features to look out for

Endowment plans and flexible cover plans may offer some of these features:

■ **waiver of premium option** – you stop paying premiums but the plan continues if you become ill or disabled over a long period (say, more than six months) and can't continue with your normal job. Some companies will continue the plan for you if you have a joint policy and either partner is ill or disabled

■ **total disability cover** – some companies will pay out the death benefit if an accident or illness leaves you unable to work again

■ **accidental death benefit** – if you die as the result of an accident, the plan pays out an extra lump sum

■ **inflation linking** – you can take out further plans or increase your cover (or premium) in line with changes in the Retail Prices Index

■ **special event cover** – a further plan can be taken out or your cover can be increased on marriage or the birth (or adoption) of a child without you having to prove you are still in good health

■ **family income benefit** – if you die, the plan pays out a regular tax-free income for a given number of years rather than a lump sum

■ **low-start option** – for the first year of your plan, premiums are reduced to, say, half the normal amount. Then they will increase by, say, 20 per cent a year for five years or 10 per cent a year for 10 years, and be level for the rest of your plan. This option usually costs more in the long run

■ **stop-start option** – if you are made redundant or suffer financial hardship, you may be allowed to stop paying premiums for a limited period (up to two years, say) and keep your policy going. You will have to make up for these

missed premiums at a later date though
- **increasing or extending options** — you may be able to increase your cover or extend the term of the policy without having to prove that you are still in good health
- **term insurance** – if you die within a given period, the plan pays out an extra lump sum. Check, though that it isn't cheaper to take a separate term insurance policy.

If you already have a unit-linked policy

Over the years, unit-linked policies have changed a great deal. If you already have a unit-linked policy, you may find it is different to the types of policies now available which are described in this chapter. It would be unwise to cash in an old-style policy in favour of a new one without considering the surrender value and the cost of setting up a new policy. What is more, your life cover will be more expensive now that you are older than when you took out your policy.

The Government still subsidises the premiums on policies taken out before the Budget in March 1984 – see p104.

Choosing a company

Sadly, there is no foolproof way of picking a company whose policies are going to perform better than other companies'. In particular, just because a company's funds have done well in the past doesn't mean that they will do as well in the future. But, when choosing a company, there are a number of things to watch out for:
- whether the company has a good choice of funds – and, if you want to switch between funds, includes a cash fund (which can be a useful temporary home for your money when prospects for shares, property and fixed-interest investments all look bleak)
- what the company's charges are (and if these are spelled out in the policy document)
- whether the company makes any charge for cashing in the whole or part of your bond or policy, what you get if you cash your plan in early and how cash-in values are calculated
- whether the company offers a *withdrawal scheme* (ie partial cash-in) for single premium bonds and whether income withdrawals have to be on a regular basis or can be on an irregular basis to suit your circumstances. Check if the policy or bond is split into a series of policies to allow simple and tax-efficient cashing-in

■ if the company offers an *additional premium facility* so that you can add to your investment without having to take out a new policy each time (see p338), should you want to increase your investment

■ what the company's switching charge is (one 'free' switch a year is fairly common), and whether you can switch just some of your units

■ the size of the funds and how they are split between different types of shares or property. Funds range in size from less than £1 million to over £1 billion (£1,000 million) – you may feel happier to go for a larger fund. Also check that a property fund is not too heavily invested in just one locality, or too dependent on one huge office block, say. (Some companies provide reports which list the properties in the fund)

■ with a managed fund, the size of fund (see above), and how the investments are split between different sectors – though this, of course, could change.

If things go wrong

It's important to realise that although the performance of your bond or policy depends upon the performance of a fund of investments, investors *do not own the investments.*

However insurance companies, but not friendly societies (to which different legislation applies), are covered by the Policyholders Protection Act. This effectively says that, if your company goes bust, you'll get back 90 per cent of what you were owed when the company failed. If your policy has benefits, such as guaranteed cash-in value, which are considered *excessive*, you may get back less than 90 per cent of what you were owed.

These plans will also be covered by the Financial Services Act allowing you to take up complaints with the relevant Self Regulating Organisation. See Chapter 5 for details of these and other useful organisations.

21

GUARANTEED INCOME AND GROWTH BONDS

These are investments issued by insurance companies which are suitable for lump sums. You have to invest your money for a fixed period (usually four or five years but it can vary between one and ten years). In return you normally get a fixed rate of return for that period.

With an **income bond**, the return is paid out as a regular income (usually yearly but some companies will pay monthly). With a **growth bond**, the return is left to accumulate, and paid out when the bond comes to an end.

If you die before the bond comes to an end, the insurance company normally pays out the amount you originally invested plus, with growth bonds, the return accumulated to date.

The insurance company normally arranges for the return from an income or growth bond to be free of income tax at the basic rate. If you pay tax at no more than the basic rate (even after adding what you make on the bond to the rest of your income) you should get the return quoted in the ads. But if you or your husband or wife are 65 or over (or approaching 65) see p353.

If you've got a lump sum to invest, *and* you don't mind locking your money away for a time *and* you want a fixed return for this period, an income or growth bond may be suitable for you. But remember inflation will reduce the value of the fixed return. Alternatives to consider include local authority loans, National Savings Certificates, bank and building society high interest accounts, and bank or finance company fixed term deposits. Don't invest in a bond if you may need to cash it in early. Some insurance companies don't allow you to do this, and with the others, you may get back less than you originally invested.

If you don't pay tax – or pay more than basic rate tax

If you don't pay tax at all, you'll get more than the quoted return with some types of bond. But if you pay tax at the higher rate, the return is likely to be lower than the rate quoted in the ads. To find out how you'd be affected, see *How to choose a bond* below.

How bonds work

Bonds are set up in different ways, often using one or more life insurance policies with or without one or more annuities. The mechanics needn't concern you, though your age or tax position will usually make certain types of bond a better buy for you than others. For devotees, *Types of bond*, opposite, gives brief details of how the types of bond most commonly available when this book went to press work. But note that bonds are normally available only for limited periods of time, and the mechanics of newly issued bonds change from time to time.

How to choose a bond

For a list of which companies issue which types of bond, get a copy of the most recent issue of *Planned Savings* or *Money Management* magazine (see p362). But because bonds may be available for a short period only, the returns listed in such a magazine may soon be out of date.

Telephone the companies offering the best returns on suitable bonds and ask for details of their latest bonds. If you're not a basic rate taxpayer, ask them what someone in your tax position would get from their bond (after tax). Then choose the bond which gives the best return for the period you want to invest for. You could ask a couple of brokers to do this work for you.

In general:
■ if you do not pay tax or you are liable for less tax than the insurance company deducts, you're likely to get the best returns from a deferred annuity bond
■ if you pay tax at the basic rate you will probably find the endowment type of bonds the most attractive
■ if you pay tax at the higher rate, a series of single-premium endowments may well give you the best returns *or*, if you can arrange for the bond to end in a year when you pay only basic rate tax (after you've retired, perhaps) one single-premium endowment bond.

Warning: if you cash in all (or part) of a bond based on an endowment policy, your 'total income' (see p95) is increased. For most people, this has no significance at all. But if you get the special income tax allowance called age allowance, for people who are 65 or over, you could find that your tax bill rises – see p54 for details.

Note that *deferred annuity bonds* generally give a better return the older you are.

Types of bond

Single-premium endowment

Your investment buys a single-premium endowment policy which has guaranteed bonuses. You can choose whether to have these bonuses paid out to you as income or reinvested for growth (or you may be able to have part paid out, part reinvested). At the end of the term, you get back your original investment plus bonuses you haven't cashed in.

Annuity bonds

With a growth bond, your money is used to buy a deferred annuity – an agreement which promises to start paying out an income at the end of the term. But there's a cash option, under which you can take a guaranteed lump sum instead.

With income bonds, part of your original investment goes to buy an immediate annuity – an agreement to pay out a regular income for the duration of the bond.

Series of single premium bonds

Your bond is divided up into a series of single premium policies – one to provide an income for each year of the term and one to return the original lump sum at the end of the term.

Tax

Very briefly, the tax treatment is as follows:

Annuity bonds

With bonds based on a deferred annuity with a cash option,

the proceeds are liable to tax at your highest rate on the profit you make (but you may get top-slicing relief).

With bonds based on an immediate annuity, the life insurance company deducts tax from the income at the basic rate. However, part of the income will be tax-free because the Inland Revenue considers this to be repayment of capital (see p361).

Higher rate taxpayers will have to pay any higher rate tax due to the taxman separately. If you are a non-taxpayer or you are liable to less tax than the company deducts, you can claim the tax back.

Endowment bonds

There is no tax to pay on either the income or the final payout for basic rate taxpayers, because this has already been paid by the insurance company. Non-taxpayers can't claim this tax back, though.

With a single endowment bond, you can take income of up to five per cent of the investment each year until the end of the bond's term without paying any tax. If income of more than five per cent is taken, a higher rate taxpayer may have to pay some tax (but see p335).

With a series of endowments, an endowment policy is cashed in every year to provide the income. This income is effectively tax-free.

At the end of the term the proceeds from an endowment bond are free of tax unless you are a higher rate taxpayer, but you may get top-slicing relief (see p103 for details).

22

ANNUITIES

You may come across annuities either in connection with pensions, or as a form of investment you buy yourself. In this chapter, we concentrate on annuities you buy yourself, separately from a pension: for more on annuities tied to pensions, see Chapter 14.

An annuity you buy yourself is probably only worth considering if you've reached your 70s. You hand over a lump sum to an insurance company in return for a guaranteed income for the rest of your life. The older you are when the annuity begins, the larger the income it gives you. For example, in return for £10,000, a 75-year-old woman who paid tax at 25 per cent could (in April 1988) have got an after-tax income of about £1,440 for life.

On people who live for years and years, the insurance

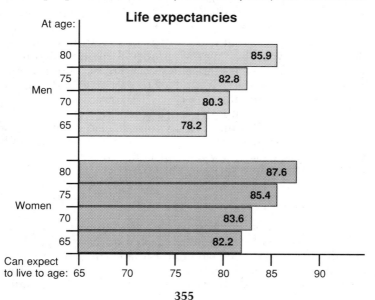

Life expectancies

At age:

Men
- 80: 85.9
- 75: 82.8
- 70: 80.3
- 65: 78.2

Women
- 80: 87.6
- 75: 85.4
- 70: 83.6
- 65: 82.2

Can expect to live to age: 65 70 75 80 85 90

company will make a large loss. On those who die early, the company will make a handsome profit – because with most types of annuity, however soon you die after buying it, you get none of your lump sum back. Table 1 on p355 shows what age you can expect to live to, if you're 65, 70, 75 or 80. You'll see that someone who has already reached 80 can be expected to live a greater age than a 70-year-old.

People who buy annuities tend to be healthier than those who don't – the insurance companies allow for this in the income they offer. In this chapter we look at the various different types of annuity that are available, and their pros and cons. On p363 you'll find details of home income schemes – where you borrow money to buy an annuity, using your home as security.

Types of annuity

This chapter deals with immediate annuities. With these, the company starts paying you the income 'immediately' – which normally means half-yearly, starting six months after you buy it. There are also deferred annuities – where you pay a lump sum now and arrange for the income to start further in the future (in five years' time, say). Deferred annuities form the basis of many personal pension plans.

The most common type of immediate annuity is a level annuity, where the income is the same each year. For a given outlay, this type gives you the largest income to start with – though, of course, inflation will erode its buying-power over the years. Another type is an increasing annuity, where the income increases at regular intervals by an amount you decide upon when buying the annuity. Unit-linked annuities are offered by a few companies – with these, your income is linked to the value of a fund (eg of property) and so goes up and down in amount.

The basic type of annuity stops when the person buying it dies – a single life annuity. But you can also get annuities which carry on until both the person buying the annuity and someone else, usually a wife or husband, are dead. These are called joint life, last survivor annuities.

Variations

The figures we quote in this Chapter assume that the company pays you half-yearly, starting six months after you buy the annuity, and that no payment is made after you die. You can, however, usually get any of the variations opposite. Some are fairly costly in terms of a reduced yearly income.

■ First payment to be made at the time you buy the annuity. The same outlay gives rather less income than the normal version.

■ Payments to be made more frequently than half-yearly (ie quarterly or monthly). The same outlay gives a smaller yearly income than an annuity paid half-yearly – the more frequent the payments, the smaller the income.

■ First payment to be made a year after you buy the annuity, then at yearly intervals. The same outlay gives a higher yearly income than an annuity paid half-yearly.

■ An extra, proportionate, payment (made after you die) for the period between the date you receive the last half-yearly payment and the date you die. This will give less income than the normal version.

■ Some of the payments to be made **guaranteed** – ie paid out by the company for a minimum number of years even if you die early. The same outlay gives you less income than the normal version – how much less depends on your age and the length of the guaranteed period (commonly, five or ten years).

■ A payment (made after you die) of the difference between your outlay and the income paid out so far by the company. You get less income then the normal version.

■ With a joint life, last survivor annuity, less income to be paid after the first person dies – often half or two-thirds of the amount paid while both are alive. The starting income will be higher than normal.

The income you get

This depends on a number of things – in particular your age when you buy the annuity, the type of annuity you go for and the level of interest rates in general at the time you take the annuity out. A woman gets a lower income than a man of the same age – women, on average, live longer than men. Joint life, last survivor annuities pay lower amounts too.

Insurance companies tend to vary their annuity rates frequently and at short notice, but what you get stays at the rate that applied when you bought the annuity. The Table overleaf gives you some idea of the rates being offered in early April 1988. With the increasing annuity you'll find two rates of return in the Table – one for the year in which the annuity is bought, and one for five years later.

Basic rate tax will normally have been deducted from the annuity income before you get it. The income you get from an annuity consists partly of interest and partly of a return

After-tax yearly return from annuities in April 1988

age when you buy annuity	level annuities			increasing annuities (5% compound a year)	
	if you pay no tax	if you pay tax at basic rate of 25%	if you pay tax at rate of 40%	if you pay tax at basic rate of 25% first year	sixth year
	%	%	%	%	%
Man					
65	14.0	12.8	12.0	9.0	11.4
70	15.9	14.2	13.2	11.0	14.0
75	18.7	17.1	16.0	13.8	17.7
80	23.0	21.3	20.3	18.0	22.9
Woman					
65	12.6	11.3	10.5	7.5	9.6
70	14.0	12.3	11.3	9.0	11.5
75	16.1	14.4	13.4	11.2	14.3
80	19.2	17.5	16.6	14.4	18.4
Man 75, woman 71	12.9	11.4	10.5	9.0	11.0
British Government stock (undated)	8.9	6.7	5.3	6.7	6.7

of the capital you invested, and each part is treated differently for tax purposes – see p361.

For comparison, we have included in the Table the return available on undated British Government stocks in early April 1988. Like annuities, these give you a guaranteed income for the rest of your life – but unlike annuities, the money invested in stocks is still yours to do with as you wish. You can leave the stocks to your heirs when you die, or you can sell them at any time (though there's no guarantee of what price you'll get for them). With an annuity, you normally get none of your original investment back.

Inflation

When deciding whether to buy an annuity you should consider the effect that rising prices will have on the buying-power of your income. For example, a woman of 70 who buys an annuity could expect to live for about another 14 years. If prices rise at around 5 per cent a year, each £100 of income she gets at the start will be worth only £50 or so in 14 years' time – and, of course, the current low level of inflation may not continue. To see how rising prices might reduce the buying-power of an annuity, look at the Diagram overleaf.

To protect the buying-power of your capital you could consider investing in index-linked National Savings Certificates (p176) – cashing them in if you need income – or index-linked British Government stocks (p294).

An annuity would then be worth considering for *part* of your remaining money if you're over 70 or so.

Why an annuity is a gamble

Whether or not an annuity proves to be a good buy in the long run depends on:
■ how long you live. Obviously an annuity will be a better buy if you live for years and years after buying it, than if you die soon after investing your money. If you are in poor health, you'd be wise to steer clear of annuities, and invest your money elsewhere
■ what happens to interest rates after you have bought your annuity. The annuity income offered by an insurance company is related to the general level of interest rates at the time you buy. If, later on, interest rates go up, companies are likely to offer better annuities – but you'll be stuck with your relatively poor-value-for-money annuity. On the other

hand, if interest rates go down, companies will offer poorer annuities – and you'll be sitting pretty
■ the extent to which inflation will erode the buying-power of your income.

But you don't know how long you're going to live, and you don't know what's going to happen to interest rates or to inflation – so you can't know if an annuity will turn out to be a good buy or not.

Fall in buying-power of income from an annuity (annuity bought for £10,000 by 70-year-old man)

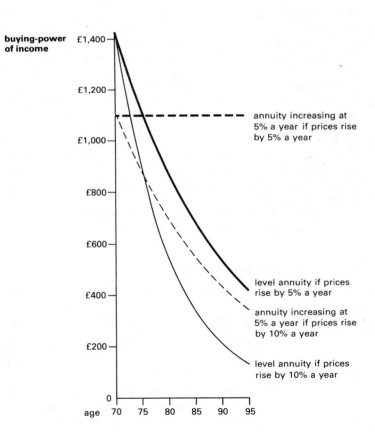

Should you buy an annuity?

Once you have bought an annuity – and handed over your money – you can't go back on the arrangement. So you shouldn't buy one without pausing for thought. You should first make sure your dependants would have enough to live on when you die. Then consider how much you want to leave your family (or favourite charity), how much you want to put by for a rainy day, and how much you want to leave available for holidays, replacing your car, colour television, and so on. You could consider spending part of what is left on an annuity – *provided* the extra income you get compared with what you'd get from another type of investment is large enough to compensate you for handing over part of your savings for good.

Which type?

For most people the choice is between a level or increasing annuity. With these types you know just how many £££ of annuity income to expect each year. You can get unit-linked annuities, where your income is linked to investment performance. With these your income will vary from year to year, and may be very low in some years.

Choosing between a level and an increasing annuity is more difficult. An increasing annuity offers some protection against inflation – but not much, unless you're prepared to accept a low starting income. You can see from the Diagrams that in terms of buying-power it would take some six years for the yearly income from an increasing annuity to overtake a level one. It would take much longer for you to receive the same *total* buying-power. And you may not live long enough to be better off from the increasing annuity. It might be better to go for a level annuity, investing what you don't need at once to draw on later in retirement.

Tax treatment

Part of the income from an annuity is treated as your initial outlay being returned to you – and is tax-free. The remainder counts as interest, and is added to your investment income.

The amount of the tax-free part is worked out according to Inland Revenue rules. It is fixed in terms of £££, not as a proportion of the income from the annuity. For each type of annuity the tax-free amount is based on your age when you buy the annuity, the amount you pay for it, and how often the income is paid. The older you are when you take out the annuity the higher the capital part of the income you get, and the higher the total amount of income. This is because the older you are the shorter the period the insurance company expects to have to pay the income for.

With increasing annuities, the tax-free amount normally increases at the same rate as the income from the annuity increases. With unit-linked annuities the tax-free amount stays fixed, whether the income rises or falls.

An annuity is treated in this special way only if you buy it voluntarily with your own money – for example if you use a lump sum from your employer's pension scheme.

The insurance company normally deducts tax at the basic rate from the taxable part of your annuity income before paying you. If you are liable for less tax than the insurance company deducts, you can claim tax back from the taxman. If you pay tax at higher rates you'll have to pay extra tax.

If your income from all sources – including the taxable part of the annuity – is below certain limits, you can apply through the insurance company to have your annuity income paid without deduction of tax. Check with the taxman.

From which company?

Our Table on p358 gives an indication of the sort of return available in early April 1988, but companies' rates can change frequently. To choose a company yourself, get an up-to-date copy of *Money Management* – £2.85 from Central House, 27 Park Street, Croydon CR0 1YD – which regularly compares companies' immediate annuity rates.

If your age is close to those used by the magazine, get quotations from companies which do well for that age. But things may well have changed since the magazine went to press. So it might be as well to go to an insurance adviser too. Some subscribe to computer systems which list annuity income from different companies.

Company safety

The Policyholders Protection Act (see p325) gives you protection should your insurance company go bust. However, you'd still be faced with a lot of anxiety while it was all going on. To avoid this, you may do as well to avoid very new or very small insurance companies. Get your insurance broker to check for you.

Home income schemes

If you're elderly and own your home, you may be able to boost your income with a home income scheme. A 75-year old man, for example, with a £20,000 loan could boost his after-tax income by about £1,560 a year. A woman of 75 would get about £1,100.

How the schemes work

You get a loan based on the security of your home. The loan is used to buy an annuity from an insurance company. While you live, you get the income from the annuity from which basic rate tax and interest on the loan has been deducted. When you die, the loan is repaid out of your estate (possibly by the sale of the home) before inheritance tax is worked out. (Note that with some schemes, called **reversions,** you sell all or part of your house to the company. Any increase in the value of the house then goes to the company, not to you.)

Everyone, taxpayer and non-taxpayer, gets tax relief on the full amount of the loan interest (provided the loan is not more than £30,000). This means that basic rate taxpayers and non-taxpayers have their interest payments reduced by 25p in each £ (in the 1988–89 tax year). See Diagram overleaf for an example of how this works in practice.

If you pay tax at more than the basic rate, you can claim extra tax relief from the taxman.

The nuts and bolts

The schemes are available for freehold houses, and for leasehold property with a substantial part of the lease still to run (50 to 80 years, depending on the company). When you apply for a scheme, your home will be valued by an independent valuer – you pay the fee, but it may be returned if you take out the scheme. The most you can usually borrow is a percentage (60 to 80 per cent) of the market value of your home.

The interest rate is normally fixed at the time you take the loan, and so is the income from the annuity. This means that the income you get from the scheme won't change as time passes. However, there are schemes where the interest rate varies – we don't recommend them, because if interest rates rise, your income would drop.

How a home income plan works

[1] You get this tax relief even if you don't pay tax. If you pay higher rate tax you'll have to claim back the extra tax relief from the taxman.

You mortgage your home to an insurance company and get in return an annuity of, say, £3,200 a year

The company also deducts mortgage interest after deducting basic rate tax relief – say £1,500 [1]

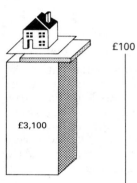

£100

£3,100

Before paying you this, the company deducts basic rate tax of, say, £100 from the taxable part of the annuity – which leaves £3,100

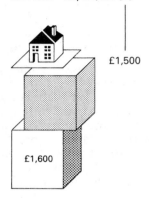

£1,500

£1,600

So company hands you £1,600

You may be able to take part of the loan in cash in return for a rather lower income. There's often a minimum loan – commonly £15,000 or so.

If the house is occupied by two people – husband and wife, or brother and sister say – the annuity is arranged so that it continues for as long as either is alive. You generally have to be at least 70 to be eligible for a home income plan (somewhat older if you're a couple applying).

Pros and cons

The value of your home is likely to go up year by year, after you've taken out the loan. You may be able to use the increase in value to get a further loan and buy another annuity. In this way you might be able to increase your income in line with inflation.

With an ordinary annuity, inflation reduces the buying power of your fixed income, and there's not much you can do about it. With these schemes, inflation still reduces the buying power of your fixed income, but it correspondingly reduces the value of your debt to the insurance company. So rising prices don't wholly work against you.

On the other hand, you'd be almost certain to get a better after-tax increase in your income by paying cash for an annuity (if you could do so) rather than mortgaging your home. And if it's likely you'll have to sell your home (to move in with relatives or into an old people's home, say) think twice before going for a home income plan. If you do move later on, you'll have to repay the loan, and may get left with a rather low fixed-income annuity.

If you get state benefits such as income support or housing benefit, a home income plan could mean that you'll lose some or all of that benefit. So get advice (from your local Citizens' Advice Bureau, for example) before signing on the dotted line.

Suitable for you?

A home income scheme is worth considering if you need the extra income, provided you're at least 70 (or preferably older). But you'd almost certainly get a better after-tax increase in your income by paying cash for an annuity (if you could do so) rather than mortgaging your home. Steer clear of reversions and variable interest rate schemes. And remember that you can't cancel an annuity and get your money back.

23

COMMODITIES

You might think that investing in commodities is a way of investing your long-term savings so that they stand a chance of keeping pace with inflation. Investing in commodities can give you a very bumpy ride though. Chapter 25 tells you about investing in things like stamps, antiques and wine. Here we deal with a different group of commodities – raw materials which can be bought and sold easily in large quantities on organised markets based in the city of London. The main raw materials which come into this category fall into two groups: *metals* such as copper, lead, silver, zinc and *soft commodities* such as cocoa, coffee, rubber, sugar and gas oil. Direct investments in commodities are not generally suitable for the small investor, or for money you cannot afford to lose.

How commodity markets work

Private investors can buy and sell commodities in two main ways:
■ for delivery straight away
■ for delivery on an agreed date in the future.

For delivery straight away

You can buy or sell copper, for example, which has already been mined, and is being stored in a warehouse. In the trade, this is known as buying or selling physicals or actuals; and the price you pay is known as a spot price. You have to pay – in full – for the commodity at the time you buy it. And you have to buy at least a minimum amount – 25 metric tons of copper, for example (which would have cost around £33,500 at the time this book went to press).

The commodity will be kept in a warehouse – and you'll have to pay charges for storing and insuring it.

If you buy a commodity for delivery straight away, you are hoping that the price of the commodity will go up and you'll eventually be able to sell it at a profit (after taking account of buying and selling costs, and storage and insurance charges).

For delivery on an agreed date in the future

This is the usual way in which private investors buy and sell commodities. You agree *now* to buy or sell a fixed amount of, for example, copper at a fixed price for delivery on some agreed date in the future. In the trade, this is known as dealing in futures and your agreement is known as a futures contract. There are rules about how far in advance you can arrange to buy or sell each commodity – eg up to three months with copper, and up to 17 months or so with cocoa. If you agree to buy or sell cocoa in December 1988, say, you are said to be dealing in *December 1988* cocoa.

If you buy a commodity for delivery in the future, you are hoping that its price will rise above the price you've agreed to buy it at – and that you'll be able to sell it at a profit before it is due to be delivered.

But you can also make a profit if you expect the price of a commodity to fall. You can agree to *sell* rather than buy, December 1988 cocoa, for example, at a fixed price. You then have to buy – before December 1988 arrives – the cocoa you've agreed to sell. If the price of December 1988 cocoa does indeed fall below the price you've agreed to sell at, you will be able to make a profit on the deal. But if it goes up in price, you'll end up having to buy your cocoa at a higher price than the one you've agreed to sell at – and so make a loss on the deal.

You don't have to pay out the full cost of the futures contract you are dealing in – only a deposit (of perhaps 10 per cent of its value). But this doesn't mean that it's only your deposit you can lose. You will indeed lose a 10 per cent deposit if the value of a futures contract you've bought goes down by 10 per cent by the time you sell it. But if the price goes down by 50 per cent before you sell, you'll lose five times that amount. In practice, if the price falls, your broker (see p376) will ask you for more money (known as a margin call). If you don't hand over this extra money, he's likely to insist that you sell your futures contract straight away and accept the loss you've already made.

Trading in futures is not long-term investment

A private investor (often called a speculator) who deals in commodity futures is not making a long-term investment. He is gambling on what will happen to the price of a commodity over a relatively short period. If he buys December 1988 cocoa, for example, it's what happens to cocoa prices before then that decides whether he wins or loses his bet.

He may believe – quite correctly perhaps – that cocoa prices will double over the next five years. But he can't buy a futures contract which lasts that long. Buying December 1988 cocoa doesn't make sense unless he believes that cocoa prices are going to go up more than other people expect over the period before then.

Commodity options

A commodity option gives you the right to buy or sell a commodity futures contract at its current price at any time up to an agreed date. The amount you have to pay to buy an option varies widely – depending on what is expected to happen to the price of the particular futures contract you are interested in.

The advantage of taking out an option to buy a futures contract is that it gives you the chance of making a profit if the price of the commodity goes up – whilst at the same time limiting the amount of money you can lose if the price of the commodity falls, to the amount you paid for the option. The main disadvantage is that the price of the futures contract has to go up by at least the amount you paid for the option before you start making a profit.

How the markets are organised

London is one of the main centres in the world for commodity futures trading. There isn't one large market where all commodities are traded – there are several. For example, trading in aluminium, copper, lead, nickel, silver, and zinc is organised by the London Metal Exchange while futures and options trading in cocoa, sugar and coffee is handled by London FOX, the Futures and Options Exchange.

All the markets work in much the same way. Trading in each commodity takes place according to a set of rules – which lay down standards for the quality of the raw material, and fix things like the minimum amounts that can be traded.

Why futures markets exist

Futures markets enable people who trade in commodities – eg raw material producers (such as mine owners and farmers), manufacturers (such as chocolate firms) and wholesalers – to reduce the risk they face of losing money because of changes in the prices of commodities. Futures markets allow the raw material producers to get a guaranteed price for raw materials they haven't yet produced. And they allow manufacturers to know exactly how much they'll have to pay for raw materials they'll need in some months' time.

The private investor (or speculator), who has no intention of producing or using commodities, is one of the people who take on the risk that the producers and manufacturers want to avoid. The private investor is the person who loses if, say, he has bought December 1988 cocoa and the price falls before he can sell it. But he is the person who gains if the price goes up before he sells it.

How commodity prices vary

Commodity prices in general

The Chart opposite shows how the *Financial Times* index of commodity prices has changed between July 1952, when the index was started, and October 1985, when it was suspended following the collapse in the tin market (see p376). We've adjusted the index to take account of inflation – so the Chart shows what's happened to commodity prices, compared with UK prices in general. Note that when the index started, commodity prices were almost as high as they had ever been – due mainly to shortages caused by the Korean War.

The Chart shows two main things:
■ compared with prices in general, the commodity price index fell fairly steadily between 1952 and 1972
■ prices tend to go up and down quite quickly. A change of five per cent in a month is common.

Prices of individual commodities

The charts on pp372–374 show the average monthly prices (*not* adjusted for the full in the buying power of the £) of three commodities – sugar, coffee and cocoa – since the beginning of 1983. You can see that all three commodities fluctuated enormously in price during this period.

Commodity prices 1952–1985

Index based on Financial Times Index of Sensitive Commodity prices, corrected for fall in buying-power of £, using monthly level of the Index of Retail Prices, compiled by the Department of Employment.

Index of
commodity prices

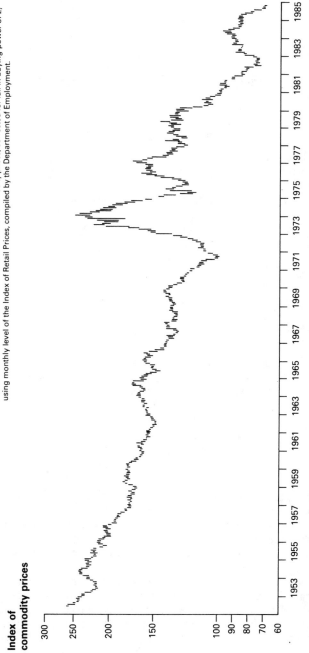

Sugar – average monthly price

The price of cocoa varied the least but still almost doubled from 1983 to 1985 and then fell back to below 1983 levels during the next three years. The prices of coffee and sugar (which is priced in dollars) were even more volatile over the short term. Today's prices for coffee and cocoa are lower than their prices in 1983.

So to judge from what has happened in the past, it seems that you can expect a bumpy ride if you invest in commodities. Their price may well double or halve in a year or two. You can, of course, make a profit on commodities even when their price is falling if you are successful in your use of futures or options contracts (see p369), but you should never under-estimate your possible losses.

What commodity prices depend on

The prices of most commodities depend on supply and demand. In the end, the demand for a commodity comes from us – the consumers. To make the things which we want to buy, firms have to buy raw materials – for example, copper is needed for making electrical wire and copper pipes, cocoa for making chocolate.

If firms want to buy more of a commodity than is available, its price will rise. This may persuade producers that it will be profitable to produce more (for example start another copper mine, or plant more cocoa trees). But it may take some years before any more copper or cocoa is actually produced. The production of some other commodities –

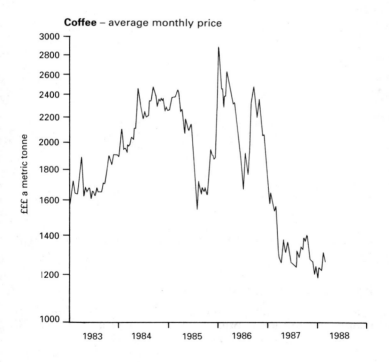

Coffee – average monthly price

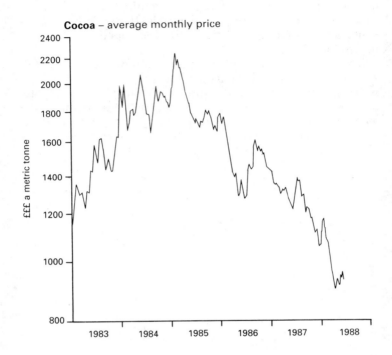

Cocoa – average monthly price

sugar, for example – can be increased within a year or so of producers deciding to produce more (weather permitting).

Prices in the long-term

There's no way of predicting with certainty, what will happen to commodity prices over the long-term – the next 20 or 50 years say.

You might think if that the world economy grows, and the total amount of goods and services produced in the world goes up, the price of raw materials would tend to rise in response to increased demand. But if new and better ways of producing raw materials are found, if new producers come into the market, or if cheap man-made alternatives to some raw materials are developed, commodity prices *may* go down over the long-term.

Prices in the short-term

Commodity prices have fluctuated a lot from one year to another, and even from one month to another. These fluctuations can be the result of a number of things. The main ones seem to be:

■ **natural disasters.** Droughts, floods, hurricanes, disease, and so on, may damage crops – and so lead to higher prices for commodities such as sugar, coffee and cocoa. Conversely, good harvests may lead to lower prices. Natural disasters can damage mining areas too — causing reduced production and high prices for a commodity such as copper.

■ **booms and slumps.** In the past, most economies have had periods of boom (with low unemployment and a high rate of growth of the amount of goods and services produced) followed by periods of slump (high unemployment, little –if any – growth in the amount of goods and services produced). In the boom, firms need to buy more raw materials in order to increase the amounts they produce – so raw material prices tend to rise. In a slump, firms cut back on the amounts they produce and the amount of raw materials they buy – so raw material prices tend to fall. In the early 1980s, much of the developed world experienced a slump at some time – and commodity prices, in general, fell.

■ **political problems.** For example, if a war breaks out, or a political revolution takes place, in an area of the world where a large proportion of the world's supply of a particular commodity is produced, the price of that commodity is likely to rise – as a result of fears that supplies of the commodity will be reduced.

■ **the exchange rate of the £.** Most of the world supply of commodities is bought by foreign firms – who naturally work out their cost in foreign currencies, such as US dollars and German marks. If they continue to pay the same price for their commodities, and if the exchange rate of the £ (ie the number of US dollars, German marks, and so on, you can get for a £) goes down, the price of commodities in terms of £££ will go up. Conversely if the exchange rate of the £ goes up, the price of commodities in terms of £££ will go down.

Commodity price agreements

With some commodities, the main producing and consuming countries have got together to try to reduce price fluctuations. Most of these efforts haven't been very successful – there's always temptation for some country to break an agreement by exporting more than it is supposed to. And not all producing countries may join an agreement in the first place.

The best known commodity price agreement is probably the one for oil, run by OPEC (the Organisation of Petroleum Exporting Countries) – but this depends on the co-operation of producing countries only. The UK is not a member of OPEC.

In October 1985, The International Tin Council, which controlled the price and supply of 52 per cent of tin production, defaulted on huge debts. The London Metal Exchange suspended tin trading and the price of tin collapsed from around £9,000 per tonne to around £3,500 per tonne. Tin trading has not yet been re-started on the London Metal Exchange.

How you can invest in commodities

You can invest directly in commodities in two ways:
- by buying and selling commodities through a commodity broker
- by putting money into a fund which has been set up specially to invest in commodities.

Buying and selling through a broker

Investing in physical commodities isn't a practical idea for most people. The minimum quantities you can buy are very large – for example 25 metric tons of copper (which would have cost around £33,500 at the time this book went to press), or 50 metric tons of sugar (which is priced in dollars, but in sterling would have cost around £6,400). And with many commodities – such as cocoa and coffee — you run the risk of your commodity deteriorating in quality before you sell it.

If you deal in futures, you don't have to pay out such large sums of money, and you don't have to worry about the quality of your commodity. You have to put down only a deposit – perhaps 10 per cent of the value of what you're buying or selling. But the risk of losing a large sum of money is still there. Suppose, for example, you bought the minimum possible quantity of cocoa for delivery in a year's time.

You might have to put down a £1,000 deposit at the time you arrange the deal. But then if the price of cocoa fell, you'd have to hand over more money to the broker. And if the price fell by 50 per cent before you decided it was time to get rid of your cocoa you would have lost around £5,000 (half of the £10,000 the cocoa was worth when you arranged the deal).

You may be able to join a syndicate of people who pool their money and invest in commodities. Some commodity brokers run such syndicates. And, in some cases, there's a guarantee that you can't lose more than the amount of your original investment. But you might face problems about getting your money out when you want to. And there's still a fairly high chance of losing a lot of money.

Commodity funds

Putting money into a fund which has been set up specially to invest in commodities has three main advantages. First, it allows you to invest in commodities even if you can afford to lose only a more modest amount (perhaps, say, £3,000, though £5,000 or £10,000 may be a more common minimum investment). Secondly, you can choose a fund which guarantees you won't lose more than the amount you put into the fund. Thirdly, most of the funds invest your money in a lot of different commodities – something you couldn't do yourself without investing a good deal of money. This means that if one commodity does particularly badly, it won't have a disastrous effect on the value of your investment.

For legal and tax reasons, the commodity funds which are available to the public are based outside the UK – often in the Isle of Man, or the Channel Islands. And they aren't allowed to send their booklets, prospectuses and so on, direct to members of the public. If you want these, you'll have to ask for them to be sent via a professional adviser – such as a bank manager or stockbroker. However, this may change in the future if, as a result of regulations currently under discussion, some funds are allowed to operate in the UK.

How commodity funds work

Commodity funds work in much the same way as unit trusts. The fund is divided into a number of units – and your stake in the fund is represented by the number of units you own. The value of a unit is roughly the value of the fund divided by the total number of units.

But one major difference between these commodity funds and most unit trusts is that most unit trusts are *authorised*, formerly by the Department of Trade and Industry, but since the implementation of the Financial Services Act, by the Securities and Investments Board (see Chapter 5). This means that the trust deed, which spells out how the trust works, has been looked at and approved. There are also rules about how the prices of units should be worked out. There are not the same safeguards with these commodity funds, though if commodity funds were to be based in the UK, they would also have to be authorised.

Most of the commodity funds can invest in both commodity futures and physical commodities. But a few invest only in physical stocks of just one commodity – for example copper or silver.

The performance of the funds which deal in just one commodity depends, on the whole, on what happens to the price of that commodity. But how your investment fares if you invest in a fund which deals in futures depends, to a large extent, on the skill of the fund managers. Since these funds started there have been some vast differences in performance. For example, assuming all income had been reinvested in the fund, if you'd invested £1,000 in 1983, it would have been worth over £2,837 five years later if you'd chosen the best performing fund. If you'd chosen the worst, £1,000 would have dwindled to £908 or so (worth only around £711 in terms of buying-power).

All the funds have minimum investments – perhaps, say, £5,000. And all make charges – perhaps an initial charge of 5% of the amount you invest, a yearly charge of 2% of the value of the fund and, in some cases, a 'performance' fee of, say, 10% of any increase in the price of units. Some of the funds pay out an income, but some don't. And the funds vary in how often the unit price is calculated and, therefore, how long you may have to wait to buy or sell units – with some this happens daily, with others you may have to wait a week or possibly even longer. Some of the funds – but not all – have independent trustees or custodians who look after the fund's cash and the bits of paper which say what assets the fund owns.

For a list of some of the commodity funds, details of how they've done in the past and how to contact the managers, see a magazine such as *Money Management*, £2.85 from Central House, 27 Park Street, Croydon CR0 1YD (Telephone 01-680 3786).

Commodity unit trusts

A commodity unit trust allows you to invest indirectly in commodities. Authorised unit trusts are not, at present,

---

Tax

How any profits you make from investing in commodities will be taxed is far from certain.

Profits from buying and selling *physical* commodities are likely to be treated as trading profits — and so taxed as earned income. A loss might count as a trading loss and you could set it off against the total of your income from all sources, but not against capital gains.

Just one isolated venture into the commodity *futures* market is likely to be treated as giving rise to a capital gain (or loss). But if you make a profit from a series of transactions, or invest as a member of a syndicate run by brokers or by a professional manager, this is likely to be treated as investment income. In this case, a loss could be set off only against profits of the same kind, or against certain other income. For more on tax, see Chapter 7.

---

allowed to invest directly in commodities but only to buy the shares of companies which do so, since this is considered less risky. The value of units in the trust then goes up and down with the share prices of the companies the trust invests in – it doesn't depend directly on commodity prices. Investment trusts (see p265) cannot invest directly in commodities either.

Is commodity investment for you?

Buying physical commodities and storing them in the hope that their value will rise isn't a practical idea for most people. You have to invest several thousand pounds to buy the minimum possible quantity of just one commodity. And with commodities such as cocoa and coffee you run the risk of the stocks deteriorating in quality before you sell them. What's more, there's no guarantee that commodity prices will, in the long run, rise as quickly as prices in general.

Buying and selling commodity futures is a way of gambling on what's going to happen to the price of a commodity over a relatively short period — two years at the most. It could be a way of making, or losing, a lot of money in a short period. One large firm of commodity brokers estimated that 95 per cent of commodity speculators who take their own investment decisions lose money.

If you decide that – despite the drawbacks – you do want to invest in commodities, putting your money in a special commodity fund has advantages. In particular, with some funds, it will limit the amount you have to be willing to risk losing.

24

INVESTING ABROAD

At present you are free to invest world-wide. But there's no guarantee that this will always be the case. Until 23 October 1979, exchange control restrictions meant that there were all sorts of barriers to investing overseas – for example, you had to get Bank of England permission to transfer money abroad to buy a house, and you had to change money via what was known as the 'dollar premium' (which could have meant a poor rate of exchange).

You may decide to invest abroad for two main reasons:
■ you reckon that you'll get a better return on your money than with UK investment – taking account of the return (both income and capital growth) in terms of local currency and the effect of changes in the exchange rate of the £
■ you want to spread your money around different countries in the hope of cutting down the risk of your investments, as a whole, doing very badly.

Below we look in more detail at these reasons. But bear in mind that investing overseas should form only part of your overall investment strategy. The first two chapters of this book give general advice on how to plan your investments – and can be applied not just to UK investments, but to overseas ones too.

Better return abroad?

Just as you might compare different investments in the UK to check which would give you the best return, so you should consider overseas investments as an alternative to UK ones. For example, you may have decided that a British Government stock paying a high income meets your investment needs. It could be worth checking whether a similar foreign investment could offer the prospect of a better return. The same goes if, for example, you are looking for a capital gain from unit trusts, or want to put money in a bank deposit account.

When comparing the returns don't just look at the return in local currency (eg the rate of interest you'd get on your deposit account). You need to be aware that ups and downs in the exchange rate can affect your total return. Suppose, for example, you invest £100 in the US, at an exchange rate of $1.80 to the £ – ie you invest $180. If you get interest of 15 per cent, at the end of the year you'll have $207 (ignoring, for simplicity, any tax and any cost of buying and selling the investment). You discover that the £ has gone down a lot in value over the year compared with the $ and that the exchange rate is now $1.50 to the £. In this case, you'd get back £138 (ie $207 ÷ 1.5), giving you a total rate of return of 38 per cent – more than twice the 15 per cent you get in local currency.

Of course, things may not work out in your favour in this way. For example, you may find at the end of the year that the £ has gone up in value and that the exchange rate is now $2.10 to the £. In this case, you'd get back about £98.60 (ie $207 ÷ 2.1), which is less than the £100 you originally invested, despite the 15 per cent your money has been earning.

In short, it's good for your overseas investment if the exchange rate of the £ goes down against the currency concerned. It's bad if the exchange rate of the £ goes up. But beware – a country offering high interest rates may well have a currency which is falling against the £ (see *Warning* opposite).

Cutting risks

It's all very well to go for the best return on the money you invest, but few people are willing to face the risk of losing a lot of it in the process. One way of cutting down this risk is to spread your money around different types of investments – eg putting some in British Government stocks, some in shares, some in a building society and using some to buy a house. The chance of *all* these different investments doing extremely badly is lower than the chance of just one of them turning out to be a dud. Of course, reducing your risk of loss in this way also reduces your chance of winning the jackpot.

Spreading your investments around different countries is another way of cutting down your risk. Although the economies of (and the health of investments in) some countries may, at times, move up and down more or less together (for example Canada and the US, Singapore and Hong Kong), this is not true of all countries. For example, the problems faced by the Far East are quite different from those faced by Germany, and different again from those faced by the US.

Short-term fluctuations in exchange rates can have a dramatic effect on the value of your investment, but by choosing investments in a cross section of countries you reduce your risk of all of them doing badly at once.

Another way of reducing the effect of short-term fluctuations in exchange rates is to take out a **forward exchange contract**. This is a way of buying or selling foreign currency for delivery at a date in the future. Your bank should be able to give you more information.

Where to invest

Overseas, as in the UK, there is a wide range of investments. For a summary of the main types, see pp390–398.

In the next few pages, we've looked at how the two factors – exchange rates and return in local currency – have interacted for several different countries over a sample period (from 1980 to the end of 1987).

Exchange rate of the £

You can see from Diagram 1 that, over the period in question, the exchange rate of the £ tended to go down against most of the other currencies we looked at. Diagram 2 shows the gain you would have made (ignoring buying and selling costs and the interest you might have got) if you had bought £100 worth of each of the currencies in Diagram 1 at the end of 1980, and changed it back into £££ at the end of 1987. Diagram 2 also shows the yearly rate of return these gains represent. You can see that you could have achieved a rate of return of just over 12 per cent (compound) a year – simply by turning your money into Japanese yen. You'd have lost out only with Australian $ and French francs, where the £ has generally done quite well over the period in question. Of course, even with other currencies, small gains could be wiped out by the costs of buying and selling.

Warning

Just because you could have made large gains over the period shown, it doesn't mean the same will apply in the future.

Diagram 1: Exchange rate of the £

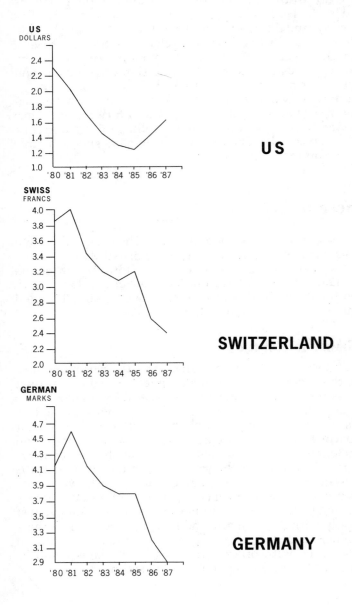

Diagram 1 contd: Exchange rate of the £

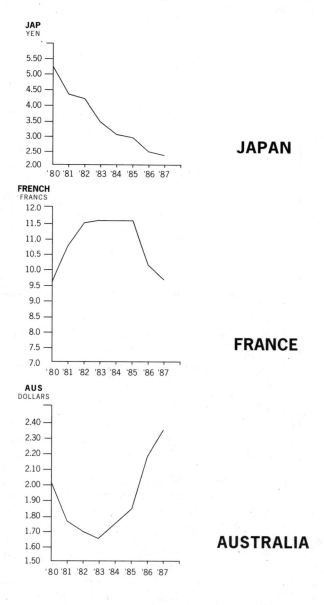

JAP YEN

JAPAN

FRENCH FRANCS

FRANCE

AUS DOLLARS

AUSTRALIA

Diagram 2: Gains made on foreign currency 1980 – 87
(ignoring buying and selling costs. Percentages show equivalent yearly return, compounded)

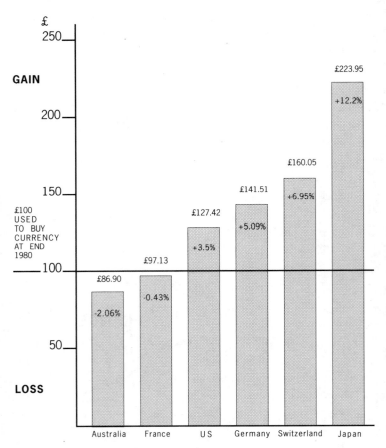

Indeed one of the major problems in choosing where to invest is trying to predict what will happen to exchange rates in the future. The £ could rise against other currencies, and your gains could be wiped out.

In the long term, one of the key factors affecting exchange rates is inflation – if the rate of inflation in one country is considerably higher than in another, the first country's exchange rate is likely to fall relative to the second. You can see from Diagram 3 that during the period when the exchange rate of the £ tended to be falling, the inflation rate in the UK was generally higher than in the other countries we looked at.

Diagram 3: Inflation Rates

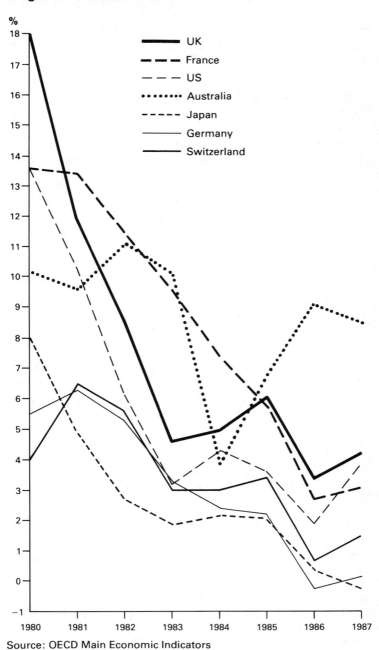

Source: OECD Main Economic Indicators

The moral is, *don't* invest in a particular country just because you get a high interest rate. If the currency is going down relative to the £ (perhaps because inflation has been high), your extra interest could be wiped out by exchange rate losses.

The return in local currency

Diagram 4 shows how the returns on stocks issued by the governments of the different countries compared over the period of 1980 to 1987. You can see that in the UK returns were generally above average, but were outstripped consistently by both Australia and France.

This was at least partly because the interest rate a country has to offer to attract foreign investors must reflect, to some extent, how people expect that country's exchange rate to move in future. And, over the period, foreign investors tended to be wary of the UK's record of high inflation rates and a falling exchange rate against the yen, mark and Swiss franc.

Diagram 5 looks at share prices from 1980 to 1987. You can see that all the markets we looked at rose significantly over the period in question. If you'd been clever you could have made a bomb, but timing was all important. The world-wide crash in share prices in October 1987 hit share prices hard, and wiped off much of the huge gains shareholders had made in the 'bull' market which had dominated throughout the 1980s. However, as a long term investment, shares have consistently outstripped the rate of inflation, even taking the crash into account.

The total return

Exchange rate changes, and the return in the local currency, are the key factors in working out what an overseas investment is worth to you. Diagram 6 draws these factors together, and gives the average yearly rate of return for government stocks and shares bought at the end of 1980 and sold at the end of 1987. The shaded bars give the return in local currency, the other bars the return adjusted for the changes in the exchange rate.

You can see that, with government stocks, although UK investments came out quite well in terms of local currency, other countries did better when changes in exchange rates were taken into account.

Warning The graphs we've shown are for a sample period to show how exchange rates, local rates of return and total

Diagram 4: Return on government stocks [1]

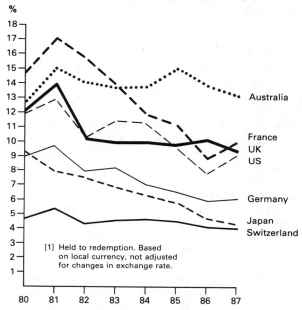

[1] Held to redemption. Based on local currency, not adjusted for changes in exchange rate.

Source: OECD Main Economic Indicators

Diagram 5: How share prices have done [1]

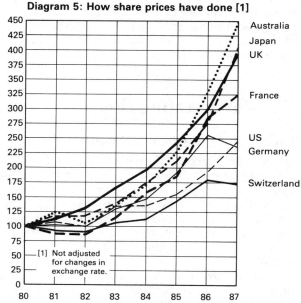

[1] Not adjusted for changes in exchange rate.

Source: OECD Main Economic Indicators

returns are inter-related. Future rates of return may be quite different.

Should YOU invest abroad?

If you've got several thousand £££ to invest, putting some of it abroad is worth considering. Though you can't rely on getting a better return than in the UK, spreading your money among different countries could cut down the risk of your investments, as a whole, doing badly. Bear in mind that the outcome of your investment depends not just on how well it does in terms of local currency, but also on what happens to exchange rates. And what will happen to exchange rates over the next few years – in the light of what happens to relative inflation rates, how long North Sea Oil lasts, and political developments throughout the world – is anyone's guess.

Because your investment depends so much on exchange rates, investing abroad is not the place for money where you want to be quite sure of how much you'd get at short notice – so not a home for your emergency fund, say. Investing indirectly – for example through UK-based unit trusts or investment trusts specialising in foreign investment – would cut down on administrative problems, and would be less risky than direct investment (in foreign shares or foreign government stocks, say). Read on for the pros and cons of different ways of investing abroad, and see p396 for the tax implications.

Ways of investing abroad

Foreign currency bank accounts

High-Street banks will open foreign currency accounts for UK residents. These can be either current accounts (ie you can draw cheques on them), or deposit accounts (where interest is paid). Some accounts may offer current account facilities and pay interest if a certain balance is maintained. You may, however, have to pay charges. You don't need to have a UK account with a bank to be able to open a foreign account.

Interest rates can vary from day to day. In general, the more you invest the higher the rate of interest you can get. If you have to give notice to withdraw your money the rate of interest is normally fixed for this period. Note that

Diagram 6: Average yearly return 1980 – 1987

Ignoring buying and selling costs and assuming
all income reinvested
Source: OECD main economic indicators

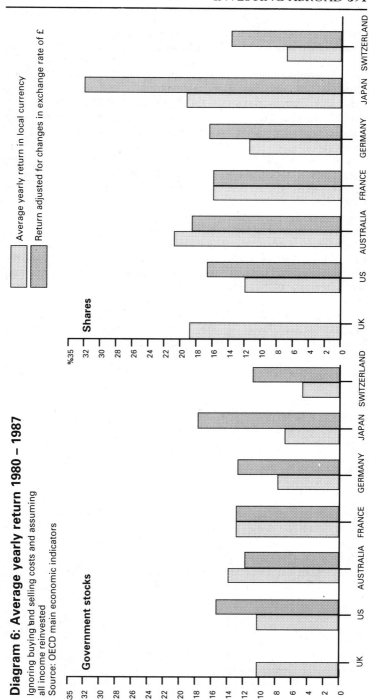

interest rates – and the minimum amount you have to invest – vary from bank to bank. For example, in mid March 1988, the minimum investment for seven days' notice of withdrawal ranged from the equivalent of US $1,500 to $10,000. And the interest rate for such deposits ranged from 6 per cent to nearly 9 per cent for Australian dollars, from just under 3 to around 6.5 per cent for French francs. There were similar variations for other currencies, so shop around before opening an account.

You can now also get accounts denominated in **European Currency Units** (ECUs). This is the currency of the European Community based on all the national currencies in the Community.

Points to watch

■ Current accounts don't normally pay interest – and you may pay charges for operating them. So it's not worth having one unless you travel a lot in a particular country, or plan to live there part of the time.

■ Some foreign banks with branches in this country will also open accounts for UK residents. They tend to offer rates of interest similar to (or somewhat lower than) those given by our High-Street banks. You could also open an account direct with a bank abroad – beware, though, of any local exchange control restrictions.

Points about tax

Interest on UK-based accounts is paid after deduction of composite rate tax (the equivalent of basic rate tax). Interest will be paid without deduction of tax only if the account is held offshore – in the Channel Islands, say.

Unit trusts

Many unit trusts invest overseas rather than in the UK. Some of these are based in the UK, some in places like the Channel Islands and Isle of Man (known as offshore funds). And, of course, many other countries have their own unit trusts. Some trusts spread their investments internationally, others specialise in particular areas – eg US, Far East, Australia. Most invest in shares, but some invest in government stocks, Eurobonds or put money on deposit. A few specialise in investing in foreign currencies. Investing through a unit trust means that you can get a stake in a spread of investments in an overseas country for a relatively low minimum investment (say £500) – and that you don't have to get involved in the administrative problems associated with investing directly in overseas stocks and shares (see p395). See Chapter 16 for more details about unit trusts.

Money Management magazine (subscription details from Central House, 27 Park Street, Croydon, CR0 1YD) gives lists each month of which UK unit trusts invest where and how they've performed in the past (though, of course, this is no guide to the future).

Points to watch

■ Unit trusts are not a home for money you might need at short notice. They should be considered, in the main, as a long-term investment (seven years or more, say) – though they can also be used for short-term speculation if you're prepared to take a higher risk.

■ If you invest via UK-based unit trusts (but not offshore funds), you get the protection of the Financial Services Act (see Chapter 5).

Points about tax

Distributions from UK-based unit trusts are paid with only UK tax deducted, while distributions from most offshore funds are paid with little or no tax deducted. So there are no problems with reclaiming tax held back by foreign governments. With foreign-based unit trusts, distributions are normally paid with some tax withheld by the foreign government. You'll have to arrange to get a credit for any tax deducted – see p400.

Investment trusts

Investment trusts are companies which, in turn, hold the shares of other companies (see p265 for more details). Many UK investment trusts hold overseas shares (perhaps specialising in particular areas of the world, such as the US, Far East, Australia). UK investment trust shares can be bought and sold on the London Stock Exchange. Details of UK investment trusts are published annually in a directory available from the Association of Investment Trust Companies, 16 Finsbury Circus, London EC2M 7JJ. Monthly statistics on where the companies invest and how they've performed are printed on the second Saturday each month in the *Daily Telegraph*.

Investment trusts also exist in other countries – and a few of the major foreign ones are quoted on the London Stock Exchange.

Points to watch
■ As with unit trusts, investing through a UK investment trust spares you the administrative problems you would face with overseas shareholdings. You'll also be protected under the Financial Services Act.
■ Investment trusts are not a home for money you might need at a short notice. They should be considered, in the main, as a long-term investments (seven years or more, say) – though they can also be used for short-term speculation.

Points about tax
As for unit trusts.

Foreign currency funds

These offer a means of investing in a range of currencies without opening individual bank accounts. You buy units in a fund (rather like buying unit trusts). The investment managers then shift the money in the fund around among a range of currencies, in the hope of taking advantage both of high interest rates and favourable exchange rate movements. So, in effect, you are staking your money on the skill and luck of the managers. Some of the funds are based in the Channel Islands (offshore funds), and operate like unit trusts. Others are UK-based and are linked to life insurance.

Points to watch
■ These funds give the opportunity of investing in currencies for a relatively low outlay – the minimum investment ranges from £1,000 to £10,000. But the funds all charge an annual management fee – often around 0.75 to 1 per cent.
■ Currency funds are *not* recommended as a home for money you can't afford to lose. You are taking on substantial currency risks.

Points about tax
UK-based funds pay interest after deduction of basic rate tax, so higher rate taxpayers may have to pay more tax. Since January 1984 offshore funds have had the choice of taking either 'accumulator' or 'distributor' status. Funds with distributor status have to distribute at least 85 per cent of their income, and you are taxed on this at your top rate of income tax. When you sell units, you pay capital gains tax on any increase in their value, but you qualify for the annual tax-free slice (see p105). Accumulator funds accumulate income in the price of the unit, but any profits made are taxed at

your top rate of income tax when you sell the units. So which type of fund is better for you will depend on your tax position.

Government stocks and company stocks

Just as the UK government raises money through issuing British Government stocks, so there is a wide range of stocks issued by foreign governments and bought and sold on foreign stock exchanges. Some of these are also traded on the London Stock Exchange.

Many companies, including foreign ones, also issue fixed interest securities which work in a similar way to government stocks. These normally pay higher interest, reflecting the fact that a company has more chance of going bust than most governments.

Points to watch

■ As with shares, there is a certain amount of administrative hassle and extra cost in dealing in foreign stocks on foreign stock exchanges (see p398). It may be simpler to invest through a unit trust that specialises in foreign stocks.
■ Remember that some governments may be offering high interest rates to offset a falling exchange rate. It's probably as well to stick to countries with strong governments.

Points about tax

Gains on foreign stocks are liable to capital gains tax – unlike gains on British Government stock, which are tax-free. Interest payments are generally made after deduction of some foreign tax. So you may have to arrange to get a credit for the tax deducted (see p399).

Shares

Shares in foreign companies can be bought and sold on their local stock exchanges, and some foreign companies' shares are traded on the London Stock Exchange too. But buying and selling them can work out very expensive. For foreign dealings done abroad, you have to pay the commission rates applying in the relevant country (as well as UK commission if you use a UK broker). This isn't a suitable way of investing in foreign companies unless you've got enough money to get a good spread of companies (and preferably of countries) – say £10,000 to £20,000 or more set aside for investment in foreign shares. The rest of us would be better advised to invest via unit trusts or possibly investment trusts.

Points to watch
■ Shares are not a home for money you might need at short notice. They should be considered, in the main, as a long-term investment (seven years or more, say) – though they can also be short-term speculation.
■ Some countries' protection for shareholders is less extensive than ours – it may be as well to stick to large, well-established stock markets (such as US, Japan, Netherlands).
■ It's likely to be difficult for you (or your adviser) to have detailed knowledge about a lot of foreign companies, and the economic environment in which they're functioning. Even those in the know may find it harder to keep up to date than those on the spot. And there are likely to be administrative hassles in collecting your dividends, and so on – see p398.

Points about tax
Dividends are normally paid with some tax withheld by the foreign government. So you may have to arrange to get a credit for the tax deducted – see p399.

Eurobonds

Eurobonds are a way in which international borrowers (for example, governments, large companies and international institutions like the World Bank) raise money. The bonds – which pay interest – are generally issued in a particular currency (eg dollars, German marks) and are quoted on various stock exchanges. Eurobonds issued by companies (rather than governments, and so on) normally pay a slightly higher rate of interest, reflecting the higher risk of them going bust.

Points to watch
■ Eurobonds come in fairly large units – $1,000 for example. The minimum investment is around $50,000, and many dealers won't deal with members of the public. You may do better to go for a unit trust specialising in Eurobonds.
■ The interest rate may be fixed, or may be changed at set intervals.
■ Interest rates on Eurobonds generally reflect interest rates in the country of the currency they're issued in.

Points about tax
As with foreign stocks, capital gains on Eurobonds are liable to capital gains tax. Interest is paid without any foreign tax

being deducted. But the interest is liable for UK tax, and you must declare it on your Tax Return.

Property

Buying property abroad is full of pitfalls for the unwary. For example, the costs of buying and selling are usually considerably greater abroad than they are in the UK: perhaps 10 per cent on both buying and selling. If you need to borrow money to buy the property, you may find it difficult to get a loan from a UK institution. There may be severe restrictions on taking your money out of the foreign country again if you decide to sell. And there's always a chance that, at some time in the future, the political climate in the country might change and foreigners won't be welcome. You should certainly get professional advice before contemplating an investment in property abroad.

If you haven't the money to buy a property outright, you could buy a timeshare. This will give you a set number of weeks in your holiday home every year. Organisations exist for timeshare 'swaps' if you don't want to go back to the same place every year, and you can sometimes arrange to swap dates as well. But a timeshare may turn out to be a very poor investment – you may find it hard to sell and what you sell it for could be much less than you paid in the first place. There have been many reports of high-pressure selling of timeshares, so beware of being pushed in to an unsuitable deal. The trade association for the industry is the Timeshare Developers' Association, 23 Buckingham Gate, London SW1E 6LB.

Points to watch

■ Always visit a home before buying – don't rely on glossy brochures. Try to spend a fair bit of time in the area, and see the house at different times of the day, and even in different seasons.

■ Check carefully on things like the reliability of local water, electricity supplies, sewerage; and on the structure and surroundings of the house you have in mind.

■ Planning permission for new buildings is easier to get in many countries abroad than in the UK; your idyllic country retreat may become the centre of a concrete jungle.

■ If you are planning to retire abroad, be particularly cautious. And check on medical facilities.

Points about tax

Gains you make on selling property abroad are liable to capital gains tax in the UK. Income you get from letting property is taxed as investment income, and you must declare it on your Tax Return. You can deduct any expenses incurred abroad in managing and collecting the income (eg paying an agent). If some foreign tax has been deducted, you'll have to arrange to get a tax credit.

Unit-linked life insurance

Some life insurance companies run funds which invest abroad. These work a bit like unit trusts. For details of how single-premium and regular-premium policies work, see Chapter 20.

Cost of buying and selling foreign currency

Unless you're investing in UK-based foreign investments (eg a unit trust) you're likely to have to exchange the £££ you want to invest for foreign currency. And when you cash your investment, you may have to turn your foreign currency back into £££ again. In both cases, you'll be charged for the transaction (the charge may be hidden in that different exchange rates will be used depending on whether you're buying or selling foreign currency). If you're changing a lot of money – several thousand £££, say – you may get a better deal than with smaller amounts. And if you're dealing through a stockbroker or other agent you may be able to benefit from favourable exchange rates he or she can get.

Administrative problems

If you have foreign investments you have to make arrangements in the foreign country for the share certificate (or whatever) to be held by an agent (for example a bank or stockbroker) and passed on to the new owner when you sell, and for dividends, interest, and so on, to be collected and sent on to you. You could make these arrangements yourself or ask a UK agent, such as a stockbroker, to make them for you. Either way, there'll be a fee to pay – and it could be high.

Tax on overseas investments

The tax treatment of investments held abroad (as opposed to UK-based foreign investments) can be extremely complicated. But even if you plan to hand over your tax affairs to advisers, a bit of background knowledge would help you to understand what they're up to.

Income tax

In general, if you're a UK resident all your income is liable to UK tax, whether or not it is brought into this country. So if, say, you have a bank deposit account in Switzerland, you have to declare the interest you get from it in your Tax Return, even if you keep the interest (or spend it) abroad. When converting foreign income into £££, use the exchange rate applying at the time it was due to be paid to you (not when you actually changed it into £££).

Income from overseas investments is often taxed in the country in which it originates – so two lots of tax could be charged on one lot of income. The UK government has made agreements with a wide range of countries to limit the extent to which income may be taxed twice. Under one of these *double taxation agreements* the amount of tax which a foreign government deducts from income before it reaches you is reduced. And the tax actually deducted is allowed as a tax credit against the UK tax charged on the same income.

Suppose for example, that you're entitled to £1,000 in dividends from the US. Tax at 30 per cent would normally be held back by the US taxman before paying over the dividends to non-US residents.

However, because of our double taxation agreement with the US, only 15 per cent is withheld – ie you get £850. If, say, you're liable for tax in the UK at 40 per cent on your £1,000 gross dividends, there'd be £400 tax to pay. But the £150 you've paid in tax to the US would be allowed as a credit against the £400 of UK tax you're liable for – so you'd have to hand over to the taxman £250, not £400.

If you are liable for no UK tax (or less than has been deducted under a double taxation agreement), there'll be no further UK tax to pay – but you can't claim back the extra foreign tax you've paid.

In general, double taxation agreements mean that tax on dividends is withheld at a rate of 15 per cent. With interest payments the rate at which tax is withheld varies more between countries.

For more details of how double taxation agreements work, see Inland Revenue leaflet IR6 (available free from your tax office).

How to get your relief

If your foreign income is paid to you through an agent (eg a bank) in the UK, who passes it on to you after deducting basic rate tax, the agent should allow for any double taxation agreement when doing his sums.

But if the income is paid direct to you from abroad, you have to apply for double taxation relief yourself – and until you do so, you may find the income arrives with substantial amounts of foreign tax withheld, and no credit against UK tax allowed for it. To get the foreign tax reduced, get an application form from the Inland Revenue, Inspector of Foreign Dividends, Lynwood Road, Thames Ditton, Surrey KT7 0DP. To get the withheld foreign tax allowed as a credit against your UK tax bill, apply to your Tax Inspector.

When UK tax is due

Your tax bill is normally based on the foreign income you get in the preceding tax year – ie your tax bill for the 1988–89 tax year would be based on the foreign income you got in the 1987–88 tax year. Special rules apply in the first three and last two years in which you get foreign income of this type – in the same way as for UK income not taxed before you get it (see p96).

Other tax deducted

In certain countries, foreign dividends are paid after deducting tax other than personal income tax. And non-residents · may not be able to reclaim this tax. So before investing in a particular country, check that the return you hope to get allows for *all* the tax deducted.

Capital gains tax

Gains you make on overseas investments are liable for UK capital gains tax in the normal way (see p104). In general, you'll be taxed on gains whether or not you bring the sales proceeds into the UK. Your capital gain will be the difference between the value of the asset in sterling when you acquired it, and its value in sterling when you disposed of it – using the exchange rates that applied at the relevant times. Note that gains you make on foreign currency – for example, currency held in a bank deposit account – are liable for capital gains tax in the normal way (unless you got the currency for holidays or living expenses abroad).

There's normally no foreign capital gains tax to pay if you're a UK resident. However, gains on selling a foreign home may be taxed in the country where the home is. And if you have a permanent home in certain foreign countries (eg a country cottage in California) or spend substantial parts of the year there, you may find that you're treated as a resident of that country and are liable for local capital gains tax. Any foreign tax you pay is allowed as a credit against your UK capital gains tax liability.

Inheritance tax

UK inheritance tax is charged on foreign assets in the normal way – see p113. A similar tax is likely to be charged by the country in which the assets are situated.

The foreign inheritance tax (or its equivalent) is normally allowed as a credit against UK inheritance tax.

Note that there are likely to be delays (perhaps lengthy ones) and complications in obtaining probate for assets held abroad in your name, on your death – it may be better to have them held in the name of a UK agent, such as a bank.

25

ALTERNATIVE INVESTMENTS

If you are worried about inflation taking off again, you may want to look for less conventional investments to stake your money on in the hopes of showing a profit. And it's certainly possible to show that, over the last 20 years, an investor in certain alternative investments could have more than maintained the buying power of his or her savings.

The Diagram on p21 shows how gold sovereigns and antique furniture have performed over three different periods since 1968 compared with investing in shares, buying a home and so on. We've given rates of return over different periods of time because the success of your investment depends very much on when you buy and when you sell. You can see from the Diagram that antique furniture did particularly well – the return from it more than kept pace with inflation, and produced higher rates of return than most of the conventional investments we've illustrated. But presenting the investment potential of alternative investments in this way can be misleading. If *you* had been investing in 1968, you might have chosen to buy things which didn't do nearly so well – such as the *wrong* piece of furniture.

Which alternative investment to go for?

Limited supply plus growing demand is what to look for in an alternative investment. Things like old stamps, Georgian silver and Roman coins are available in limited quantities – there is no way that more can be produced (forgeries apart). So if more people want to own them – or the same number can afford to pay more (because of inflation, say) – prices will go up.

But limited supply, on its own, is not sufficient to make a good investment. For example, limited editions (see 410) are produced in quantities of a few hundred or a few

403

thousand. But they are unlikely to prove good investments unless people will want to buy them in the future.

Nor is a high level of demand enough to make a good investment. For example, many collectors will snap up new issues of British stamps (for example the Royal Wedding issue was widely bought when the Duke and Duchess of York got married in 1986). But if several million are issued, it's unlikely they will become valuable. For the investor, only stamps in fairly short supply and which are popular with collectors are likely to gain significantly in value.

Should YOU put your money in alternative investments?

If you're thinking of alternative investments, you should consider investing only part of your savings in this way – not more than 10 per cent, say – and certainly not your emergency fund or money you can't afford to lose. And bear in mind that:

■ because of the expenses of buying and selling, such as auctioneer's commission or dealer's mark-up, you may not make a profit unless you keep your money invested for a fairly long time – say, five years or more

■ money invested in this way won't give you a regular income. And you may have to pay for storage, insurance and so on (see opposite)

■ fashions in collecting change; what may have been a steadily appreciating asset 10 years ago, may no longer be so much in demand now. You may even make a loss when you come to sell

■ you may find it hard to decide on what price to ask when you sell – and, unless you sell at an auction, some haggling with buyers is likely to be involved. Going for a quick sale could mean a poor price.

Alternative investments have one advantage which most other types of investment lack – you can get pleasure out of finding and owning the things you invest in. Indeed, you're more likely to invest successfully if you do take an interest in them. And if your investments turn out to be unsuccessful, you at least have the consolation of owning a stamp collection, a set of prints or whatever.

On pp407–13 we look at a few of the wide range of alternative investments available. Bear in mind that these are included as examples only – we are not suggesting that these investments in particular are ones you should go for. But reading pp407–13 should give you hints on what to watch out for even if you decide to specialise in an area we haven't mentioned.

How should you invest?

The golden rule is **avoid investment from a position of ignorance.** Here are a few tips:

■ **find out about the things you want to invest in** *before* **you spend any money.** Read books and magazines on the subject, join societies for collectors of the things you are interested in, visit exhibitions, study auctioneers' catalogues and dealers' price lists, talk to experts. See pp414–415 for a few details about societies, specialist magazines, useful addresses, and so on

■ **start small.** Buy a few low-priced items in a narrow field, to get to know the things you are collecting. Develop your knowledge before spending more – and then stick to the field you are expert in

■ **aim for items in very good condition.** You might have to settle for a poor quality item – to complete a set, say. But, in general, two or three items in good condition are likely to do better than several tatty ones

■ **shop around.** Prices are likely to vary considerably between dealers – so don't be afraid to haggle over prices

■ **be sceptical of 'guarantees'** (to buy back the things you invest in at double what you paid for them after five years, say). These 'guarantees' are only as good as the dealer who gives them – no good at all if he or she goes bust

■ **invest in things which are collected world-wide** – so that the price you get when you sell won't necessarily be reduced if UK demand slumps.

Ahead of the crowd?

You can make money if you invest in things which other investors haven't cottoned on to which subsequently become popular with collectors. You can't expect to be right every time (or even most of the time) with this sort of speculation. If you're only in it for the money, and other speculators do catch on, you may need to be good at spotting when a craze is reaching its height so that you sell before prices start tumbling.

Storage and insurance

Careful storage may be important with things like stamps, wine, paintings, say. Damp, sudden changes in temperature, sunlight, insects and so on could reduce (or even wipe out) the value of the things you collect.

You'll also need to insure your valuables against things like theft or fire. Typically, this might cost around £5 to £7 a year for each £1,000 of cover as part of a normal house contents policy (more if you live in a high-risk area). Some house contents policies also offer cover against accidental damage, as an optional extra. If you want all-risks cover (which includes accidental damage cover, for example), this might cost between £20 and £40 or so a year for each £1,000 of cover.

Before you decide on a policy, check the terms of the insurance carefully. There may be an unwelcome restriction, such a low limit on the amount of cover for individual items. You might prefer to buy a special insurance policy for your collection. Consult the *Insurance Buyer's Guide* (available from Kluwer Publishing, 1 Harlequin Avenue, Brentford, Middlesex TW8 9EW at £15, including postage and packing – or try your local library).

If your collection is worth a lot of money (more than a few thousand pounds, say), the insurance company is likely to insist on a safe, special locks and burglar alarms. The insurance company is also likely to ask for proof of your collection's value, so it's sensible to keep photographs of it, as well as a regularly updated professional valuation. A professional valuer (or a dealer) may charge perhaps one and a half per cent of what he values your collection at. Remember to review the level of your insurance regularly – whatever the value of your collection.

Alternatively you could store your collection in a bank's strongroom – insurance may be less if you do this. The bank makes a charge for storage – from £2 to £5 a year for an envelope, say, up to £30 a year or more for a bulky item. Bank storage costs are considerably higher if you want to rent a safe deposit box – but these can be difficult to get. Some dealers will also store and insure the things you buy from them – this may seem the simplest solution, but remember that you could have problems if the dealer you store with goes bust.

What about tax?

Because there's usually no income from investing in things, there's usually no income tax to pay (unless the taxman decides you are carrying on a trade or business and taxes your profits as income).

You might be liable for capital gains tax if you make a gain when you sell or give away things you have invested in. But the first £5,000 a year of gains are normally tax-free. So are gains on things like antiques, jewellery and other tangible moveable objects which you sell for £3,000 or less. You may even get some relief if the gain is over £3,000. Note that if you give things away you may not have to pay any tax that's due if you and the recipient apply for *hold-over relief*. For more details on capital gains tax, see pp104–113.

However, beware of trying money up in something just because of favourable tax treatment – the tax situation *could* change.

You will normally have to pay VAT on the things you invest in if you buy from dealers.

Some alternative investments

Busted bonds

Collecting busted bonds is also known as *scripophily*. You collect old share certificates in companies which have collapsed, or government stock certificates issued by countries which have since had revolutions and repudiated their debts.

There are two distinct markets for busted bonds. The first is for bonds where there is some chance of at least part of the debt being repaid by the defaulting country. In 1987 the Government of the USSR redeemed some of its bonds, and the 4,500 British applicants were offered an interim payment of 10 per cent of the face value of their bonds. It's expected that in the end, the successful claimants will receive about double this initial figure. The Chinese and Bulgarian authorities are also in the process of redeeming bonds they defaulted on when the communists came to power, though the settlement sums being offered range from only about 8 per cent of face value (for the Chinese bonds), to as much as 40 per cent on some Bulgarian Sterling Bonds. You should bear in mind, though, that some rare bonds will be more valuable as collectors' items than the amounts you'd get by redeeming them.

The other market is for bonds and share certificates which definitely won't be redeemed. Their value lies in their appeal to collectors – because they are associated with a specific historic event (for example some were issued by the confederate states during the American Civil War) or because they are particularly attractive or scarce. These can be bought from dealers, at auctions, and so on.

Collecting busted bonds developed as a hobby in the early 1970s. The market has always been volatile, and investors made huge gains between 1978 and 1980. But the bubble soon burst, and over the next few years prices were forced sharply down as there were not enough genuine investors to support the market. However the market recovered slightly by 1988, and genuine collectors are always on the look-out for bonds to add to their collections.

The market is currently of greater interest to the collector than the speculator. There are plenty of bonds to be had for between £15 and £50. These *may* turn out to be a worthwhile investment in the longer term, but for now busted bonds should be looked on as a hobby for the enthusiast.

Wine

Laying down vintage wines and ports has been, at times, a highly profitable investment. A 1955 vintage port laid down in the early 60s might have set you back around £12 for a case of 12 bottles. But if you'd sold that same case at auction in early 1988, you *might* have got up to £540 (after auctioneer's commission) – equal to an average yearly return of just over 16 per cent. The return is free of tax unless the taxman reckons you've gone into the wine trade and taxes the gain as your business profits.

Even over a much shorter period of time, the gains made on fine wines can be worthwhile. A 1982 vintage claret would have cost you around £60 for a case had you bought it from a wine merchant in 1983. In March 1988, auction room prices were as much as £380 for a case of some of the finest vintage. Again this figure is after deducting auctioneer's commission, as private individuals without a licence are not allowed to advertise or sell any alcohol except via an auctioneer or wine merchant.

Vintage wines must be stored in carefully regulated conditions to maintain their quality and value, so unless you are in the enviable position of having your own suitable cellar, you will have to pay yearly storage and insurance costs to a wine merchant. For storage you can currently expect to pay from £2.50 to £5 per case per year, and the insurance premium will be around one per cent of the wine's value.

Not all wine bought for investment can be expected to produce a high return for you. You have to be careful not to get in on the tail-end of a particular fashion, and must be prepared to tie up your money for at least five years. But a knowledge of what you're buying should help you enormously. Well-selected fine wines can best be relied upon to improve in value, and in recent years have consistently outpaced inflation. And even if your investment doesn't produce a good cash return, you can at least have the pleasure of drinking it.

Stamps

Apart from what they cost to use for postage, stamps are intrinsically worthless bits of paper. But they are avidly collected by very large numbers of people all over the world, some of whom are prepared at times to pay very large sums of money for stamps which are extremely rare, or of historical interest.

While there are many stamps and other items of postal history which would have given you a good return on your investment over most of the last twenty years, some stamps have increased in value much more than others – and values can fall as well as rise.

Stamps which, in the past, have shown some of the largest increases in value have included examples (in fine condition) of rare nineteenth-century issues – sometimes called classics. However, some investors have had their fingers burnt by innocently following the advice of a few unscrupulous dealers who have sold them 'investment' portfolios. The stamps turned out to be over-priced, not of the best quality and did not continue to appreciate at the rate that dealers claimed had applied in the past. The prices of some stamps fell dramatically between 1979 and 1980, making them difficult to resell – even back to the dealers they were bought from.

If you want to invest seriously in stamps, you will have to approach this as a hobby first, and get to know a lot about them – through studying catalogues and auction results, visiting dealers, joining a philatelic society and so on. Small variations in printing and watermarks – and even the sheet from which the stamp has been torn – can affect the price drastically. The condition of the stamp is also very important. Stamps with printing errors and occasionally forgeries can be worth much more than ordinary stamps.

Buying special issues of modern commemorative stamps is unlikely to be a good investment because they are generally issued in very large quantities. Don't take catalogue prices as fixed values of stamps, or proof of increases in value. Catalogues show the prices at which a dealer would hope to sell stamps in first-class condition; he'd normally pay much less to buy the stamps. The prices fetched at auctions are a more reliable guide.

Limited editions

Many things are sold as limited editions – eg plates, porcelain figures and prints. There are basically two ways to produce a limited edition:
■ the number to be sold is specified at the outset – 50, 500 or 5,000, say
■ the number sold is the number ordered or bought by a certain date – for example, 50 if only 50 are sold by that date, 50,000 if that is the number sold. With this method the total number to be sold (important in evaluating scarcity) is normally known only after you've agreed to buy.

There are variations on these themes. For example, with some limited editions, the limit mentioned in the advert may only apply to the UK, and more of the item may be sold in other countries.

Of course the investment potential of limited editions depends not only on the number produced, but also on the demand for them from collectors. And with many limited editions, there's little hope of a big demand – so even if only a few dozen were issued, you'd be unlikely to make a lot of money by investing in them.

With some limited editions you may find that it's not the limited nature of the item which makes it profitable but the intrinsic value of the material they're made from. A set of commemorative silver ingots say, may be worth more for their silver content as scrap than as fully made up ingots, so they could make you money in times when silver prices are high.

Forestry

Clearing land and planting trees for the production of timber is one way you can watch your investment grow physically, as well as in terms of its value. But investing in forestry, or commercial woodlands, should be seen as a strictly long-term process. Timber takes, on average, about 25 years to produce an income, so it may be more likely that your children will get the benefit of the investment rather than you. The benefits last for a long time though, as timber is felled and sold over a long period.

The Government offers incentives to investors, in the form of grants to plant trees. Until March 1988 there were also substantial tax incentives, because the costs of planting and maintaining the trees could be used to reduce your tax bill on other income. This incentive now continues only for people who already owned or tenanted commercial woodlands on 15 March 1988, and will stop altogether in 1993. However the proceeds from the sale of trees are now tax-free.

Direct investment in forestry is pricey, and your minimum outlay would have to be in the region of £40,000. If you don't want to tie up so much for so long, you can invest a much lower figure in part-shares of a forest, available from forestry management companies.

There is increasing demand for timber, so the long-term prospects look good. However, in the past, a lot of the attraction of forestry investment came from the favourable tax treatment. Now that the tax rules have changed, make sure you can put up with the disadvantages before you invest. You have to be prepared to tie up quite a lot of money for a very long time — so someone looking for a quick return should look elsewhere.

Diamonds

Diamonds have always held a fascination with investors, but since the early 1980s they have proved to be a very poor investment. Prices for investment quality stones reached their peak in 1980, but more recently the returns have been less than half of what you could have expected to get then.

There used to be three ways of investing in diamonds: buying them over the counter, buying from a diamond investment company, or putting money into a scheme which in turn invested on the diamond market. But with the heavy losses made by investors over the last six to eight years, you'll be lucky if any investment company or scheme will deal with you – that's if you can find one.

Buying diamonds over the counter

You can buy diamonds from a jeweller, or a diamond merchant, or at an auction; they may be loose or mounted in jewellery. When you want to sell, you can hawk the stones around dealers, or put them in an auction. But, as *Which?* discovered the hard way, there are serious drawbacks to investing this way. In 1970, *Which?* bought some diamonds (mounted in jewellery, and loose). Since then, they've hawked them around jewellers and dealers several times – most recently in the summer of 1985. Each time, the prices they'd have fetched were very disappointing – a building society would have given a better return on the money involved.

Buying and selling loose diamonds over the counter seems to be a mug's game. Even if you get good value when you buy (and you've no way of being certain about that), the dealer's mark-up – which can be as high as several hundred per cent – is likely to make them a poor investment, even over a ten-year period. And particularly if you're looking for a sale on the spot, offers from dealers are likely to be on the low side. Most can't accurately establish the value of a diamond on the spot – though having certificates from a specialist diamond-grading laboratory might help in some cases.

As for diamonds mounted in jewellery, you're unlikely to show a profit on *new* jewellery for a very long time. The investment market for *antique* jewellery is more like that for antique furniture or porcelain, say, than for loose diamonds. Putting antique diamond jewellery into an auction may be the best way to sell.

Buying from diamond investment companies or through investment schemes

Until the dramatic fall in investment diamond prices in the early 80s, there were several diamond investment companies willing to sell private investors high-grade unmounted stones, usually with a certificate describing the size and quality of each stone. However, over the last few years, some of these companies have gone into liquidation, and the ones still surviving are not doing any new business. The picture is much the same for the various investment schemes that were available. In the current climate the few that remain don't represent a good investment for the private investor.

Gold

For thousands of years, gold has been looked on as a store of wealth, and many people the world over believe that gold is a good asset to hold in times of political upheaval. But if you are tempted to invest in gold be prepared for a bumpy ride. For example, the highest price for one troy ounce of gold in 1986 was £307.98, but the year's lowest price was around 30 per cent less. Even daily fluctuations can be alarming, so gold isn't suitable for the faint-hearted.

For an indication of how gold has performed over longer periods, see the Diagram on p414. Note that this shows rates of return for gold sovereigns rather than bullion. Nowadays, you can buy and sell gold in any form. Here we look at buying gold coins (not to be confused with the rare coins that collectors go for) and gold bars. Other ways of investing include buying gold shares (eg the share of companies that mine gold); buying units in a unit trust that specialises in gold shares and dealing in gold futures. For how gold futures work, see p368.

The main ways of buying and selling coins and bullion are through banks, coin-dealers, jewellers and stockbrokers – or through the bullion-dealing companies that make up the London Gold Market. It's probably advisable to steer clear of jewellers because they tend to have high mark-ups. Note that if you invest via intermediaries such as stockbrokers, you will have to pay commission on buying and selling.

Bear in mind that the price at which a coin or bar is offered for sale will be higher than the current value of the gold in it. On top of the value of the gold content you'll have to pay a *premium* for the cost of manufacture and distribution of the coins. Premiums for particular coins fluctuate according to supply and demand, and it's possible for your investment to show a gain (or loss) without the price of gold changing. Note that bullion and foreign coins (but not post-1837 sovereigns and Britannias, the new British gold coins) are liable for capital gains tax – see p106.

Most of us couldn't possibly afford to invest in gold bars in the standard sizes in which they are traded (400 troy ounces – around $12^1/_2$ kilograms), though it is possible to obtain much smaller sizes – from 1 kilogram down to a 1 gram 'wafer'. But the very small bars are not usually a sensible investment as the tinier the bar, the higher the premium. Small bars are often sold to be made up into jewellery. You can do this with coins too, but if you want to sell your pendant, or whatever, you may get a very poor price.

In the Table overleaf we show the prices at which you could have bought and sold single sovereigns, Britannias and gold bars in March 1988. Until 1982, gold coins were often a better bet for the small investor than gold bars because they were normally exempt from VAT. But, from the end of March 1982, this exemption was withdrawn, unless they are bought and held in an offshore bank. Note that world trade in gold is transacted in US dollars – so the current exchange rate between the dollar and the pound will affect gold prices. When you sell, you may have to pay an assay fee – ie for checking that your bar actually is gold and doesn't just look like it.

Buying and selling gold at 8 March 1988 [1]

Gold price: £238.28 for one troy ounce

	gold content		prices	
	troy ounces	grams	to buy [2] £	to sell back £
Coins				
Queen Elizabeth II Sovereign	0.24	7.32	59	55
Britannia 1oz	1.00	31.10	256	243
Britannia 1/2 oz	0.50	15.55	129	123
Britannia 1/4 oz	0.25	7.77	67	64
Britannia 1/10 oz	0.10	3.11	28	27
Bars				
1 kilogram	32.15	1,000	8,044	7,642
1/2 kilogram	16.07	500	4,022	3,821
100 grams	3.21	100	804	764
20 grams	0.64	20	161	153
5 grams	0.16	5	45	43

[1] Retail prices for single bars and coins. Selling prices do not include any assay fee.

[2] Including VAT on buying prices.

A few sources of information

Books

The Successful Investor by Robin Duthy (Collins, £15)

Diamonds by Eric Bruton (NAG Press, £18.95)

Miller's Antiques Price Guide 1989 (Miller's Publications Ltd, £14.95)

Which? Wine Guide 1989 (£9.95 from Consumers' Association, Castlemead, Gascoyne Way, Hertford SG14 1LH)

Scripophily by Keith Hollender (£9.95, available from Herzog, Hollender, Phillips & Co, Mardyke House, 16–22 Hotwells Road, Bristol BS8 4UD)

The Antique Collectors' Club publish specialist books on art and antiques. (Write to 5 Church Street, Woodbridge, Suffolk IP12 1DS for a list)

Standard catalogues

Stamps of the World 1988 (Stanley Gibbons Publications, 2 volumes, £15.50 each)

Coins of England and the United Kingdom 24th Edition (Seaby Numismatic Publications, £9.95)

Societies

There are lots of societies, local and national. Here we give a very small selection. For societies near you, see the *Directory of British Associations* (ask at your local library). This lists national societies and federations who will be able to put you in touch with any local branch or group.

British Association of Numismatic Societies Dept of Coins and Medals, Manchester Museum, The University, Oxford Road, Manchester M13 9PL

The Antique Collectors' Club (for address see the entry under books)

The British Philatelic Federation, 107 Charterhouse Street, London EC1M 6PT

The Bond and Share Society Hobsley House, Frodesley, Dorrington, Shrewsbury, SY5 7HD

Magazines and journals

Too many to name. Look in large newsagents (eg John Menzies, W.H. Smith) for magazines about your speciality — or see *Willings Press Guide* or *Benn's Media Directory* at your local library.

Antique and Collectors' fairs

These are listed under 'Collecting' in the 'Leisure' section of *Exchange & Mart* (available at newsagents) and are often advertised in local newspapers.

Auctions

Here we list the largest auction houses in London. For local auction houses, see *Yellow Pages* under auction rooms, specialist magazines, and local newspapers.

Bonhams Montpelier Galleries, Montpelier Street, London SW7 1HH

Christie's 8 King Street, St. James's, London SW1Y 6QT

Phillips 7 Blenheim Street, London W1Y 0AS

Sotheby's 34 New Bond Street, London W1A 2AA

Buying and selling gold

London Gold Market members prepared to deal with the public:

Mocatta & Goldsmid Ltd (01-628 2825)

NM Rothschild & Sons Ltd (01-280 5000)

Sharps Pixley Ltd (01-623 8000)

All High Street banks except Lloyds will sell you gold coins (normally only Sovereigns), but only National Westminster Bank will buy them back. Britannia Building Society sells Britannia coins through its branch network.

INDEX

INDEX

accidental death benefit **347**
accountants, as advisers **84–5**
accumulation and maintenance
    trusts **60, 61, 62, 71**
accumulation trusts **60, 68, 283–4**
    CGT **112**
additional premium facility **338,
    348, 349**
additional voluntary contributions
    203–4, 216
advertisements **18, 75**
advice **76, 81–92**
    accountants **84–5**
    banks **85–6**
    best advice rules **75**
    building societies **86**
    choosing an adviser **82–4**
    independent insurance advisers
        and brokers **87–8**
    independent investment
        advisers **86–7**
    insurance company
        representatives **88–9**
    merchant banks **89**
    solicitors **89–90**
    stockbrokers **90–1**
    types of **81–2**
age allowance **16, 52–3, 353**
alternative investments **17, 19, 20,
    38, 40, 120, 403–15**
    busted bonds **407–8**
    diamonds **411–12**
    forestry **410–11**
    gold **17, 412–14**
    guarantees **405**
    how to invest **405**
    insurance **404, 406**
    limited editions **403, 410**
    pleasure from **404**
    stamps **409–10**
    storage **405, 405–6**

    supply and demand **403–4**
    taxation **406–7**
    wine **408–9**
    world-wide appeal **405**
annuities **14, 41, 51, 120, 203,
    355–65**
    choosing type **361**
    company choice **362**
    company safety **362**
    deferred **218, 225, 233, 356**
    guaranteed payments **357**
    immediate **218–19, 233–4,
        356**
    income amounts **357–9**
    income tax **100**
    increasing **356, 361**
    joint life, last survivor **235, 356,
        357**
    level **356, 361**
    life expectations **355**
    payment intervals **356–7**
    risks **359–60**
    single life **356**
    tax treatment **361–2**
    tax-free income from **95**
    see also home income
        schemes
annuity bonds **353–4**
antiques *see* alternative
    investments
Appropriate Personal Pensions
    (APPs) *see* personal pension
    plans
art galleries, gifts **115**
Association of Futures Brokers
    and Dealers (AFBD) **79**
Association of Investment Trust
    Companies **393**
authorised businesses **74–5**
    interim authorisation **75**
average pay schemes **207–8**

banks
  as advisers **85–6**
  deposit accounts **27, 39, 121,
    166, 167**
  fixed-term fixed interest **167–8**
  fixed-term variable interest **167**
  foreign currency accounts **390–2**
  higher-rate deposit accounts **167**
  interest **27, 99**
  notice accounts **121, 168**
  regular savings schemes **36, 167**
  savings accounts **27, 122**
  Scottish **166**
  security of investment **165–6**
  term accounts **121**
best advice *see* advice
best execution rules **75**
beta analysis **249**
bid price auction **297**
bonds
  annuity **353–4**
  broker managed **339**
  busted **407–8**
  choosing **353–3**
  guaranteed income and growth
    100, 128, 351–4
  lump sum investment **351**
  qualifying corporate **106, 107**
  single premium *see* single-
    premium bonds
  taxation and **100, 352, 353–4**
  working of **352**
British Government stocks **38,
  287–302, 359**
  accrued interest **292–3**
  buying and selling **302**
  capital gain (or loss) **294**
  choosing **299**
  conventional **122**
  coupon **290, 291, 295**
  cum- and ex-dividend **292**
  dated **288**
  income (interest) yield **293**
  index-linked **23, 40, 50, 51, 123,
    294–7, 359**
  information and advice **299, 302**
  interest rate changes **291**
  life of **290**
  names **288, 290**
  new issues **297–8**
  nominal value **288**
  prices **292–3**
    reasons for change **290–1**
  rate of return **26**
  redemption date **290**
  tap stock **297**
  tax-free gains **106, 107**
  taxation of **96, 101, 298–9**
  total return **294**
  undated **288**
  unit trusts and **272, 302**
  workings of **287–91**
British Merchant Banking and
  Securities Houses Association
  89
British Savings Bonds **174**
broker managed bonds **339**
building societies **17, 19, 36,
  151–63**
  advice from **86**
  agents **153**
  cash machines **153**
  children's accounts **159–60**
  choosing a society **163**
  choosing accounts **161–2**
  combination accounts **160**
  current accounts **159**
  fixed-rate bonds **158, 162**
  friendly society bonds **160–1**
  guaranteed premiums **155**
  instant access accounts **39, 123,
    157–8, 162**
  interest **99, 154–6**
    see also interest rates
  limited companies **152**
  monthly income accounts **158,
    162**
  notice accounts **124, 153, 157,
    162**
  ordinary shares **124**
  paying in **152–3**
  penalty charges **156, 157, 158**
  safety of **151**
  savings accounts **125**
    regular **158–9, 162**
  SAYE **36, 37, 95, 106, 126,
    159**
  services offered **152**
  term shares **125, 153, 156–7,
    161**
  withdrawals **153**
Building Societies Ombudsman
  86
Building Society Choice **163**
Business Expansion Scheme
  106–7, 263–4
  tax relief **264**
busted bonds **407–8**

capital accumulation plans **342**
capital gains tax **104–113**
  allowable expenses **105**
  allowable losses **105**
  alternative investments **406–7**

amount of **105–6**
assets as 31 March 1982 **111**
chargeable gains **105**
children and **71–2**
final value **105**
gifts **111**
gold **413**
hold-over relief **71, 72, 111, 407**
house purchase and **148**
indexation allowance **105, 107, 110**
indexation factor **110**
initial value **105**
marriage and **112–13**
overseas investments **400–1**
reduction of **113**
retirement and **49, 50**
shares **111–12, 241**
single-premium bonds **334, 338**
tax-free gains **106–7**
trusts and **72**
unit trusts and **111–12, 284, 334**
working out gain **105**
capital growth
  investing for **23**
  unit trusts for **38**
CAR *see* interest rates
cash funds **220**
cashing-in
  early **19, 22, 24**
  endowment policies **319, 320**
  for income **24–5**
  long-term investments **16**
  National Savings Certificates **173, 177**
  single-premium bonds **339**
  unit-linked regular income plans **344–5**
charities, gifts to **106, 115**
Chartered Association of Certified Accountants **80**
children
  building society accounts for **159–60**
  inheritance tax and **115**
  investing for **55–72**
  life insurance proceeds to **61, 62, 68**
  parents' income tax and **55, 58, 68**
  single persons allowance **58**
  special investments for **58–9**
  taxation and **67–72**
  trusts *see* trusts
  under 18 but married **58**
  unit trusts **61–2**
  see also dependants' benefits;

education; heirs; school fees
code of business rules **75**
cold-calling **76, 78**
commissions **75, 78–9, 232**
  share sales **252, 253**
commodities **38, 126, 243, 367–79**
  buying and selling through broker **376–7**
  commodity funds **377–9**
  delivery in future **368–9**
  delivery straight away **367–8**
  futures dealing **368–9**
  gambling not investing **369, 379**
  markets **369–70**
  options **369**
  prices **370–3**
    long-term **374–5**
    price agreements **376**
    short-term **375**
  supply and demand **373–4**
  taxation **379**
  unit trusts **378–9**
commodity funds
  charges **378**
  minimum investments **378**
  performance fee **378**
  unit trusts **378–9**
company loan stock **101, 261**
compensation scheme **77**
contracting out *see* SERPS
convertible loan stock **261**
coupon **290, 291, 295**
covenant payments **114**
currency deals *see* overseas investments
customer agreements **75, 84**

Daily Telegraph **163, 393**
death benefits
  accidental death **347**
  single-premium bonds **338**
  unit-linked regular income plans **341**
  see also dependants' benefits
debentures **261**
deferred annuities **218, 225, 233, 356**
deferred pension **47, 205**
dependants' benefits
  family income benefit **315, 347**
  personal pension plans **205, 216, 229, 235**
  single-premium bonds **338**
  unit-linked regular income plans **341**
  see also life insurance

dependent relative house
  occupation **148**
dependent relative support,
  inheritance tax **115**
deposit administration schemes
  220–1, 225, 230
diamonds **411–12**
disability cover **204, 347**
  permanent health insurance **204**
discretionary trusts **60, 69, 71**
  income tax **100**
distribution trusts **284**
dividends **241, 256–7**
double taxation agreements
  399–400

early cashing *see* cashing-in
earnings rule **48, 191**
education *see* educational trusts;
  school fees
educational trusts **63–4**
  taxation and **64–5**
emergency fund **14, 18, 39**
  investing of **22**
  updating amount **22**
employee benefit trusts, gifts to
  115
employee share schemes **262–3**
  profit-sharing **262**
  share option schemes **262–3**
employer's pension schemes **46–7,
  134, 200–11**
  additional voluntary
    contributions **203–4, 216**
  average pay schemes **207–8**
  changing jobs **205–5**
  dependants' benefits **205, 216**
  early retirement through ill-
    health **204**
  final pay scheme **200–2**
  FSAVC **203–4**
  guaranteed minimum **205, 206**
  inflation proofing **202**
  life insurance **205**
  money purchase schemes **206–7,
    209–10**
  permanent health insurance **204**
  PPP compared **208–11**
  preserved pension **205**
  protected right **206**
  voluntary **200**
endowment bonds **353, 354**
endowment policies **127, 311–26**
  assets **316–17**
  bonuses **314–15, 317–18**
    regular **314**
    reversionary **314, 316–18**
  terminal **314**
  buying policy **324–5**
  cashing-in policy **319, 320**
  choosing a company **324**
  company safety **325–6**
  complaints procedure **326**
  ending early **318–22**
  family income benefits **315**
  flexible **322**
  investment in long-term fund
    316
  investment not insurance **315**
  liabilities **317**
  loan against policy **319–20, 321**
  low-cost **322**
  non-profit **322**
  paid up **319, 320, 321**
  returns on **315–16**
  selling at auction **31**
  suitability of **323–6**
  surplus (or excess) **317**
  surrender value **319**
  taxation of **318**
  unit-linked **342**
  unitised with-profits **322**
  whole life policies **322–3**
  workings of **311**
  see also life insurance
equalisation payment **112**
equity funds **220, 329, 330**
Eurobonds **396–7**
European Currency Units **392**
exchange rates *see* overseas
  investments
executive plans **226**
experienced investors **76, 79**

family income benefits **315, 347**
final pay pensions **46, 49, 200–2**
finance companies
  deposits **27, 121, 168**
  fixed-term fixed interest **168–9**
  interest **99**
  notice accounts **121, 169**
  savings accounts **122**
  security of investment **165–6**
  term accounts **121**
Financial Intermediaries,
  Managers and Brokers
  Regulatory Association
  (FIMBRA) **79**
Financial Services Act *see* legal
  protection
Financial Times **243, 299, 331,
  370**
fixed interest funds **220**
fixed trusts **60, 69, 70–1**

flexible cover plan **342, 344**
foreign investments *see* overseas
   investments
forestry **410–11**
forward exchange contracts **383**
friendly societies
   building societies and **160–1**
   investments **161**
FT-Actuaries All-Share Index **249**
fundamental analysis, shares
   247–9
futures *see* commodities

gearing **148–9**
gifts **111**
   see also inheritance tax
gilt-edged securities *see* British
   Government stocks
gold **412–14**
   sovereigns **17, 20–1**
growth bonds *see* bonds

heirs
   investing for **15, 16, 24**
   proceeds of life policy to **24, 61,
   62, 68, 116, 323**
   see also children; dependants'
   benefits
high investment plans **342**
hold-over relief **71, 72, 111, 407**
holidays, saving for **16**
home income schemes **41, 51,
   128, 363–5**
   age limits **364**
   independent valuation **363**
   reversions **363, 365**
   rising house prices and **364–5**
   state benefits and **365**
   variable interest rate schemes
   363, 365
   working of **363–4**
home responsibilities protection
   188, 189, 192
house purchase **14, 127**
   as investment **143–5**
   capital gains tax **148**
   dependent relative occupation
   148
   future prices **149–50**
   gearing **148–9**
   inflation hedge **145, 147**
   overseas property **397–8, 401**
   prices **141–3**
   running costs **145**
   second homes **145**
   tax relief on mortgage interest
   146

trading down **41, 51, 52**
two mortgages when moving
   146
   see also home income schemes;
   property

income
   cashing investments to give
   24–5
   changes over time **15**
   from savings in retirement **48**
   from single-premium bonds **334,
   336**
   investing for extra **40–1**
   investing for fixed **16**
   investing for income later **23–4**
   investing for income now **22–3,
   38**
   monthly income **158, 162**
   reinvesting to build capital **25**
   risk to **19, 22**
income bonds *see* bonds
income tax **94–104**
   allowances **95**
   alternative investments **406**
   annuities **100**
   double taxation agreements
   399–400
   gross income **95**
   interest paid gross **96–7**
   life insurance and **101–4**
   outgoings gross **95**
   overseas investment **399–400**
   parents', and childrens' income
   55, 58, 68
   rates **95**
   retirement and **49, 50**
   taxable income **95**
   top-slicing relief **103–4, 338, 345**
   total income **95**
   see also investment income
independent insurance advisers
   and brokers, advice from **87–8**
independent investment advisers,
   advice from **86–7**
Independent Schools Information
   Service **63, 64**
index-linked investments **17, 23**
   British Government stocks **23,
   38, 40, 50, 51, 123, 294–7, 359**
   National Savings index-linked
   SAYE **183–4**
   see also Index-Linked National
   Savings Certificates
Index-Linked National Savings
   Certificates **23, 36, 38, 40, 50,
   51, 132, 176–9, 296, 359**

amount of holding **176**
cashing **177**
fifth anniversary bonus **178**
growth of **176–8**
old certificates **178–9**
RPI and **178**
indexation allowance **105**
capital gains tax **107, 110**
indexation factor **110**
inflation **16–18**
index-linked investments **17,
295–6**
see also index-linked
investments; interest rates
inheritance tax **24, 113–16**
annual exemption **115**
chargeable transfers **114**
children and **62, 68, 69–71, 115**
dependent relative support **115**
gifts on marriage **115**
life insurance and **115-16**
maintenance payments **115**
overseas investments **401**
PETs **114**
school fees and **65, 67**
small gifts **115**
tax-free gifts **114–15**
trusts and **59**
whole life policy to pay **323**
insider dealing **250**
Institute of Actuaries **80**
Institute of Chartered
Accountants in England and
Wales **80**
Institute of Chartered
Accountants in Ireland **80**
Institute of Chartered
Accountants of Scotland **80**
insurance
for alternative investments **404,
406**
permanent health insurance **204**
see also life insurance
Insurance Brokers Registration
Council (IBRC) **80, 87**
Insurance Buyer's Guide **406**
insurance company
representatives, advice from
88–9
Insurance Ombudsman Bureau
98, 326
interest in possession trusts **60,
69, 70–1**
interest rates **25–8, 27**
compounded annual rate (CAR)
154
gross equivalent **27–8, 154**

CAR **28, 154**
gross rates of return **27–8**
guaranteed premium **155**
local authority loans **305**
net **27, 28, 154**
CAR **28**
tiered **155–6, 157, 162**
times of payment **154**
true rate of return **26–7**
variable or fixed **154–5**
see also inflation
International Tin Council **376**
investment
abroad *see* overseas investments
advice *see* advice
aims **22–5**
alternative *see* alternative
investments
choices **29–41**
early cashing *see* cashing-in
for children *see* children
income *see* investment income
long-term *see* long-term
investments
lump sum investment **31–3, 36**
non-taxpayers **58–9**
regular review **25, 51**
safe **38**
short-term *see* short-term
investments
strategy **13–16**
tax planning **37–8**
see also savings
investment income
basic tax deducted **97, 99**
composite rate tax deducted
99–100, 155
surcharge **95**
tax-free **95–6**
taxable but not taxed **96–7**
Investment Management
Regulatory Organisation
(IMRO) **79**
investment trusts **38, 129**
companies **265–6**
overseas investments **393–4**
savings plans **37**

jewellery *see* alternative
investments
joint life, last survivor annuities
235, 356, 357

Law Society of Northern Ireland
80
Law Society of Scotland **80**
Law Society, The **80**

legal protection 73–80
  advertisements and illustrations 75
  authorisation 74–5
  best advice rules 75
  best execution rules 75
  code of business rules 75
  cold-calling 76, 78
  commissions 75, 78–9
  compensation scheme 77
  complaints procedure 77–8
  cooling-off period 76
  customer agreements 75, 84
  experienced investors 76, 79
  fit and proper businesses 75–6
  FSA 74–7
  historical 73
  independent advice 76
  self-protection 78–9
  separation of moneys 76
Life Assurance and Unit Trust
  Regulatory Organisation
  (LAUTRO) 80, 232, 283, 326
life insurance 13–14
  CGT tax-free gains 106
  employer's pension schemes 205
  endowment policy 116
  for the unhealthy 15
  income tax and 101–4
  inheritance tax and 115–16
  non-qualifying policies 102
  premium relief 104
  proceeds to heirs 24, 61, 62, 68, 116, 323
  protection-type 39
  qualifying policies 101
  retirement and 48
  taxable gain 53–4, 102–3
  term 14, 116, 315, 323, 346, 348
  top-slicing relief 103–4
  whole life policy 116, 323
  see also unit-linked life insurance
limited editions 403, 410
loan-back facility 222
  pension mortgages 223–3
loan stock
  company 261
  convertible 261
  see also loans
loans
  gearing 148–9
  local authority 27, 99, 101, 129, 304–6
  temporary local authority loans 306

see also loan stock
local authority, gifts to 115
local authority benefits 50–1
local authority investments 303–9
  loans 27, 99, 101, 129, 304–6
  security of 304
  stocks 308–9
  temporary loans 306
  yearling bonds 130, 307–8
London FOX 369
London Gold Market 413
London Metal Exchange 369, 376
long-term investments 38
  buying a home 14
  early cashing 16
lump sum investment 16, 31–3, 36, 39–40
guaranteed income and growth
  bonds 351

maintenance payments,
  inheritance tax 115
managed bonds 329, 330
managed funds 220
marriage
  capital
  capital gains tax and 112–13
  children under 18 58
  inheritance tax and gifts 115
married women's pensions 53, 189–90
maximum investment plans 342
merchant banks, advice from 89
mergers 260–1
Money Management 340, 352, 393
money purchase schemes 46, 195–6, 197–8 206–7, 209–10
monthly saving 16
mortgages
  pension mortgages 222–3
  see also house purchase
museums, gifts to 106, 115

national heritage bodies, gifts to 106, 115
National Savings Certificates 95, 131, 171–6
  cashing certificates 173
  death of holder 173
  general extension rate 174
  interest payment method 171–2
  investing in 33rd issue 172–3
  old certificates 173–5
  rate of return 26
  reinvestment certificates 172
  tax-free gains 106
  value for money 174–5
  see also Index-linked National

Savings Certificates
National Savings Deposit Bonds
96, 132, 182
National Savings Income Bonds
96, 133, 181
interest paid **27**
National Savings index-linked
SAYE **183–4**
National Savings Investment
Account **39, 58–9, 131, 180–4**
income tax on **97, 101**
rate of return **26**
National Savings investments **23,
171–86**
gift tokens **184**
see also individual investments
National Savings Ordinary
Account **39, 95, 96, 97, 101,
130, 179–80**
interest paid **27**
National Savings Stamps **177**
National Savings Stock Register
96, 298
National Savings Yearly Plan **36,
37, 95, 133, 182–4**
SAYE **106**
National Trust, gifts to **106, 115**
net relevant earnings **236–7**
net working capital **248**
non-profit making bodies, gifts to
115
notice accounts
banks **121, 168**
building societies **124, 153, 157,
162**
finance companies **121, 169**

occupational pensions *see*
pensions
Office of the Banking
Ombudsman **85**
offshore funds **393, 394**
ombudsmen **77, 85, 86, 88**
OPEC **376**
open market option **218, 221, 233**
options **261–2**
traded **262**
overseas investments **381–401**
administrative problems **398**
company stocks **395**
cutting risks **382—3**
eurobonds **396–7**
exchange controls **381**
exchange rate fluctuations **382,
383, 383–8**
foreign company deposits **99**
foreign currency **398**

bank accounts **390–2**
funds **394–5**
forward exchange contracts **383**
government stocks **395**
investment decision **390**
investment trusts **393–4**
property **397–8, 401**
returns
from UK and **381–2**
in local currency **388**
shares **365–6**
spreading investments **382–3**
taxation **399–401**
total return **388–90**
unit-linked insurance **398**
unit trusts **392–3**

pension mortgages **222–3**
pensions
average pay schemes **207–8**
changing jobs **47, 205–6, 209**
deferred **47, 205**
final pay schemes **46, 49, 200–2**
home responsibility protection
188, 189, 192
index-linked **46, 202**
lump sum in addition **46**
money purchase schemes **46,
195–6, 197–8, 206–7, 209–10**
preserved pension **205**
'Section 226' schemes **217**
self-employed *see* personal
pension plans
SERPS *see* SERPS
tax-free lump sums **202–3**
tax relief on premiums **50**
transfer payments **47, 205–6**
see also employer's *and* state
pension schemes; personal
pension plans
Pensions Management **233**
permanent health insurance **204**
Personal Equity Plans (PEPs) **38**
discretionary **264–5**
non-discretionary **265**
reinvested income from **96**
tax relief **107, 265**
Personal Insurance Arbitration
Service **88**
personal investment consultants,
advice from **86–7**
personal pension plans **14, 41,
49–50, 134, 213–37**
additional life insurance **230**
additional voluntary
contributions **203–4, 216**
administration charges **209, 229**

advantages of **213, 215**
age at commencement **217, 227–8**
age at retirement **217, 228–9, 233**
Appropriate PP **196–7, 216, 223–4, 234, 235**
cash funded **218–19**
commissions **209, 232**
contracting out with APP **196–7**
death before retirement **229**
deferred annuities **218, 225, 233**
dependants' benefits **205, 216, 229, 235**
deposit administration **220–1, 225, 230**
disadvantages **215–16**
employer's schemes compared **208–11**
executive plans **226**
guaranteed pensions **219, 225**
immediate annuities **218–19, 233–4**
index-linked **234–5**
inflation and **215–16, 226–7, 234–5**
level or increasing pensions **234–5**
loan-back facility **222**
lump sums **215, 229, 233–4**
money purchase schemes **215–16**
net relevant earnings **236–7**
non-profit **219, 225**
open market option **218, 221, 233**
paid up **228**
payment amount **226–7**
phasing retirement **229**
policy choice **230–2**
premium payment **221**
qualification for **216**
regular-premium policies **221, 225**
reinstating paid up policy **228**
retirement through ill health **228–9**
reversionary bonuses **219**
security of **232**
single-premium policies **221**
stopping paying **221, 223, 228**
taxation and **226–7, 236–7**
terminal bonuses **219**
unable to pay premiums **223**
unit-linked **219–20, 225, 230, 234–5**
unused tax relief **237**

with-profits **219, 225, 226, 230**
Personal Pensions Handbook **230, 231–2**
PETs *see* potential exempt transfers
Planned Savings **340, 352**
Policyholders' Protection Act **232, 325, 349**
political parties, gifts to **115**
potential exempt transfers **114**
pound cost averaging **285, 331**
power of appointment trusts **61**
premium bonds **135, 184–6**
  gift tokens **184**
  prizes **95, 106, 185–6**
  workings of **185**
profit margins **248**
property **17, 19**
  funds **220, 329, 330**
  overseas **397–8, 401**
  see also house purchase
protected right **195, 196, 206**
protection *see* legal protection
Public Works Loans Board **304**
purchases, savings for **24**
purchasing power **17, 19, 40**

qualifying corporate bonds **106, 107**

Recognised Professional Bodies (RPBs) **74, 80**
relief *see individual forms eg* hold-over relief
Retail Prices Index **110**
  index-linked National Savings Certificates and **178**
retirement
  abroad **397**
  age allowance **16, 52–3, 353**
  annuities *see* annuities
  calculating needs **48–9**
  claiming benefits **50–1**
  cutting expenses **50–1**
  death before **229**
  dependants *see* dependants' benefits
  earnings rule **48, 191**
  income sources **43–8**
    from home **51, 52**
    from savings **48**
    working after **47–8**
  investing for **43–54**
  life insurance policy gains **53–4**
  planning **15, 16**
  reviewing investments **51**
  spending in **49–50**

taxation after **52–5**
taxation from 1990 **54**
through ill health **228–9**
see also pensions
return on capital employed **248**
reversionary bonuses **219, 314, 316–18**
reviewing investments **25, 51**
rights issues **259–60**
risk **17–18, 19–22**
  lump sum investment **39–40**
  spreading **19**
  to capital **19**
  to income **19, 22**
  see also legal protection

safe investments **38**
Save As You Earn *see* SAYE
savings **34–5, 36**
  for holiday **16**
  for purchases **24**
  for special event **36–7**
  regular **16, 36, 37**
  see also investment; SAYE
SAYE
  building society **36, 37, 95, 106, 126, 159**
  National Savings index-linked SAYE **183–4**
  National Savings Yearly Plan **106**
  share option schemes **136, 262–3**
school fees **14, 15, 37, 62–7**
  capital schemes **62, 63–4, 64–5**
  composition fees **65–6**
  educational trusts **63–5**
  employer's help **64**
  Government Assisted Places Scheme **64**
  grants and scholarships **64**
  income schemes **63, 66–7**
  investment bonds **64**
  investment needed **64, 66**
  ISIS **63, 64**
  loans or overdraft **67**
  opting out **66**
  taxation and **64–5, 67**
scripophily **407–8**
SEAQ *see* Stock Exchange Automated Quotations System
Securities and Investments Board (SIB) **74, 79**
Securities Association, The (TSA) **80**
self-employed persons, pensions *see* personal pension plans

Self-Employed Retirement Annuities **217**
self-protection **78–9**
Self-Regulating Organisations (SROs) **74, 79–80, 349**
SERPS **46**
  APP **196–7, 223–4**
  calculation of pension **193–4**
  contracting out **194–200**
    choosing **197–200**
  guaranteed minimum pension **195, 197**
  married women **189–90**
  money purchase scheme (COMP) **195–6, 197–8**
  pension given by **192–3**
  people not covered **191–2**
  protected rights **195, 196**
  widows **190**
share exchange scheme **339**
share option schemes **37, 136**
  approved **263**
  SAYE **262–3**
shares **17, 19, 21–1, 38, 136**
  aggressive and defensive **249**
  bets analysis **249**
  buying **251–2**
  capital gains **241**
  certificates **254–5**
  CGT **111–12**
  choosing methods **246–51**
  commissions **252, 253**
  consideration **253**
  contract levy **253**
  description of **255**
  direct investment in **19, 241–61**
  dividend **241, 256–7**
    cover **257**
    yield **257**
  fundamental analysis **247–9**
  hunches **250**
  insider knowledge **250**
  mergers and takeovers **260–1**
  monitoring in newspapers **255–8**
  name and par value **256**
  new issues **259**
  options *see* share option schemes
  overseas investments **365–6**
  price **256**
    price earnings ratio **257–8**
    spread **251**
  rights issues **259–60**
  scrip (bonus) issues **259**
  selling **252–4**
  settling up **254–5**
  spreading investment **243–6**